Knickerbocker Commodore

John Drake Sloat. (Braun Research Collection, Autry National Center, Los Angeles; 92.140.1detail.)

Knickerbocker Commodore

The Life and Times of John Drake Sloat, 1781–1867

BRUCE A. CASTLEMAN

excelsior editions
State University of New York Press
Albany, New York

Cover image of Commodore John Drake Sloat, unknown artist, 1846.
Courtesy of the Navy Art Collection, Naval History and Heritage Command.

Published by State University of New York Press, Albany

Printed in the United States of America

Excelsior Editions is an imprint of State University of New York Press

For information, contact State University of New York Press, Albany, NY
www.sunypress.edu

Production, Diane Ganeles
Marketing, Fran Keneston

Library of Congress Cataloging-in-Publication Data

Castleman, Bruce A., author.
Knickerbocker commodore : the life and times of John Drake Sloat, 1781–1867 / Bruce A. Castleman.
pages cm. — (Excelsior editions)
Includes bibliographical references and index.
ISBN 978-1-4384-6151-9 (hardcover : alk. paper)
ISBN 978-1-4384-6153-3 (e-book)
1. Sloat, John D. (John Drake). 2. Mexican War, 1846–1848—Biography. 3. Ship captains—United States—Biography. 4. United States. Navy—Officers—Biography. 5. Monterrey, Battle of, Monterey, Mexico, 1846. I. Title.

E403.1.S6C37 2016
973.6'2092—dc23
[B] 2015036645

10 9 8 7 6 5 4 3 2 1

To Penny Castleman

Contents

Illustrations

Figures

Table

Preface

Let me state emphatically and unequivocally at the outset that I consider the 1846–1848 war with Mexico to have been a war of aggression on the part of the United States against a weaker neighbor. This book is in no way intended to justify the Mexican War, even though it is a biography of a United States Navy officer who played an important role in the conquest of Mexican California. By accepting the role of his biographer, I sought to understand how the commodore in command came to be the man that he was, and in so doing, to contribute to the historiography of the antebellum United States and its navy.

Rear Admiral John Drake Sloat is one of those historical actors whose memory has receded from common recognition into the fog of historical recollection. Like a number of my Latin Americanist colleagues who also trained in United States history, I shifted my research focus northward after retiring from university teaching. While reading California history looking for a new research possibility, I came across the controversies surrounding Sloat's actions at Monterey in command of the United States Navy's Pacific Squadron. I have been fortunate to have had two distinct careers in my adult life, and the first was as a seagoing officer in the United States Navy for twenty years. Commodore Sloat, to use the rank title by which he is more commonly remembered, stood at an intersection of my own background and interests. So I ended up researching the life of a New Yorker whose trail of records is mostly on the opposite coast of the one on which I live.

Because the sources were scattered far and wide, I traveled to many places and piled up a large debt to many people and institutions, only some of whom can be named here. W. Jeffrey Bolster, Michael Crawford, Todd Creekman, Timothy Francis, John Schroeder, and Gene Smith all encouraged me in this work and provided their insights into maritime and navy history. Christine Hunefeldt and Charles Walker encouraged me in this project and helped me to deepen my knowledge of Andean history in the nineteenth century. Cornelia Bush, Ann Roche, Jean Krish, and Pat Schwetje found documents and guided me through records of local institutions of Goshen, New York. Diane Norman did the same for Norwich, Connecticut. Frank Sloat, a distant cousin of the admiral, kindly shared his genealogical research. Robert Chandler pointed me toward sources about antebellum mail steamers. Wayne Franklin, Rochelle Tuck, and Jeff Walker shared their understanding of James Fenimore Cooper. Steven Lubar shared his work on the Naval Lyceum even before it appeared in print. David Pelfrey of the National Park Service cleared up some misconceptions that this steamship sailor had about sailing ship equipment.

A work of this sort could never be done without the help of archivists and librarians, and I have enjoyed the collegial cooperation of so many. Christopher Damiani of the Historical Society of Pennsylvania provided letters of Thomas Truxtun. Eileen Keremitsis and Allison Moore of the California Historical Society's North Baker Research Library, Gina Bardi and Ted Miles of the San Francisco Maritime National Historic Park Research Center, Jennifer Bryan of the U.S. Naval Academy Nimitz Library Special Collections Branch, and Janice Torbet of the San Francisco Public Library all pointed me in the right direction on a variety of topics. I also thank the San Francisco Public Library for its support through its own extensive collections, and for obtaining many necessary books from other libraries. I am also indebted to the staffs of the New York Public Library, the Patricia D. Klingenstein Library of the New-York Historical Society, the Library of Congress, the Bancroft Library, the libraries of the University of California at Berkeley and at Davis, the Episcopal Diocese of New York, and the Athenaeum of Portsmouth, New Hampshire. As a naval officer, John Drake Sloat was a federal person and so most of his paper trail lies in the various branches of the National Archives of the United States. Trina Yeckley of the Northeast Region–New York branch first showed me how to wend my way through the system. I also benefited from the assistance of the staffs at Archives I and Archives

II in Washington, D.C., and the branches in Waltham, Massachusetts; in Philadelphia; and in San Bruno, California.

I also thank the editorial staff of the State University of New York Press and am especially indebted to Amanda Lanne-Camilli and Jessica Kirschner for their support of the wide range of efforts required to bring this book into existence. Each of the two anonymous peer reviewers provided incisive and insightful comments on the manuscript. Of course, I alone bear complete responsibility for any errors or shortcomings that remain.

The illustrations for this book became a sort of extra chapter unto themselves. My thanks go out to Marilyn Van Winkle of the National Autry Center, Claudia Jew of the Mariners Museum, Karen Paige and Keli Skoglund of the California State Library, Tracie Logan of the U.S. Naval Academy Museum, and at the Navy History and Heritage Command, Pam Overmann, curator of the Navy Art Collection, and Lisa Crunk, curator of the NHHC photograph collection.

Iris Engstrand helped develop my interests in California history and, along with other mentors such as Robert Patch and Eric Van Young, did her best to make me into a historian. A graduate seminar in biographical writing with the late Ray Brandes has served me time and again in conceiving and researching this project.

Without the logistical support of my wife, Penny Castleman, the many arrangements for travel in pursuit of John Drake Sloat would never have been so smooth. Without Penny's cheerful and unending emotional support, the manuscript would never have been written at all, and to her I dedicate this book.

CHAPTER ONE

Indecision at Monterey?

On July 7, 1846, landing parties of sailors and marines from ships of the United States Navy's Pacific Squadron occupied the Mexican town of Monterey, the capital of the department of California. Commodore John Drake Sloat, the squadron commander, issued a proclamation to the inhabitants declaring that, from that day forward, California was annexed to the United States.[1] Hostilities had finally broken out between the United States and Mexico, but the commodore had not yet received official notification that war had actually been declared. Sloat had arrived in Monterey aboard his flagship, the frigate *Savannah*, almost one week earlier. The Pacific Squadron had sailed from Mazatlán after Sloat learned that combat had taken place along the Rio Grande between Mexican and United States forces. By the end of July, Captain Robert F. Stockton had relieved Sloat as the commodore of the Pacific Squadron, and Sloat had left for New York.

A large monument to Commodore Sloat stands on the grounds of the Presidio of Monterey, and some streets and schools are named in his honor. But few among the general public who travel on those streets seem to have any idea who he was. Several published histories of California appeared in the nineteenth century that took critical views of many American figures involved in California during the war with Mexico, including John Drake Sloat, Robert Field Stockton, and John Charles Frémont. Among the most prominent voices, historian Theodore Hittell opined that Sloat acted wisely in Monterey, whereas Hubert Howe Bancroft (not related to George Bancroft) and Josiah Royce argued that the commodore had a timid and vacillating nature that led him to act hesitantly and risk failure of his assigned mission in California.[2]

Among students of the Mexican War, Commodore Sloat's actions in command continue to provide grist for the mills of historical controversy. Interpretations appearing after 1900 take either of two approaches. Some criticize Sloat sharply for not acting sooner than he did in Mazatlán and also after arriving in Monterey. Authors from this school of thought use words like "Nervous Nellie," "dithering," or "hypochondriac" to describe Sloat. The historian K. Jack Bauer best exemplifies this most critical viewpoint. In his 1969 book about the naval aspects of the Mexican War, Bauer blisters Sloat with scathing denunciations and portrays him as timidly quavering in a situation that demanded decisive action. Five years later, Bauer authored a work on the entire war in which he toned the rhetoric down somewhat, and in a 1980 book chapter about George Bancroft as secretary of the navy, Bauer stated that while Sloat was "overly cautious," his proclamation of annexation was a good approach to the situation as it existed at that point in time. Bauer also criticized Secretary Bancroft's actions and, in all three of these works, heaped criticism on Commodore Robert F. Stockton as well.

Commodore Sloat has received kinder treatment from other modern historians of the Mexican War. Such writers tend to sympathize with his fear of repeating the colossal blunder of Commodore Thomas ap Catesby Jones, who in 1842 occupied Monterey in his mistaken belief that the United States and Mexico had gone to war. Some note Sloat's age and sickliness. Bernard DeVoto added that Sloat was a "navy fuss-budget." Robert Selph Henry and John S. D. Eisenhower have seen Sloat as ensnared in a predicament caused by unclear, contradictory orders from Secretary Bancroft.[3]

Some officers of the age of sail navy, such as Stephen Decatur, are the subject of several biographical studies. Most others, of course, have none at all. The corpus of "commodore biographies" comprises a large and important part of the history of the United States Navy in the age of sail. The years from the navy's founding in 1798 until the end of the War of 1812 have attracted a fair number of studies, some of the interest relating to the bicentennial of that war. Studies of the period between 1815 and 1861 do exist but in much smaller numbers than for the preceding years. The biographical literature comprises a very important part of the naval historiography of those later antebellum years.[4]

There is one earlier biography of Rear Admiral John Drake Sloat, who was promoted to that rank on the retired list after the Civil War. Edwin Allen Sherman's *The Life of the Late Rear Admiral John Drake Sloat* appeared in 1902.[5] Major Sherman served as the secretary of the Sloat Monument Association of California, an organization founded to raise the monument on the Presidio of Monterey. Sherman's adoring book reflects its author's mission and is also rife with fulminating ad hominem attacks against anyone who had criticized Sloat or whose words might have been construed that way. Triumphalist and celebratory, the work is unreliable but by no means completely worthless. It does contain some outright falsehoods, and some of them will be pointed out in this essay. Sherman seldom identified his sources, but it appears that much of his information came from an anonymously authored magazine article that appeared in 1849 and also from descendants of Sloat. One great-grandson was present at the dedication of the monument. I have chosen to treat Sherman's book as a sort of family memoir of a departed ancestor that requires corroboration before accepting anything it says. Sherman created a historical record that needs revision, and this book will make that contribution.

Wondering how a high-ranking naval officer such as Sloat could possibly be "timid" sparked the research that led to this biography. After all, he had been decorated by Congress for his key role in capturing a British frigate during the War of 1812 and later led United States Navy forces in the capture of an elusive and fearsome Caribbean pirate. To understand Commodore John Drake Sloat's actions, one must understand something about the man himself and the experiences that shaped him. That goal requires studying the life course that brought him to Monterey that fateful July. The surviving historical record does not support "getting into his head" in any psychological sense. However, we can peer over Sloat's shoulder and look out at things as he saw them. That is not enough. We must also consider situations and settings that affected his thoughts and actions, even though they were sometimes beyond his radius of personal influence.[6] He first entered the United States Navy soon after it was founded and was placed on a retired list in 1855. His career spanned almost the entire period between the navy's beginnings and the Civil War. Then just as now, much of navy life was mundane and unexciting. But at different times and in varying degrees, Sloat's life also touched a wide range of important historical issues and processes beyond what might be expected in the biography of a high-ranking officer in the United States Navy. He played an important role in the territorial expansion of the United States. In his role as commandant of the navy yard at Portsmouth, and later at Norfolk, Sloat was the chief operating officer of industrial enterprises in a period of rapid changes in technology. But there is still more. The practices of Hudson Valley landowners, the suppression of Caribbean piracy, attempts to overthrow the government of Peru, the American maritime labor market, and the expansion and urbanization of New York City, all had their impact on the life of this long-serving naval officer and prominent New Yorker.

CHAPTER TWO

Upstate Knickerbocker

John Drake Sloat was born in Sloatsburg, New York, on July 26, 1781. His father, John Sloat, sometimes spelled "Slot," "Sloot," or "Slott," had been killed by a fellow American soldier on April 4 of that year, reportedly after failing to give the proper password when challenged by a sentry. Some sources identify the father as a Continental Army captain, but others say he was a private in a company commanded by Captain Steven Sloat, the future commodore's grandfather. In either case, the militia company in Sloatsburg protected West Point from a British attack via the Ramapo Valley, which parallels the larger Hudson Valley just north of New York City. Sloatsburg lies some thirty miles north-northwest of New York City. At the time of John Sloat's unfortunate demise, General George Washington's main force had not yet left its encampment across the Hudson River in White Plains for the final confrontation with Lord Cornwallis's British troops at Yorktown, Virginia. Within two years, John Drake Sloat's mother, Ruth, also died. Her parents, Joseph and Amy Drake, raised their grandson in nearby Goshen, about thirty miles northwest of Sloatsburg.[1]

No documentary record of much substance survives from John Drake Sloat's youth, but there is some information about each side of his family. Also, historians have studied various aspects of life in New York along the lower Hudson River, and their work informs us about the sort of place in which Sloat grew up and gives some idea about the experiences that he likely had.

Ethnicity was one important aspect of Hudson Valley life in the late eighteenth century. John Drake Sloat was primarily of Dutch descent. Biographer Edwin Sherman declared that the Drakes of Goshen were a collateral branch of Sir Francis Drake's family, but that is a patent falsehood. That error about the Drakes is repeated in at least one published biographical blurb.[2]

John Drake Sloat's paternal grandparents were Steven Sloat (b. March 25, 1726, Hackensack, New Jersey; d. October 11, 1806, Sloatsburg) and Marretje Van Duser (b. February 23, 1729; d. July 29, 1807, Sloatsburg). They were of Dutch descent, and some of Steven's ancestors had been in North America since before 1673. Steven and Marretje were married in Sloatsburg in 1753 and had four children: John, Isaac, Elizabeth, and Marretje (also listed as Mary). John Sloat (b. 1754, Sloatsburg; d. April 4, 1781, Sloatsburg) married Ruth Drake (b. September 11, 1761, Goshen; d. ca. 1782, Sloatsburg or Goshen) in Goshen's Presbyterian Church on March 17, 1778.[3]

Figure 2.1. Birthplace of John Drake Sloat in Sloatsburg, New York. (Photo by author.)

Ruth Drake's parents were Joseph Drake (b. August 10, 1720, Goshen; d. August 12, 1807, Goshen) and Amy Carman (b. August 14, 1727; d. August 15, 1804, Goshen). The records do not reveal Amy's origins. Joseph Drake's mother was Martha Oldfield (b. 1698, Queens County, New York; d. February 6, 1779, Goshen) whose father was also born in Queens and whose mother came from La Rochelle, France. Joseph Drake's father was Jan Dratz (b. 1687, Kings County, New York; d. 1779), who took the Anglicized name John Drake sometime before his marriage to Martha on Long Island, New York, on February 24, 1719. John Drake's parents were Jan Dratz (b. 1644, Amsterdam) and Aeltjie Brouwer (b. 1662, Gowanus, Brooklyn, New York).[4]

In the decades of the eighteenth century that followed United States independence, established Dutch families in the Hudson River region experienced significant social change as families of English descent arrived in increasing numbers.[5]

Dutch landholding and tenancy patterns in North America are usually portrayed as mammoth landholdings concentrated in the hands of a very few families. The ongoing historiographical debate about whether those large "manors" were predominately feudal or capitalist in nature need not receive extensive consideration here. The landholders rented parts of their lands to tenant farmer families, and the people who actually worked the land had precious little chance to own any of it. As with Bacon's Rebellion in Virginia, resentment against the power of a wealthy few led to conflict. After quashing the rebellion led by Jacob Leisler that took control of southern New York during 1689–1691, King William III appointed the Earl of Bellomont to be governor of New York. Bellomont served as governor until his death in 1701, and while little change took place in the more northern reaches of the Hudson, he did manage to annul land grants in what are now the counties of Orange, Rockland, and Ulster. Goshen is in Orange County, and Sloatsburg is in Rockland County. In these counties, independent, landowning farmers became the norm. One historian finds that average holdings there were in the range of two thousand acres. By comparison, Judge William Cooper at one time held more than 750,000 acres, mostly in Otsego County.[6] The land grants created new opportunities for individual land ownership and brought in settlers like the Slots/Sloats from Hackensack and the Dratzes/Drakes from Brooklyn.

The Sloats were prominent in the area around the village that bore their name. A large land tract that included the village itself had been passed down to Steven Sloat through his wife's family. They had a large house in the village along the road and a large farm just to the west where the Orange County–Rockland County line meets the New Jersey state line.[7]

Joseph Drake was also prominent in Goshen town and Orange County. St. James's Episcopal Church of Goshen became a formal parish in 1801, and Joseph Drake was one of its six founding vestrymen. The Goshen tax rolls for 1800 list three hundred individuals, six of whose assessments show them as significantly richer than the others. Joseph Drake was not one of those six, but he was among the wealthiest 10 percent. Drake's estate was valued at about four thousand dollars in a New York state tax assessment in 1800, and a study of counties farther upstate indicates suggests that Orange County gentry were rather better off than the most well-to-do tenants of the large estates around Albany. Joseph Drake owned parcels of land at a number of places around Orange County and resided on a two-hundred-acre farm near Chester, which is just outside of Goshen.[8] The Goshen area later became a predominately dairy-producing center, but before 1810, Orange County farmers also grew wheat and raised livestock for sale in New York and Albany markets via both the river and overland turnpike routes.[9]

Another indicator of Joseph Drake's prosperity and status is his ownership of slaves. The 1790 federal census records that he owned four slaves and that in 1800 he still had two. Most people in the Hudson Valley could not afford to own slaves, but the typical slave owner there owned three persons in bondage. Steven Sloat had five slaves in 1790 and three in 1800. Chattel slavery is usually associated today with tobacco and cotton states in the American South, but it also existed to a significant degree in the Hudson Valley region. Dutch farmers had never objected to slavery on any philosophical or religious grounds, and they vigorously opposed New York's gradual emancipation law that passed in 1799.[10]

The well-known historical figure Sojourner Truth came from the Hudson Valley instead of the American South, as many might initially suppose. Her experiences record clearly that New York slavery was no less brutal than was South Carolina or Mississippi slavery. Sojourner Truth was auctioned in an estate sale in 1808 or 1809 for one hundred dollars. The nine-year-old girl was whipped mercilessly by her new owners. Sold again a year later for seventy New York pounds ($175), she was also abused physically and sexually by her new owners. One study of Southern plantation records revealed that in any given year, a typical force of ten slaves received seven floggings of sufficient severity to be entered in a plantation's permanent records. Still another analysis of slavery emphasized the institution's inherent brutality and concluded that brutality inevitably affected the master class as well as the slaves.[11] No surviving record tells us about John Drake Sloat's personal experience with slavery, or whether or not his grandfather was a brutal master. But the composite record does reveal unpleasant and important truths about Hudson Valley society that many might prefer to overlook. Suffice it for now to say that John Drake Sloat grew up in a slave-owning, capitalist agricultural society that produced goods for market.

Records from the one primary school that existed in eighteenth-century Goshen were unfortunately destroyed in a fire, and once again we are left to fill in the blanks using indirect and circumstantial evidence to learn about John Drake Sloat's formal education before he joined the United States Navy. Major Sherman reports that he attended local schools. The primary school in Goshen was founded by none other than Noah Webster in 1782. Webster taught in Goshen for about a year and then returned to Connecticut. While in Goshen, Webster produced the first version of the famous *Blue-Back Speller* that became a standard text in American primary schools. The *Blue-Back* replaced an English speller used widely in the North American colonies, and the new book had a decidedly nationalistic slant. Most likely the teacher who took over after Webster departed would not have changed the text. It was viewed as an advance in the day but today might be seen as focused on rote memorization. Any formal education beyond the minimum reading and writing remained a privilege of birth into an elite family. Sloat did not attend Columbia or any of the New England colleges. As was often the case in the United States in the 1790s, his post-primary education probably came from a local clergyman or a hired tutor.[12] His letters in the National Archives suggest to this author that Sloat wrote as well as any of his colleagues and better than quite a few of them.

One glimmer in the archival record briefly shines a direct light on Sloat's youth. On September 23, 1795, Joseph and Amy Drake sold a parcel of land to one Thomas Payn. For three hundred New York pounds, equivalent to $750, Payn took title to forty-nine acres of land near Minisink, to the west of Goshen. Fourteen-year-old John Slott (Sloat) was a witness to the conveyance.[13] This suggests an early familiarity with real estate transactions that will be seen to stand him in good stead. It also hints that young John Sloat functioned as an integral member of the Drake family and not as an inconvenient orphan in the house.

Nothing in the record suggests what led teenaged John Drake Sloat to want to go to sea. Only today's lower Manhattan comprised the total urban settlement of New York City, but it was already a burgeoning international port. Federal census records show that its population had increased to about sixty thousand between 1790 and 1800, and the growth continued apace for years to come. Undoubtedly an exciting city to visit from rural Goshen, New York also served as a base of the fledgling United States Navy. When an elite family's son wanted to go to sea, he usually sought an officer's berth in the navy.

CHAPTER THREE

Mr. Midshipman Sloat

The newly created navy to which John Drake Sloat sought an appointment was created in 1798 as part of the response by President John Adams and the Congress to deteriorated relations between the United States and its Revolutionary War ally, France. Of course, France had struggled in the throes of revolutionary turmoil since 1789 and also fought a war with Great Britain since 1793. The United States negotiated Jay's Treaty with Great Britain the following year, during the second term of President George Washington. That treaty contained accommodations of British goals that angered the French. Corsairs sailing under French letters of marque captured hundreds of U.S. merchant ships in the following years. Sometimes they did so right off the entrances to American ports, but the bulk of the guerre de course took place in the Caribbean. Marine insurance rates skyrocketed, especially for voyages to Jamaica.

Attempts at diplomacy by President John Adams with the French Directory failed, and the "XYZ Affair" further inflamed passions in the United States when the cash-strapped French government attempted to extort loans and personal bribes before any meaningful diplomatic negotiations could begin. Congress abrogated the old Franco-American treaty and authorized the completion of warships whose construction had been interrupted during Washington's presidency after the threat of Algerian commerce raiders in the Mediterranean had subsided. A separate Navy Department was created, and Benjamin Stoddert joined President Adams's cabinet as the first secretary of the navy.[1]

The new administration resumed construction of the six frigates. Three were to be rated at forty-four guns: *United States*, *Constitution*, and *President*. The remaining ships would be rated at thirty-eight guns:

Constellation, *Congress*, and *Chesapeake*, the last of which entered service rather later than did the others. Each frigate was built in a different seaport: Philadelphia, Boston, New York, Baltimore, Portsmouth (New Hampshire), and Norfolk, respectively. Public subscriptions raised money to build still more ships, such as the *Essex* and the *Philadelphia.* Frigates such as these were full-rigged ships, that is to say, with three masts carrying square sails, plus jibs and spankers fore and aft. They were meant for long-range cruising in wartime and to match or exceed in firepower any opponent except for a ship-of-the-line, the bulky battleship of the age of sail. A frigate had to have tall masts to carry a comparatively large spread of sail and a large complement of sailors and marines to handle all the sails and simultaneously to man all the guns in battle.[2] Other types of ships will be discussed in this essay at the points where they first appear in the narrative of John Drake Sloat's life.

Finding personnel to sail these ships into harm's way was no small challenge. There were no experienced naval officers in the United States, but there were merchant ship masters, and some of those had combat experience as privateers. Some of them also had experience in Britain's Royal Navy, but not as commissioned officers. Copying the British system to train the next generation of naval officers, each ship carried a number of midshipmen. Usually in their middle to late teen years when appointed, midshipmen were essentially lieutenants-in-training. The title stems from their battle station amidships, from whence to relay orders and reports aft to the ship's commanding officer on the quarterdeck, which was a sail warship's control station. Much of their true purpose, of course, was fulfilled as they trained in seamanship and other naval arts while cruising at sea in times of both war and peace.

The historian Christopher McKee has studied at great length the formation of the United States Navy officer corps. Secretary Stoddert wanted the midshipmen's warrants to go to well-educated young men of good character and with good connections. McKee's analysis shows that many of the midshipmen warranted in 1800 had lost one or more parents. A large minority were eighteen years of age or older, a fact from which McKee infers that those young men may have started out on another career path. Only a few had any university education, some had been to a secondary academy, but the majority received their education from local tutors. Most had no direct experience of the sea, but the navy lieutenant's commission that each midshipman sought offered the prospect of an exciting job that paid well enough and carried a great deal of prestige.[3] John Drake Sloat appears to have fit rather closely Secretary Stoddert's mold. Although perhaps a bit unusual in coming from a rural area, the eighteen-year-old youth conformed well to the archetype developed by McKee.

The secretary of the navy required a letter of recommendation from a person of substance who could personally attest to a prospective midshipman's suitability and qualifications, but the National Archives do not contain any such letter to Stoddert on Sloat's behalf. A San Francisco newspaper carried in 1896 what appears to be a Sloat family tradition. The young John Drake Sloat supposedly went to the Executive Mansion in Philadelphia, marched into President John Adams's office, and declared that he wanted to become a midshipman in the navy. Startled but impressed, Adams is said to have sent the youth down to see Stoddert.[4]

The story as published seems quite far-fetched, and if not a complete fabrication, perhaps it changed and grew embellished over the years of its retelling. John Drake Sloat may very well have gone to Philadelphia to seek a midshipman's warrant, armed with appropriate letters of introduction by reputable citizens of Goshen that he could have learned he needed from speaking with naval officers in New York City. Another lad from an upstate New York elite family who was possessed of a desire to go to sea followed a similar path. After he ran away to sea, family exertions obtained for James Fenimore Cooper a midshipman's warrant in the navy.[5] Whether John Drake Sloat had been to sea in any capacity before entering the navy, or had spent the last years of the 1790s in the Hudson region and New York City, remains anybody's guess.

Modern biographers find John Adams an often irascible man, and an always reserved and formal one. Adams even described himself exactly the same way. As president, he did take a particular interest in midshipmen and recognized their importance to the future of the navy that he worked so hard to create. But he delegated almost all aspects of running the Department of the Navy to Secretary Stoddert.[6] Whether John Drake Sloat actually spoke with the president, was redirected to the secretary of the navy's office by a presidential assistant, or figured out on his own that he really needed to call upon Benjamin Stoddert remains obscure. But whatever he did, it worked. On February 12, 1800, Secretary

Stoddert wrote to John Drake Sloat and appointed him a midshipman in the United States Navy. James Biddle and Edward Biddle, scions of the prominent Philadelphia family, also received midshipman's warrants on that date.

One month later, Secretary Stoddert ordered Midshipman Sloat to report for duty onboard the frigate *President* and to place himself under the command of Lieutenant Isaac Chauncey. Shortly after reporting to the *President*, Sloat became an apprentice mason in St. Andrew's Lodge No. 9, of the Ancient York Masons.[7] The historian Samuel Eliot Morison contends that as the fastest ship in the navy, the *President* was a particularly prized assignment for officers.[8] The newly built frigate was then fitting out in New York harbor. Captain Thomas Truxtun would take command in July, and Lieutenant Chauncey would stay on as one of the ship's officers.

Figure 3.1. *United States Frigate* President, by Jean-Jérôme Baugean, ca. 1814. (Courtesy of Navy Art Collection, Naval History and Heritage Command.)

Captain Truxtun was to take the *President* to the West Indies as the commodore in command of the U.S. squadron that pursued French corsairs in those waters. Just when Sloat was ordered to the *President*, Truxtun had returned in March 1800 from a West Indies cruise in the frigate *Constellation*. He had just defeated and heavily damaged the French frigate *La Vengeance*.[9] Assignment to a fine ship under the command of a highly regarded captain who took very seriously his responsibility to the navy for training its future officers augured well for Midshipman Sloat's future.

The *President* sailed from New York in September and headed for the island of St. Christopher, today often known as St. Kitts, located less than one hundred miles from the French stronghold of Guadeloupe. The ship's log reports sighting and giving chase to many a sail around the Leeward Islands, but not one turned out to be French. There were no prizes to be taken. The Convention of Môrtfontaine, signed on September 30, 1800, agreed to an end to the Quasi-War. The governor of Guadeloupe informed Truxtun when he learned of it, but the American declined to stand down from anti-corsair cruising until he received formal instructions from his own government. In January 1801, Commodore John Barry arrived at St. Christopher in the frigate *United States* with a squadron to relieve Truxtun and the *President* on station, and Truxtun informed Barry of the diplomatic developments. On January 21, 1801, Truxtun directed Lieutenant Andrew Sterett to have the ship ready to sail home with the squadron on February 1. The *President* entered Hampton Roads, Virginia, on February 19.[10]

The five-month cruise without capturing a single prize must have been an unhappy and frustrating one. Truxtun felt ill during much of it, and he appears to have been a difficult commanding officer even at the best of times. One seaman assaulted Lieutenant Sterett with a marlinspike. Midshipman John King drew a bayonet and brandished it at Lieutenant Chauncey. King was on board as *President*'s sailing master and so was probably an officer of some experience instead of a fresh-caught young gentleman aboard for training. (Because Sloat would later serve in that capacity, a discussion of the role of the sailing master is reserved for a subsequent chapter.) Midshipman Edward Biddle died on board, probably from yellow fever. He had come aboard with his older brother James to the extreme dismay of their mother, whose unhappy premonitions and worst fears came sadly true. James Biddle and John Sloat remained friends throughout their lives. Midshipman Lewis Warrington also reported to the *President* at some point during Sloat's time on board and became the namesake of Sloat's firstborn son.[11] During this particular cruise, the *President* probably suffered from morale problems among the officers and the crew. Disappointments in not sharing any part of prize money awards from captured ships must have been keenly felt, along with not finding any opportunity for personal glory.

But the Quasi-War cruise in late 1800 of the *President* squadron can be viewed as a success in terms of national goals and interests. France failed in one major objective because its guerre de course did not force the United States to actively support its war against Britain. Insurance rates for West Indies voyages had returned to acceptable levels before the guerre de course was suspended. Caribbean seaborne trade was important to the United States, and that trade had become safer. Of course, that was not due solely to Commodore Truxtun's efforts, or even solely to the American squadron's actions. The Royal Navy also campaigned actively against French West Indies corsairs, and the French themselves had critically evaluated the effectiveness of their earlier policy choices.[12]

As one of twenty midshipmen aboard the *President*, John Drake Sloat probably found the wartime cruise to be a life of routine in very cramped quarters. Commodore Truxtun subjected midshipmen to a steady and intense training program. Historian McKee writes in detail about the development of the navy's "young gentlemen," and some discussion of their training appears in most of the biographies of various age of sail commodores. Before the founding of the United States Naval Academy in 1846, midshipmen were trained aboard ships at sea. They received instruction in mathematics, navigation, seamanship, gunnery, and other technical aspects of a warship officer's profession. Some of that instruction could continue while the ship lay in New York harbor. At anchor in a port, of course, there would have been no opportunity to handle the large frigate itself, but certainly a great deal could be learned by handling the ship's boats under sail on a regular basis. There were eight ship's boats in each of the three forty-four-gun frigates, ranging from twenty to thirty-four feet in length.[13] The *President* had such an abnormally large contingent of midshipmen that their training experience might have been diluted in some degree. But there was more to developing naval officers than the merely technical aspects.

In a famous quote that midshipmen at the U.S. Naval Academy in this author's day were required to memorize, John Paul Jones wrote that a naval officer must indeed be a capable mariner but also a great deal more than that. An officer must be a gentleman of liberal education, refined manners, punctilious courtesy, and the nicest sense of personal honor . . . not to mention the soul of tact, patience, justice, firmness, and charity![14]

What Jones was getting at was the great importance in acculturating Sloat and the other midshipmen into the navy's ways and developing the sense of duty and honor that the navy wanted in its officers. In short, the new navy wanted to establish an institutionalized process of social reproduction. The navy needed to assimilate these midshipmen and, in turn, wanted the midshipmen to assimilate the navy. In the United States Navy, a midshipman was a warrant officer. He did not yet have the commission to which he aspired. The secretary of the navy issued the warrant by the direction of the president, but no Senate advice or consent was required. The same words from 1800 appear on the midshipman's warrant received by this author in 1969. When visiting foreign ports, midshipmen learned the diplomatic aspects of their profession. They often developed a reputation for carousing ashore as well, but during the *President*'s Quasi-War cruise, there would have been little opportunity for Sloat or the other nineteen midshipmen to do that. Instruction and tutoring of the young gentlemen was a primary duty of the ship's chaplain, but in this case, Truxtun sent Chaplain Robert Thomson off the ship because he did not get along with the ship's lieutenants. Those same lieutenants would have had to fill in as instructors. In theory at least, a ship's commissioned officers were also the models by example of what the midshipmen should strive to become. Besides Captain Truxtun, the wardroom of the *President* included the following lieutenants on the 1800 Quasi-War cruise: Andrew Sterett, Isaac Chauncey, John Dent, Godfrey Wood, John Clagett, and Charles Gordon.[15]

McKee finds that even in ships with smaller contingents, this system of training, development, and acculturation frequently did not work as well as hoped. Even so, senior officers complained about the results on one hand and stoutly defended the system on the other.[16] Commodore Charles Morris wrote about his own experience at that time while serving as a midshipman in a different frigate. Morris stated that, including even those who had commanded merchant ships, the officers of the new United States Navy had only the most rudimentary knowledge of celestial navigation and other advanced scientific subjects that would later become basic knowledge for a naval line officer.[17] The system did have faults, but by and large it did meet the navy's needs for many years—or at least as the products of that navy system perceived the navy's needs to be.

Peace and politics soon upset Midshipman John Drake Sloat's applecart. The end of the Quasi-War meant that the rapidly expanded United States Navy would be reduced in size. While the *President* cruised in the West Indies, Thomas Jefferson was elected to be the third president of the United States. President John Adams and the Federalists feared that the Jeffersonian Republicans would reduce the navy's strength to what they saw as an unacceptable degree. The Federalists decided to act first and passed the Peace Establishment Act in March 1801, just before Jefferson's inauguration. The reductions in force were severe, but Federalists feared that the Republicans would cut even more if they took office and had a fresh hand. The fleet was to be reduced to thirteen frigates and the other thirty-six ships were to be sold. Seven of the retained frigates laid up in navy yards "in ordinary," which is akin to being mothballed in a reserve fleet. The officer corps would be substantially reduced, retaining nine of the twenty-eight captains, none of the seven masters commandant, thirty-six of the 110 lieutenants, and 150 of the 254 midshipmen. The enlisted strength of the fleet would be reduced substantially as well, probably to 2,500–3,000 total sailors to crew the six active frigates. Obviously a reduction of such proportions would save a great deal of money.[18] A list of officers who served in the *President* during the Quasi-War names thirty midshipmen as retained and four discharged under the Peace Establishment Act. John Drake Sloat was one of the latter four. In another letter, Truxtun reported information to newly installed secretary of the navy Robert Smith meant to be passed to Captain Richard Dale, in which he states that the *President* had a large number of midshipmen aboard and that more were on the way. None of the young gentlemen is mentioned by name. Later correspondence stated that Midshipman Sloat had been discharged only because he had been ashore in sick quarters when the *President* sailed for the Barbary Coast in 1801. Possibly Commodore Truxtun delayed the discharge as long as he could. Commodore Richard Dale replaced Truxtun in command of the *President* squadron on May 22, 1801, in Hampton Roads, Virginia. Records say that Sloat was discharged on the preceding day, but the other three midshipmen were discharged earlier than that. He would have received four months' severance pay, a total of seventy-six dollars. There would be no "dancing and wenching in the Mediterranean" for John Drake Sloat.[19] At least not as a United States Navy midshipman.

CHAPTER FOUR

Schooner Skipper

John Drake Sloat had fifteen months' service as a midshipman under his belt and was just shy of his twentieth birthday when struck by the Peace Establishment Act. He turned to sailing in U.S. merchant ships, perhaps in the hope of one day returning to the navy. Most of the captains brought into the fledgling navy had years of merchant marine experience. Many lieutenants and midshipmen took furloughs without pay to gain practical seamanship experience on merchant voyages, a practice encouraged by the Navy Department in recognition that the experience to be gained in the frigates was simply insufficient. Most of the furloughed junior officers made only one such voyage, either as a mate or as a deck seaman. Two of Sloat's fellow midshipmen from the *President* made merchant voyages after receiving lieutenants' commissions. Lieutenant Archibald Kearney did so well financially and enjoyed the merchant service so much that he resigned his commission a few years later. Lieutenant James Biddle, on the other hand, made one voyage to Asia and vowed never again to sail in a merchant ship. In 1806, newly appointed Midshipman Thomas ap Catesby Jones failed to find a "suitable berth" and decided instead to study navigation theory ashore before receiving an active duty posting.[1] In the years before the War of 1812, John Drake Sloat would make at least fifteen voyages as ship's master, in other words, as the captain. These voyages are documented in the shipping news sections of newspapers and sometimes also by surviving records of the U.S. Customs Service. Gaps in the coverage of these records may mean that Sloat spent those times ashore, or that he made other voyages for which no documentation survives.

The trail first appears with the arrival in Philadelphia on March 30, 1802, of a brig, a square-rigged vessel with two masts. The ship had made a voyage from Norfolk that lasted six days, but the vessel's name is illegible, and its master is identified only as "Sloat."[2] Possibly this is not John Drake Sloat, but if it is not, then this is the only appearance of another master named Sloat in the shipping news during the first decade of the nineteenth century in the United States. Sloat may have spent the nine months since leaving the *President* as a mate or a deckhand on a merchant ship.[3] But on the other hand, men who today would be considered very young for such responsible positions frequently did sail as masters of American merchant ships in the years around 1800. A single voyage as a deckhand often led to the next one as a ship's officer.[4] Young Sloat's Quasi-War cruise on the *President* might have been all he needed to get a merchant schooner command, especially if he or one of his grandfathers bought some shares in the voyage.

A study of Baltimore maritime shipping investment patterns shows that around 1790, mariners owned 100 of 575 total shares of ships registered in that city. Another historian finds that in general, shipmasters did not own part of the ship or a share in the trade, but if one did, his interest was usually one-sixteenth of the total. Shares in ships were most usually divided in halves, thirds, or quarters among merchants who owned ships. Cargoes could be shipped on consignment, but shipowning merchants usually purchased the cargoes and then sold them at their ships' destinations. Captains frequently could ship some cargo of their own on a voyage. They bore considerable responsibility for the sale of cargoes away from home port and therefore routinely received commissions on the sale of the cargo once it was delivered.[5] John Drake Sloat came from a family of some affluence, and so he may have had access to the funds needed to purchase some capital in his merchant marine voyages. Unfortunately, we are left to speculate on those financial matters because the customs registry documents do not survive in the archives.

"The fast sailing schooner *John Vining*, J. D. Sloat, master," advertised on July 20, 1803, that cargo space was still available and that anyone desiring to consign freight or book a passage to Surinam should apply to the captain on board, or to Joseph Wood at 263 Pearl Street, New York. A subsequent report indicates that on the following August 20, the schooner cleared for Guadeloupe.[6] There was no indication whether or

Figure 4.1. Detail of *New York from Long Island*, unknown artist, ca. 1800. (In Stokes, *Iconography of Manhattan Island*, vol. 3.)

not Sloat planned to continue to Dutch Surinam in the Guyanas after calling at French Guadeloupe. This author was unable to locate a record that *John Vining* had returned to New York, but that most likely means that no newspaper happened to publish a report of its return.

Figure 4.2. *View of the Great Harbor of Pointe-à-Pitre, Guadeloupe*, after an early nineteenth-century drawing by Ambroise Louis Garneray. (Historical Images of Guadeloupe, Wikimedia Commons.)

In December 1803, John Sloat cleared again for the West Indies, this time as master of the schooner *Only Daughter.* On February 23, 1804, the *Only Daughter* sailed homeward from St. Jago, Cuba. (Santiago de Cuba.) The schooner was boarded the next day by a party from a British frigate, HMS *Desire*, a Captain Whitby commanding. Whitby told Sloat that he had recaptured three American brigs of New York and two schooners of Philadelphia. This is most likely the same Captain Henry Whitby who later commanded HMS *Leander.* Whitby precipitated a diplomatic incident in 1806 and was indicted for murder in New York City when a poorly aimed warning shot killed the helmsman of an American merchant ship. Whitby later continued an aggressive pattern of boarding and searches but appears to have allowed Sloat and the *Only Daughter* to proceed. Sloat sailed past the easternmost point of Cuba and was boarded once again. Just two days after the British boarding, a French privateer with a captured brig in company boarded the *Only Daughter.* Sloat said that he saw eleven captured American ship masters on board the privateer, but his report as published in the shipping news does not indicate why the Frenchman did not also capture Sloat and the *Only Daughter.* The American schooner continued to New York with a cargo of coffee and cigars for John B. Church and V. Du Pont, arriving on March 26 after a thirty-one-day voyage from Santiago.[7]

John B. Church was also the merchant for the next voyage. This time, Sloat sailed as master of a square-rigger, the ship *Clarissa.* On May 9, 1805, the *Clarissa* departed for Santiago de Cuba and returned to New York on August 7 with a cargo of coffee, sugar, and logwood. This last is a source of natural dye, either red or blue depending on the acidity.[8] Sloat's last port of call on this voyage before New York was Baracoa, on the Atlantic side of the southeastern end of Cuba.

A month later, John Sloat cleared for Havana, sailing as master of the brig *Hannah,* for John D. Martin of New York. He may have gone to Havana first, as reported in the shipping news, but by December 7, the *Hannah* had entered the Caribbean. The ship foundered off Jamaica on that date and was lost. A Rhode Island–based sloop, the *Louisa,* rescued the lucky crew of the *Hannah* and took them to Charleston, South Carolina. Sloat returned from there to New York as a passenger aboard the brig *Venns.*

Sloat again sailed for the tropics just three weeks after returning from the *Hannah* disaster. This next voyage is particularly significant from the historian's point of view because it is better documented than most. Not only are both the departure and arrival published in the news, but the foreign clearance filed upon departure with U.S. Customs in New York City is one of the few that survives in the archives. The schooner *Polly*, 101 tons burthen, was cleared for St. Thomas, in what was then the Danish Virgin Islands. The customs document records the cargo carried in the *Polly* to the Caribbean: flour, shoes, nails, chinaware, hats, dry goods, chairs, and other furniture. *Polly* sailed on February 4, 1805. The schooner then returned to New York on April 9 after an eighteen-day voyage from Fort-Royal, Martinique, with a cargo of sugar, coffee, and cocoa. After a two-week turnaround, Sloat again planned to sail in the *Polly* for St. Thomas, but the documentary trail vanishes at that point.[9] Sloat's route and cargoes follow a typical pattern of the time. The American market absorbed some but not all of these commodities. Many of the cargoes from Caribbean islands would be re-exported by American buyers to Europe for transport in American-flagged ships. The British Rule of 1756 held that, for instance, if France required in peacetime that sugar cargoes from Martinique to French ports be carried in French-flagged ships and Britain and France then went to war, the French shippers could not switch to American-flagged ships and claim the rights to protection of neutral ships. But if an American merchant bought the Martinique cargo in New York and then shipped it to Bordeaux in an American ship, then neutral rights applied. Britain allowed this practice to continue for several years before changing its policy in 1805 and began to consider American merchant ships bound for France as legal prizes that were eligible for capture on the high seas.[10]

John Sloat may not have taken the *Polly* to sea again. A ship named the *Nancy*, of which Sloat is listed as the master, was reported to be loading in Bordeaux for New York. At the time, thirty-six American ships were in Bordeaux awaiting cargo. No other record of this voyage appears in newspaper or government records. This report appeared in early October 1805, and so the master who informed the newspaper would have seen the ships in Bordeaux some four to eight weeks beforehand.[11] If the *Nancy* sailed for New York around the same time as did the ship from which the paper got its report, then it would have arrived around October. That timing fits the rest of the evidence, and so Sloat probably did make that voyage to Europe. The *Polly* left Martinique a few weeks before the French fleet arrived there under Admiral Villeneuve, and the battle off Cape Finisterre in northwest Spain between British and French squadrons took place on July 23, when the *Nancy* would have been in Bordeaux. The major British naval victory at Trafalgar took place on October 20, 1805. Trading in French ports at the height of the naval war between Britain and Napoleon's France must have been a rather risky business, even more so than the West Indies trade.

Sloat returned to the West Indies as master of the schooner *Hunter* in November 1805. Eight days out of New York, the *Hunter* ran aground on rocks off Bermuda. The crew was saved as was part of the cargo. Here again, the record goes dark, until Sloat appears in mid-1806 as a passenger aboard the sloop *Rainbow*. The British detained the *Rainbow* after it sailed from French Martinique and took it to Tortola in the British Virgin Islands. There, officials confiscated some of the coffee carried in the *Rainbow*'s hold. Quite a long time would pass before Sloat would again be found trading with the French.

Possibly due to the mishap in Bermuda, John Drake Sloat began to sail out of Baltimore instead of New York, although U.S. Customs records indicate that his first voyage from the Maryland port was as master of a vessel registered in New York City. He sailed the 113-ton schooner *Vigilant* from Baltimore for Danish St. Thomas on August 4, 1806, and returned from Dutch Curaçao on October 23 with cocoa, wood, and skins. The departure clearance shows that the *Vigilant* carried a crew of fifteen including the master.[12] On Christmas Day of 1806, Sloat sailed as master of the 153-ton ship *Fame*, en route to Leghorn (Livorno), Italy. The *Fame* was registered in Baltimore. The return voyage was first through Barcelona and then to New Orleans, which part took eighty days and then another forty-two days sailing back to Baltimore, arriving on October 9, 1807.[13] There, Sloat probably received letters advising him that the remaining two of his grandparents had died.

Marretje Slot passed away on July 28, 1807, at seventy-eight years of age. She had received a life estate in the will of Steven Slot, John Drake Sloat's paternal grandfather. Steven's will had been probated the year before and so would have been carried out after Marretje's death.

The will had been signed on August 20, 1792, when John Drake Sloat was eleven years old. John was to receive thirty pounds in the "current money," which would equate to seventy-five dollars. He also got his choice of beds and its appurtenances, Steven's wagon and tack, and his pleasure sleigh. Steven also willed a slave named Tone to John Drake Sloat. The 1800 census shows Steven owning three slaves, and he had owned five at the time of the 1790 census. John Drake Sloat's uncle Isaac got all the land and was directed to give him seventy pounds when he turned twenty-one years of age. Perhaps he got the seventy pounds, equal to $175, in 1802 from his still-living grandfather. He probably could have used it at that time. His two aunts, Elizabeth and Mary, divided the rest of the personal estate equally and also received equal shares in a New Jersey land parcel. Inheritance divisions such as this one favoring Isaac Sloat were quite traditional. Maintaining a family lineage was more important than any individual member of the family, and while others were to be given something, one heir would receive the bulk, which would serve as the basis for the continued economic prosperity of the family.[14]

Joseph Drake, John Drake Sloat's maternal grandfather, died just two weeks later on August 12, 1807. His wife preceded him in death. Drake's will was signed on February 12, 1807. His instructions were to sell everything and divide the proceeds between his living daughters and his grandson, John Drake Sloat. A few items were left to other family members, including cash totaling £120. If the 1800 tax rolls cited earlier accurately assessed Drake's wealth, then John Drake Sloat would have received about eight hundred pounds, or two thousand dollars. A codicil to the will, signed on June 11, 1807, provided for the emancipation of Drake's two slaves, Jack and Hannah, within six days after his death.[15] Edwin Sherman's 1902 biography states that Sloat inherited twelve slaves from his grandfather Drake and immediately manumitted them.[16] This is another example of the inaccuracies in Sherman's book. Grandfather Drake freed Hannah and Jack, and we have no record of Tone at all, although quite possibly John Drake Sloat did manumit Tone if he was still living and still a slave at the time of Marretje or Steven Sloat's death. Drake's insistence that manumission of Hannah and Jack occur so shortly after his death differs from the extant practice among Hudson Valley slave owners, even after New York's gradual abolition law went into effect in 1799. If a will called for manumission, it was usually some years after the death of the testator.[17]

At this point in the narrative, it is appropriate to pause and consider the preceding information about Sloat's merchant voyages in historical context. John Drake Sloat sailed as master in the first decade of the nineteenth century. The usual risks that went along with merchant sailing in the Atlantic world were amplified by the Napoleonic wars. To sail in the Mediterranean added even more risk of being boarded or captured by Algerian or Tripolitan commerce raiders. The United States had extensive trading ties with the Caribbean islands, just as it had done in colonial days, and so pirates of the Spanish Main also figured along with British or French threats to neutral shipping. In particular, the port of Baltimore carried an extensive trade with the West Indies. Fast schooners carried flour and tobacco south and returned with coffee, cocoa, sugar, rice, indigo, and cotton from the tropical Caribbean.[18]

Many of Sloat's voyages to the West Indies were as master of just such schooners. Historian Howard I. Chapelle contends that the majority of American maritime trade at that time was carried in schooners, and a recent statistically based study of the cocoa trade confirms that finding. These fore-and-aft-rigged ships almost always had two masts in the decade before the War of 1812. Those schooners were built for speed and so sacrificed cargo capacity to obtain sharp lines. Their fore-and-aft rigs enabled them to sail at a closer angle against the wind than could a square-rigged vessel. A fast and well-sailed schooner was a difficult ship to catch. A typical merchant schooner would have been between seventy and one hundred feet long, with a cargo capacity of seventy and one hundred burthen tons.[19] A burthen ton was a unit of volume, not weight, that equated to ninety-four cubic feet. A one-hundred-ton schooner such as Sloat's *Polly* would have had the cargo space of about four present-day shipping containers, the most commonly seen containers having a volume of 2,400 cubic feet. Brigs such as the *Hannah* and full-rigged ships such as the *Clarissa* might have had the capacity of two hundred to as much as four hundred burthen tons, respectively.

Records of crew size do not survive for any of Sloat's voyages except for the *Vigilant*, but fifteen men seems an unusually large crew for a schooner. One report from the United States consul at Bordeaux records that a brig from New York sailed with a crew of eight. The consul at La Rochelle later reported that another brig navigated with a crew of eleven, including the master.[20] The historian Ira Dye writes of two brigs during the War of 1812 that sailed with crews of seven and nine.[21] Let us compare merchant and naval ships. The frigate *President* was 173 feet long, a little more than 1,500 tons burthen, and carried a crew of about 450, including seven commissioned officers and twenty midshipmen.[22] One can easily imagine how seamanship development among frigate officers could become problematic from the lack of practical opportunity, as historian McKee concludes. Contemporary commenters concur. In *Two Years before the Mast*, Richard Henry Dana shows how merchant ship officers, especially mates but also masters, routinely dirtied their hands doing tasks that a commissioned naval officer would never do. Herman Melville's *White Jacket* and James Fenimore Cooper's *Afloat and Ashore* and *Miles Wallingford* all corroborate the point. His years in the merchant service gave John Drake Sloat a tremendous wealth and depth of seamanship experience.

The men who sailed as crew with Sloat were probably as young as he was. No crew list survives from any of his voyages. The typical American sailor went to sea at about twenty years of age, and the vast majority of them moved to livelihoods ashore within nine years. The storied grizzled old salts could be found, but they were the exceptions that proved the rule. About one-third of American seaman were illiterate or could barely read or write. The seamen generally came from towns and cities and not from farms. About one in five overall was of African descent, but this proportion was higher in ships such as the *Vigilant* that sailed out of Maryland and the Chesapeake. About one in ten seamen sailing from Northern ports was black. Hiring of seamen would later be taken over by exploitive agents known as "crimps," who frequently "shanghaied" sailors by nefarious or tricky methods to deliver them to ships in return for a fee. A more thorough discussion of crimping appears in a later chapter. But before the War of 1812, shipmasters usually hired their own crews on the waterfront.[23]

A shipmaster typically received a wage of fifty dollars per month throughout the decade preceding the War of 1812. A mate made thirty dollars monthly in 1800, but that declined by two dollars with the end of the Quasi-War. When the Peace of Amiens ended and the war between Britain and France resumed in 1804, a mate's wage rose back to between thirty and thirty-two dollars. An able seaman's monthly wage went from twenty to thirteen dollars between 1800 and 1803 and returned to twenty dollars around 1804. When the threat of British impressment was particularly high after 1809, the seaman's wage rose to twenty-five dollars. The year 1815 brought not only the conclusion of the War of 1812 and the fall of Napoleon but also a drop in seamen's monthly wages to fourteen dollars. Seamen on the New York waterfront could be a contentious lot, and in 1802 they went on strike demanding higher wages. They dismantled one schooner and stowed its sails. City authorities had the ringleaders arrested, and the strike itself failed when owners and masters hired strikebreakers to round out their crews. Its failure notwithstanding, this groundswell labor action by seamen who had no trade union organization was a remarkable event. Underlying the problem was the economy itself. During the period 1800 to 1812, the cost of living rose steadily while wage rates remained steady or declined. Either way, the loss of purchasing power equated to a loss in real wages.[24] By comparison, a United States Navy lieutenant received pay and rations equal to fifty-eight dollars each month, an able seaman got eleven dollars, and an ordinary seaman earned nine dollars.[25]

The United States merchant marine profited greatly from trading under its neutral flag during the years before 1812. American exports were in demand, and freight rates were high. The profits justified the risks. The dollar value of exports from New York doubled between 1797 and 1807. Growth slowed during the year-long Peace of Amiens, but when war resumed between Britain and France, the maritime carrying business again boomed. The cargoes listed for Sloat's various voyages are typical of those traded on the Caribbean and the European shipping routes for the period.[26] One risk was impressment of seamen from American ships by Royal Navy men-of-war on the high seas. Probably the most famous and most egregious example came on June 22, 1807. The frigate *Chesapeake* had just sailed from Norfolk and was fired upon and then boarded by a party from HMS *Leopard*, a frigate of the Royal Navy. Claiming that four *Chesapeake* sailors were actually their king's subjects, the British impressed them then and there. One was determined to be a Royal Navy deserter and that unfortunate man was soon hanged.[27] The uproar in the United States led to President Thomas Jefferson getting the famous, or perhaps infamous, Embargo Act through Congress. Departures to foreign ports by American vessels were prohibited. The embargo was repealed in March 1809 just as Jefferson left office, it having had virtually no effect on Britain at all. It did have a devastating effect on American ocean trade.[28] It also had a devastating effect on sailors. At least five hundred ships sat idle in New York harbor alone, and in Salem, Massachusetts, soup kitchens fed more than a thousand seamen per day.[29]

John Drake Sloat's name does not come up in a computer search of the shipping news during 1808. Some shipowners and masters did break the embargo and sail anyway. Sloat appears to have been one for following the law rather than breaking it, and it thus seems unlikely that Sloat would have been one of those very few who broke the embargo. Coastal shipping did increase during the embargo, and Sloat may have switched to that arena until international trade was again legal under the American flag. Throughout 1809, he sailed as master of the 152-ton *Financier.* This large schooner sailed out of Baltimore but was registered in New York. Sloat arrived in Baltimore from New Orleans on January 5 of that year. *Financier* next appears at one of the Mississippi River's mouths, waiting to go up to New Orleans. Sloat then shuttled twice between New Orleans and Havana and made a side trip to Campeche, Mexico; the schooner recorded yet another trip to Havana and then left New Orleans for home on October 6. Sloat reported that his schooner was pursued off Matanzas, Cuba, by two seventy-four-gun ships of the line, two frigates, one brig, and one schooner. The *Financier* appears to have given the pursuing squadron the slip and arrived back in Baltimore on November 2, 1809.[30]

The year 1810 saw John Sloat as master of a full-rigged ship trading between the Atlantic coast of the United States and ports in Britain and Ireland. Congress had reopened legal trade with Britain in May 1810.[31] On July 4, 1810, there appeared the following in the *Boston Commercial Gazette*:

> The American captains at Dublin celebrated the 4th July in a becoming manner. Capt Robins, of Philad, and Mr. Dunlap, of N. York, presided. The elegant ship *Oneida*, capt. Sloat, was decorated in the most superb manner; and the different

> American vessels in the harbor displayed their flags. The greatest harmony prevailed, and the company amounted to forty-seven in number.[32]

Oneida returned to New York with a cargo of linens and Irish porter on August 28. Sloat then cleared for Liverpool on September 26, 1810. One report from another shipmaster places Sloat and the *Oneida* at Liverpool discharging cargo in late November. The return voyage across the Atlantic to New York took forty-eight days, and *Oneida* arrived there on January 21, 1811, with three passengers and a cargo of coal, dry goods, and hardware.[33]

The trail of John Drake Sloat at this point again ducks into the shadows. In March 1811, Congress reinstituted nonimportation against Britain, breaking off commercial relations altogether. Throughout 1811, the United States slid toward a war with Great Britain that neither country really wanted. Historians have long debated the causes of the War of 1812, but Alan Taylor points to three disputes that together led to the American declaration of war: the British Orders in Council that interfered with American maritime commerce, the continued impressment of American seamen into the Royal Navy, and British alliances with Native American nations that interfered with the westward expansion of the United States. In his history of American foreign policy, George C. Herring contends that this last cause was self-inflicted by the Americans.[34]

On May 16, the twenty-gun corvette HMS *Little Belt* mistook the forty-four-gun frigate *President* for a French ship and gave chase in hopes of taking a prize. Accounts differed as to which ship fired first, but once the fight began, the *President* quickly pounded the smaller ship even though the *Little Belt* fought well. Needless to say, the *Little Belt* affair inflamed passions on both sides of the Atlantic.[35] Diplomacy failed, and war was clearly expected by many as the year ended. John Drake Sloat was in the Norfolk area at the beginning of 1812.

CHAPTER FIVE

Sailing Master

At the dawn of the year 1812, a squadron of American warships repaired and groomed its vessels in the Norfolk area as the United States Navy actively prepared for the war that would later be declared against Great Britain. The squadron included some of President Jefferson's ill-starred gunboats, as well as the brig *Nautilus*, the sloop-of-war *Wasp*, and the thirty-eight-gun frigate *Congress.* The pennant of the squadron commander, Commodore Stephen Decatur, flew in the forty-four-gun frigate *United States.*

Stephen Decatur was already one of the most storied sailors in the history of the United States Navy and remains so to this day. Many biographies of Decatur have appeared over the years, including no fewer than four such books between 2004 and 2006 alone. In 1812, his fame stemmed from the Barbary Wars. The frigate *Philadelphia* ran aground in Tripoli harbor and was captured along with the crew in October 1803. Lieutenant Decatur led a disguised boarding party that sailed into Tripoli harbor on the night of February 16, 1804. They recaptured the *Philadelphia* after hand-to-hand combat, set the ship ablaze, and then withdrew. For this action that restored the national and naval honor lost when the ship fell into Tripolitan hands, Decatur was promoted directly from lieutenant to captain, bypassing the rank of master commandant. At least one well-regarded officer, Lieutenant Andrew Sterett, resigned his commission in furious resentment after being bypassed in seniority, but Decatur's reputation was firmly established.

How John Drake Sloat met Stephen Decatur remains obscure. Throughout the period when Midshipman Sloat served aboard the *President*, Lieutenant Decatur served in the *United States* and in the brig

Norfolk for part of 1800 while the *United States* underwent repairs. Decatur returned to the *United States* and was aboard when that ship relieved the *President* in the West Indies during the Quasi-War with France. The two may have met during the turnover in the Caribbean, or possibly they were introduced years later just before Sloat returned to the navy. One mutual point of contact was Captain Isaac Chauncey, who had served with Decatur during the Barbary Wars in the Mediterranean and who had been a lieutenant aboard the *President* during the 1800 Quasi-War cruise.

Sloat must have been very interested in returning to the navy, or else he would not have gone to great lengths to do so. It is difficult to imagine a thirty-year-old master mariner who sailed his own ships for several years being willing to return as a mere midshipman. Returning as a lieutenant without ever having held a commission also seems unlikely in view of the large number of midshipmen eagerly seeking the few available lieutenancies. But another avenue did exist, however narrow it was. One could become a sailing master and try it from there. Chauncey persuaded Sloat to apply for a sailing master's warrant. Secretary of the Navy Paul Hamilton assured Sloat that if war was declared on Great Britain, then he would be commissioned a lieutenant.[1] John Drake Sloat was appointed Sailing Master, United States Navy, with his warrant dated January 10, 1812, and ordered to report to the commandant of the navy yard at Gosport, Virginia, which is near Norfolk.[2] The *United States*' incumbent sailing master was promoted to acting lieutenant on February 12, and Sailing Master Sloat joined the ship on February 21.[3]

In becoming a sailing master, Sloat took a position that suited well his own purpose, but one that was on its way to obsolescence. The term "sailing master" actually had two meanings. It referred to a position aboard a warship. It was also the rank title of the person who was expected to hold that position. Just as one could be a purser, a boatswain, or an assistant surgeon, a warrant officer could be a sailing master.

Sailing masters had existed aboard English warships and in other navies for centuries. Before standing professional navies came into existence, a warship captain was a warrior sent by the monarch to command a military force at sea, but he was often a landsman who knew nothing of ships and the sea. To back him up, then, a master mariner was brought aboard to handle the nautical aspects under the captain's command. By the late eighteenth century, the Royal Navy had a solid corps of professional

Figure 5.1. *USS* United States *under Full Sail*, unknown artist. (Courtesy of Photo Collection, Naval History and Heritage Command.)

naval officers. They came from elite backgrounds suitable for one to hold a British king's commission, but they were trained seamen. The United States Navy was created very much in the Royal Navy's image, but at a time when the sailing master had become a bit superfluous, as Christopher McKee's magisterial social history of the early U.S. Navy officer corps demonstrates.[4] In the modern U.S. Navy, the position most closely resembling the sailing master is the navigator, who is a commissioned officer of appropriate rank to supervise officers of the deck on watch if the commanding officer or the executive officer is not physically present.

The historian Will Fowler lays out a daily routine at sea of the famous *Constitution*, a near sister of the *United States.* The sailing master would be on deck at dawn to observe the weather and review the deck log. In the morning, he adjusted the trim of the ship, both fore and aft as well as port and starboard. The sailing master also instructed the midshipmen each morning. In the afternoon, he supervised the cleaning of the hold, the stowage of which was another matter under his cognizance. Toward sunset, he conferred with the captain about the night orders to be written for the lieutenants who stood watch as officer of the deck while the captain and the sailing master were asleep below decks.[5] Celestial observations of the sun could be done at any time, but those of stars could only be done at morning and evening twilight because that is when the stars and the earth's horizon can both be seen well enough to get an accurate measurement with a sextant or a quadrant.

These duties could place the sailing master in a supervisory role over lieutenants who outranked him. Also note that the sailing master was not in charge of a division of the large number of able and ordinary seamen who comprised the bulk of the ship's labor force and gun crews. That duty belonged to each of the lieutenants. The sailing master normally had some master's mates, who were petty officers who assisted him on a rotating basis around the clock. A ship's sailing master did not always have to be a warranted Sailing Master, U.S. Navy. An experienced midshipman could be taken on as sailing master. These midshipmen were ready in all respects to become lieutenants but were waiting for a vacancy to open so they could be commissioned. This already common practice would become the norm after the War of 1812 as officer promotions slowed down. Whether sailing master or midshipman by rank, a ship's sailing master received pay and rations of fifty-two dollars per month, which was considerably more than a midshipman's nineteen dollars.[6] Considering the sailing master's duties, John Drake Sloat's extensive experience as a merchant mariner, and his earlier knowledge of navy ways from his midshipman days, it seems that Commodore Decatur made a very good choice for the sailing master of the *United States*. That choice would serve him well.

The three forty-four-gun frigates had originally been meant as sister ships and were derived from one basic plan. The *United States* was built in Philadelphia, the *Constitution* in Boston, and the *President* in New York. The *United States* was the first one to be finished and was fitted out in 1797. Captain John Barry, the first commanding officer, had made substantial design changes while he supervised the construction. In particular, the stern area had been expanded with a "round house," which created

Figure 5.2. Main deck of the frigate USS *Constitution*, looking aft. *Constitution* was a near sister of the *United States.* Sailing Master Sloat's watch and battle station was on the quarterdeck, located at the aft end of the ship. (Photo by author.)

larger quarters for the commanding officer. That made the *United States* heavier than the other two frigates and more difficult to keep properly trimmed at sea. Being the slowest of the frigates quickly earned the ship the somewhat inglorious nickname "Old Wagon." Southern live oak hull timbers made for a strong ship against enemy cannon fire. Adding heavier armament than originally planned exacerbated the sluggishness problem at sea. The gun batteries on sailing ships could be changed rather easily, and commanding officers did so according to their predilections. Commodore Decatur preferred guns that fired twenty-four-pound rounds, as opposed to the eighteen pounders used by many British captains.[7] As a combat platform, the "Old Wagon" fired a heavy broadside but required a high degree of seamanship for effective employment in combat against a nimble adversary ship.

For several weeks after Sailing Master Sloat reported aboard the *United States*, repairs to the ship continued under Commodore Decatur's supervision. When the repairs were complete, the frigate sailed north to New York and there joined the squadron under the command of Commodore John Rodgers. Besides Decatur's "Old Wagon," the squadron comprised the brigs *Argus* and *Hornet* and the frigates *Congress*, rated at thirty-eight guns, and the *President*, the last being Rodgers's flagship.

President Madison signed on June 18, 1812, the declaration of war against Great Britain that he had requested from the Congress. Within a few days, the squadron put to sea. Secretary Hamilton ordered it to cruise the Atlantic and to prey upon British shipping. By keeping the ships together, he hoped to have enough strength to deal with whichever portion of the several hundred ships of the Royal Navy they might encounter. That navy, of course, was largely deployed against France. The American squadron encountered a great deal of fog and found few ships to take as prizes as it cruised near the English Channel, then by Madeira, and back toward the U.S. Atlantic coast. The departure to sea from New York took

Figure 5.3. *USS* United States *and HMS* Macedonian (October 25, 1812), unknown artist after Thomas Birch. (Image courtesy of U.S. Naval Academy Museum.)

place so hastily that the ships did not take on a full load of provisions. Vegetables and fruits soon ran out, and a scurvy outbreak soon followed. They arrived off Sandy Hook just as the *Constitution* also returned to New York, having defeated the thirty-eight-gun frigate HMS *Guerrière* in action at sea. Commodore Rodgers argued that his cruise had also been a success because it had pulled many British ships away from raiding American merchant ships. Even so, one Royal Navy squadron continued to prey upon American shipping along the coast with substantial success.[8] Historians today continue to disagree about Rodgers's degree of success. It seems beyond debate, however, that the sailors in the ships themselves felt unhappy with the results. Secretary Hamilton was also disappointed and changed his operational concept. The ships would split up and operate independently so as to cover larger areas. On October 8, 1812, the squadron got underway and returned to the Atlantic.

Commodore Decatur took the *United States* and the *Argus* when the squadron divided up at sea. The *United States* had been cruising singly west of the Canary Islands and southeast of the Azores when the long-sought opportunity finally presented itself. As the sun rose on October 25, lookouts sighted what turned out to be the British frigate HMS *Macedonian.* The British lookouts reported the American frigate to their captain John Carden, who turned his ship toward the *United States.* The two ships closed range on roughly opposite courses. Then, the *United States* turned around to a parallel course. Decatur intended to maintain a distance that favored his twenty-four-pound guns over the *Macedonian*'s eighteen pounders. The *United States* again reversed course away from the *Macedonian* and headed on a parallel course but in the opposite direction. As the ships passed, the American frigate fired a ranging broadside that fell short. As it had been a double-shot broadside and the rest would be single shot, Decatur had the range he wanted. The *Macedonian* then turned toward the *United States* to close the range and came all the way around to a parallel course. The *United States* responded with a quick turn away and back again in a try to maintain the longer range. The faster-sailing *Macedonian* began to close again, but heavy broadsides began to batter the British ship. In fairly short order, the *Macedonian* lost the top halves of all three masts. The *United States* backed the mizzen topsail in order not to pull ahead and then raked the *Macedonian* again, bringing down the rest of the Britisher's mizzen mast. Filling the mizzen topsail, the "Old

Wagon" then moved ahead and made quick battle repairs to some damage. Once again returning alongside the now crippled *Macedonian*, the *United States* made ready to fire another broadside when Captain Carden struck the *Macedonian*'s colors and surrendered. At some point during the battle, Sailing Master Sloat received a minor wound to his face.[9]

Five days passed while temporary repairs were made to the *Macedonian* to make her able to sail again, with a prize crew under the command of Lieutenant William Henry Allen, who had been aboard the frigate *Chesapeake* when HMS *Leopard*'s press gang boarded her in 1807. As first lieutenant of the *United States*, Allen was second-in-command to Decatur, and so to him went the honor of serving as prize captain. They set sail in company toward Montauk Point at the east end of Long Island. The "Old Wagon" continued to justify the nickname when on several occasions the damaged *Macedonian* had to shorten sail and slow down to remain on station. The two ships made landfall on December 3, 1812. The *Macedonian* entered Newport, Rhode Island, and the *United States* went to New London, Connecticut.[10] The deck log of the *United States* shows that Sailing Master Sloat remained aboard and stood watch as officer of the deck in regular rotation during this transit.

How much credit for the *Macedonian* sea battle should belong to Sailing Master John Drake Sloat? The U.S. Navy's traditional approach is to give the officer in command full credit for every success and usually full blame for any failure or even mere shortcoming. Many commanding officers then magnanimously point to their officers and men as being behind it all. In his post-action letter to Secretary Hamilton, Commodore Decatur did just that and said that everyone performed so splendidly that it would be impossible for him to single out any particular person. He then singled out Lieutenant Allen for the ship's superb gunnery and attributed it to the first lieutenant's effective training program. Decatur probably did that because he intended to press the secretary to nominate Allen for a double promotion to captain. That would be an extraordinary reward, like he had received for burning the *Philadelphia*. Decatur perhaps did not think that getting a lieutenancy for his sailing master would be extraordinarily difficult.

Present-day biographers of Stephen Decatur such as Leonard Guttridge, John Schroeder, and Spencer Tucker make no mention of the frigate's sailing master. Similarly, biographer Cyrus T. Brady wrote in 1900 that the "masterly manner" in which the *United States* was handled during the *Macedonian* battle earned the admiration of the British officers and any veteran seamen who knew enough to understand. Shortly after Decatur's premature and much-mourned death in 1820, S. Waldo Putnam wrote in that vein, and John H. Schroeder recently did the same. But some present-day historians suggest a contrary view. James Tertius deKay echoes Ira Dye's contention that Decatur was an "indifferent sailor." Dye gives credit for good shiphandling to Decatur on that day at least but concludes that Allen's gunnery gave Decatur his victory over the *Macedonian.* DeKay goes on to say that Decatur preferred to give his sailing master general intentions and then expected him to carry them out. Tucker particularly emphasizes the importance of maneuver in the battle between the *United States* and the *Macedonian.* Robert Allison points out some contemporary criticisms of Decatur's shiphandling during the subsequent Algerian war of 1815.[11] Such criticisms would wound deeply any seagoing naval officers who received them. Seamanship is a part of their core self-identity. That being said, this author's experience is that some officers are better shiphandlers than others, and an enviable few seem to have a knack for what comes a little harder to most. Decatur showed great wisdom by getting a sailing master with that knack, and one with the experience in seamanship that Sloat had gained in his years of merchant service. A good leader would do that. In 1812, Decatur's superb service reputation derived from a close combat commando-style raid, and his ketch was conned into Tripoli at night by Salvatore Catalano, an Italian pilot who knew that harbor well. All in all, it may well be unfair to implicitly disparage Commodore Stephen Decatur's seamanship or to try to take away anything from his memory. But it would also be unfair, through omission or otherwise, to deny Sailing Master John Drake Sloat substantial recognition for his own seamanship in the defeat and capture of HMS *Macedonian.*

The nation certainly did give recognition to Commodore Decatur, and the city of New York did to all the "Wagoneers" in particular. The frigate sailed across Long Island Sound and passed through the Throgs Neck on New Year's Eve Day en route to an East River anchorage. Along with Captain Isaac Hull, late commanding officer of the *Constitution* that was then at sea off Brazil, and Master Commandant Jacob Jones and the crew of the *Wasp* that had been victorious over HMS *Frolic,*

Decatur and the *United States*' crew were feted at dinners and theatrical celebrations throughout the city. They paraded in formation to these celebrations through the streets filled with admiring citizens. About a fifth of the crew was of African descent and, at this event at least, they sat right alongside the other sailors. One British sailor, a *Macedonian* seaman who had avoided repatriation to Halifax to remain in the United States, wryly wondered whether the welcome extended to the sailors would continue once their prize money was gone, but for the moment, exuberance reigned in the streets.[12]

Bringing the *Macedonian* into port entitled the personnel of the *United States* to cash rewards of prize money. Under the applicable laws of the day, if the prize ship was of lesser force than the captor ship, then the United States government kept half the prize ship's value and the other half was distributed among the captor crew. If the prize was a stronger or equal ship than the captor, then the captor crew received a double reward by splitting the prize ship's entire value. Commodore Decatur filed a claim that the *Macedonian* mounted forty-nine guns and the *United States* had but forty-four. The *Macedonian* actually did carry forty-nine but was rated at thirty-eight. The *United States* carried more than fifty but was rated at forty-four and was also a somewhat larger ship with a much larger crew. Using different standards for the comparison probably fooled nobody, but Decatur's stretch of the truth prevailed and the "Wagoneers" split $200,000 among themselves.[13]

The commanding officer received 15 percent of the prize money. Stephen Decatur's $30,000 was the largest U.S. prize award of the War of 1812. The smallest awards of *Macedonian* prize money, to landsmen and ship's boys, were of two hundred dollars. The lieutenants, the sailing master, and the captain of marines shared in a 10 percent portion. Other fractions were designated for various groups of warrant officers, marine lieutenants, sergeants and corporals, petty officers, midshipmen, and so on.[14] The *United States* carried six lieutenants, Sailing Master Sloat, and two lieutenants of marines. Lieutenant John M. Funck was killed during the action, but perhaps his share went to his next of kin. The senior marine lieutenant perhaps received the share intended for the captain as commander of the marines on board. Sloat then would have received as little as one-eighth or as much as one-sixth of the officers' portion, which would amount to between $2,500 and $3,333. At a minimum then, he received a lump sum equaling at least six years of his regular salary for the *Macedonian* action.

The official papers submitted about the ships' relative strength perhaps did not sink to the level of an outright false official report on the part of Commodore Decatur. But this episode may have been a sort of object lesson to Sloat and the other officers on selectively "gilding the lily" when submitting reports and documents.

At the same time that the prize award matter unfolded, Commodore Decatur also took up the matter of promotions for Lieutenant William Henry Allen and Sailing Master John Drake Sloat. Historian Christopher McKee writes extensively about these two cases. Decatur attempted to get Allen promoted directly to captain and to get Sloat commissioned a lieutenant. Recall that Decatur himself had been promoted two grades for the *Philadelphia* burning. Also, the first lieutenant of the *Constitution*, Charles Morris, had just been double promoted to captain after that frigate captured HMS *Guerrière* in the summer of 1812. Just like Decatur's promotion during the Barbary Wars, Morris's promotion had caused some resentment on the part of those over whom he had jumped on the seniority list.[15]

But in the short time that had passed since Morris's good fortune, Paul Hamilton had been replaced on January 19, 1813, as secretary of the navy by William Jones. The latter was a much more effective official and seems not to have felt bound by any of Hamilton's promises. To Decatur's chagrin, Lieutenant Allen "only" received an immediate promotion to master commandant and command of the brig *Argus*.[16] Sailing Master Sloat also encountered unexpected difficulties. Secretary Jones denied Decatur's request for a lieutenancy for his sailing master. Sloat himself then wrote to Jones but heard nothing back for several weeks. Interestingly, Sloat contended that his appointment as midshipman was still in effect, although Navy Department records clearly state otherwise.[17] As there were no increases in pay based on longevity in service, nor any retirement system at all, the point was perhaps moot.

Decatur allowed Sloat to go personally from New York to Washington to press his case. Besides the recommendations of his own commanding officer, he also carried a letter from Allen who said that he would be pleased to have Sloat as one of his own lieutenants on board the *Argus*. The record contains no mention of any letter from Thomas

Truxtun about Sloat's discharge under the Peace Establishment Act, and so we are left to speculate as to why not. Truxtun lived in New Jersey close to the post road leading from New York to Baltimore, and so it would have been easy for Sloat to stop there. Perhaps being sick ashore when Truxtun left the *President* was a cover story, but one must remember that *President* shipmate Isaac Chauncey supported the scheme for Sloat to return as a sailing master and then to seek a commission. Truxtun's biographer notes that Truxtun opposed the war with England, and so as a Federalist, his letter might have done more harm than good in dealing with a Madison administration official. The picture painted by biographer Eugene Ferguson of Truxtun ashore in retirement suggests a tempestuous, cranky old man whom most might prefer just to leave alone.[18] Sloat's case seems to have depended on his own letters and those of Stephen Decatur.

Secretary Jones's reluctance to promote Sailing Master Sloat derived in large part from his concerns about the large number of midshipmen who were competing for a dwindling number of lieutenancies as the navy officer corps filled out and stabilized. A few exceptions did occur, however, and Jones rationalized this one by taking note of Decatur's strong recommendation and the peculiar situation that led to Sloat's discharge under the Peace Establishment Act. John Drake Sloat received an appointment as acting lieutenant on April 28, 1813. He followed up with another letter to the Navy Department, in which he enclosed a copy of his appointment letter as midshipman so that he would receive appropriate seniority placement among the new lieutenants when the group received the consent of the Senate. He also reminded the secretary of his earlier personal visit to Washington and declared his wish to be remembered as more than just another name on the list of sailing masters.[19] His lieutenant's commission became permanent when the Senate confirmed it on July 24 of that year. Historian McKee observes, "Sailing Master Sloat's story delineates the combination of native ability, determination, and powerful support required if a sailing master was to gain the lieutenant's rung on the ladder of rank."[20]

Armed with a commission and a lesson in the importance of politicking with secretaries of the navy, John Drake Sloat returned to the *United States* as a junior lieutenant in the wardroom. He had considerably more nautical experience than did his equals on the naval seniority list, and he was also considerably older. Consider as examples, two contemporaries: Lieutenant Matthew Calbraith Perry was thirteen years younger than Sloat but had the same date of rank. James Biddle was only two years younger than Sloat but had come aboard the *President* as a new midshipman at the same time during the Quasi-War as did Sloat. Biddle was promoted from lieutenant to master commandant at the same time that Sloat became a lieutenant.[21] As will be seen in the following chapters, both advantages and disadvantages would stem from the age and experience differences between John Drake Sloat and other navy officers of the same seniority.

CHAPTER SIX

Blockaded Lieutenant

While the administrative machinations to get Sailing Master John Drake Sloat commissioned as a lieutenant carried on during the spring of 1813, the frigate *United States* prepared in New York harbor for another war cruise. The strategic situation had dramatically changed. Stung and humiliated by American victories at sea, the British increased Royal Navy strength in the western Atlantic. They declared a blockade of the coasts of the United States and brought up the ships to enforce it. By May 1813, two British frigates and two ships of the line, the most powerful type of warship in the Napoleonic era world, patrolled off the entrances to New York harbor. Commodore Decatur proposed that the *United States* and *Argus* slip out to the Atlantic, but Secretary Jones sent the *Argus* on a different mission. Instead, the brig *Hornet* and the newly refitted prize frigate USS *Macedonian* joined Decatur's squadron. The three ships moved down to Sandy Hook. A British ship of the line and a frigate moved up to oppose the American departure, and Decatur waited for the right weather to get past the stronger force. That weather never came. Decatur decided to reach the Atlantic via Long Island Sound. The three American ships returned to the East River between Brooklyn and Manhattan. On May 24, 1813, they moved toward the Hell's Gate, the same treacherous passage they had used to get to New York from the New England coast months before. By that time, the secretary of the navy had given Lieutenant Sloat his acting commission and the *United States* had a new sailing master. This second transit through the Hell's Gate did not go as well as the first one. They arrived at low tide so that the currents would be at a minimum. But the *United States* ran lightly aground and had to wait for the tide to rise and float the ship. While sailing on toward Long Island Sound, lightning struck the *United States* and damaged several spars. The *Macedonian* had been following astern and backed all sails from fear of colliding with the *United States*, whose magazines appeared in danger of exploding from ignition by the lightning. Repairs were made, and then the ships fought headwinds before finally reaching Montauk Point five days later on May 29. Two British ships awaited there and more quickly appeared. Heavily outnumbered, Commodore Decatur headed for New London and the safety of Connecticut's Thames River. The American ships anchored in the river, and the British would keep them caged there for the rest of the war.

The United States Navy suffered another reverse just at that time. The frigate *Chesapeake* sailed from Boston on June 1, 1813, but HMS *Shannon* immediately intercepted and gave battle. Captain James Lawrence was killed during the fight. His ship was captured by the British and taken to Halifax flying the Royal Navy's White Ensign atop the Stars and Stripes.

The spectacular successes of American naval ships during 1812 and in early 1813 on the high seas were a bright side of the war. The rest of it had not gone so well. In August 1812, General William Hull was defeated near Detroit. Attempts to cross the Niagara River from western New York into present-day Ontario resulted in failure. Great Britain declared a blockade of the United States coast and enforced it.

Since some international maritime legalities will also figure in a later chapter, it is useful to discuss them here. The *United States* and *Macedonian* are often said to have been "blockaded" in Connecticut by British naval ships, but that is something of a misnomer. Legally speaking, a blockade exists when a belligerent nation places its ships off the entrances to enemy harbors and ports to keep vessels from going in or out. The purpose is to interrupt maritime commerce. In a declared blockade, belligerent nations' warships have the right to visit and search merchant ships anywhere on the high seas, including those of neutral nations. An attempt to run through a blockade begins as soon as the blockade runner sails for a blockaded port, no matter how far away it is. Liable for capture from that point on, a blockade-running ship and its cargo are subject to condemnation in a prize court. A blockade must be formally declared, and to be recognized under international law, it must be effective in that a ship attempting to breach the blockade will probably be caught.[1] These concepts do not apply to a tactical situation between combatants when British warships off shore prevented American warships such as the *United States* from getting to sea. Those same enemy ships, in this case, also enforced the maritime blockade declared by the British against commercial shipping bound for American ports.

Nothing trains for service at sea like actually being at sea does. But time spent in port can be put to good use. The "Wagoneers" settled into a routine of training and drills. In particular, the training of gun crews could be maintained at a high level through regular practice. Commodore Decatur and Lieutenant Allen had done that for years before the *United States* fought against HMS *Macedonian*.[2] Allen was gone, of course, having been given command of the *Argus*, and others also transferred in and out of the New London squadron's ships. Lieutenant Matthew Calbraith Perry had reported to the *United States* from the *President* in the fall of 1813.[3] Thirteen years younger than Sloat, Perry had been promoted from midshipman to lieutenant with the same date of rank, although junior to the former sailing master by a few numbers on the seniority list. Perry's older brother, Master Commandant Oliver Hazard Perry, had just won the Battle of Lake Erie in September 1813, which was the first step in enshrining the Perry name's prominence in American naval history. John Drake Sloat and Matthew Calbraith Perry would cross paths many times in the decades that followed, and the two seem to have been good friends.

The patriotic delirium that had erupted when Decatur brought a British frigate to New England as a prize eventually subsided. "Mr. Madison's War" enjoyed little popularity among New Englanders, even though that region was substantially and directly affected by the British Orders in Council and by impressment of seamen. Maritime trade was New England's lifeblood, and the blockade strangled it. Present-day readers should keep in mind that ideas of nationhood and loyalty that exist in the United States today were not well formed in 1813, and that in 1814, New England states seriously contemplated secession before the war ended. New London was home to a mix of Republicans who supported President Madison and the Federalists who often opposed the war. Frustrations in getting the American squadron out of New London and back to sea created a national cause célèbre.

New Londoners and Connecticut militia proved reluctant in assisting the squadron and even in improving the fortifications protecting their

Figure 6.1. Detail of "Map of the southern part of the state of New York including Long Island Sound, the state of Connecticut . . ." Pettipaug is at center, New London, Norwich, and Stonington are at right. British blockading ships usually stood off the mouth of the Thames River near Fisher's Island. (Courtesy of the Library of Congress.)

harbor. Commodore Decatur accused them of aiding and abetting the British enemy after he failed to break out of New London beginning in December 1813. The newspaper *Boston Patriot* repeated a story from the *New-London Gazette* entitled "Traitors." On Sunday evening, December 12, 1813, a report circulated that the American squadron would put to sea before morning. Blue lights shone from both the New London and the Groton sides of the Thames and signaled a warning to the British ships.[4]

On the morning immediately after the December 12th blue lights incident, a small British sloop entered New London harbor. The first and second lieutenants each took a gunboat and a party of men to the harbor mouth to oppose the sloop, which then withdrew without fighting. The two officers are not identified by name in the log, but they would have been the two most senior of the lieutenants aboard the *United States*, John Gallagher and George C. Read. Decatur used navy equipment and personnel to strengthen New London shore defenses. Three days after the sloop incident, Lieutenant Sloat and a party of sailors took two eighteen-pound guns up to Fort Trumbull, which commanded the Thames River approaches to New London.[5]

Furious, Decatur wrote to the secretary of the navy and complained about the New Londoners' alleged treachery. It was not an isolated incident, and similar events took place on at least two other occasions. On January 9, 1814, blue lights appeared again on each side of the river and were answered by British ships. This time, American military and naval officers clearly saw the signal exchange. On the evening of March 19, 1814, a large snow and rain storm approached New London. Commodore Decatur hoped to take advantage of the poor visibility and escape past the British ships. He ordered the officers of the three ships to return aboard. Soon afterward, blue lights went up like rockets, and a British ship acknowledged the signal by firing guns at regular intervals.[6]

Just before the second incident in January 1814, the *Connecticut Gazette* responded that the report in December was scandalously false and stated that the blue lights were fired from British boats close in to shore and not from the heights above the Thames River. The *Connecticut Gazette* editor opined that the lights were only signals between British ships and their own boats, which they had sent in close to the shore. In February, he again took exception to Decatur's claims following the first blue lights incident. The commodore's letter had by then been shared with Congress, and a Connecticut congressman expressed outrage on the floor of the House of Representatives at the accusations of treason leveled at his constituents.[7]

Many Americans for years had harbored suspicions that Britain had employed subterfuges and underhanded methods to weaken the independent United States. In that context, Decatur's railings do not seem as outlandish as they might at first.[8]

Commodore Decatur probably went too far in accusing most of an entire city of outright treason, but there was indeed considerable antiwar sentiment there. American officers sometimes endured spoken slights while visiting ashore, and observers at the time commented on the cordial treatment afforded British officers from the *Macedonian* as they awaited parole and prisoner exchange. British officers from the blockade squadron visited New London regularly as they came ashore under flags of truce and traded openly for goods. Decatur of course knew all this, and he also knew that the British consular office in New London remained in operation even as the war progressed. James Stewart served as the British vice consul in New London. He had lived there for several years and, with his wife Elizabeth, was a well-known figure about town. After his squadron was cornered in New London, Decatur succeeded in having Stewart banished from the city to an inland residence.[9]

Elizabeth Stewart and the couple's children continued to reside in New London. While the record here is murkily obscure, she could easily have run a small spy network from the consular residence, which commanded an excellent view of New London harbor.[10] It also would have been an easy matter for the British to recruit a couple of spies among New Londoners or to have sent incognito agents ashore daily, since British boats seem to have moved along the coast at will. Any knowledgeable observer could have reported signs that the squadron meant to sail from the New London anchorage to which it had moved downriver in December 1813. Since cancelling officers' shore leave would have been one such clear signal of intent, it does seem strange that Decatur did not keep them aboard more often, even when the weather was good. Their sudden disappearance from New London streets might not then have been so noteworthy.

Three additional British ships-of-the-line hovered off New London by the spring of 1814. A predawn raid on April 8 against Pettipaug (now Essex) along the Connecticut River resulted in the destruction of twenty-eight American privateer ships. An American pilot guided the British boats up the river, and he ultimately received two thousand dollars for one night's treason. Connecticut militia responded in force, and Decatur sent marines from the ships in the Thames led by Captain Jacob Jones of the *Macedonian*. But none of them got to the Connecticut River banks in enough time to interfere with the British raiders' withdrawal to their ships off shore.[11]

The standoff had lasted for nine months before Secretary Jones decided to break it off. Both the *United States* and the *Macedonian* would move far out of reach. Commodore Decatur would take command of the *President* in New York and try a breakout from there. Captain Jacob Jones would leave the *Macedonian* for the Great Lakes and take a large contingent of personnel to that front. On April 20, 1814, the crews hove the two frigates up the Thames and anchored at a point three and one-half miles downriver from Norwich, Connecticut. The *United States* and the *Macedonian* kept a few guns each that pointed down the Thames just in case a British raiding force managed to get past the Connecticut militia garrisons in the forts astride the banks of the Thames and then take down the chain that the Americans placed across it.[12]

Another matter remained before Jones and Decatur departed. The American prisoners of war captured by HMS *Shannon* in the battle off Boston with the *Chesapeake* had been exchanged and returned to the United States Navy. Courts-martial awaited several of them. The trials took place on board the *United States.* Commodore Decatur served as the president of the courts. Members included Captain Jones, Master Commandant James Biddle of the *Hornet*, and eight lieutenants from the three ships. John Drake Sloat was one of the lieutenant members, and over the years to come, he would serve on many courts-martial, including most of the significant ones. Lieutenant William S. Cox, nineteen years of age, was the only American commissioned officer to survive the fifteen-minute battle unscathed. Lieutenant George Budd had been wounded during the battle at the same time that the other two lieutenants were killed. Cox had only been aboard the *Chesapeake* for a few days when the frigate met the *Shannon.* He was charged with cowardice and deserting his post. Cox had accompanied the mortally wounded Captain Lawrence below decks and then returned. The court concluded that Cox should have remained on deck and convicted him of neglect of duty and conduct unbecoming an officer. Even though those were lesser offenses than cowardice, Cox was dismissed from the navy. Historian James E. Valle argues that the punishment better fit a conviction of the original charge of cowardice. William Brown, the ship's African American bugler, took fright and hid under a boat during the battle. He was convicted of cowardice and sentenced to three hundred lashes with a cat-of-nine-tails. That sentence was reduced to one hundred lashes, either by President Madison or, according to one contemporaneous newspaper report, by Decatur as president of the court. Valle charges that "the implacable" Decatur was "pre-disposed to look for evidence of cowardice and dishonorable behavior." Other critics of Decatur agree that he was looking for scapegoats.[13]

Lieutenant Gallagher "and crew" departed the *United States* for the *President* on May 7, 1814. Lieutenant Matthew C. Perry also transferred to the *President* around that time. Commodore Decatur's pennant was hauled down and he soon departed for New York. Lieutenant John Drake Sloat became the senior officer on board the dismasted *United States*, which for all intents and purposes had been converted into a floating artillery battery. Besides a few sailors for gun crews, the *United States* and the *Macedonian* shared a contingent of marines including one sergeant and two corporals. Decatur had promised to write his instructions to Sloat, but they never arrived. The lieutenant decided to write directly to Secretary of the Navy Jones and asked if he had any instructions to forward. If Jones sent a reply, it does not survive in the record.[14]

A few months of independent duty for Sloat passed as the war continued in other areas. Closer to Norwich and New London, Americans launched attacks against British ships using various experimental "torpedo" designs by steamboat inventor Robert Fulton, but they all came to naught. The use of "newfangled technology" provoked a British reaction. In July 1814, Royal Navy ships under the command of Commodore Sir Thomas Hardy landed a regiment of infantry and forced the surrender of the small American garrison at Eastport, Maine, located on Moose Island across Passamaquoddy Bay from Canada. In early August, Hardy struck at Stonington, Connecticut. American militia, including reinforcements rushed from New London some ten miles away, repulsed the British forces.[15] Had a landing succeeded and been reinforced, then a serious threat to the *United States* and the *Macedonian* by an assault over land might have materialized. The British operations from the sea against Pettipaug, Eastport, and then Stonington highlight some of the difficulties in projecting power inland from a fleet offshore, and Sloat likely remembered them when he invaded California years later.

An interesting break in the frigates' routine came when troops delivered British consul James Stewart to the *United States* for confinement. He had made his way to an island off shore, where his family joined him only to see him captured shortly afterward by a raid on September

21. Stewart did not stay aboard very long, as negotiations between the blockade commanders and American authorities resulted in the consul's parole to New London for the rest of the war. Captain John Shaw arrived on October 19 to take command of the Old Wagon.[16]

Lieutenant Sloat made at least one visit to the New York City waterfront to recruit sailors. One sailor whom Sloat had enlisted on December 26, 1814, for service aboard the *United States*, deserted and then enlisted under a different name under Captain David Porter's command. Sloat discovered the trick and formally requested that Captain Porter send the sailor under orders so that he could be taken to the *United States* at her Thames River anchorage.[17]

Historians generally contend that the British blockade was quite effective as a war measure, but Wade Dudley concludes that the close British blockade was actually quite permeable. American privateers slipped through it all the time. Especially in New England, ships sailed in and out while the British watched because the British themselves were part of the commerce. In a broad sense, Dudley's and Goldenberg's conclusions seem credible, but the contradictory conclusions of other historians such as Hickey and Horsman may be the difference between a glass partially full and one partially empty.[18] In either case, the British blockade ships off New London did keep two important United States Navy ships from operating at sea for the duration of the war.

In defending their ships against inland raids, Lieutenant Sloat and his *Macedonian* counterpart, Lieutenant Benjamin Booth, had support from the local militia. State militia units had often proved problematic during the war, particularly during the various campaigns across the Niagara River into Upper Canada. Some militia units outright refused to cross the river and leave United States soil. Connecticut had long been a bastion of anti-Virginia sentiment that manifested itself as opposition to Presidents Jefferson and Madison. Governor Roger Griswold refused to send militia out of Connecticut on Canadian campaigns, and the state legislature supported him.[19] In New London, Commodore Decatur faced great reluctance to cooperate with the navy on the part of militia brigadier general Jorah Isham.[20] Sloat and Booth enjoyed better luck in Norwich. Around the time that the British first cornered the *United States* in New London, the Connecticut militia's Twentieth Regiment mustered under the command of Lieutenant Colonel Freeman Tracy, who was assisted by majors Stephen Allen and James Gordon.[21]

Lieutenant Sloat's association with Major Gordon proved a fruitful one. The Gordon family had a nineteen-year-old daughter, Abby. On November 27, 1814, John Drake Sloat and Abby Gordon were married in Norwich.[22]

No personal letters survive from which to glean a fuller picture of what she was like, and extant documentation tells us very little about Abby herself. A picture of a solid, quite well-to-do middle-class family will emerge in subsequent chapters, and it seems reasonable to speculate that Abby and John had a classic "separate spheres" sort of relationship.[23] Fourteen years younger than her husband, Abby was born in Norwich on November 6, 1795. It was probably viewed as a good match all around. John Sloat had a commission in the United States Navy, which in those days carried a significant degree of both prestige and social status, but as Samuel Eliot Morison notes, probably not on the highest rungs of society.[24]

James Gordon was a merchant in Norwich and a citizen of some prominence as one would expect of a major in the local militia. Among other interests, Gordon owned a 280-ton ship that had been built in Norwich just as the United States declared war on the British kingdom.[25] James Gordon's ancestors had been in Norwich for several generations, and Abby's mother Susan (née L'Hommedieu) had also been born there.[26] Within a few weeks of the nuptials, Gordon sold a house and lot in Norwich to his new son-in-law for three hundred dollars. This would be the first of several real estate purchases in Norwich by Sloat in the years to come. In comparison with other grant deeds in the Norwich land records, the sale price looks like a very good deal for Sloat.[27]

The War of 1812 drew to a close and ended with the signing of the Treaty of Ghent in Belgium in December 1814. The news reached New London in February. All New Londoners celebrated, as did the sailors of the opposing navies. The British ships rigged full-dress flags and fired salutes, and rounds of dinners and fetes preceded the British departure from New England waters.[28]

The United States Navy had to make adjustments after the war was over. Many officers would find themselves "awaiting orders" on half pay, or on furlough without any pay. The advantage to being furloughed was that one could leave the country and pursue one's interests without first getting the permission of the secretary of the navy. Otherwise, one could pursue personal interests at the place where one awaited orders and was available for immediate assignment should a billet become open on a ship or at a shore station. In the small navy of that day, the secretary of the navy himself controlled those assignments. Normally, the secretary gave great leeway in choosing lieutenants and warrant officers to the captains and masters commandant that he chose to command ships and navy yards. The navy list had more captains, masters commandant, and lieutenants than the fleet and shore establishment had billets for.[29] One needs little imagination to realize how much politicking and jockeying would take place in the scramble for those positions.

Lieutenant Sloat traveled to New York in late February or early March 1815, and there he met with Benjamin W. Crowninshield, the new secretary of the navy. Sloat requested an assignment to the frigate *John Adams*, a ship much smaller than the "Old Wagon." But on March 16, he wrote again to Crowninshield. Sloat reiterated his wish to remain in the navy but asked for a furlough. He said that he had been offered "command of one of the largest and finest" American merchant ships. His commanding officer, Captain John Shaw of the *United States*, had recommended that Sloat take that offer. If a furlough was not feasible, then Sloat still wished to be assigned to the *John Adams*.[30]

John Drake Sloat's claim about the merchant ship opportunity seems rather embellished. The ship was a newly built pilot-boat schooner, the *Transit*, of forty-eight burthen tons. That is only half the cargo capacity of the *Polly*, on which Sloat had sailed as master ten years earlier. As a pilot-boat schooner, the *Transit* had very sharp lines and was built for speed and not for cargo capacity.[31] By May 23, the *Transit* had fitted out and was advertised for charter or for sale by Messrs. Griswold and Griswold of 68 South Street, New York. The Griswolds ranked among the most important shipowners in New York City, and that surname appears often in documentary records from Norwich. The New York gentlemen were likely kin to the Connecticut family, which in turn probably had dealings with Major Gordon. Sloat wrote to Crowninshield and offered to carry dispatches to France in the "fast schooner *Transit*."[32]

After having gone to so much trouble since early 1812 to get back into the navy, one must wonder about the sudden return to the merchant marine. The most plausible explanation is the simplest one: money. Sloat and the owners of the *Transit* possibly figured they would make a fast trip to France and take on a cargo of high-value luxury goods that had long been unavailable in the United States. A fast sailer with a good skipper could arrive in an American port ahead of other, slower ships. When Sloat got the offer in mid-March, neither he nor the owners in New York could have known that Napoleon Bonaparte had just returned from Elba on February 26 and that the European war was about to reignite.

The *Transit* cleared New York for "Nantz" (Nantes) on June 3, 1815.[33] As Sloat sailed past Sandy Hook, Bonaparte had marshaled the French army and moved toward Belgium, where he would meet final defeat around Waterloo after a series of battles between the 15th and the 18th of June. Of course, in no way could Sloat have known of those developments as he blithely sailed across the open ocean for the first time in nearly three years.

The *Transit* arrived at Nantes and Sloat found a tumultuous situation in France. Napoleon Bonaparte had abdicated and gone to Rochefort on the Bay of Biscay, from where he hoped to go on to the United States. British naval ships waited off the French coasts to prevent an escape. An intriguing story appeared in a magazine just after Sloat returned from California in 1846. Edwin Sherman also used it in his biography. The story states that agents of Napoleon approached Sloat about an escape. Sloat agreed to hide the emperor on board and slip out to sea en route to the United States.[34] Such stories are often quite murky and dubious, but this one is quite possibly true. The dates fit perfectly with when the *Transit* would have arrived in Nantes. Bonaparte's agents would likely have made a number of parallel requests in different French ports, and an aide wrote not long afterward about one of them. General Charles Lallemand contacted the master of an American vessel anchored at the mouth of the Gironde, and that skipper agreed to take Napoleon on board. Another member of Napoleon's coterie had found a French naval officer then commanding a Danish merchant ship who was also willing to embark the emperor.[35] But those machinations came to naught, and Bonaparte surrendered to Captain Frederick Maitland of HMS *Bellerophon* on July 15. Maitland's memoir mentions nothing of any attempts to escape in an American merchant ship.[36]

A daring and remunerative intrigue no longer being possible, Sloat turned to the mundane business at hand. If he had hoped for a quick turnaround to get home ahead of the competition with high-priced luxury goods, then he was disappointed. The *Transit* remained in Nantes for almost three months before sailing on September 22. The schooner arrived in New York on November 9, 1815, loaded with brandy, silks, and linens for the firm of Stevenson and Goodwin.[37]

Abby gave birth to a son, Lewis Warrington Sloat, on November 27, 1815, most likely in Norwich where she would have stayed with her parents. The infant was obviously named in honor of Master Commandant Lewis Warrington, who had been a midshipman in the Norfolk area and then assigned to the *President* around the time that Sloat left the navy.[38] On February 15, 1816, Lieutenant Sloat acquired another house in Norwich. He bought the house in which his parents-in-law lived.[39] The trail of records here disappears again, except for one short voyage as master of the *Expedition* carrying barrel staves from Edenton, North Carolina, to New York. That ship arrived just as his furlough ended in June 1816.[40] Lieutenant Sloat then joined the other officers that awaited orders in a peacetime navy.

CHAPTER SEVEN

The First Luff

Lieutenant John Drake Sloat's return from furlough to naval duty resulted in a paradox for a sailor. It meant giving up sailing ships at sea and awaiting orders ashore in New York City for a navy assignment. In short, Sloat was "beached" for the time being. His earlier furlough had prevented him from any chance of sailing with Commodore Stephen Decatur's squadron in the brief war against Algeria in 1815 and also made him unavailable for any of the lieutenant billets aboard Commodore Isaac Chauncey's flagship, the ship of the line *Washington*, which sailed for an extended cruise in the Mediterranean just before Sloat returned to navy duty. One naval officer published an anonymous letter to the editor of *Niles Weekly Register* at the end of 1815. The correspondent complained about the large number of commissioned officers in the navy and how few billets there were for them. He opined that the old captains were good but the new lieutenants were not. He called for a major reduction in the size of the naval officer corps.[1]

Unlike the Quasi-War and all the wars after 1815, there was no major force reduction in the United States Navy following the War of 1812. But the fleet was still small, and the navy had more officers on its rolls than it did places for them to serve afloat or ashore. Those without jobs received half their basic pay and no ration allowance. Sloat's earlier benefactor, Stephen Decatur, had become a naval commissioner, one of the three naval officers who advised the secretary of the navy on matters of all sorts. The secretaries controlled officer assignments and often allowed commanding officers great leeway in their choices of lieutenants, but opportunities were few and far between in the first few years after the Treaty of Ghent. Most prized for lieutenants were commands of armed schooners, followed by being first lieutenant, the senior-most of the lieutenants aboard a larger ship commanded by a captain or a master commandant. This "first luff" was the second in command, as the U.S. Navy had not yet created today's executive officer position. No recorded comment from Sloat survives on this matter, but historian Samuel Eliot Morison found lieutenants Matthew Calbraith Perry and Raymond H. J. Perry, brothers themselves, commiserating about the difficulties that faced "old lieutenants."[2] Sloat was older than the two brothers Perry.

Registers of navy and marine corps officers began to be published annually in 1815. The registers for 1818, 1819, and 1820 show Sloat as assigned in New York, but not to the navy yard there. In other words, he awaited orders in New York. The 1820 register lists 202 navy lieutenants, twenty-seven of them senior to Sloat. Fourteen of those twenty-seven also awaited orders on half pay. John D. Sloat does not appear in the New York City directories for any of those years, and no personal correspondence survives to indicate his whereabouts except for the short voyage from North Carolina mentioned earlier.

One surviving piece of official correspondence suggests that Sloat spent a great portion of those years in Norwich. On June 7, 1818, while in Norwich, Sloat wrote to Secretary of the Navy Benjamin Crowninshield. He requested assignment to the navy schooner *Alert*, which he had heard was in need of a new commanding officer.[3] Sloat may have learned about the *Alert* possibility from correspondence received in Norwich, but it seems more likely that he heard the rumor in New York itself, where he would have been in contact with other naval officers. His request for command of the *Alert* came to naught. In the preceding October, Lieutenant Matthew Calbraith Perry had also attempted to get command of the *Alert*, and the secretary replied that he knew nothing of any plans of the incumbent commanding officer to leave the ship.[4] Sloat probably made other requests for particular assignments to the secretary of the navy before 1820, but no documents survive in the archival records.

In March 1819, Sloat sold a house and barn in Norwich for $2,500. Land records describe it as located on Main Street in a district called "Chelsea Society," and it appears to be the house in which Major Gordon and his family had lived.[5] That sale was to a different person. City directories for Norwich covering the years from 1816 to 1820 unfortunately do not survive. Two records from Norwich, and none at all from

New York, do hint that much of Sloat's time awaiting orders was actually spent in Norwich.

Lieutenant Sloat's fortunes in the United States Navy took a decided turn for the better in 1820. He wrote a letter to Smith Thompson, President James Monroe's secretary of the navy since the preceding year. The letter was written from New York and dated March 2, 1820. Saying that he had heard that an opening ashore had just occurred at the Portsmouth Navy Yard, Sloat requested assignment as second in command there until he could get to sea. It appears that the request was approved rather quickly, because Sloat wrote again three months later from Portsmouth. No sooner did he arrive in Portsmouth than he requested a transfer to sea duty. Noting that he had not had service at sea for some time, Sloat requested command of the new schooner then under construction at Portsmouth.[6] He did not get command of that vessel, the *Porpoise*. Several armed schooners were then under construction in different navy yards. These smaller warships reflect an important shift of priorities in the United States Navy's missions, but further discussion of that will be taken in a subsequent chapter because Sloat eventually did get one of the schooners.

At the time that her husband requested to go to sea in command of the *Porpoise*, Abby Sloat was six months pregnant. Jeanette Eliza Sloat was born at the navy yard on September 19, 1820. The newborn girl and her older brother Lewis were baptized at St. John's Episcopal Church in Portsmouth, New Hampshire, on November 4, 1820. Two other "Navy juniors" were also baptized on that day: Lucia Chauncey Porter, born in April 1816, and newborn Bolton Smith Porter, born on August 30, 1820. They were the children of Master Commandant and Mrs. John Porter. Each couple served as witnesses for the other's two children.[7] John Porter was the younger brother of Commodore David Porter, a hero of the War of 1812 then serving as a navy commissioner. It appears that John Porter suffered from alcoholism. The infant later served in the navy under the name William C. B. S. Porter and was lost at sea in 1860 while a lieutenant in the sloop *Levant*. Fitz John Porter, a third child of John and Louisa, graduated from West Point and served as a major general in the Union Army before being court martialed and cashiered after the Second Battle of Bull Run. He cleared his name and won reinstatement many years later.[8]

Lieutenant Sloat's initial request for assignment to Portsmouth had been to replace another lieutenant as second in command, but both Porter and Sloat were sent to the yard at around the same time. Naval officer registers from the immediate period show most navy yards as having one lieutenant assigned in addition to the captain who was the yard commandant. It was unusual to have both a master commandant and a lieutenant to serve at Portsmouth, then under the command of Captain Charles Morris. Navy yards of those days doubled as shipyards and naval stations, but Portsmouth, New Hampshire, never served as home port to any sizeable portion of the active fleet. The harbor was small, subject to fog, and the Piscataqua River had a rapid current. But a sizeable number of skilled tradesmen lived in Portsmouth and Kittery, where they were available for hire on a regular basis.

Contrary to the present practice at naval shipyards, individual tradesmen were normally hired according to need and were not part of the permanent personnel of the antebellum navy yard. In October 1820, when the *Porpoise* was building on the ways, 159 workmen and laborers were employed at the Portsmouth Navy Yard. The yard bears the name of the New Hampshire city, but it actually lies on Piscataqua River islands that are part of Kittery, Maine. The latter town was still part of Massachusetts when the yard was established. At the time that Lieutenant Sloat was assigned there, no bridge across the river yet existed between Portsmouth and Kittery. Ferries carried workmen living in Portsmouth to their jobs in Kittery until the first bridge was constructed in September 1822. Navy yards not only built ships, but their shops also frequently fabricated items such as anchors, blocks or pulleys, and other things to outfit ships under construction in a different yard. At other times, commercial enterprises supplied such equipment under contract.[9]

Line officers such as Morris, Porter, and Sloat performed managerial and supervisory duties at the navy yard. In his autobiography, Morris devotes only a few lines to his years as commandant of the Portsmouth yard, but he called it "useful and agreeable employment."[10] Responsibility for things getting done rested with them, and their signatures appeared on correspondence and reports of various kinds. Other navy officers were also assigned to the Portsmouth Navy Yard, including Surgeon Robert Thorn, Purser Nathaniel Lyde, and Sailing Master Nathaniel Stoodley. Although some other yards numbered a boatswain and a carpenter among their navy warrant officers, such was not the case in Portsmouth in 1820 and 1821. A detachment of marines, including Captain Samuel Watson and First Lieutenant Thomas English, provided physical security for the yard. There were even two midshipmen, Daniel Goodwin and Michael Mahony. The two young gentlemen came to the yard from the seventy-four-gun ship of the line *Independence.* Each had been a midshipman for about six years before coming to Portsmouth, and like many midshipmen, each had left the navy by 1824 without getting a lieutenant's commission.[11]

The records do not indicate if the two midshipmen were considered not to be worthy of commissioning and promotion, but the U.S. Navy officer career ladder was becoming more difficult to climb. The young organization founded in 1798 became stable and bureaucratized in the peacetime years after 1815. John Drake Sloat's unique situation stemmed from his years in the merchant service. He had served as a midshipman in the *President* with James Biddle and Lewis Warrington, among others. Although slightly younger than Sloat in years, they ranked as captain and master commandant while Sloat waited behind the roadblock as a lieutenant. He had a wealth of personal shiphandling and seamanship experience that others could never gain on a navy frigate. Some other contemporaries by age had commanded the small gunboats that were President Thomas Jefferson's pet project. But the gunboats were coastal and harbor vessels. As it remains today, the United States Navy was a "blue-water" institution that placed little value in "brown-water" sailing.

Lieutenant Sloat was a dozen or more years older than most of his contemporaries by date of rank. The most notable of them is undoubtedly Matthew Calbraith Perry (1794–1858), who commanded the expedition that led to the establishment of relations between the United States and Tokugawa Japan. Recall that Sloat and Perry served together in the *United States,* bottled up in Connecticut's Thames River. By 1821, Sloat had been to sea in a frigate as a midshipman and as the sailing master for significant periods of time. But his only experience underway as a frigate lieutenant was the attempted breakout across Long Island Sound that ended in New London. At forty years of age, Sloat was still not so old that being older than his contemporaries in rank would be a detriment.

Lieutenant Sloat pushed harder for command of the *Porpoise.* In January 1821, he wrote again from Portsmouth, reiterated his request of six months earlier, and appended four letters of recommendation. The first letter was from Commodore Stephen Decatur, written in May 1818 when he served as a naval commissioner. The national hero had died in March 1820 in a duel with Commodore James Barron. The other letters came from Captain Samuel Evans, commanding the New York Navy Yard; Captain Lewis Warrington, commanding the frigate *Guerrière*; and Master Commandant John B. Nicolson, who had been a lieutenant aboard the *United States* during the *Macedonian* battle and was then awaiting orders in Philadelphia.[12] This second request also met with disappointment. Command of the *Porpoise* went to Lieutenant James Ramage, then based ashore in Norfolk after having commanded another navy schooner, the *Hornet*.[13] As noted earlier, officer assignments remained the prerogative of the secretary of the navy. It may appear here than John Sloat bombarded the secretary with requests for assignments, but perusing the officers' letters file in the National Archives reveals that such was the norm. Those with the best of connections, such as the navy connections of Matthew Calbraith Perry or the political connections of Robert F. Stockton, had to do the same.

At this point, Lieutenant Sloat seems to have set his sights a little lower. By the spring of 1821, he had been relieved at Portsmouth by Thomas Wyman, a lieutenant much junior to Sloat, even though Secretary Thompson had just told Commodore Morris that as long as a master commandant was assigned, there was no need for a lieutenant to be also assigned to the Portsmouth Navy Yard. Sloat went back to New York to await orders.[14] The family of four took up residence in Manhattan at the corner of Canal and Mercer streets, and their furniture arrived by sloop in New York on April 10, 1821.[15] Lieutenant Sloat then sought assignment to the *Franklin*, a seventy-four-gun ship of the line preparing for an extended cruise to the Pacific under the command of Commodore Charles Stewart.

A prompt reply came from Secretary Thompson. He informed Sloat that Stewart would be allowed to choose his first lieutenant, and should he choose Sloat, then he would get those orders. Within another two weeks, Sloat appears to have met with Stewart. Sloat then wrote Thompson and stated that the commodore had authorized him to say that his only objection to Sloat as first lieutenant was that he had already told Lieutenant William Weaver that he could have the job if the secretary approved. Sloat requested permission to travel to Washington to call personally on the secretary.[16]

It remains unclear if Sloat actually made that journey to the national capital. His self-reported synopsis of service states that he reported to the *Washington* for duty on June 4 and then to the *Franklin* on August 6. The *Washington* also lay in New York harbor during those two months. The *Franklin* departed from New York on October 10. The absence of a listing in the following year's New York City directory suggests that Abby and the two children went to Norwich and spent the next couple of years with her family while Sloat was away at sea.[17]

Claude G. Berube and John A. Rodgaard's biography of Commodore Stewart discusses in detail the events of the *Franklin*'s cruise to the Pacific.[18] Because John Drake Sloat made only the earliest part, it will suffice here to say that it was a difficult deployment in many respects, some of which stemmed from the presence on board the flagship of Mrs. Delia Stewart. The naval register for 1822 shows ten lieutenants assigned to the *Franklin*, a number far larger than normal.[19] Lieutenant William M. Hunter was senior to Sloat and was also assigned to the ship by the secretary. To Hunter instead of to hopeful Sloat, or to Stewart's choice Weaver, went the position of first lieutenant, the second in command. The *Franklin* deck log records no transfer of Lieutenant Hunter, and the 1823 naval register shows him as still on board the ship. It appears that Lieutenant Sloat did not ever act as first lieutenant of the *Franklin*.

Also aboard the *Franklin* was Midshipman Charles Wilkes (1798–1877). He is best remembered for commanding the United States Exploring Expedition (1838–1842) and for his role in the Trent Affair during the Civil War. As a midshipman, Wilkes had been one of the thirty-two young gentlemen who sailed from New York aboard the *Franklin*. Wilkes wrote extensive commentaries about the *Franklin*'s officers, as well as about dozens of other persons that he met throughout his naval career. Commodore Stewart was a slack officer, Lieutenant Hunter was a failure, Lieutenant Thomas Hamersly was a blackguard, Lieutenant William Ramsay had a bit of Miss Nancy about him, and so on. Wilkes wrote that Sloat was no seaman, timid, fearful of responsibility, and a "most inefficient" and "exceedingly conceited" officer whom the midshipmen scornfully referred to as "grandmother."[20] It is often true that midshipmen and young officers harbor idealistic but unrealistic expectations of the experienced officers who command them. Such officers often temper their views over the years as they gain personal experience that changes their perspectives, but not so with Charles Wilkes. He began writing his 944-page autobiography in 1871, a full half-century after sailing on the *Franklin*. Vituperative vitriol permeates the book from cover to cover. Wilkes had nothing good to say about practically anybody. Excepting, of course, himself. One historian writes that Wilkes "incorporated the worst of Ahab and Bligh."[21]

Contradictions and discontinuities between Wilkes's memory and the documentary records are understandable and do not completely negate the utility of his autobiography as a historical source. As for his opinions of his colleagues and other persons, Wilkes's comments must be considered carefully and in the context of when they were made and the scornful bitterness of the man who made them. Even so, they must not be discarded out of hand because they are germane to the controversies that would surround Sloat's actions during 1846 when commanding the Pacific Squadron.

The *Franklin* set a southeasterly course to clear the easternmost point of Brazil. Initially, Lieutenants Ebenezer Ridgeway and Thomas Hamersly alternated as officer of the deck in a port-and-starboard watch rotation, but by October 20 they had been joined on the watch bill by Lieutenants Henry Henry and James A. Perry. The latter was a younger brother of Matthew Calbraith Perry, and on the next day, Lieutenant Henry Ogden also joined the watch rotation. Daily latitude entries appear in the deck log, and these would have been taken by measuring the angle between the sun and the horizon at local apparent noon, when the sun crossed the longitude meridian of the ship's location. A major warship of the early nineteenth century could have carried chronometers that would allow observations of the sun at other times and of the stars at morning and evening twilight, but the deck logs from the *Franklin* and other ships seen by this researcher contain no record other than the daily latitude. Latitude observations at local apparent noon are the only position information appearing in the deck log, and those can be done without a chronometer if the navigator uses one daily value for the position of the sun instead of the minute-by-minute values available in modern nautical almanacs. This clearly corroborates the finding of historian Frederick C. Leiner that chronometers were not in wide use in the United States

Navy even into the 1820s. In other words, they were latitude sailors, not much different than Magellan or Columbus.[22]

The *Franklin* crossed the equator on November 18, 1821. At nine o'clock the next morning, the main topsail was backed to bring the ship to a stop to receive on board "His Serene Majesty Neptune, Amphitrite, Triton, and their attendants." Those in the crew crossing the equator for the first time were initiated into the Order of Shellbacks. This ceremony has in recent times come under criticism for its hazing and degradation of the "pollywogs" who were crossing the equator for the first time. Given the ferocity of discipline in the antebellum United States Navy, one must imagine that the "frolic" in 1821 could have been harsh indeed. Lieutenant Sloat was by that time a salty mariner with much experience at sea, but he had not been across the equator. The record does not show how such an officer would have been handled in the ceremonies. On November 30, the *Franklin* made landfall as Rio de Janeiro's famous Sugar Loaf hove into view.

Figure 7.1. *Rio de Janeiro*, ca. 1860. (In Énault, *L'Amerique Centrale et Meridionale.* Courtesy of the Bancroft Library, University of California, Berkeley.)

The ship entered Rio de Janeiro harbor that same day and remained there until December 10. A British warship was also there, and improper preparation left wet powder in some of the *Franklin*'s guns, which in turn caused the ceremonial exchange of saluting gunfire to go awry. The ship took on water and fresh provisions, which doubtless included rum. Several midshipmen became severely intoxicated while on shore leave. There is no indication that any of the crew except officers were given liberty to go ashore at all. The commodore and his lady were presented at court, where Mrs. Stewart's proficiency in Portuguese garnered a good degree of social favor.[23]

This visit took place at a tenuous time in Brazilian history. Some Latin American countries had established their political independence by December 1821, but Brazil was still a separate kingdom within the Portuguese Empire and would remain so until September 1822. Ships of Britain's Royal Navy evacuated King João VI and the Portuguese court from Lisbon to Rio de Janeiro in 1808 when French troops invaded the Iberian Peninsula. He continued to rule the far-flung empire from South America after Bonaparte's defeat. Circumstances in Portugal required his return in early 1821. He left Prince Pedro in Brazil as regent and told him that if an independence movement arose there, then Pedro should declare independence and place himself on a Brazilian throne. Some factions in Brazil did not support independence from Portugal, and at the time of the American squadron's visit, that crisis was simmering but had not yet boiled over into armed conflict.[24]

The *Franklin* got underway and headed south for Cape Horn. Lieutenant Sloat made his first appearance in the deck log as officer of the deck on January 4, 1822. The *Dolphin* became separated from the *Franklin* near Tierra del Fuego on January 7. The seas at the southern tip of South America are famously rough, but they are better in the Southern Hemisphere summer than at other times of the year. One sailor was lost overboard and drowned. Midshipman Wilkes later blamed the officer of the deck, Lieutenant Ridgeway, for failing to handle the ship properly and recover the unfortunate sailor. The *Franklin* anchored in Cumberland Bay in the Juan Fernández Islands on January 29, finding the *Dolphin* already there since four days earlier. Two days later, both ships sailed for Valparaíso, Chile, quickly covered the roughly three hundred miles to the coast, and anchored there on February 6. Once again, the *Franklin* made a mess of the gun salute, and Wilkes blamed this one on Sloat. The squadron would remain in Valparaíso for more than three months.[25]

The governor of Valparaíso paid a customary courtesy visit to the *Franklin*, but since that city is not the Chilean capital, the level of diplomatic exchange remained lower there than it had in Rio de Janeiro with its Portuguese prince regent. Chile was then independent, but an independence war still raged in Peru. Chilean ruler Bernardo O'Higgins feared the Spanish presence to the north and wanted to support the independence forces there. Commodore Stewart would openly support the royalists in South America, but that did not clearly manifest itself until after Sloat left the *Franklin*.[26]

Another sad incident took place on March 20. A boat from the *Franklin* took some officers ashore for what was recorded in the deck log as a "sporting party." The boat capsized in the surf and several drowned. Among those lost were Lieutenant James Perry and Midshipman Jack Creamer, who was himself a former shipmate of Sloat's from the *United States*. Creamer had been a nine-year-old ship's boy on the "Old Wagon" on the day that HMS *Macedonian* was captured.[27]

Even with the death of Perry, the *Franklin* had more lieutenants than were needed. William Hunter was still aboard and outranked John Drake Sloat. There was no advantage in pay to serving as first lieutenant instead of one of the other wardroom lieutenants, but the "First Luff" was the second in command. Also importantly, to serve in that senior position appears to have been important to Sloat and his hopes for future assignment and promotion. He was detached on May 4, 1822, and embarked in the frigate *Constellation* along with Lieutenant Ramsay, a midshipman, and a ship's boy. The *Constellation* sailed for home as the Southern Hemisphere winter set in. The *Franklin* cruise continued for more than two years, during which the independence wars in Peru continued until after Stewart and the *Franklin* had returned to the United States. The navy's primary mission was to protect United States merchant ships and commercial interests, in particular against the blockades declared by both royalists and independence governments. The United States maintained that the blockades were illegal under international law because neither side had sufficient fleets to enforce them. U.S. naval officers often took the side of the royalists, and the diplomats ashore sometimes failed to maintain neutrality as well. Berube and Rodgaard's discussion of this point suggests that royalists adroitly maneuvered Stewart on several occasions. After their return to the United States, Commodore Stewart and Lieutenant Hunter both faced court-martial charges for improper conduct but were exonerated.[28] Lieutenant William Weaver also faced charges relating to fraud and misappropriation of government property, for which the court sentenced him to be cashiered from the navy.[29] Lieutenant Sloat must have felt fortunate not to become embroiled in the controversies that stemmed from the *Franklin* cruise.

Sloat would have arrived in the United States about July 1822. The next several months are a gap in the archival record, but he did receive the assignment as first lieutenant that had eluded him on the *Franklin*. He was assigned to the thirty-eight-gun frigate *Congress*, under the command of Captain James Biddle. A friend and shipmate of Sloat's since they were midshipmen together in the *President* during the Quasi-War, Biddle was actually a year younger than his new first lieutenant. The incumbent first lieutenant, William Howard Allen (1791–1822) received command of the schooner *Alligator*, where he would be killed in action against West Indies pirates. The *Congress* also deployed to the Caribbean in an antipiracy role.[30]

A ship's first lieutenant held duties and responsibilities that belong to the executive officer in today's United States Navy. "First Lieutenant" today refers to the officer in charge of deck seamanship, but in Sloat's navy he was second in command to the commanding officer, be the latter a captain, a master commandant, or a fellow lieutenant. The first lieutenant managed the sailing frigate's daily routine. He assigned the ship's seamen to divisions under the other lieutenants. Unless the wardroom was shorthanded, the first lieutenant did not stand in the officer of the deck watch rotation. He was responsible to the commanding officer for ship's discipline. A commanding officer needed a first lieutenant to carry out his policy intentions in running the ship, and so it was very important that the two officers got on well and that they understood each other.[31]

The *Congress* sailed for the West Indies in November 1822. On December 20, 1822, the ship was at anchor in La Guaira, in the republic of Gran Colombia, which is in present-day Venezuela. Captain Biddle and Midshipman Samuel Du Pont had left the ship to visit Caracas, at that time a departmental capital located inland about ten miles from the beach at La Guaira. They returned at six in the evening as the weather

Figure 7.2. *James Biddle, Esq., of the United States Navy.* (Courtesy of the Navy Art Collection, Naval History and Heritage Command.)

worsened. By the time they reached the shore line, a hurricane had arrived in full force and they could only watch from there.

Lieutenant Sloat had the ship's boatswain pipe all hands on deck for duty as the winds increased in strength. He urged them to stay with the ship and promised them full pay and rations until they reached the United States should the *Congress* be lost. The main anchor chain broke, as did all but one of the other anchors that Sloat had set out to hold the ship. That last anchor dragged along the bottom but held enough to prevent the *Congress* from being dashed on the rocks. Able Seaman Daniel Winton later stated that Lieutenant Sloat's leadership of an all-hands effort saved the frigate, whereas each of the other twenty-two ships in the harbor had been wrecked. By the next morning, the waters had calmed enough to allow Captain Biddle to return aboard in a raft lashed together from logs. Once aboard, the captain heaped praise on his first lieutenant for saving the ship in front of his very eyes. The *Congress* then sailed for Willemstad, Curaçao, for repairs and to replenish the lost and damaged equipment. The 140–nautical mile trip would have required two or three days. The *Congress* remained on station in the West Indies for several months afterward but did not catch any pirates. Biddle's biographer notes the difficulties faced by large ships in chasing small, coastal pirate vessels but also concludes that Biddle lacked drive and enthusiasm for antipiracy operations.[32]

Seven months in the *Franklin* and six more as first lieutenant in the *Congress* added up to more than a year as a lieutenant on a major ship conducting operations at sea. That seems to have done the trick. With Captain Biddle's concurrence, Sloat wrote to Secretary of the Navy Smith Thompson and requested to be detached from the *Congress.* They would remain good friends in the years to come, so it seems unlikely that Biddle wanted to get rid of his first lieutenant. Sloat probably felt that he needed at that point to get a ship command before any promotion decision, and so would have needed to be available to take such a post as soon as it became available. The *Congress* was slated to transport Caesar Rodney to his post as U.S. Minister in Buenos Aires. Rodney's family, including many daughters, traveled with him, and the voyage records indicate that it was nothing but headaches.[33] Lieutenant Sloat probably considered himself fortunate to have escaped it, and he would soon receive the schooner command that he had sought unsuccessfully a few years earlier.

CHAPTER EIGHT

Pirates in the Caribbean

Upon detachment from the *Congress,* Lieutenant John Drake Sloat returned to New York. He undoubtedly spent some time with his family in Norwich. Their absence from the annual New York City directories suggests that they decided to remain in Connecticut because Sloat did not plan to stay in New York for any great length of time.

Sloat began to press harder for a schooner command. The *Shark* had returned to New York on July 8, 1823, from antipiracy patrols in the West Indies. He appears to have met with his friend and former shipmate, Lieutenant Matthew C. Perry, who then commanded the *Shark.* Three days later, Sloat wrote Secretary of the Navy Smith Thompson and requested command of the *Shark.* He had been informed that Perry intended to give up command of that ship. Sloat emphasized how strongly he wanted the job, and how he hoped nobody junior to him would get it. He went on to add that he actually preferred the *Grampus* over the *Shark,* because the former schooner was somewhat larger and because the *Grampus* schedule would also allow him more time to prepare his family for an extended separation.[1]

Shark and *Grampus* were two of five topsail schooners built for the United States Navy in 1820 and 1821. The other three were *Alligator, Dolphin,* and *Porpoise,* the last being the one that Sloat had asked for as soon as he got to the Portsmouth Navy Yard a few years before. The United States Navy needed small, fast ships for antislavery patrols off the West African coast and antipiracy patrols in the West Indies. The smaller ships that the navy had at the end of the War of 1812 were no longer fit for service. The square-rigged frigates had practically no chance in the Caribbean against the pilot-boat schooners used by many pirates who could hide among the shoals and inlets of the Antilles islands in places inaccessible to large warships designed for open-ocean service. Four of the schooners were built to the same plan at different navy yards, but *Grampus* was a little larger and had an improved design to mount a swivel gun in addition to the cannons in gun ports along the port and the starboard sides. The *Grampus* was ninety-seven feet long, had a beam of twenty-four and one-half feet, and drew between eleven and twelve feet of water. This draft amounts to only three feet less than the frigates of the day, so shallow shoal waters still posed a problem. It appears that the schooners' advantages stemmed more from their faster speed and their better maneuverability from sailing closer into the wind than could the square-riggers. The *Grampus* carried five ship's boats, each between thirteen and fifteen feet in length.[2]

The five naval schooners played an important role in the Caribbean, where pirates posed an increasing threat to United States merchant ships. Spanish authorities seemed to turn a blind eye as buccaneers used

Figure 8.1. *Capture of the Privateer* Palmira *by the USS Schooner* Grampus, by Irwin Bevan. The topsail schooner rigging configuration is clearly visible. This action took place prior to Lieutenant Sloat's taking command. (Reproduced by permission of the Mariners' Museum, Newport News, Virginia.)

Cuba and Puerto Rico as sanctuaries. Although no clearly documented Spanish policy to that effect existed, some historians conclude that they resented the widespread support in the United States for independence movements in Latin America.[3]

Smith Thompson resigned as secretary of the navy and was replaced in September 1823 by Samuel L. Southard, a former U.S. senator from New Jersey. Sloat appears to have called on Southard in Trenton before the latter took up his new post in Washington. Following that meeting, Sloat met with Thompson, who was a fellow New Yorker. Thompson told Sloat that he had intended to give him a schooner command and authorized Sloat to say that in a letter to Southard. Sloat lost no time in writing to the new secretary, first in October and then again in early November. Secretary Southard then waited three weeks to reply. Southard told Sloat in no uncertain terms who was in charge. Southard would deal with Sloat's request when the *Grampus* needed a new commanding officer. He stated that he could not see that Sloat had any particular right to the *Grampus* command, and that the officer who received the assignment would be the one who best fitted the needs of the Navy Department. The first of Sloat's two letters does not survive in the records, but Sloat must have written something about his fears of some disparaging references against him in departmental files. Southard bluntly told Sloat that his supposition was incorrect, and that Sloat should remember that the Navy Department may not always see things in the same light as an individual officer.[4] Having first put the lieutenant in his place, Southard soon afterward ordered Sloat to command the *Grampus*. On December 12, 1823, Sloat left New York and journeyed to Norfolk to take his command.[5]

The *Grampus* was assigned to the West Indies squadron then commanded by Commodore David Porter, whose area of responsibility included not only the West Indies and the Gulf of Mexico but also the west coast of Africa, for which the Navy Department had not yet established a separate squadron. Porter's first orders to Sloat included a visit to Cape Mesurado in present-day Monrovia, Liberia. After several weeks in the tidewater area preparing for deployment, the *Grampus* sailed on February 28 for the coast of Africa. The schooner arrived at Cape Mesurado on April 4, 1824, and delivered a cargo of arms and ammunition to the American colony there.[6]

The American Colonization Society promoted the settlement of free African Americans in West Africa, and this movement led to the founding of Liberia. President James Monroe strongly supported the colonization movement in the United States. The motives of the movement were complex ones that are still the subject of historical debate. It can be seen as benevolently intended. Or it can be seen as a profoundly racist attempt to rid the republic of any free black population. The motives of the white founders of the American Colonization Society aside, present-day readers should recognize that most of the free black population decidedly did not want to leave the United States at all. However, some did go, and with the backing of Lieutenant Robert F. Stockton, then commanding the schooner *Alligator*, established the colony by a tenuous treaty with the local king.[7]

All did not go well. The Cape Mesurado colony had come under attack from neighboring kingdoms since it was founded. The closest one was the Kru kingdom, whose people had a coastal maritime tradition and spoke a Mandé language. Nicknamed "King Boatswain" by Europeans, King Sabsu of the Krus had served in his younger days onboard British merchant ships. Understandably, the Krus viewed the colonists as invaders. In November 1823, Cape Mesurado endured a siege and the residents repulsed two separate Kru attacks on the colony. Serendipitous aid came from a passing British ship laden with armaments.[8] Communications of the time being slow, it makes sense that when President Monroe learned of the attacks on Cape Mesurado, he would have sent military supplies. Communications of the time being slow, it would take until the following April for aid to arrive there.

The *Grampus* remained at Cape Mesurado for eight days. Sloat gave tools that would enable the colonists to repair twenty of their muskets that were then unavailable for service. The stone fort at the cape mounted five cannon of different sizes and had several more in storage. The colony had remained cut off from local trade after surviving the siege. The show of force in the form of a United States warship led to a reopening of trade by King Sabsu. Sloat reported to Porter that the Cape Mesurado colony appeared secure at that time. It had good soil, and the colonists had begun cultivation in earnest. They had good sources of fish and an abundant supply of timber from which they had built good houses. Sloat stated in his report that one reason for his writing this was to provide evidence that strengthened the colonization movement's case against increasing criticism. Contention over the matter, and of course over the issue of slavery in the United States, intensified in the aftermath of the Missouri crisis of 1820. Whether Lieutenant Sloat wrote from wishful thinking or from superficial impressions based on a short visit, historical studies of the Cape Mesurado colony usually contradict his rosy report. The colony continued to suffer at the hands of the Kru, and tropical diseases made it a "death trap."[9]

After a brief and fruitless look along the African coast for slave ships, the *Grampus* then returned across the Atlantic and visited several Mexican ports. Near Martinique harbor on May 10, an incident occurred between the *Grampus* and a merchant ship. The *Grampus* approached the ship to visit and search for pirates, but the merchant ship attempted to evade the navy schooner. Eventually, the merchant hove to and received the *Grampus* boarding party, which found no evidence of wrongdoing. Sloat reported that the ship's cargo and equipment seemed fitted for the African slave trade and surmised that to be the reason the merchant shipmaster attempted to evade the *Grampus.* Rigging became fouled between the two vessels, and the shipowner later submitted a damage claim to the Navy Department. Sloat contended that the collision resulted from several mistakes in seamanship by the master of the merchant ship, and that appears to have ended the story.[10] After replenishing food and water supplies, Sloat then cruised to St. Thomas, San Juan, and the Mona Passage between Hispaniola and Puerto Rico in search of pirates. Finding none, he continued the fruitless search along the Cuban coast and called at the port of Matanzas.[11] The *Grampus* then continued on to Mexico and made short visits to the ports of Campeche, Veracruz, and then Tampico. Sloat heard a rumor that a pirate vessel had been operating near Campeche and conducted a search there that yielded no results.[12] No incidents of note took place during any of those visits, although Sloat did just miss the execution of Agustín de Iturbide near Tampico during the following month. Iturbide had been the emperor of Mexico following its independence from Spain in 1821. He had been overthrown in 1823 by Miguel López de Santa Anna in a coup that led to the establishment of a federalist constitution.[13] That constitution had not been promulgated when the *Grampus* sailed from Hampton Roads, so perhaps the visits were intended to look in on United States interests in Mexico during a period of internal turmoil.

The *Grampus* then returned to New York and anchored off Staten Island on July 17, 1824. The New York Navy Yard conducted repairs and replaced equipment as necessary for several weeks. Abby, Lewis, and Jeanette Sloat moved to New York then and took up residence at 96 Spring Street near the corner with Broadway. On September 2, Lieutenant Sloat again left his family behind when the *Grampus* sailed for the Caribbean. The *Grampus* arrived in St. Thomas on October 22 and spent a week there before a short patrol along the Puerto Rican coast and then returning to St. Thomas. Also present in St. Thomas was the schooner *Beagle*, under the command of Lieutenant Charles Platt.[14]

The *Beagle* had just returned to St. Thomas from Fajardo (or "Foxardo," as often spelled at the time) on the eastern end of Puerto Rico. A large quantity of goods had been stolen from an American company's warehouse in St. Thomas and it was believed that Fajardo-based pirates had the loot. Platt set sail to investigate. Initially things went well, but

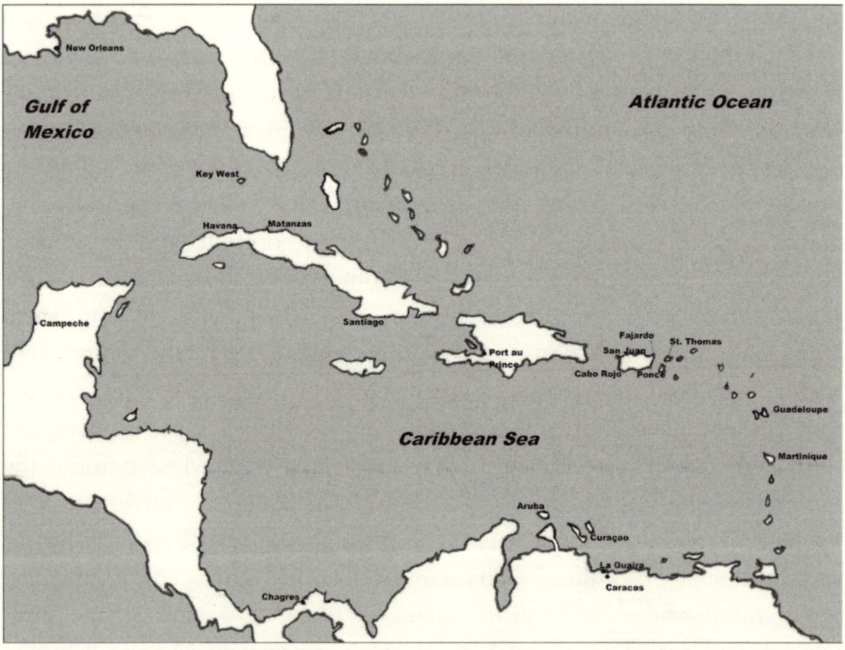

Figure 8.2. Map of the West Indies. (Map by author.)

the alcalde of Fajardo then turned against Platt, who had come ashore in civilian clothes with another lieutenant and their pilot. Accused of being a pirate himself, Platt sent for his uniform and his commission to be brought from the *Beagle*, but the alcalde pronounced them forgeries. Kept at first under arrest, Lieutenant Platt and his retinue were soon hooted out of town as they returned to the *Beagle*, which then returned to St. Thomas.

Sloat arrived at St. Thomas in the *Grampus* soon after, and Platt told him what had happened. Platt later testified that Sloat then asked him what he had expected. Commodore Porter, in the frigate *John Adams*, arrived in St. Thomas on November 12. Platt reported to Porter what transpired in Fajardo a few days earlier. The infuriated commodore immediately undertook a punitive expedition.

The *John Adams*, *Grampus*, and *Beagle* sailed in company for Fajardo. The landing party consisted of about one hundred sailors and marines from the *John Adams*, led by Commodore Porter in person and Master Commandant Alexander J. Dallas of that ship. The frigate had to anchor out of the harbor because of the shallow depth. The *Grampus* towed the landing force to shore in boats from the *John Adams*. The *Grampus* then anchored under the gun emplacements that defended Fajardo, and Sloat had his guns trained on the defenses should they open fire. Landing force elements quickly seized and spiked the Spanish cannons, while Porter and Dallas led the main column toward the town. Meeting the alcalde, Porter handed him a letter that demanded atonement and explanations for the insults to the American officers. Porter threatened that the "total destruction of Foxardo will be the certain and immediate consequence" of not submitting to his demands. The alcalde quickly capitulated, formal apologies were made, and three hours after it had first landed, the United States force withdrew and returned to Danish St. Thomas.[15]

Commodore Porter filed an immediate report to Secretary Southard outlining what he had done. The squadron commander commended the conduct of every officer and man of the three ships as meeting entirely with his approval.[16] Porter expected a full round of accolades from his country. He did not get them. Instead, Captain Lewis Warrington was sent to relieve him, and Porter received orders to report forthwith to the nation's capital to account for his actions. A court of inquiry recommended that he stand trial. The general court-martial in July 1825 convicted David Porter of insubordination, conduct unbecoming an officer, and, most importantly for our purposes, of disobedience of orders by invading Fajardo. Infuriated and disgraced, Porter resigned from the United States Navy and obtained a commission in the Mexican navy.[17]

Upon hearing of Porter's recall to Washington, Lieutenant Sloat wrote and expressed support for his commodore. He expressed sincere regret about Porter's recall and declared that with each passing day, he became more firmly convinced that invading Fajardo, and meting out the treatment to its officials that had been done, were both necessary and proper.[18] This letter creates some confusion about Sloat's meaning when he asked Platt what he expected, before their commodore arrived in St. Thomas. Sloat may have meant that Platt should have expected such a reaction because he landed in civilian clothes in Spanish territory, or perhaps because Sloat assumed that the alcalde of Fajardo was corrupt and thus acted as he did. Master Commandant Dallas and Lieutenant Platt testified at the Porter trial, but the *Grampus* still remained on station in the West Indies. In his absence, Sloat's written statements and letters were admitted as evidence, even though the court rejected for lack of authentication the statements of the alcalde of Fajardo that had been forwarded to it by the captain-general of Puerto Rico via the Spanish legation in the United States.[19]

Secretary Southard's directive to Commodore Porter in 1823 instructed him to fight piracy on the seas. He was not to interfere with local authorities at all. Units of the West Indies squadron could follow pirates ashore into unsettled areas, but this hot pursuit was prohibited if it meant contact ashore with local residents.[20] As historian David F. Long observes, Porter was not in hot pursuit of pirates into Fajardo. He did invade Spanish territory and exact demands upon local officials.[21]

Relations between the United States and Spain were at a tenuous point in late 1824 when most of Spain's mighty American empire had been lost to independence. President James Monroe, Secretary of State John Quincy Adams, and the other members of the cabinet shared particular concerns about a Franco-Spanish campaign into the Western Hemisphere after the Bourbon monarchy was restored in France. They also harbored concerns about British intentions and those of Russia in the Pacific coast regions of North America. The president promulgated the historic Monroe Doctrine in 1823. The United States promised to respect European colonies that then existed in the Western Hemisphere but declared it would oppose any attempt to expand those colonial possessions.[22] In no way could the commander-in-chief tolerate this clear violation by Commodore Porter of declared U.S. policy and of orders of the secretary of the navy that had been in consonance with that policy.

Any naval officer must have known the penalties for disobedience of orders. Discipline and the authority of the chain of command are part of the very soul of any military establishment. A captain could punish a seaman by flogging or withholding the rum ration, but a court-martial was the only punitive tool available to the secretary of the navy in cases involving commissioned officers. One might wonder why, with so much to lose personally, Porter acted as he did in November 1824. But in another sense, Porter's actions might come as no surprise. Officers in the antebellum United States Navy possessed a very keen sense of personal honor. John Drake Sloat was never involved in a duel, but dueling was endemic among the United States Navy officer corps. Naval officers, including young midshipmen, were more than willing to kill each other over perceived slights that modern readers would find trifling. Historian Long shows that Commodore David Porter was a contentious person. Perhaps he wore his pride even more touchily on his sleeve than did most of his colleagues. Secretary Southard's principal fear about the trial was that the officers comprising the court-martial would acquit Porter.[23]

The historian Michael Birkner also reminds us that theft from a warehouse, not piracy at sea, was the immediate cause of the Fajardo affair. But Birkner disputes Long's contention that Secretary Southard did not get along well with Porter, arguing instead that the secretary had no choice but to deal directly with the commodore's insubordinate conduct. At a meeting in Washington on December 2, 1824, cabinet members concluded that the United States had no right to pursue pirates onto Spanish territory in either Cuba or Puerto Rico. Even though Commodore Porter enjoyed popular support in some quarters for his actions at Fajardo, Secretary Southard insisted that a commodore could not commit unauthorized acts of war.[24] The secretary also had declared his desire that commodores not commit actions for which they could be court-martialed.[25] That must also mean that Southard wanted his officers to fear the prospect of facing such a trial.

Porter thought he reacted to the treatment of Lieutenant Platt by the alcalde of Fajardo appropriately and with decisive initiative and avenged an insult to the honor of the United States. Whatever their personal opinions of their colleague David Porter or of the events at Fajardo, the outcome must have been an eye-opener for naval officers who could have seen it as initiative receiving punishment instead of praise. At the very least, it could have planted seeds of doubt whether they could count upon the government in Washington to back them up when they served in changing circumstances on far-off stations.

Lieutenant Sloat continued antipiracy operations as the *Grampus* cruised the West Indies, calling at various islands before returning to St. Thomas. The *Grampus* again left the Danish colony and cruised along the southern coast of Hispaniola, at that time united under independent Haitian rule. After a five-day visit to Port-au-Prince, the *Grampus* returned to St. Thomas on January 9, 1825. This ship's log entry for January 2 records the punishment of seaman James Richards with six lashes. This is the only entry recording corporal punishment on the *Grampus* while Sloat was in command. The research for this biography of course led to a number of ships' logs, and quite a few commanding officers used flogging on a regular basis. This gruesome subject will figure importantly in a later chapter. The *Grampus* spent most of January in St. Thomas.[26]

The mere presence of a warship in their vicinity seems to have deterred pirates. A Spanish squadron of two forty-gun frigates, a corvette, and four transports carrying four thousand soldiers arrived in San Juan. The French consul at St. Thomas told Sloat in confidence that he thought the Spanish ships might really be heading for Chagres on the Panamanian isthmus, then part of independent Gran Colombia. Their actual destination turned out to be Havana. Lieutenant Sloat reported hearing rumors that a pirate from Cabo Rojo, on the southwest coast of Puerto Rico, had attacked shipping in the Mona Passage by Hispaniola. He sent the *Beagle* to investigate. A few days later, the *Grampus* put to sea and chased a pirate ship that escaped. Sloat then put a cutter in the water that continued the chase and captured the pirates.[27] The United States Navy had built the five schooners because the large frigates could not go into restricted waters. But the schooners themselves faced that same problem, and the use of even smaller craft offered a solution.

Sloat established a regular sailing schedule for escorted convoys, and the *Grampus* sailed in and out of St. Thomas regularly for the next several weeks. He recommended to Secretary Southard that the *Grampus* should

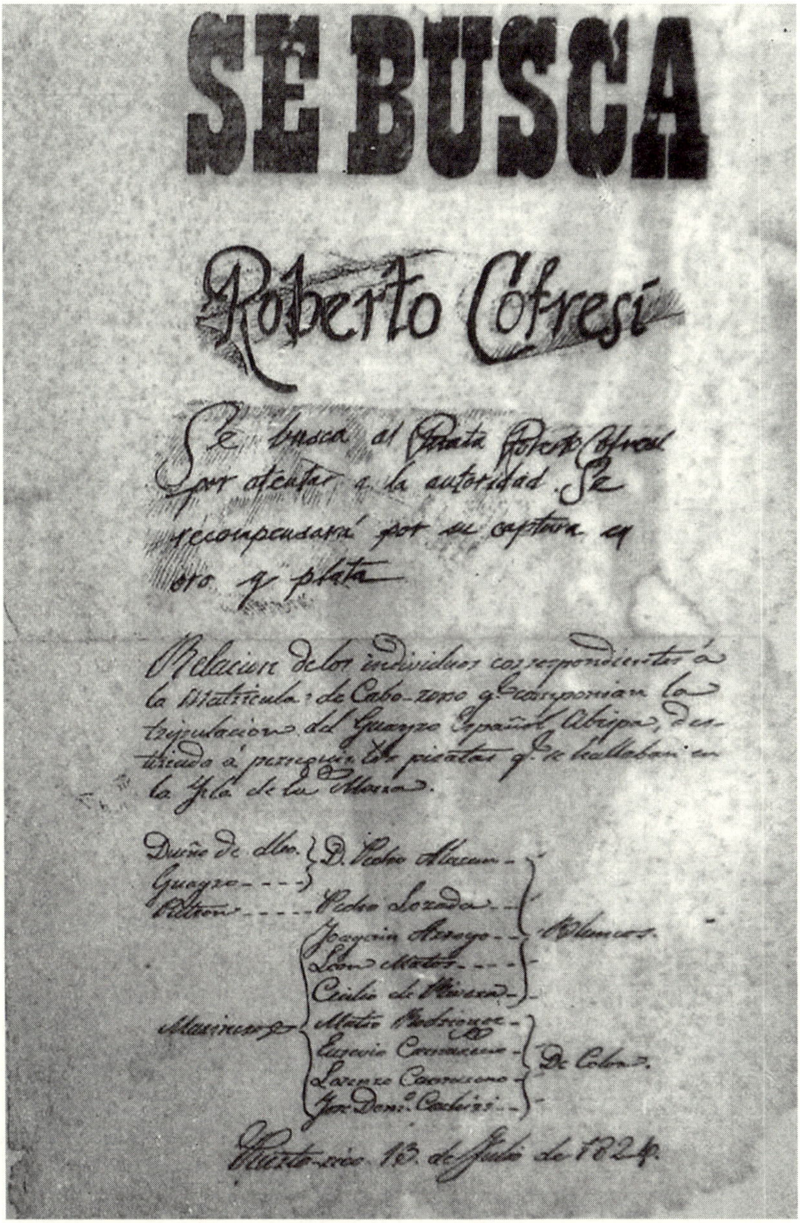

Figure 8.3. Poster offering a reward of gold and silver for the capture of the pirate Roberto Cofresí, for the owners of his ship, and seven sailors in the crew. Three sailors were "white" and four were "of color." (Image from Wikimedia Commons.)

return to the United States to get a new set of sails because the cost of buying them in the Caribbean would be very high.[28]

At the end of February, Lieutenant Sloat won a major victory in the campaign against West Indies piracy. Three sloops had just been taken by a pirate in the Mona Passage. Sloat and Peter Carl Frederik von Scholten, the governor of St. Thomas, coordinated a plan. Von Scholten placed St. Thomas under embargo to deny the pirates any advance warning. Local merchants lent two small sloops for Sloat's use, and they sailed with the *Grampus* on February 28. The ships arrived at Ponce on March 3 without having captured their quarry. They were on the verge of abandoning their effort when a lookout sighted a sail that appeared to belong to a suspected pirate vessel. Sloat ordered Lieutenant Garrett J. Pendergrast and twenty-six others back into a sloop. Pendergrast chased the ship eastward along the Puerto Rican coast for twenty miles, cornering it in Boca del Infierno. After a forty-five-minute battle, the pirates ran their sloop aground and fled ashore, leaving behind two killed in action against the Americans. They were captured in Guayama by the local military commander and handed over to the government in San Juan. Including Roberto Cofresí, the pirate captain, most of them received serious wounds during the battle. The sloop and the *Grampus* reunited in St. Thomas, where the sloop was returned to its owner. The American force suffered no personnel casualties.[29]

The *Grampus* then sailed for San Juan. Lieutenant Sloat called upon Captain-General Miguel de la Torre and offered to make available any witnesses that might be needed at trial. De la Torre thanked Sloat but said none were necessary because the captives had confessed and would be punished forthwith. Sloat did visit the condemned Cofresí in prison before his execution, and the pirate said he had not attacked any United States ships in at least eighteen months but added this was only for lack of an opportunity. Sloat remarked that he had only learned from de la Torre just how important the capture of Cofresí was to the Spanish officials in Puerto Rico.[30]

The capture of Roberto Cofresí did not mark the end of West Indies piracy, but pirate attacks in the region occurred thereafter with markedly diminished frequency. Cofresí himself, or "Cofrecinas" as he was known to Sloat and de la Torre, continues to enjoy a sort of cultural immortality after his execution. As a kind of seagoing Robin Hood, Cofresí became a symbol in some circles of Puerto Rican nationalism. Fear of slave revolutions such as took place in Haiti kept the American-born creole elites in Cuba and Puerto Rico loyal to the crown, while independence struggles raged elsewhere in the Spanish empire. Roberto Fernández Valledor has extensively studied the Cofresí myth and especially its cultural evolution as it was repeatedly reinvented over time. The role of the United States Navy in his capture is frequently absent from the folk tales. Ursula Acosta made a careful study of the Cabo Rojo pirate that counters the popular heroic vision, but Cofresí continues to be viewed as a marginalized person pushed to an outlaw's life as he resisted political oppression by Spanish colonial authorities. The subject of social banditry is a complex and fascinating study, and it does seem that Roberto Cofresí fits that mold.[31] Lieutenant John Drake Sloat may have disappeared from Puerto Rican legend, but at the time of the action, he received a great deal of professional credit for the capture of Cofresí. Because the error appears in a very well-known book, one should note that the renowned historian Samuel Eliot Morison mistakenly gave Sloat's credit to Lieutenant Francis Gregory, Sloat's predecessor in command of the *Grampus*.[32]

In an April 1825 letter, Sloat reported that Cofresí had, in fact, been executed in San Juan and reiterated the need for the *Grampus* to return to the United States for maintenance. Secretary Southard ordered the ship to return to Norfolk right away, but the *Grampus* did not arrive in Norfolk until August 7. Sloat was ordered to deliver the *Grampus* to the commandant of the Norfolk Navy Yard for repairs. A week later, Sloat requested leave to visit his family during the refit of the *Grampus*. Secretary Southard suddenly decided to send the *Grampus* back to sea without delay and directed Sloat to return to the ship. Sloat reluctantly asked to remain in New York because some private affairs urgently required his attention. The nature of the personal emergency does not appear in the record, but Secretary Southard granted Lieutenant Sloat a six-month leave and ordered a replacement to command the *Grampus*.[33]

CHAPTER NINE

New York Interlude

The Sloat family, John, Abby, ten-year-old Lewis, and four-year-old Jeanette, settled into a reunited life together in New York City. The family had probably stayed in Norwich while Lieutenant Sloat commanded the *Grampus* in the West Indies. Sometime in 1825, they again took up residence at 93 Grand Street in Manhattan, and the city directories indicate that they remained there for three years. They lived one block away from Lieutenant Matthew Calbraith Perry and his family. Perry biographer Samuel Eliot Morison remarks that the residential neighborhood lay two miles on foot across Manhattan to the ferry that crossed to Brooklyn and the New York Navy Yard. Another former shipmate of Sloat's, Commodore Isaac Chauncey from his *President* days, served as commandant of that yard. These officers all shared a social life of the middling to upper-class sort, although a lieutenant on leave got only half of his normal forty-dollar salary each month.[1] Some of Sloat's sources of additional income remain obscure, but he did continue to own real property in Norwich and presumably shared some business interests with his father-in-law, James Gordon.

Lieutenant Sloat returned once again to the task of obtaining assignment to a full-time post with full pay. In January 1826, he wrote to Secretary of the Navy Southard and asked for command of the receiving ship in New York.[2] Receiving ships were ships of the line used as barracks barges, providing quarters for enlistees who had not yet been sent to an active ship of the fleet for duty. Command of such a ship would be like commanding a shore installation, which is to say, essentially administrative in nature. The job did, however, call for a master commandant, and so perhaps Sloat expected to be promoted soon. He did not get the assignment. In 1825, seven lieutenants received promotions to master commandant, and they were the first ones in five years. Three lieutenants made master commandant the next year, each with March 26, 1826, as his date of rank: William M. Hunter, who commanded the receiving ship in Philadelphia; John D. Sloat, awaiting orders in New York; and Matthew C. Perry, then serving in the Mediterranean as first lieutenant of the *North Carolina*, from which he was immediately ordered home and assigned to command the Naval Rendezvous in Charleston, South Carolina.[3]

The new master commandant now had to go through the same motions as when he returned from furlough as a lieutenant. To get an assignment from the secretary of the navy, Sloat wrote letters asking to be assigned to openings that he heard might occur. In April 1827, to use one example for which the documentation survives, Master Commandant Sloat requested command of the sloop-of-war *Lexington*, having heard that Master Commandant William B. Shubrick was about to resign that command. Sloat attached a very positive endorsement from Master Commandant George Budd, who then commanded the New York receiving ship that Sloat had sought earlier. The endorsement from a peer is interesting, because Budd himself might very well have wanted the *Lexington* command. Budd, who outranked Sloat by several years, did receive a sloop-of-war command the next year, so perhaps he knew that he was slated for the *Natchez* when he wrote on Sloat's behalf. A few months later, Sloat reacted to news that Master Commandant Daniel Turner was to give up command of the Naval Rendezvous at Boston and ordered to sea in command of the *Erie*. Sloat requested the Boston billet until he could get sea service. He did not get that either, and the subsequent year's register of naval officers lists Master Commandant Sloat as being on leave of absence.[4]

Without a navy assignment for the time being, John Drake Sloat appears to have spent the next couple of years in the real estate business. In May 1826, he bought a lot at Houston Street and Broadway for two thousand dollars. Two years later, he purchased an adjacent lot for another $1,250. The Sloat family would eventually take up residence on this property, but in 1828 they remained at nearby 93 Grand Street. Presumably he rented out the Houston Street property during this time.

In July 1826, Sloat bought three lots on the southwest corner of

Grand and Mercer streets in Manhattan. He paid six thousand dollars for the lots and then sold them in September 1827 for $7,500. The fifteen hundred dollar profit in little more than one year equated to more than a United States Navy captain's basic pay for one year, and slightly more than two years' pay for a master commandant. A month after selling the Grand and Mercer streets property, Sloat paid $10,300 for two properties on the south side of Bleecker Street between Mercer and Green streets. (Now part of the New York University campus.) He turned around and sold some of the Bleecker Street property in May 1828 to a widow in Newport, Rhode Island. In August 1828, Catherine Jones Clinton, the widow of recently deceased New York governor DeWitt Clinton, purchased another piece of the Bleecker Street property for $13,500. Sloat retained the remainder of the Bleecker Street property until 1833, when he sold that third piece for another twelve thousand dollars.[5]

The property sale to Catherine Clinton is quite interesting. Governor DeWitt Clinton of New York died in office on February 11, 1828. The governor left behind a widow and minor children with practically nothing to support them. Catherine claimed that she was unable to purchase a gravesite for her late husband's remains following the lavish official state funeral. The casket was interred in the vault of a friend in Albany. One wonders where six months later, Catherine Jones Clinton came up with the money to purchase real estate in New York City. A biographer of DeWitt Clinton notes the acquisition by Freemasons some years later of a collection of silver vases that had been taken from the estate by a creditor of the governor. The group of Masons returned the silver to Clinton's heirs. Clinton had been a Mason, and so was Sloat.[6] Perhaps a group of Masons arranged the financing, or possibly the widow's own family came to her aid. This essay does not require a resolution of that question. But at the very least, this particular transaction hints at the New York social and business circles in which John Drake Sloat moved. He probably did not take a financial loss in this transaction.

Sloat still owned two pieces of property in Norwich, Connecticut, one of which was his father-in-law's residence. He acquired more Norwich property in October 1828. This involved a somewhat more complicated exchange. Sloat bought one lot from a Gurdon Corning of Rensselaer City, near Albany, New York. He bought the adjacent lot from a minor for whom Corning served as guardian. Each lot cost $570.

He then sold the lot that had been the minor's to Corning himself for fifty-five dollars. Sloat thus added to his Norwich landholdings the lot that had belonged to Corning. This land undoubtedly was rented out as well, probably with Abby's father acting as Sloat's local agent. Norwich had become an increasingly prosperous textile-producing town, but New York was for Sloat a more lucrative market. These successful dealings suggest that John Drake Sloat possessed considerable acumen regarding real estate. This is not surprising when one recalls from an earlier chapter that, even as a teenager, he had been exposed to the property transactions of his grandfather Joseph Drake in upstate New York and signed as a legal witness the execution of at least one deed of sale. Sloat probably learned a great deal about land transactions from his grandfather Drake.

By the War of 1812, real estate values in New York City had risen more than 700 percent since the Revolution. New York continued to grow out of lower Manhattan after the Treaty of Ghent ended the war and the British blockade off Sandy Hook and off Montauk Point on Long Island. Well-to-do people began to seek escape from the increasingly less hospitable environment of the lower city. In the 1820s, they moved in ever larger numbers to the Hudson Square area, south of Houston Street by the Hudson (or North) River and to an area centered on Bleecker Street and Broadway where John Drake Sloat bought and sold properties as just described. He was not the only shrewd investor there. John Jacob Astor pulled a great deal of capital out of his shipping and trading concerns to invest in Manhattan real estate. Astor later said that he wished he had gone even more heavily into New York land investments because they were so profitable. Sloat also profited, but of course on a smaller scale because he started smaller. The fact that he could start at all shows that he was well off to begin with. It took money to make money.[7] Because he would spend several more years in New York City after a later assignment at sea, a more in-depth consideration of Sloat's class position in New York society is deferred to a subsequent chapter.

Master Commandant John Drake Sloat resumed his efforts to obtain an active duty navy posting in June 1828 and requested command of the New York Navy Rendezvous. Commodore Isaac Chauncey, Sloat's shipmate from midshipman days in the Quasi-War with France, had commanded the New York Navy Yard for several years and presumably lent his support to the request. Sloat remarked in his letter to Secretary

Figure 9.1. *South St. from Maiden Lane*, by William James Bennett, 1828, showing the busy waterfront of New York City. (In Phelps-Stokes, *Iconography of Manhattan Island, Vol. 3*.)

Southard that he would be especially pleased to get the job because New York City was his residence. The secretary granted Sloat's request. A discussion of duty at the rendezvous will appear in a later chapter, because Sloat only held the post for a few months but would later hold the same billet for several years. At the end of August 1828, recruiting requirements had been met and Sloat requested from Southard leave subject to twenty-four-hour recall by Commodore Chauncey. The purpose for the leave did not appear in the text of the letter request. Most likely, he wanted to accompany thirteen-year-old Lewis Warrington Sloat to boarding school in Connecticut. The youth's name first appears in the 1828 roster of students at Plainfield Academy, a secondary school in the town of that name a few miles away from Norwich. Interestingly, the Plainfield Academy catalog lists Warrington, as he was apparently called by his family, as being from Norwich instead of New York. Abby's father,

Major James Gordon, served as a trustee of that school.[8] Sloat's tenure at the rendezvous ended when Southard offered him command of the sloop-of-war *St. Louis.*

In 1825, Secretary Southard, and the John Quincy Adams administration, obtained congressional authorization for the construction of ten new sloops-of-war. Sometimes called corvettes in other navies, these ships were square-rigged with three masts and mounted between eighteen and twenty-two guns each. Including the *St. Louis*, the ten sloops in the 1825 program each carried eighteen guns. In the United States Navy, masters commandant served as their commanding officers instead of captains. A sloop was smaller than a frigate and therefore less costly to operate while

Figure 9.2. *City of Washington from Beyond the Navy Yard*, by William James Bennett, ca. 1832. Navy yard facilities are clearly visible in the foreground along the Anacostia River. Note also the previous dome on the Capitol building. (Courtesy of the Library of Congress.)

still able to perform most of the missions required of the larger ships. At the risk of emphasizing the obvious, the sloop could be in as many places as could a frigate or a ship of the line. The crew numbered about two hundred, or about one-half of a frigate's complement. The700-ton *St. Louis* was 127 feet long, thirty-three feet nine inches abeam, and drew sixteen feet of water. She was built in the Washington Navy Yard on the Anacostia River during 1827 and 1828.[9]

Because the ship was brand new, Sloat perhaps did not have to wrangle with the Washington Navy Yard about repairs to the degree that frequently appears in the letters from commanding officers of older ships. The initial entries of the *St. Louis*'s deck log record in excruciating detail the equipage that was brought on board, from sails and sextants down to fish hooks. Apparently due to the ship's destinations in the Pacific, *St. Louis* received national ensigns of Chile, Buenos Aires, the Brazilian empire, Mexico, and Colombia to go with the normal flag bag's British, French (Bourbon restoration), Spanish, Portuguese, and Russian banners.[10]

Sloat did face quite a few problems in obtaining a full crew for the *St. Louis.* Soon after taking command, he requested that Secretary Southard increase the sloop's allowance of seamen so that each gun crew would consist of ten men instead of the eight then allowed. He argued that in each of his earlier ships, ten-man gun crews had been standard. Southard appears to have ignored Sloat's petition, as no reply appears in the record. Weeks later, at the end of January 1829, Sloat reported that the *St. Louis* was ready for sea in all respects except for manpower. He reported a shortfall of forty able seamen! A sloop's allowance consisted of sixty able seamen, fifty ordinary seamen, and ten ship's boys, so the *St. Louis* was evidently very undermanned.[11]

Before sailing down the Potomac River and Chesapeake Bay to Norfolk, Master Commandant Sloat concluded that one of the *St. Louis*'s warrant officers was a drunkard. Accordingly, he requested that Carpenter Isaac White be replaced, and Carpenter William Wines came aboard in White's stead.[12] A matter about the commander of the *St. Louis* marine detachment proved to be a more difficult problem. Second Lieutenant Landon N. Carter commanded that detachment in 1829. Carter had five years in grade as a second lieutenant. The *St. Louis* was one of the replacement ships for the Pacific Squadron, along with the frigate *Guerrière* under the command of Commodore Charles C. B. Thompson. *Guerrière* was allowed two marine officers, but only Second Lieutenant Theodore Bainbridge was actually aboard. Bainbridge had been commissioned for little more than a year, and the commodore probably had concerns about his readiness to command a marine detachment on foreign service. No training program for marine officers then existed at all. They did not come from the United States Military Academy at West Point like army officers did, and neither they did spend years as midshipmen. Like navy pursers (supply officers) of that time, marine officers received direct appointments from civilian life and then learned on the job. Lieutenant Bainbridge clearly had not had much time to learn. Lieutenant Carter ended up being transferred to the *Guerrière*, and Bainbridge stayed aboard the frigate. No other marine officer could be found to make the three-year cruise in command of the *St. Louis* marine detachment. The navy register for 1829 lists a total of forty marine first and second lieutenants. Only two second lieutenants were without orders, and several other ships were also below their allowance for marine officers.[13] Options were limited.

A vastly different situation existed with navy lieutenants. The 1830 navy register lists 258 lieutenants, of whom eighty-eight were awaiting orders, on leave of absence, or on furlough. The *St. Louis* had an allowance for four lieutenants. The reader by this point doubtless realizes that favoritism and personal politics played crucial roles in navy officer assignments. The secretary of the navy controlled each assignment and could allow the commanding officer as much leeway as he wished concerning the assignment of subordinate officers to a ship or shore billet. The navy registers for Samuel Southard's years as secretary suggest that getting command of a sloop-of-war was for a master commandant mostly a matter of waiting for his individual turn. Sloat and Southard did correspond about which lieutenants would be assigned to the *St. Louis*, and Sloat made known his views without being overly insistent. Lieutenant Thomas Pettigru was already a member of the *St. Louis* wardroom but apparently did not wish to make the cruise. This seems to have chagrined Sloat, who had by then spent years seeking jobs such as the one that Pettigru then had but seemed not to appreciate. He wrote to Southard that Pettigru by rights ought to be made to go on the cruise, but that if the secretary wanted to indulge the lieutenant, then he should go ahead and replace him. Pettigru went on a leave of absence. Sloat stated that Lieutenant John Kelly wanted to go to the *St. Louis* and that he would like to have him. William V. Taylor, the ship's first lieutenant and a former warrant sailing master like Sloat, came down sick. Sloat said that Taylor did not want to be detached but he was probably too sick to stay on the ship, and Sloat needed a first lieutenant. Commodore Thompson of the *Guerrière* was willing to let Lieutenant Charles Caldwell of that ship become Sloat's first lieutenant. Adding to the problem was that Lieutenant Hugh D. Scott of the *St. Louis* was also sick. In the end, Taylor went ashore, Kelly stayed ashore, Scott recovered, and Caldwell stayed on the *Guerrière.* Secretary Southard ordered Lieutenant Andrew Fitzhugh to the *St. Louis* as first lieutenant. The other wardroom lieutenants were Scott, John E. Prentiss, Joseph Morehead, and Edward B. Boutwell. The *St. Louis* thus sailed with one navy lieutenant more than nominally allowed. The sailing master was Midshipman Andrew H. Foote, who had passed the examinations for promotion to lieutenant and who would later achieve fame during the Civil War. In that billet of course, Midshipman Foote received a sailing master's pay, which was almost as much as the lieutenants got. Twelve other midshipmen rounded out the officer complement. Some of the required materials for the midshipmen's education and training proved difficult to locate, and Sloat asked Secretary Southard to come up with two substitute texts and to provide two globes as well. The senior midshipman was Guert Gansevoort, who years later would play a key role in one of the most dismal events in the pre–Civil War history of the United States Navy.[14] Gansevoort served as first lieutenant of the brig *Somers* when a midshipman, a petty officer, and a seaman were executed by hanging after being charged with plotting mutiny.

The shortfall of seamen in the *St. Louis* crew finally got resolved. On February 5, a draft of fifteen men arrived on board from the Naval Rendezvous in Portsmouth, New Hampshire, and twenty-three more sailors transferred over from the *Guerrière.* All was in readiness. The *St. Louis* and the other ships in the squadron moved from Norfolk to an anchorage in Hampton Roads and, on February 14, 1829, sailed past Cape Henry and headed south into the Atlantic.

CHAPTER TEN

South American Cruise

The *St. Louis* and the *Guerrière* made their way toward Brazil and points farther south. The *St. Louis*'s log suggests an uneventful passage, punctuated by naval routine. Officers came on watch and were relieved a few hours later. Passed Midshipman Andrew Foote fulfilled his daily duties as the ship's sailing master and recorded the latitude based on his daily observations of the sun with a sextant. On March 4, 1829, the *St. Louis*'s crew mustered at quarters for inspection by the commanding officer. Evidently Master Commandant Sloat found them unsatisfactory, because three days later, he again inspected his crew at quarters. Happily, the *St. Louis*'s log contains no record of the crew being mustered to witness punishment (by flogging) although this would happen later in the cruise. Logs from his various cruises in command of United States Navy ships suggest that Sloat seldom resorted to the cat-of-nine-tails or the smaller colt to whip his men into line.[1] The same cannot be said of more than a few of his contemporaries. The *St. Louis*'s crew included many men who were new to the ship, having come from the *Guerrière*, and others who were completely new to the navy, having been recruited and sent by a naval rendezvous. In its makeup then, the *St. Louis*'s crew probably typified the rest of the navy. A large fraction of the men would have been African Americans, although perhaps not a full fourth of them as had been the case seventeen years earlier aboard the *United States.* Historian W. Jeffrey Bolster's research shows that the number of black sailors declined over the first half of the nineteenth century, but in 1829, they still abounded on American waterfronts. They tended to stay in the maritime trades longer and so generally had more experience than their white shipmates.[2]

White seamen were still a majority, however, and they tended to give up the maritime trades after a few years. To put it mildly, seamen did not enjoy the approbation of polite society. They were considered rootless vagabonds and ruffians whose alcohol consumption caused them to stand out even in a society that, by today's standards, drank quite heavily as a matter of daily routine. Not surprisingly then, seamen stood out as potential beneficiaries (or targets) of social reformers. Many movements for political and social change grew out of the religious movement known in the United States as the Second Great Awakening. One of those movements specifically meant to ameliorate the sufferings of men of the sea. A sort of religious revivalist group appears to have emerged on board the *St. Louis*. It must have had Sloat's approval merely to exist on the ship, but most likely Midshipman Foote led it at least in the earliest months of the cruise. Foote's biographers present the picture of a quite serious and sober individual, whose father sat as a United States senator from Connecticut during the *St. Louis*'s South American cruise. He had passed the examinations for a lieutenant's commission but remained a "passed midshipman" while waiting for a vacancy to occur in the naval officer corps. Foote was a member of the American Seamen's Friend Society, as were Lieutenants John W. Mooers and Robert D. Robb, both of whom reported aboard the ship at later points during the cruise. The society hoped to free seamen from entrapment in cycles of debt and alcoholism, in other words, to save them from the iniquities of their lives. It established reading rooms and boarding houses and provided reading material for sailors on ships at sea. Bible study and evangelical meetings played important roles in the American Seamen's Friend Society programs. Historians have concluded that such well-intended efforts produced little real effect on the behavior of seamen, both in naval and in merchant service.[3]

John Drake Sloat does not appear to have been an especially outwardly religious individual. He was born a Presbyterian but then joined the Protestant Episcopal Church at some later point. The Episcopal Church has always been formalistic, hierarchical, and reserved in comparison with more aggressively evangelical denominations. Most likely, Sloat would have given leeway to subordinates like Foote, Mooers, and Robb as long as their activities did not interfere with the ship's operations or cause divisive impacts on morale.

Figure 10.1. Map of South America, ca. 1830. Boundaries approximate and subject to dispute. (Map by author.)

The squadron continued southeast around Pernambuco and then southwest toward Rio de Janeiro. The *St. Louis*'s log contains no mention of festivities upon crossing the equator, but recall that the *Franklin*'s log of seven years earlier did record the arrival on board of King Neptune and his court. The traditional ceremonies most likely did take place on board the *St. Louis.* The ship continued south and made landfall off Cabo Frio on March 27, 1829. It then took three days to cover the eighty-odd nautical miles to the Brazilian capital at an average speed of advance of less than two knots. The ships sailed past the Sugar Loaf mountain and anchored in the bay off Rio de Janeiro on March 30.[4]

The final days of the voyage were obviously quite calm, but some of the earlier parts appear to have been much rougher. The *Guerrière* sprung so many leaks in her timbers that Commodore Thompson elected to remain at Rio de Janeiro to recaulk the ship, which was an extensive job. Sloat wrote to a friend in Portsmouth, New Hampshire, that the *St. Louis* was the best "sea boat" that he had ever sailed in. If the seas had been like glass the whole way from Norfolk, then Sloat would not have had much basis to admire the sloop's seakeeping ability. Sloat also remarked upon the *St. Louis*'s speed. He said that had his ship not been held back by the rest of the squadron, then he would have sailed the sloop from Norfolk to Rio de Janeiro in thirty days instead of the forty-five that actually elapsed. This letter from Sloat was the basis of a Portsmouth newspaper article, but the recipient's name unfortunately does not appear in it.[5] The uniformed navy staff had all turned over at the Portsmouth Navy Yard in the years since Sloat left it. He could have written to someone stationed at the yard whose personal connection is not evident or to some civilian friend in Portsmouth or Kittery. A few stray letters and references such as this newspaper article are all that we have, since this author has found no luck in locating personal letters of John or Abby Sloat. At any rate, the *St. Louis*'s first commanding officer appears to have been well pleased with his ship.

The *St. Louis* sailed alone from Rio de Janeiro on April 6, 1829, after spending one week in the Brazilian capital. Entries in the ship's log from one month afterward report several days of heavy weather along the track south to Cape Horn. The South Atlantic seas must have been particularly rough for such an unusual log entry to have been made. Two more weeks passed before the *St. Louis*, averaging two or three knots, passed around Cape Horn on May 19 and 20 and then headed north in the Pacific waters off Chile. The sea conditions must have improved because the sloop-of-war averaged a little more than five knots after rounding the Cape Horn and arrived in Valparaíso on June 6. Sloat reported to Secretary Southard that the passage from Rio de Janeiro had been quite rough, and that he found no American naval ships in Valparaíso.[6] After taking on water and fresh foodstuffs in the Chilean port, the *St. Louis* sailed on June 10. She anchored by Isla San Lorenzo off Callao, Peru, on June 19.[7] The Peruvian port would serve as the central base of operations in the months to come.

Seven years had passed since John Drake Sloat detached from the *Franklin* in Valparaíso. As a ship's lieutenant, he would have been more of an observant bystander, but as commanding officer of the *St. Louis*, he would participate more directly in affairs outside the physical limits of his ship. In 1822, Chile had established independence under Bernardo O'Higgins, and Simón Bolívar had done much the same for Gran Colombia, which included present-day Colombia, Venezuela, and Ecuador. Struggles between royalist and independence forces continued in Peru and what would become Bolivia. Defeat at the battle of Ayacucho on December 9, 1824, reduced Spain to toeholds that would in turn be lost in 1826. But by 1829, Gran Colombia stood on the verge of dissolution as a nation-state.[8] The mission of the United States Navy squadron in the region remained as it had been during the independence wars, to protect American shipping and commercial interests. The political stage in 1829 was different, but no less delicate than it had been before.

Commodore Charles Stewart in the *Franklin* had some problems as squadron commander in the Pacific. He personally sympathized with the royalists, which frequently put him at odds with American diplomats ashore. Not long after Sloat left the *Franklin* in 1822, a man came to Mrs. Delia Stewart in Callao with a hard-luck story of shipwreck and asked for help. She played a crucial role in arranging his embarkation and transport. He left the ship in Quilca, near Arequipa in southern Peru. The man turned out to be a royalist officer who escaped from patriot-held Lima. The Peruvian government protested formally to the United States. Following Stewart's return to the United States, the battle-proven hero from the War of 1812 found himself charged with several counts of conduct unbecoming an officer and was tried by a court-martial. The charges included having transported the royalist officer. The commodore claimed in his defense that he knew nothing about what had happened until the royalist had left the ship. Stewart's sympathetic biographers note that the commodore must have been the only person aboard who did not know about the passenger's presence, which to this author suggests a low state of order and discipline aboard the *Franklin*. The court-martial convened in Washington during August 1825. The court found Stewart not guilty of that particular charge.[9]

Sloat had no part in the trial, but he was doubtless aware and interested in it. The antebellum navy was a small organization, and Charles Stewart was one of its most celebrated heroes. At the time of the trial itself, Sloat was on leave in New York and Connecticut after his West Indian cruise in command of the *Grampus*. There was a lesson from Stewart's troubles for other officers to heed in the future. It was well that the court acquitted Commodore Stewart, but it would have been better had his cruise as squadron commander in South America been such that he had never been tried. A pitched battle at sea during a declared war was one thing. Complicated diplomatic situations were quite another. Taken together, the experiences of Porter after Fajardo and of Stewart after the *Franklin* cruise can only have highlighted to naval officers the need for care and for caution in the exercise of their responsibilities if they wished to avoid personal disgrace and the loss of their careers.

The fluid political situations in Peru and Gran Colombia created a morass-like environment in which a misstep by a naval officer charged with protecting his own country's interests became much more difficult to avoid than it might have been in, for instance, Amsterdam or Constantinople. Historians of Latin America of this period tend to take a long-term view of the postcolonial struggles and intrigues between caudillos (military strongmen) as newly independent political entities went through the throes of defining and creating viable nation-states. A governmental change took place in Peru, on average, once a year in the first two decades after the Battle of Ayacucho, and its constitution went through five rewritings.[10] This study of John Drake Sloat, however, requires detailed attention to the sequence of events in order to understand the specific struggles and intrigues to which he was a close witness and, at times, even an involved participant.

A few months before Sloat and the *St. Louis* arrived in Callao, three generals, Agustín Gamarra, Antonio Gutiérrez de la Fuente, and Andrés de Santa Cruz, allied with each other and overthrew José de la Mar, the sitting president of Peru. La Mar had seized upon the fractious situation that faced Simón Bolívar in Gran Colombia. Taking advantage of a rebellion in southwestern Gran Colombia against Bolívar's rule, invading Peruvian forces crossed the northern border. They occupied the port city of Guayaquil in an attempt to split off the coastal department that under colonial rule had been part of the Audiencia de Quito. Guayaquil is a low-lying coastal city with a warm tropical climate and was the capital of a department characterized by plantation agriculture. Quito is a high mountain city and remained a bastion of Quechua-speaking Andean culture as it had been under Inca rule centuries earlier. Annexing a slice of Gran Colombia to Peru was perhaps an achievable goal, but it was

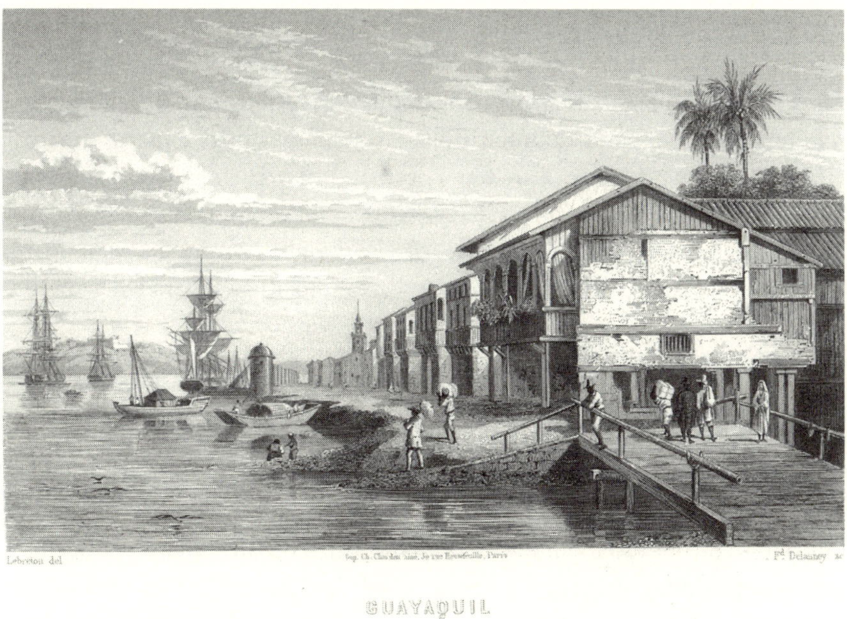

Figure 10.2. *Guayaquil*, ca. 1860. (In Énault, *L'Amerique Centrale et Meridionale.* Courtesy of the Bancroft Library, University of California, Berkeley.)

not to be. Gran Colombian forces led by Marshal Antonio de Sucré and General Juan José Flores defeated La Mar near Cuenca at the Battle of Tarqui on February 27, 1829. The defeated Peruvian president was forced to withdraw from Guayaquil and was soon overthrown. Simón Bolívar had left his capital in Bogotá to deal with the rebellion, and he continued his journey south meaning to hold together his wobbly confederation. Bolívar arrived in Guayaquil on July 21.[11]

After spending two weeks in Callao, Sloat had sailed north on July 4. Out of concern for the safety of large amounts of United States citizens' property in view of the ongoing political struggles there, Commodore Charles C. B. Thompson ordered the *St. Louis* to visit Guayaquil. Following port visits at Guanchaco near Trujillo, and Payta near Piura, the *St. Louis* anchored in the Gulf of Guayaquil on July 26 and then moved to the port city itself four days later.[12]

Bolívar and Flores had already quelled any disorder in Guayaquil when Sloat arrived. The appropriate diplomatic formalities followed. The ship's log reports that General Flores and other Colombian officers visited the *St. Louis* on August 2. They were formally honored with a fifteen-gun salute. No other formal visits aboard the sloop are recorded. Sloat feted the Colombian officials in apparently grand style and later requested reimbursement of one hundred dollars for his personal expenses in that affair. Excluding rations, a master commandant then received sixty dollars per month as salary, and a navy lieutenant received forty. On August 19, Sloat's mission completed, the *St. Louis* sailed from Guayaquil and returned to Callao, stopping again at Payta and then Guanchaco on the way south.[13]

The city of Guayaquil may have been quiet for the moment, but the country of Gran Colombia still teetered on the precipice of dissolution. Bolívar's writings from those weeks bemoan his country's impending dissolution. Bolívar was ill during that month in Guayaquil, and historian John Lynch contends that he already suffered from the tuberculosis that killed him in the following year. By the time of the liberator's death, a strong secessionist movement in the north had succeeded in creating an independent Venezuela. Bolívar's loyal subordinate, Juan José Flores, later led both Quito and Guayaquil into an independent Ecuador, apparently conceding that South American realities could not sustain Bolívar's dreams of Pan-American unity.[14]

The Guayaquil port visit seems rather a dull story in some ways. A peacetime diplomatic mission was successfully carried out without incident, but that is important to this study of John Drake Sloat. The absence of drama stands in stark contrast to Porter at Fajardo, nor did Sloat create the kind of embarrassment to his country that Stewart had done a few years earlier. But some discrepancies exist among the source documents. Sloat made his claim for reimbursement in the spring of 1832, shortly after the *St. Louis* returned to the United States from the cruise. Almost three full years had passed since visiting Guayaquil. Sloat's letter to Secretary of State Edward Livingston states that he received Bolívar and his officers "in appropriate style." The *St. Louis* log book, however, reports only that Flores and a retinue came aboard, and Bolívar's name does not appear at all. The absence of an archival record does not prove that something did not take place, but this case is different. The gun salute would have been rendered to the ranking official in a visiting party, and so it appears that Bolívar may not have come aboard the *St. Louis.* A head of state would have received a salute of twenty-one guns instead of fifteen. A scenario in which General Flores was the senior visitor comports with biographer Lynch's conclusions about Bolívar's illness. Some other formal meeting or reception may well have taken place ashore. But the State Department document appended to Sloat's claim as published in the records of Congress recommends paying Sloat one hundred dollars for entertaining Bolívar and others aboard the *St. Louis.* That document also records the reception as taking place on July 10, 1829, which it clearly cannot have done. The *St. Louis* did not arrive in Guayaquil until more than two weeks later.

Why the discrepancy? Sloat's claim carried recommendations from the secretary of state, the secretary of the navy, and even President Andrew Jackson himself that Congress pay the claim. Perhaps Sloat's memory was faulty, but this seems unlikely, and he would have only recently submitted the ship's log book to the secretary of the navy, assuming he had already submitted it and did not keep a transcribed copy for himself. Perhaps Sloat and others felt they needed to bring Bolívar into the claim for fear that Congress might deny it if General Flores was the recipient of the fete. Certainly, the Jackson administration had its difficulties with Congress in 1832, with the Bank of the United States renewal issue being at the forefront when Sloat's claim went forward.[15] The truth may have been shaded, or the records selectively framed toward the goal of getting Sloat reimbursed for out-of-pocket expenses undertaken in the national interest. Similar claims had been denied in the past, such as Secretary of the Navy Southard's disapproval of Master Commandant Thomas ap Catesby Jones's request in January 1828.[16] But any way that one looks at it and however minor they may be in the grand scheme of things, the official documents on this matter do contain outright contradictions. Questions such as these will appear again in this study, but let us return our focus to Master Commandant Sloat and the *St. Louis.*

After two weeks in Callao, Sloat again weighed anchor on October 10 and stood out to sea. Within a few hours, Commodore Thompson's flagship hove into view, bound for Callao. The *St. Louis* followed the *Guerrière* back to Callao and remained there until November 27. The squadron maintained an ongoing, official United States presence at this South American maritime crossroads. The *St. Louis* again cruised north from Lima, called at several Peruvian ports, and then returned to Callao on January 5, 1830.

Routine matters of naval administration punctuated life aboard the *St. Louis.* Lieutenant Edward Boutwell left the ship and returned to the United States. He was replaced by Lieutenant Robert Robb, who came over from the *Guerrière.* A court-martial convened to hear charges against two sailors. The record does not include the charges against the men, but one Horace Farewell received fifty lashes on the day that the *St. Louis* got underway from Callao.[17] As had been the case when he commanded the *Grampus*, Master Commandant Sloat seldom resorted to flogging as a means of punishment. Twelve lashes was the maximum allowed without a court-martial conviction. A sentence of fifty lashes was a heavy punishment, so Farewell must have been convicted of a serious offense such as mutinous conduct, disrespect to an officer, or attempted desertion. Historian James E. Valle finds that a typical United States Navy ship averaged one flogging punishment per week.[18] On January 9, the *St. Louis* again sailed from Callao, and on that day all hands were again mustered to witness punishments meted out to five different sailors. They received the only floggings administered on the *St. Louis* during the entire year of 1830.[19]

The *St. Louis* sailed north as before and made another brief visit to Payta, but the voyage would go much farther north this time. The sloop-of-war arrived at Panamá at the end of January and remained in that Colombian port for a week. Sloat then sailed north to Mexico and arrived at San Blas on March 21, 1830, for a three-day visit. The sloop then sailed for Mazatlán and spent more than four weeks anchored in that important Mexican port. Sloat's mission of "showing the flag" and maintaining a visible presence went very well according to an American newspaper correspondent, who reported that the *St. Louis* was the first United States Navy warship ever to visit that city. Commodore Thompson probably decided to send the *St. Louis* to Mazatlán upon learning in Callao of events that took place in Mexico in late 1829. Mexican troops led by General Antonio López de Santa Anna had defeated and driven from the country a Spanish military force that invaded in an attempt to reestablish colonial rule. Shortly after that success, however, a revolt erupted on December 4, 1829, against liberal, federalist president Vicente Guerrero. The conservative, centralist vice president Anastasio Bustamante overthrew Guerrero and took over the presidency himself just as the new year arrived. Commodore Thompson could have learned about the Mexican uprising and immediately sent Sloat north, or he may have only based his decision on the Spanish invasion on Mexico's east coast.

After deciding that his mission in Mazatlán was complete, Sloat departed on April 29 and made a quick visit to San Blas. A three-week cruise south brought the *St. Louis* back to Guayaquil, where the sloop dropped anchor on May 24 and rendered a thirteen-gun salute to the port commandant. Just ten days earlier, prominent citizens in Quito had joined under the leadership of Juan José Flores and declared Ecuador's independence from Gran Colombia. Passage of goods between the mountainous capital and the tropical port was very slow during the rainy season, but it seems likely that a post rider with the news from Quito could have reached Guayaquil by the time the *St. Louis* arrived there.[20]

The *St. Louis* sailed from Guayaquil on June 2 and arrived back in Callao three weeks later. The ship remained there for more than six months. The usual round of international formalities followed, including a visit on board by the commanding officer of a French frigate. Lieutenant Joseph Moorhead had taken sick. In a letter to Commodore Thompson, Sloat acknowledged that Moorhead wished to remain on board and not to lose his berth, but the surgeon's evaluation insisted that the lieutenant could no longer perform his shipboard duties. Sloat attached the medical report to a letter explaining the situation to Commodore Thompson. On July 4, 1830, Lieutenant Moorhead was detached and put aboard a ship for passage to the United States. On the same day, Sloat sent Ordinary Seaman Alfred Williams to a hospital for lunatics in Lima. No other documentation reveals the unfortunate Williams's fate, but most likely his was an unpleasant end.

On July 18, thirty-two *St. Louis* sailors and thirteen marines were granted liberty ashore in Callao. Their individual names appear in the ship's log. Presumably the officers and perhaps the sergeant of marines chose them as a reward for good behavior. Historian James E. Valle writes that because of the opportunities for mass desertion, liberty for sailors and marines was a rare treat in the antebellum navy. On the other hand, officers regularly left the ship on shore leave and those excursions were not entered in the ship's log. The nominal manpower authorization for a sloop-of-war included 159 persons from the commanding officer down to the ship's boys. This allowance included twenty-six commissioned and warrant officers and also the marine lieutenant, which the *St. Louis* did not have. Desertion appears to have been a problem for the *St. Louis* no less than for other ships, and perhaps far more deserters escaped than were apprehended. Purser Dudley Walker reported that Sloat regularly enlisted sailors in foreign ports and had them paid the routine advance pay. Walker complained that if they deserted as they sometimes did, then he ended up personally accountable for that part of their advance pay that had not yet been paid off through monthly deductions.[21] In November, the *St. Louis* sailed south from Callao and went to Valparaíso, Chile. This port visit lasted for six weeks and included one day of liberty for another twenty men. The ship returned to Callao on January 17, 1831.[22]

The mission of presence to protect United States commercial interests continued to dominate Sloat's life in Callao during the last half of 1830. One might use the term "gunboat diplomacy" to describe it. Sloat's efforts seem to have been appreciated by American merchant mariners. The brig *James Beacham* left Callao on January 31, and the master went out of his way to praise the help given to American ships by the United States Navy's Pacific Squadron. He mentioned in particular Master Commandant Sloat and the other officers of the *St. Louis.*[23] Sloat may have made assisting American merchant ships a priority, perhaps remembering his own voyages as a merchant master and wishing that he had that sort of support himself.

The shipping news report that praised Sloat also made mention of a growing border conflict between Peru and Bolivia. Historians of the United States sometimes dismiss with disdain the postindependence power struggles in Latin American countries and elsewhere. Reliance on United States sources frequently creates in their writings, historical stages on which United States persons act and people of other nations serve mainly as stage props, tropes of incompetence, or even outright evil. Such ethnocentric triumphalism can lead to skewed interpretations of complex situations. The tense political situation in Peru gave rise to a series of events that are important to understanding how John Drake Sloat approached problems that emerged to confront him in command. A summary overview of what follows would suffice for much historical writing, but a crucial question of this biography centers on Sloat's actions in California. The ebb and flow of the civil disturbances in Lima during April 1831 were important to Sloat's experiences and decisions. They warrant careful attention here.

There was far more afoot and at stake in Peru in early 1831 than a border dispute with Bolivia or even just personal power rivalries. Following the Peruvian defeat in Ecuador and the unseating of President José de la Mar, several local caudillos emerged to vie for overall power. Each of these men had military rank and political ability but, as historian Charles Walker emphasizes, did not necessarily have battlefield success or a record of gallantry in combat. Bolivian-born Andrés de Santa Cruz served briefly as president of Peru in 1827, but by May 1829, he had returned to Bolivia and assumed the presidency of that country. Santa Cruz attempted repeatedly to create a confederation of Bolivia and Peru. Cuzco-born Agustín Gamarra became president after La Mar. The third caudillo was Antonio Gutiérrez de la Fuente, whose power base centered on Arequipa despite his having been born near Tarapacá in southern Peruvian territory that would later be lost to Chile. Although Gutiérrez was his father's surname, he most often appears as La Fuente in the historical record. La Fuente became vice president when Gamarra acceded to the presidency. Also important to this story is Marshal Gamarra's wife, Francisca Zubiaga y Bernales, a very capable woman who exercised a great deal of power in spite of the highly gendered society in which she lived. All three of the men were former royalist officers who switched sides and joined independence forces in 1820 and 1821.[24]

As president and vice president, Gamarra and La Fuente moved to Lima and Callao, respectively, each one leaving his home city and province where he had been the prefect. As president, Marshal Gamarra faced many difficult challenges in maintaining power, due in some part to Santa Cruz's machinations to establish a confederacy with himself at its head. One of the most serious uprisings took place in Cuzco, at the very heart of Gamarra's power base. On August 26, 1830, Colonel Gregorio Escobedo attempted to overthrow the Gamarrista prefect of Cuzco. Escobedo failed, but Gamarra left the national capital for Cuzco and remained there for several months while confronting the threat across the border posed by Andrés de Santa Cruz.[25]

Gamarra left La Fuente as acting president in his absence. He treated his vice president as a friend and an ally, but La Mariscala did not share her husband's opinions on that particular score. She detested La Fuente, and the vice president reciprocated her dislike and resented her intrusions into the political sphere. Needless to say, La Mariscala was a controversial figure in Lima in her own right, but an important figure nonetheless. A number of incidents between her and La Fuente took place after Gamarra left for Cuzco. Some historians believe that Gamarra himself never really trusted his vice president. A dispute arose over wheat tariffs. When taking power, Gamarra had left in place a protective tariff structure. Acting in Gamarra's absence and without any protest from the Peruvian legislature, La Fuente lifted the tariffs on imported wheat and on rough cloth. Those actions had a negative impact on the business dealings of La Mariscala's brother. Señora Gamarra also believed that La Fuente had actively conspired with Santa Cruz, and in fact, the two men had been friends. Rumors circulated in Lima that the vice president planned to overthrow Gamarra. Colonel Francisco Vidal, an aide to Gamarra, had recently arrived in Lima from Cuzco. He set out to arrest La Fuente, but the vice president turned the tables and sent the colonel under guard to Callao. But the garrison at Callao sided against La Fuente and quickly released Vidal.[26]

Prefect of Lima Juan Bautista Eléspuru was loyal to Marshal Gamarra and an ally of La Mariscala. With her concurrence, he sent troops on April 16 to arrest La Fuente to prevent the coup d'état that they feared the vice president was about to lead. They arrived at La Fuente's residence after he had retired for the evening. Mercedes Subirat y Cossío, the vice president's wife, met the troops at the front door and delayed them while her husband attempted to escape. Dressed only in a nightshirt, La Fuente fled out the back and onto the rooftops as the troops stormed inside. They opened fire and killed a man in the darkness that turned out to be one of their own officers. Taking advantage of the confusion and the evening darkness, La Fuente disappeared into the night. He took refuge with a loyal acquaintance who provided him with a disguise. After a day in hiding, La Fuente then made his way to Chorrillos and from there hired a canoe that took him back along the shore to Callao and the gangway of the *St. Louis.* At about five o'clock in the morning of April 18, La Fuente clambered aboard and asked for asylum.

Sloat replied that he was under orders not to receive aboard anyone fleeing from the Lima political turmoil. La Fuente repeated what he had just said to the watch officer, that if he were to get back in the boat and return to Callao, then the Gamarristas would kill him. Sloat then agreed to grant only temporary protection to Vice President La Fuente, and that was subject to three conditions: first, if requested by the Peruvian government, then La Fuente would be handed over; second, that none of La Fuente's partisans could join him aboard the *St. Louis*; and third, La Fuente could send or receive letters only with his immediate family,

Figure 10.3. Detail of *View of Callao*, ca. 1817. View of the Presidio of Callao from the likely anchorage of the *St. Louis.* Vice president Antonio Gutiérrez de la Fuente's boat rounded the point at right and then came alongside. (In Shillibeer, *A Narrative of the Briton's Voyage to Pitcairn's Island.* Courtesy of the Bancroft Library, University of California, Berkeley.)

and all such correspondence would have to go through Sloat himself. La Fuente agreed and went below with Sloat to his cabin. Some dispute continues among modern historians about the subsequent conversations between the two men, but that need not concern us here.

Meanwhile, back at the presidio of Callao, the tumult continued after Major General William Miller of the Peruvian army arrived from Lima and tried to get the garrison to open up the gates of the fortress. Known as Guillermo Miller in Peru, the English adventurer arrived in South America after the end of the Napoleonic Wars. An artillery officer veteran of the Peninsular War in Spain and the War of 1812, both at the burning of Washington and the Battle of New Orleans, he served in General José de San Martín's army during the independence wars. Gamarra had appointed Miller as commanding general of a division. Miller had been in contact with Santa Cruz by letter in the months preceding the April disturbances, and La Mariscala considered him to be an ally of La Fuente. She was correct. When informed on the evening of April 16 that shots had just been fired at La Fuente's residence, Miller dressed and mustered some troops to support the vice president. By the next morning, his efforts had come to naught. Miller surrendered that same afternoon. Prefect of Lima Eléspuru then gave Miller safe conduct and written permission to embark in a neutral ship. On April 18 by means of a written letter of his own, Miller requested to come aboard the *St. Louis* and Sloat granted him protection.[27]

Minister Samuel Larned, chief of the United States diplomatic mission to Peru, well understood the fractious political situation in Peru of that day and also the attendant risks to United States commercial interests. On April 18, he sent a dispatch to Secretary of State Martin Van Buren that described La Fuente's attempt to arrest Vidal and the Gamarrista faction's counterstroke against the vice president and also General Miller's failed attempts to take control of the Presidio of Callao. Larned wrote that La Fuente had disappeared over the rooftops and his whereabouts were then unknown. The minister also remarked that La Fuente's preference for more free trade resonated with United States interests in Peru. Larned's letter must have begun to make its way to Washington before Sloat's report reached him in Lima. Sloat reported the events surrounding the arrival on board of La Fuente and Miller and emphasized that the latter carried written permission of the prefect of Lima. La Fuente wished to send a written communication to the Peruvian Congress. Sloat asked Larned if that should be allowed, as he remained unclear about the situation in Lima. Lieutenant S. Humphreys carried the letter to Lima and waited there to carry back Larned's reply. The minister wrote back right away. He applauded Sloat's actions with respect to both La Fuente and to Miller. Larned added that he found it difficult at that moment to know exactly which officials in Lima would have had the right to request that La Fuente be handed over. Larned had informed the Peruvian minister of state that La Fuente had gone aboard the *St. Louis*, and that official stated there was not any reason just then to return La Fuente to the control of Peruvian authorities. Larned went on to add that the government could change again at any time and asked that Sloat confer with himself before complying with any request for custody of La Fuente.[28]

After another two days passed, Commodore Charles C. B. Thompson arrived on the scene as the Pacific Squadron flagship, the frigate *Guerrière*, anchored in Callao Roads. Master Commandant Sloat immediately reported to his senior in command the events of the previous days. Sloat added that after the *Guerrière* had left earlier in the year, the political situation in Lima deteriorated, and thus he decided to stay in Callao Roads. The *St. Louis* was provisioned and ready for sea except for bread, which he did not want to take on board until just before getting underway.[29]

Thompson replied immediately that he concurred completely with Sloat's decision to allow La Fuente and Miller temporary refuge on board the *St. Louis*. But the commodore also expressed reservations about the refugees' continued presence on board a ship of his squadron. They interfered with the *St. Louis*'s readiness to respond to any necessary assignment, and also the longer they stayed, the more one could construe that the United States improperly began to take a side in Peruvian politics. He directed Sloat to urge La Fuente and Miller to find a different asylum. Thompson also sent an almost identically worded letter to Larned and requested that the diplomat keep in regular contact and express his views freely and frankly. While Thompson's letter was on its way to Lima, Larned went to Callao and conferred with La Fuente. Upon returning to Lima, Larned received Thompson's letter but delayed in responding until he had met with the acting president, who expressed his satisfaction with La Fuente's remaining offshore in United States custody. The ousted vice president was allowed a visit by his family and to receive his personal effects. La Fuente and Miller received passports to Chile and took passage there during May 1831 in neutral merchant ships.[30] Each would be back in Peru within a few years, but this narrative now takes its leave of them.

In the Callao affair, Master Commandant Sloat found himself suddenly faced with a delicate situation. His decision to take La Fuente and Miller on board can be viewed as disobedience of orders not to shelter any political refugees. Alternatively, one could argue that the threat to La Fuente's life transformed the situation to one for which Sloat had no previous orders and therefore had to use his own judgment. As had been the case in the capture of Roberto Cofresí, the value of consultation with diplomats and authorities ashore was clear. American diplomats and naval officers often did not cooperate with each other, often to the particular chagrin of the former.[31] Caution and prudence in the La Fuente affair earned praise and approbation, but it remains interesting to note Commodore Thompson's own caution. His expressions of concern about keeping La Fuente and Miller on board for extended periods made an important point, but they also gave the commodore some room to distance himself and disavow Sloat's early morning decision should he find that convenient or prudent. It never came to that.

On May 10, 1831, the *St. Louis* sailed from Callao, presumably without La Fuente or Miller as passengers. The itinerary looked much like earlier ones during the cruise, with visits of about two weeks' duration to Payta and Guanchaco before returning to Callao. Patrols off central Peru followed in July, and in August, Sloat made ready to return to the United States with the rest of the squadron. The three years of cruising in the Pacific afforded many opportunities, and indeed requirements, for Sloat to exercise independent command and judgment because the *St. Louis* and the *Guerrière* frequently were in different locations instead of sailing in company.

On September 7, 1831, the *St. Louis* left Callao en route to the United States. Three weeks later, she rounded Cape Horn and headed north. No intermediate stops occurred. On December 9, the sloop-of-war anchored off Sandy Hook, three years and two days after the first log book entry was made at the Washington Navy Yard.[32]

Sloat reported his arrival in New York to Secretary of the Navy Levi Woodbury and asked for permission to discharge a number of sailors who had only five or six weeks remaining on their enlistments. He asked for leave for each of his lieutenants as soon as possible, because each one of them had a family. The *St. Louis* was turned over to the New York Navy Yard and placed in ordinary. On Christmas Eve, Master Commandant John Drake Sloat commenced a three-month leave period as Woodbury had authorized.[33]

CHAPTER ELEVEN

Beached in New York

Completion of the long cruise as commanding officer of the sloop-of-war *St. Louis* marked an important milestone in the life of John Drake Sloat. No formally promulgated career progression appears to have existed in a navy where promotion was widely perceived to depend upon patronage and favoritism. But a review of the naval officer registers of the 1820s and 1830s shows that a tour in command of a sloop-of-war as a master commandant was a de facto requirement for promotion to captain. Seniority did matter, and so that promotion would have to wait another five years until Sloat reached the top of the master commandant seniority list. Also, the number of deploying sloops-of-war was substantially smaller than the number of masters commandant seeking those commands, and so a second sloop command was almost unheard of. This meant that Sloat would be "beached" in a shore assignment or, worse, simply waiting for one to become available. He did once entertain a brief hope. In December 1835, a diplomatic furor over claims payments led to a war scare with France. Sloat wrote to Secretary of the Navy Mahlon Dickerson to ask that he be given a command if a fleet were to be fitted out, reminding the secretary that he had been a "uniform friend of [President Jackson's] administration."[1] Of course, it did not come to be because diplomacy resolved the confrontation with France.

That letter shines some light on Sloat's political inclinations. Both Democrats and Whigs could be found in the navy officer corps of the 1830s. Sloat's good friend James Biddle was of course a Whig, as one would expect of a member of that family. Sloat once sent his friend a silver matchbox and made a joke about Locofocos, a humorous reference to the workers faction of the Democrats at the time. That nickname stemmed from their having used sulfur matches when another faction shut off gas to the lights during a candidate nomination meeting in Tammany Hall.[2]

Sloat would spend the next eight years in New York City, doing the routine work of the peacetime navy. No thrilling tales of nautical derring-do emerge from such a situation. Including even Commodore Charles Morris in his own autobiography, some biographers of American commodores have dismissed these long periods of their subjects' lives with a mere one or two paragraphs. Heretofore, this essay has adhered to the taut chronological scheme one would expect of a biography. But much of this next decade in Sloat's life is better understood from a thematic organization even though the chronology may repeat itself. This chapter will look at Sloat's personal life beyond the navy, his years in charge of the naval recruiting station in New York, and then his involvement in broader naval affairs.

Having been away from his family for three years, Master Commandant Sloat wasted no time in getting up to Norwich and reuniting with them. He also wasted no time in expanding his real estate holdings by buying another house and lot in Norwich for six hundred dollars. That sale was completed in just one week after he left New York, and the deed was recorded on January 2, 1832.[3] Sloat bought that house from Gurdon Corning, the same person with whom he had dealings back in 1828 before taking command of the *St. Louis.* Recall that Corning lived near Albany, New York, but he also owned property in Norwich. The earlier deals had been executed in Rensselaer City, but this transaction did take place in Norwich. A transaction so rapidly completed might mean one of two things: The first is that Sloat arrived in Norwich and immediately spotted and seized a good deal. Or second, and more likely, Abby Sloat or her father, James Gordon, had kept an eye out for such opportunities while Sloat was overseas. The New York City directories for those years do not list the Sloats as residing there, so their properties must have been rented to tenants, and the family most likely spent that time living in Norwich. They probably lived with the Gordons instead of renting a separate house. Norwich city directories for those years do not survive, but the 1830 census tally for Major Gordon's household is consistent for Abby, Lewis, and Jeanette living there while John sailed in South American waters. The 1832 directory for Plainfield Academy, in the town of that name located close by, lists seventeen-year-old Lewis Warrington Sloat as a resident of Norwich who completed his studies and graduated in that same year. He most likely boarded in Plainfield at the time, and then probably returned to live with his parents in New York and pursue a business career. The name of young Lewis's grandfather, James Gordon, no longer appeared among the members of the academy's Board of Trustees.[4]

In May 1833, Sloat sold another piece of the property at Mercer and Bleecker streets in New York City. The sale price was twelve thousand dollars. The last of John and Abby's three children came into the world soon afterward. John Drake Sloat, Junior, was born on September 18, 1833. In November 1834, an advertisement appeared in the *Norwich Courier* for the sale of Major Gordon's residence in Norwich. The advertisement described the house as one of the "most pleasant in the City" and large enough for a "genteel" family. It had two kitchens and so could easily have been split into two houses. One John A. Rockwell acted as Sloat's agent for the sale, and he had been a party in one of Sloat's earlier Norwich real estate transactions. James Gordon was by then seventy years old and seems to have met with some business reverses. He had undergone an insolvency hearing in the Norwich Superior Court in 1825, and it appears that things had not improved very much for him. No transfer of title appears in the Norwich land records, and so the attempt at sale appears to have failed. Gordon died a few years later, in February 1837. The circumstances of Gordon's business troubles remain for speculation, but one should note that Gordon had been in the shipping business when he first met his son-in-law during the War of 1812. Since that time, the effects of the Industrial Revolution transformed Norwich from an agricultural transportation center to a thriving textile mill town, and perhaps Gordon fared poorly because of the changes in the times.[5]

After Sloat turned over the *St. Louis* to the New York Navy Yard to be placed in ordinary, some additional matters stemming from the cruise still required resolution. He sought reimbursement for official entertainment expenses while in command of the *St. Louis.* While still on post-cruise leave, Sloat left his family in Norwich and traveled to Washington in March 1832. The Navy Department rejected his claim for $1,050 because no budgetary authorization existed to pay it. Since the matter related directly to national diplomacy, Sloat next presented his claim to

Secretary of State Edward Livingston. The latter agreed with the justice of the claim and recommended to President Andrew Jackson that Congress be asked to make an appropriation of funds. Just two days after he received Livingston's endorsing letter, Jackson submitted the claim to Congress on April 4, 1832. Many issues at the time, including the struggle over the renewal of the charter of the Second Bank of the United States, exacerbated a highly contentious relationship between the president and the Congress. The matter of Sloat's reimbursement passed through the Capitol Hill maelstrom without any apparent difficulty as the Committee on Foreign Affairs reported out to the House of Representatives on May 14. Congress authorized $1,360 instead of the claimed $1,050. President Jackson had recommended that a provision be made for cases like Sloat's, but the House Committee disagreed, opining that such occurrences were few and far between.[6]

Not until March 1833 did Sloat actually receive the draft. When he presented it to Secretary of the Navy Woodbury for payment, Sloat speculated that the increased award may have been for interest, or perhaps for the personal expense borne in traveling to Washington regarding the claim. He also noted that the increased award from Congress still amounted to less than his actual expenses out of pocket.[7]

Sloat's initial letter to Secretary of State Livingston stated that Antonio Gutiérrez de la Fuente was the president of Peru at the time he sought refuge on board the *St. Louis.* At best, Sloat stretches the truth here. Recall that La Fuente was actually the vice president but had been acting as the chief executive because President Manuel Agustín Gamarra went to Cuzco to confront both local rebels and the threat from Bolivia. Subsequent documents from Secretary Livingston, President Jackson, and the House Committee on Foreign Affairs all correct this error. But there is more.

Sloat's request also included one hundred dollars to reimburse him for entertaining General Simón Bolívar and other Colombian officers in Guayaquil as discussed in the preceding chapter. Passed Midshipman Andrew Foote, of Civil War fame, served as sailing master of *St. Louis* while awaiting his lieutenant's commission. A biographer of Foote, the historian Spencer Tucker, notes that a "lavish party" for Bolívar took place, but the book does not identify the author's source.[8] The *St. Louis* log book indicates only that General Juan José Flores and a retinue of officers came aboard. Bolívar perhaps did request to make a visit to the

United States warship as Sloat stated in his claim to Livingston. But recall from the preceding chapter that the Colombian liberator had fallen ill in Guayaquil. It seems inconceivable that Bolívar's arrival on a formal visit would have gone unmentioned in the log that did record the arrival of an important but still a subordinate official. The original log book seems the most reliable source here. One should also know that the *St. Louis* log contains no mention at all of Vice President La Fuente or General Miller, but neither of those two officials came aboard in a representational capacity. In the antebellum United States Navy, commanding officers submitted their ships' logs to the secretary of the navy upon completion of their cruises. Sloat had traveled to Washington to press his claim for reimbursement, and so he probably delivered the log to Secretary Woodbury while in the nation's capital. Perhaps the exaggeration was meant to ensure that a penurious government would honor his justifiable claim, and it certainly appears that Sloat did not defraud the public treasury from anything to which he was not fairly entitled. Nevertheless, there is no escaping the simple fact that the ship's log says one thing and Sloat's claim says another.

At the end of March 1832, Sloat returned to New York City and once again awaited orders on half pay. He laid out his preferences for duty assignment in a letter to Secretary of the Navy Levi Woodbury. Sloat said that he did not want duty in a navy yard unless it was the one in Philadelphia. He also stated that he would like to command a naval rendezvous north of Philadelphia. He pointed out that he had duty at the New York rendezvous for a few months before taking command of the *St. Louis* and added that it was the only shore assignment "with emolument" in which he had served.[9]

Why Sloat would not want duty at any of the navy yards except Philadelphia is baffling. One captain commented upon how undemanding he found his duties as navy yard commandant when compared with other assignments, and a master commandant later remarked that as the second senior officer at a yard, he had virtually no duties at all unless the yard commandant was called away.[10] Sloat's reservations seem not to have been about navy yard duty itself or else he would not have said that Philadelphia would be acceptable. Moreover, two of the other yards were commanded by officers with whom Sloat had served before. Isaac Chauncey commanded at New York and Charles Morris at Charlestown

(Boston). But Morris was relieved by the widely disliked Commodore William Bainbridge at around this point in time. Probably the most perplexing aspect of Sloat's declaration of preferences is that Commodore James Barron commanded the Philadelphia Navy Yard.[11] Barron was a very controversial officer, in no small part due to his having killed Stephen Decatur in a duel. Of course, Sloat's navy career owed a great deal to Decatur, and so one is left to wonder why Sloat would indicate a specific willingness to serve under a yard commandant who was widely reviled for having killed Sloat's benefactor. It seems unlikely that Sloat wanted to live in Philadelphia for its own sake, a city to which he had no particular ties, because he did not include the Pennsylvanian city among his preferences for command of a naval rendezvous. There were three rendezvouses north of Philadelphia: New York, Boston, and Portsmouth, New Hampshire. Sloat eventually did get the New York rendezvous assignment, which, New Yorker that he was, must have pleased him greatly. We will return to the years at the rendezvous shortly.

Sloat's statement that his earlier, short period in charge of the New York rendezvous was his only paid shore duty must raise our eyebrows. He had a short tour as a lieutenant at the Portsmouth Navy Yard more than a decade earlier. A history of the yard quotes budget documents that include pay and allowances for then-lieutenant Sloat. Local parish records show two of his children being baptized there.[12] It seems highly unlikely that he would have gone up to Kittery, Maine, and away from New York and Norwich, for the same half pay that he could get for awaiting orders there. A different secretary of the navy did by then hold office, and perhaps Sloat only meant to discuss his assignments since being promoted to master commandant. But Sloat's letter does not directly say that either. In any case, that particular aspect of Sloat's letter to Woodbury looks like another stretched or shaded truth, not unlike the discrepancies in the records surrounding the claim for reimbursement of expenses incurred in South America.

After two months in New York, Sloat then returned to Norwich and asked Woodbury to forward any correspondence for him to the latter city. While in Norwich, he provided an accounting of the specie shipments that he had accepted from American merchants while commanding the *St. Louis.* Commanding officers of United States warships were authorized to safeguard and to transport cash for civilian merchants. The officers were allowed to charge a fee for this armored car–like service.[13] Sloat carried $642,444.59 in commercial funds, of which his "deposit" amounted to $11,007.11. This equates to a service charge of about 1.7 percent. One-third of the deposit went to Commodore Thompson, the Pacific Squadron commander, so Master Commandant Sloat's portion came to $7,338.07.[14] A master commandant's base salary was sixty dollars per month, plus a daily allowance of five rations at twenty-five cents each. While commanding a sloop-of-war in the Pacific then, Sloat earned $1,176.25 per year. Carrying specie brought him a bonus greater than six years' pay. Over the course of the three-year cruise, carrying specie more than tripled Sloat's navy income.

John Drake Sloat spent the rest of 1832 awaiting orders in New York and presumably visited Norwich on a regular basis. He was granted a leave of absence for three months beginning on December 24, 1832. Soon afterward, he received command of the New York Naval Rendezvous, which was essentially a recruiting station. The commandant of the New York Navy Yard, located just across the East River in Brooklyn, acted not only as shipyard commander but also as the overall supervisor of all shore activities in the New York City area as well as over any navy ships that happened to be in the harbor. In his classic and adulatory biography of Matthew Calbraith Perry, renowned historian Samuel Eliot Morison reports that Perry had received the New York rendezvous command on January 7, 1833. However, the naval register submitted to Congress for the year shows that in 1832, Sloat awaited orders and Perry commanded the sloop-of-war *Concord* in the Mediterranean. The subsequent annual register shows Sloat in command of the New York Naval Rendezvous and Perry assigned to the New York Navy Yard. Master Commandant Lawrence Kearny had commanded the rendezvous, but his promotion to captain effective December 20, 1832, elevated him out of the job to await orders. The registers are one-time snapshots of assignments as of the beginning of the year, and if an officer were to be transferred twice between publication dates, the interim assignment would not appear.[15] Perry may have commanded the rendezvous for a few months and then moved across the river to the navy yard when Sloat returned from leave in early 1833, but that seems unlikely.

The New York Naval Rendezvous had an authorized staff of one master commandant, two lieutenants, one surgeon, and two midshipmen.

Besides Sloat himself, also assigned were Lieutenant Henry W. Ogden, Lieutenant J. B. Montgomery, and Surgeon David S. Edwards. No names of any assigned midshipmen appear on the naval register, although several are at the navy yard. That might have been a better place for those aspiring to lieutenancies to develop professionally, and the navy yard commandant could have sent them to assist the rendezvous whenever needed. Slowed promotions in the peacetime Navy meant that the rendezvous enjoyed a wealth of experience and maturity among its staff. Originally entering as midshipmen in 1811 and 1812, Ogden and Montgomery had been lieutenants since 1817 and 1818, respectively. Surgeon Edwards first entered as a surgeon's mate in 1818.

A naval rendezvous was opened and closed as directed by the local navy yard commandant to provide seamen for the ships of the navy as needed. Besides New York, rendezvouses existed in Portsmouth, Boston, Philadelphia, and Norfolk. Temporary ones also had existed at Carlisle, Pennsylvania, Savannah (Georgia), and Washington. The New York rendezvous was located in Manhattan on lower Broadway. Enlistments and medical examinations by the surgeon took place in the room that fronted on the street, and an administrative office adjoined in the back. The New York rendezvous was by far the largest and busiest of them. Between war's end in 1815 and 1832, the New York rendezvous shipped 12,002 of the estimated 22,157 seamen that enlisted for cruises in navy ships. Probably responding to Congress's questions on shore station budgets, the secretary of the navy reported in 1833 that since 1825, the New York rendezvous was open for recruiting during 2,448 days, which equates to somewhat more than six and one half years. The Portsmouth rendezvous was open for only three weeks in eight years, and Boston for a year and a half. Norfolk and Philadelphia each operated for four and a half years. Even though the New York rendezvous appears to have usually been open, ships generally deployed as squadrons and so the work load there was probably still rather cyclical.

The establishment of Naval Rendezvouses went back to the Revolutionary War, when Continental Navy and privateer captains set up rendezvouses to recruit seamen for their crews. These temporary affairs were frequently located in taverns and attracted enlistees with music, drink, and entertainment. A rendezvous of the standing United States Navy was doubtless a rather more sober affair, but alcohol still played

Figure 11.1. *Broadway, New-York*, by T. Marner, 1836. The New York Naval Rendezvous was located a few blocks south of this intersection. (In Phelps-Stokes, *Iconography of Manhattan Island, Vol. 3*.)

an important role. The Naval Rendezvous often relied on "crimps," men who recruited or ensnared seamen onto ships for a bounty. Many of them also kept boarding houses that catered to the maritime trade. Sailors between voyages stayed in boarding houses, often until their money ran out and they had to go back to sea. Boarding house proprietors often acted as bankers and kept accounts for their patrons who often ran up large debts. Frequently the boarding house keepers overcharged for goods and services and then collected from the victims' advance navy pay. Three months' advance was allowed, at a rate of twelve dollars per month for able seamen and ten dollars per month for ordinary seamen. Or a seaman might have conspired with a crimp to split the advance after enlisting and then disappear into the streets of New York before the crimp had delivered him from the rendezvous on Broadway to the ship of the line

North Carolina, the receiving ship anchored in the East River that then served as a barracks barge.[16]

In running the New York Naval Rendezvous, Master Commandant Sloat continued operating in a well-established mode. Toward the end of his tenure there, Sloat became the target of a complaint signed by several boarding house keepers. John Morrison and Samuel Bradley, a pair of New York crimps, initiated the complaint and got a number of other boarding house landlords to sign it. Sloat declared that when he confronted them, they expressed surprise and said that they only signed it because Morrison and Bradley had asked them to do so. Sloat wrote to Secretary Dickerson to defend himself and labeled Morrison and Bradley as "two of the most worthless pillars in the city." His predecessors in command of the rendezvous had refused to deal with them. At first Sloat did conduct navy business with the two men but quickly came to regret it when he learned of their unreliability and lack of security. Sloat added to Dickerson that he had made several recommendations to the navy yard commandant to improve the operations of the rendezvous, and that some of them had been approved.[17]

Crimps occupy a notorious niche in maritime labor history. The potential for abuse should be obvious to the reader at this point, and the whole system of crimping became a lightning rod for reformist criticism. The historian Harold Langley studied social reform in the antebellum navy and emphasizes the abuses of seamen by waterfront crimps. Comparing the life of a navy sailor with that of a Southern plantation slave, Langley contends that in some cases the slave actually came out better. Many sailors were indeed victims of this abusive system, but in two separate studies, historians Judith Fingard and Paul Gilje conclude that not all was abuse and abasement. Memoirs by seamen of the time also offer a mixed commentary. Jacob Nagle wrote about the difficulties he had to overcome when that he once fell into a crimp's clutches. On the other hand, Ned Myers said that some landlords were fair. A former shipmate of Myers, James Fenimore Cooper edited and published Myers's comments. "On the whole, their class of men are not as bad as they seem, though there are some precious rascals among them. The respectable sailor landlord is quite as good, in his way, as one could expect, all things considered."[18]

Crimping was by no means a uniquely American institution. It existed in sailor towns throughout the nineteenth-century English-speaking world and had been there for many decades. Crimps had brought men to the British army and navy at least since the early seventeenth century. By hook or crook, they mobilized a labor supply at wages far lower than would have been necessary in a free labor market. In traditional labor market situations, personal connections and traditional expectations often counted more than purely economic considerations. But the market economy underwent enormous changes in the early nineteenth century. "Modern" employers sought a docile, skilled labor force. Including the American Seamen's Friend Society discussed in an earlier chapter, reformists homed in on what they saw as the degraded existence of the common sailor, and of workers in industrial factories as well. Abolitionist movements challenged the continuation of chattel slavery. Some contended that unfree labor was ineffective and therefore philosophically indefensible, but many more opposed it on religious arguments that emerged during the Second Great Awakening. Ongoing opposition notwithstanding, crimping continued on some waterfronts even into the twentieth century.[19] But change was in the air, and ferocious resistance emerged from some quarters to oppose it. John Drake Sloat, the Naval Rendezvous, and the United States Navy itself, all had their parts in this broad picture.

Sloat submitted comments on the recruiting situation and the labor market to Commodore Charles G. Ridgely, who had succeeded Isaac Chauncey as commandant of the New York Navy Yard. Recruiting practice continued as it had for years. Before 1815, the rendezvous could recruit men easily because of the threat of impressment into Britain's Royal Navy. But by 1836, the United States Navy had come to experience difficulty in attracting able seamen. Merchant shipmasters no longer had to take inexperienced men into their crews, and merchant seaman could expect monthly pay of eighteen dollars. Other compensations raised that to the equivalent of twenty dollars. Sloat recommended that navy pay for an able seaman be raised from twelve to fifteen dollars per month, figuring that the job security would be worth the difference. He felt that the navy would get good men that way. In other words, raise navy pay so that it would be accepted freely by a sailor. One should note that five hundred dollars per year is estimated to be what a working-class family of four required to make ends meet, and that a petty officer such as a boatswain's mate made nineteen dollars per month.[20] Reformers hoped that a bill establishing a system of naval apprenticeships would attract a new type of recruit, rid the navy of the rampant alcoholism among its sailors, and also reduce the fraction of foreign-born men among them. That solution would eventually lead to a different set of problems. The bill was signed into law in March 1837, by which time Sloat was no longer in command of the New York rendezvous and so would have had no direct impact by this reform attempt.[21]

Just after assuming command of the Naval Rendezvous, Master Commandant John Drake Sloat joined a different reform group. This one came from within the naval officer corps itself and was intended as a vehicle for their own professional development. The Naval Lyceum of the United States was organized in 1833 by Master Commandant Matthew Calbraith Perry. The lyceum had its headquarters in a building at the New York Navy Yard, located in Brooklyn. It housed a collection of artifacts from around the world such as stuffed animals and birds, shells, minerals, and detailed ship models of the kind used in ship design and construction. Its initial library grew from about one thousand books to five thousand after twenty years had passed. Perry began publication of a lyceum journal entitled *The Naval Magazine*, but that project failed for lack of funds and ceased after its second year of publication. During its brief existence, *The Naval Magazine* provided a forum for a wide range of articles on subjects such as astronomy, the effects of malaria, travelogues from various parts of the world, and Commodore Charles Stewart's advocacy for establishing a naval station at Pensacola. The lyceum also maintained a collection of current newspapers and other periodicals but very tellingly prohibited the introduction of abolitionist literature in an attempt to preclude political arguments among members about the most crucial issue of the antebellum years.[22]

A comparison of the 1836 naval officers register with the list of Naval Lyceum members reveals that most of the captains and masters commandant in the navy did not belong to the lyceum. The lyceum roster included most of the lieutenants in the New York City area, and five of the six local masters commandant. Perhaps some officers became members because they feared it would be inexpedient not to join a forum with most of the officers with whom they might serve in the future. A few of the prominent names not on the 1836 lyceum roster are Commodores James Biddle and Jesse D. Elliott and Captains William B. Shubrick and Thomas ap Catesby Jones. Also absent from the list is Master Commandant Robert F. Stockton. However, Perry biographer John Schroeder finds elsewhere that Stockton did indeed belong to the lyceum, which this author would certainly expect from the one naval officer who seems most likely among all his contemporaries to challenge established norms of group thinking. Other nonmember officers may have chosen not to join the Naval Lyceum if they saw it as a sort of power clique centered on Perry and his circle of friends and associates.[23]

The lyceum also had honorary members from outside the navy. Some memberships were extended because of the person's office, such as President Andrew Jackson or Vice President Martin Van Buren. Others had membership because of their contributions to nautical science such as Nathaniel Bowditch, the author of the compendium reference, *The American Practical Navigator.* Celebrated author James Fenimore Cooper also held an honorary membership. Cooper had held a midshipman's warrant before the War of 1812 and served aboard the *Wasp.* He resigned because his intended bride did not want a marriage to an absentee husband, but he retained a deep interest in the sea, the navy, and in military affairs in general. He considered himself still to be a member of the naval officer fraternity and in particular maintained a close friendship with *Wasp* shipmate William B. Shubrick.[24] Cooper had much wealthier family roots than did Sloat, but they both came from the same slave-owning, upstate New York rural gentry. Cooper took a great interest and participated in the New York City celebrations of the capture of HMS *Macedonian.* He may have first met Sloat then. In any case, the record shows that they crossed paths often in the years after Cooper returned from Europe and Sloat was also in New York. They probably knew each other rather well beyond the lyceum.[25]

The Naval Lyceum of the United States was one part of a national phenomenon that began in the 1820s. Historian Steven Lubar finds that Matthew Calbraith Perry had belonged to a number of lyceum societies in both New York and Boston. The movement spread around the country, but lyceums were more commonly found in the Northeast and Midwest regions. As Perry biographer Samuel Eliot Morison notes, the lyceum movement found popular support by providing an avenue for adult education on a wide scale. In a later study dedicated solely to the lyceum movement, Angela Ray finds two diverging trends. In the first, lyceums held lectures on a wide range of topics for the edification of the general public. But many lyceums were founded with more specialized groups in mind, and this latter formed the basis for Perry's vision of the Naval Lyceum.[26] Even so, the Naval Lyceum did formally correspond with the board of the American Lyceum, a sort of national umbrella organization for lyceums during the 1830s.[27] John Drake Sloat's name does not appear among the authors during the short run of *The Naval Magazine.* One article deals with recruiting issues and echoes many of the concerns about sailor's pay that Sloat had expressed in official correspondence to Commodore Ridgely. The article's author remains unidentified beyond being a member of the Naval Lyceum, but his examples are all from Boston. Master Commandant Thomas Stevens commanded the Naval Rendezvous, Boston, but was not a member of the Naval Lyceum. Stevens's assistant, Lieutenant Ralph Voorhees, however, does appear on the published list of members and so he is most likely the source of that article. He did not create it, but Sloat did join the Naval Lyceum as a founding member. Most senior naval officers chose not to join it at all. The Naval Lyceum represented a serious effort to improve the United States Navy and the professionalism of its individual members, and so some degree of credit must attach to each one of them.

Routine shore duty continued until good fortune struck in early 1837. Two years had passed since four masters commandant gained promotion to captain in the spring of 1835, but as President Andrew Jackson prepared to leave office, eight new nominees received Senate confirmation. Sloat ranked second among the eight, all of whom received commissions with dates of rank of February 2, 1837. Shortly afterward, he was relieved of command of the Naval Rendezvous, having been promoted out of the job. He returned to the "waiting orders" status.[28] Perhaps in part helped by a letter signed by Sloat, Perry, and others that complained that masters commandant ranked with army majors but were paid less than army captains, a new pay scale for naval officers had been enacted in 1835. Congress raised the annual pay for a master commandant from $1,176 to $2,100 if serving ashore and $2,500 if in a sea billet. As a captain, Sloat received $2,500 per year while awaiting orders. That salary increased to $3,500 for captains serving in billets afloat or ashore. The title "Commander" replaced "Master Commandant" at that time, although commanders at that time still took precedence with army majors instead of with lieutenant colonels. Captains with less than five years in grade ranked with lieutenant colonels and then afterward with colonels, although no pay increase came with the longevity.[29] The current rank equivalencies were established during the Civil War.

Captain John Drake Sloat soon received orders to special duty. Along with Captains Lawrence Kearny and Matthew C. Perry, he began a survey of New York waters in June 1837 to make recommendations for improvements of navigational aids. New York area harbor traffic had continued to increase as the city grew and shipments of goods increased from the interior via the Erie Canal. The matter thus became an increasingly important concern. Captain Kearny was senior and therefore in overall charge. They interviewed shipmasters and harbor pilots, drew upon their own experiences, and extensively surveyed the local waters themselves from cutters and boats. Lieutenant Thomas Gedney, an officer with considerable experience in such surveys, was also assigned to this project, and the three captains credited him with its success in the final report that they submitted the following December. They recommended many changes, especially around Staten Island, Newark, and Raritan Bay by Perth Amboy. Sandy Hook, the usual landfall for ships arriving from sea, also required improved lights and beacons.[30]

Sloat had requested permission from Secretary Dickerson to travel to Washington to settle the money account for the Naval Rendezvous so his successor could take it over. The request was submitted in October 1837 during the navigational aid survey. The matter was an important one and doubtless would have been approved. But most likely Sloat did not go to Washington until after completion of the survey and preparation of all the reports, which would place the trip between mid-December and mid-January 1838. Secretary Dickerson undoubtedly had at least one personal meeting with Captain Sloat.

At that particular point in time, Dickerson was grappling with a major personnel problem. The United States Exploring Expedition was nearing readiness to sail with six ships on a voyage to explore and chart the vast ranges of the Pacific Ocean. Captain Thomas ap Catesby Jones had been designated to command the expedition but had resigned the position due to personal illness and, perhaps, personal frustration with Lieutenant Charles Wilkes, who was an expert in hydrography and surveying. Jones biographer Gene A. Smith shows that Dickerson then offered the command to Captains William Shubrick, Lawrence Kearny, and Matthew C. Perry, each of whom declined. Historian David F. Long stated that every captain in the navy refused to accept command of the Exploring Expedition.[31] Navy Department letter files contain no record of Sloat being offered the expedition command, but he ranked in seniority between Kearny and Perry and so should have been considered. Sloat could have had the opportunity to accept or decline the expedition command in a personal meeting with Dickerson. No correspondence would have been necessary and so no document would have been placed in the files. Recall that as a midshipman, Wilkes had been on the *Franklin* for a time with Sloat, and in his autobiography written in his waning years, Wilkes expressed extreme disdain for Sloat and the other officers of that ship. Neither Sloat nor Wilkes would likely have wanted to sail again with each other, particularly on a cruise that lasted several years.

Eventually, the Exploring Expedition sailed under the command of Lieutenant Wilkes alone. It was a technical success, but as an operation of the navy, the expedition was marred by problems of command and leadership on the part of Lieutenant Wilkes.[32] Those aspects are beyond the scope of this essay, but Secretary Dickerson's problems in finding an officer to command the Exploring Expedition offer intriguing insights into the officer corps of the antebellum United States Navy. The secretary of the navy had to negotiate with his subordinates. Every captain and commander in the navy forewent the opportunity for this command afloat in a time when those opportunities became increasingly hard to come by and also forewent a chance to hoist a pennant and, according to the custom of the day, use the much-prized title "Commodore" for the rest of his life. They cannot have all been simply a group of muddle-headed dullards, and future research might reveal logical reasons to avoid commanding the expedition. However, one might reasonably speculate that nobody wanted to put up with Lieutenant Wilkes, and it was impossible to replace him because he was the only officer available with the requisite hydrographic and surveying skills.

Sloat continued to "await orders" in New York with his family while residing at their Houston Street residence. Abby's father, James Gordon, died in February 1837. Her mother, Susan L'Hommedieu Gordon, and her much younger sister, Eliza Gordon, came from Norwich to live with the Sloats in New York. The Sloats continued to maintain contact with Norwich relatives and to manage real estate interests in the Connecticut city. In December 1839, eighteen-year-old Jeanette Eliza Sloat married James Bayard Whittemore, a Manhattan merchant, at St. Thomas Episcopal Church, located at that time just a few blocks from the Sloats' Houston Street home.[33] The couple continued to live with the Sloat family until the captain was posted to Maine.

Service as a member of courts-martial often punctuated the time that a senior officer waited for orders. On one such occasion, Sloat served on a court that acquitted Lieutenant A. C. Maury of neglect of duty aboard the sloop *Natchez* while deployed to the West Indies.[34] Later that year, Secretary of the Navy James K. Paulding authorized Captain Sloat, as the junior member of the court, to appoint the judge advocate for the trial. Sloat chose John McKeon, a Democratic politician and lawyer who had just lost reelection to the U.S. House of Representatives. This particular trial took place just before the Sloat-Whittemore wedding, a point of some interest because McKeon later became Jeanette's second husband.[35]

It is well at this point to interrupt the narrative and to attempt an assessment of Captain John Drake Sloat's position in society. To meaningfully place any person in a complex system of social stratification is a difficult task that seldom yields better than inexact results, and the first problem is to establish some parameters of analysis of the social structure itself. Several competing theories of social class exist in modern scholarship, and this essay draws in particular upon the general social theories of Max Weber and the writings of Edward Pessen about antebellum society in the United States. Where did Sloat and his family stand in terms of wealth, of prestige, and of power?

Let us first consider wealth. Without tax records and itemized lists of assets, assessment of wealth can be problematic. But we have seen that Sloat owned several parcels of real estate in Norwich and several others in New York City. The previously cited deed transfer records show the various Norwich properties valued at about four thousand dollars, and at the beginning of 1840, Sloat still owned Norwich real estate valued at four thousand dollars. His landholdings in New York were much more valuable. Recall that he had sold three holdings around Bleecker Street for around thirty thousand dollars. He bought the house and lot at 433

Houston Street for two thousand dollars in 1826 and would sell it for $8,500 in 1848. Except for a temporary, very sharp drop at the beginning of the Panic of 1837, Manhattan land values climbed steadily between 1820 and 1840. The values of real property owned by Sloat take no account of rental income from owned properties over the years. For reference, a brick house in the outer Manhattan wards in 1840 would command an annual rent of two hundred dollars.[36] The figures here, of course, account only for properties for which this author could find a record, and conceivably a deed transaction ended up being omitted from the land record indices. Sloat does seem to have had a head for real estate, perhaps first developed growing up in Goshen under the tutelage of his grandfather Joseph Drake. He was not the only naval officer to fare well in Manhattan real estate. Captain Uriah P. Levy had at least forty parcels there. Ira Dye's biography of Levy suggests that Levy started out with more money to invest that did Sloat, but there can be no doubt that each of them did well.[37] Another note of caution: records of real estate values say nothing about any other investments or interests, and in Sloat's case, the probate records offer little in the way of insight because a great deal remained in the unitemized estate.

So what does the foregoing mean? Some historians have suggested as a benchmark Walt Whitman's contemporaneous statement that a middling sort of individual needed about one thousand dollars a year for a middle-class sort of lifestyle. A navy captain's salary was more than twice that even if he awaited orders and had no duty assignment! Historian Pessen finds that only 1 percent of New Yorkers were worth more than fifty thousand dollars, but that group owned fully one half of the wealth in the entire city. The next 3 percent of the city's citizens held estates valued between twenty and fifty-five thousand dollars.[38] Captain John Drake Sloat appears to fit at the upper end of what Pessen marks as the upper middle class based on personal wealth alone.

Even if the recorded evidence for an antebellum person was complete in all respects, an individual's wealth still might not tell the whole story. Family connections mattered a great deal. Someone with a modest personal income on paper might have been a member of a well-to-do family and therefore have occupied a higher place in the social strata. Marriage connections mattered too. So it was with Sloat and the Gordons, and Jeanette Sloat's marriage to James Bayard Whittemore suggests a link to a very prominent New York network. The editor of the *New York Sun*, one Moses Beach, published directories of New York's richest people and sometimes attached biographical vignettes as well. Beach's wealth biographies have been thoroughly discredited as sources for collective biographical analyses, but the 1845 edition does list four different members of the Whittemore family as worth $460,000 between them. One of the four was Jeanette's widowed mother-in-law, Jane Tileston (Mrs. Samuel) Whittemore. The family owned factories in New York and New Jersey that produced cards of wool or cotton for textile mills, on machines that James's grandfather had invented and for which the heirs still owned the patents.[39] Jane Whittemore lived in a large house on grounds fronting on Grove, Christopher, and Bleecker streets. Other Whittemores lived in commodious dwellings close by. The extended Whittemore family's interests included not only textiles but also banking, insurance, and shipping. They founded two banks and one fire insurance company with offices in the Greenwich Village section of New York.[40] We have no records to tell us whether Jeanette and James Whittemore absolutely adored or totally detested each other, or if any of the parents objected to the couple's wedding. Scholars have analyzed marriage patterns from the Jacksonian era and found a high degree of social endogamy among Americans, just as it had been in the eighteenth century.[41] Although not nearly as wealthy as the Whittemores, the Sloats most likely were an acceptable match.

Power in the context here means, in general, the ability to get other people to do what one wants them to do. Sloat of course had the power that went with being a senior naval officer, but however considerable, that particular power was constrained to the naval establishment and mattered little in society at large. A great deal of unofficial power usually derives from a great deal of wealth, but to this author, that seems to refer more to the extremely wealthy such as John Jacob Astor or the scions of New York's Livingston family.[42] Assignments to senior jobs in the navy were the prerogative of the secretaries of the navy, who of course were important politicians themselves. Sloat appears not to have enjoyed any close political connections of the sort that could exert extra influence on a secretary of the navy's decisions. Captain Alexander Dallas, by way of contrast, was the son of a secretary of the treasury and the brother of a vice president of the United States. John Sloat was a Jacksonian Democrat, as he at least once reminded Jackson's secretary of the navy when asking for a posting.

He appears to have had acquaintances among New York City Democratic politicians such as John McKeon, even before that prominent politician became daughter Jeanette's second husband. As a New York state legislator from the city, McKeon had supported Jackson's stands on the Second Bank of the United States and in the South Carolina nullification crisis in the early 1830s. He held a seat in the U.S. House of Representatives from 1835 to 1837 but lost his reelection bid and returned to his private law practice, from whence Sloat had nominated him to serve as judge advocate on a court-martial as noted earlier. McKeon, of whom more will appear later, returned to Congress for another single term in 1841 and would become a major antagonist of Fernando Wood.[43] Acquaintance with this important New Yorker gives yet another indication of the circles in which Captain Sloat moved.

Prestige is perhaps even more subjective a concept than either wealth or power. Many naval officers were well connected, and the naval profession itself afforded social prestige to its officers far beyond what their salaries would otherwise command. An 1822 painting by John Searles of prominent New Yorkers at a fashionable theater identifies Master Commandant John B. Nicolson in the audience. Nicolson came from Virginia, and he was not the highest ranking naval officer assigned to duty in the city. But the artist put a senior officer in a painting meant to portray important New Yorkers rather than people who actually went to the theater on a particular evening. In their history of New York City, Edwin G. Burrows and Michael Wallace use that picture as the introduction to a chapter on the elite of New York entitled "The Medici of the Republic." Nicolson had also served with Sloat as one of the lieutenants on the *United States* in the battle with HMS *Macedonian* during the War of 1812. Sloat was a Freemason, and converted to the Episcopal Church which in New York at least, was the church of the influential and the well-to-do.[44] Besides his navy peers, his contacts included prominent officeholders like John McKeon and men of letters like James Fenimore Cooper.

If not wealthy by some standards, Captain John Drake Sloat was certainly very well off financially, was reasonably well connected politically, and a well-respected person. He could be considered almost the prototype of a Knickerbocker New Yorker of the antebellum upper middle class.

Sloat bought some land in New Brighton on Staten Island and set out to build a new residence there. The decision to move out of New

Figure 11.2. *Interior of the Park Theatre*, by John Searles, 1822. Master Commandant John B. Nicolson appears in uniform, seated third from the right in the second tier above the orchestra. (In Phelps-Stokes, *Iconography of Manhattan Island, Vol. 3.*)

York City is an interesting one. The city limits included only the island of Manhattan for most of the nineteenth century, and its population grew about 60 percent per decade from 1820 on. By 1840, New York City housed slightly more than three hundred thousand residents as it continued its northward growth up Manhattan toward Harlem. It had become an increasingly tumultuous place and an increasingly dangerous one as well. In 1835, a major fire destroyed much of lower Manhattan. Crowded living conditions in poor neighborhoods with bad sanitation caused outbreaks of cholera. Riots upset the public order, such as the one in 1837 when flour prices jumped from seven to twelve dollars per barrel as the economic Panic of 1837 set in.[45] The Sloat family rode things out in their comfortable neighborhood above Greenwich Village, but the threats to their comfortable existence were certainly palpable ones.

Figure 11.3. *View of Brighton, Staten Island, New York*, unknown artist, 1857. The Sloat residence was among those along the road from the church at left. The view is across the Kill Van Kull from Staten Island toward New Jersey. (From Wikimedia Commons.)

Only eleven thousand people lived on Staten Island in 1840. The famed regular ferry service began in the mid-1830s and made it feasible to live on Staten Island and work in Manhattan. An 1857 print of Richmond Terrace, where Sloat bought the lots for five thousand dollars, shows a pleasant suburban scene with large houses on spacious lots overlooking the Kill Van Kull beyond to Bayonne.[46] The absence of any direct evidence leaves us to speculate about why Sloat decided to move there, but the contrasts in 1840 between New Brighton and New York are starkly obvious. Sloat called it a "small cottage" in a letter to Secretary Paulding wondering if he would soon be called for service afloat or whether it would be safe for him to leave Manhattan and supervise the construction. No reply survives in the record, but within two weeks, Sloat was ordered to Philadelphia to sit on another court-martial.[47]

The trial in 1840 of Commodore Jesse Duncan Elliott excited a considerable degree of public attention. He had recently returned from a cruise in command of the Mediterranean Squadron and found himself facing a host of charges: He was alleged to have risked a sick midshipman's life by forcing him to be transferred from the *Constitution* to the *Shark*, both ships being anchored in Smyrna, Turkey (present-day Izmir). He menaced one of his lieutenants with a stick at the racetrack in Minorca. He received improper gifts of silver for which he only partially paid. He brought twenty-two livestock animals on board the *Constitution* and transported them west across the Atlantic, thereby rendering the frigate unready for action at sea. He exceeded the maximum permissible flogging punishments meted out to sailors in the squadron. And last, he failed to suppress mutinous actions of the *Constitution* crew after returning to Hampton Roads from the Mediterranean.[48]

Commodore Jacob Jones presided over the court-martial that tried Commodore Elliot, and as a member of the court, Sloat became personally embroiled in the broader Elliott controversy.[49] The court convicted Elliott and sentenced him to suspension for a period of four years. As if financial abuses and misappropriation by a senior officer were not enough, long-standing issues increased the public visibility of this trial. As a master commandant, Elliot had been second in command of the United States forces at the Battle of Lake Erie on September 10, 1813. Master Commandant Oliver Hazard Perry had overall command. The British put Perry's flagship out of action, and Perry then transferred by boat to Elliott's ship. Perry took command there and sent Elliott in a boat to rally nearby American gunboats and to bring them closer to the battle. The American ships won the battle and gained control of Lake Erie. Initially, Oliver Hazard Perry praised Elliott's actions, and those of all sailors in his squadron. Soon after, Perry accused Elliott of hanging back in the first phases of the battle. The controversy continued after the war. Perry died of yellow fever in the West Indies in 1820 and had been on the verge of pressing formal charges against Elliott.[50]

Jesse Elliott had also played a pivotal role as James Barron's second in the 1820 duel that killed Stephen Decatur. The duelers seemed on the

Figure 11.4. *Matthew Calbraith Perry*, by William Sidney Mount, 1835. (Courtesy of the U.S. Naval Academy Museum.)

verge of reconciling their differences when Elliott ordered them back to their places so the duel could proceed. When both Decatur and Barron had fired and lay wounded, Elliott fled the scene. Many believed that Decatur's blood stained Elliott's hands as well as those of Barron.[51] An influential and sizeable faction of naval officers thus had little use for Commodore Jesse Duncan Elliott.

Figure 11.5. "James Fenimore Cooper," engraving by E. Scriven after painting by John Wesley Jarvis, 1822. (Courtesy of Navy Art Collection, Naval History and Heritage Command.)

Still another problematic factor stemmed from James Fenimore Cooper. The novelist had published a history of the United States Navy in 1839, in which the account of the Battle of Lake Erie failed to attack and criticize Elliott as the Perry faction wanted. Matthew Calbraith Perry led this faction, having become the guardian of his late brother's reputation.[52] Captain Sloat, of course, was a former shipmate and long-standing friend of the younger Perry and owed his naval career to Decatur. Yet, Sloat still managed to remain on good terms with Cooper. The novelist was outraged by the severe sentence awarded to Elliott. A few months after the trial, he met with Sloat in New York, who talked with him "a great deal" and partially mollified the novelist with what Cooper called a most satisfactory explanation of the charges and findings of the court, even though he still felt the sentence to be excessively harsh.[53]

Sloat had barely got back to New York when he was ordered to turn around and go back to Philadelphia and sit on the Board of Examiners of Midshipmen scheduled to convene at the Naval Asylum on July 6, 1840. This board met periodically to examine midshipmen on all the subjects they had to master in order to receive a lieutenant's commission. Passing this examination did not automatically bring that commission because there were already many more lieutenants awaiting orders than there were billets for them to fill. But as an officer with some proven qualifications, a "passed midshipman" could serve in a number of places, not least as sailing master aboard a ship in commission as seen in previous chapters.

The 1840 Board of Examiners consisted of Commodore James Biddle, as president, and Captains David Conner, Thomas H. Stevens, John D. Sloat, and Francis H. Gregory, as members. Professors David McClure and Thomas Perry examined the midshipmen in mathematics. The five officers conducted examinations in seamanship and in navigation. Twenty-two midshipmen were examined, including John L. Worden, the future commanding officer of the *Monitor* during the famous Civil War ironclad battle. All but one midshipman passed all three of his examinations, and that one failed both mathematics and navigation.[54] Sloat would serve on the Board of Examiners again, and each time the process became more extensive than it had been earlier.

While in Philadelphia, Captain Sloat began to press Secretary James K. Paulding to give him a permanent assignment. He wrote the same sort of letters that he and others had done in earlier years as lieutenants and masters commandant, the sort of letters that detracted from Paulding's enjoyment of his cabinet office. In July 1840, he wrote twice to complain that captains junior to him had received preference for assignments that he should have filled. He asked specifically for one of three posts: command of the steam vessel then under construction in Philadelphia, the frigate *Brandywine* where Captain William Bolton was reportedly ill and needed a relief, or command of the Portsmouth Navy Yard where Commodore William Crane's tour of duty was about to end.[55] Two months later, Paulding offered Sloat a choice. He could become either the commanding officer of the frigate *Potomac*, or he could become the commandant of the Portsmouth Navy Yard. Not wishing to command a frigate that was the flagship of a commodore who outranked him, John Drake Sloat chose to return to Portsmouth.[56]

CHAPTER TWELVE

Portsmouth Commandant

On an autumn New England day in 1840, Captain John D. Sloat relieved Captain William M. Crane as commandant of the Portsmouth Navy Yard. Sloat had left New York on October 23 and completed the change of command in Kittery just four days later. At the same time, Commander Thomas Wyman took over from John C. Long as second in command and Purser Thomas Breese relieved Francis MacCauley. Both Long and MacCauley had been transferred to sea duty. Wyman had been in the navy for thirty years and Breese for twenty-five. A week after taking command, Sloat reported to Secretary of the Navy James K. Paulding that things at the navy yard were well in hand and requested leave to return to New York so he could move his family up to Maine before the winter got bad enough to prevent travel. The Sloats took up residence in the commandant's quarters by the first of December.[1]

Sloat's arrival at the navy yard happened to coincide with a rejuvenation of shipbuilding in the Portsmouth area. The industry had suffered reverses from the 1808 Embargo Act and then the War of 1812. The navy yard had never closed, but naval shipbuilding had been in the doldrums for years.[2] The geographical limitations of Kittery and Portsmouth as a fleet base, discussed earlier, of course still posed their problems, but a core of artisans skilled in shipbuilding trades still existed some twenty years later. Construction of a frigate had begun during Commodore Crane's tenure in command.

The new *Congress* represented the pinnacle of sail frigate development in the United States. The New York and Philadelphia Navy Yards each then had a steam frigate under construction. Hybrid in design, those steam frigates still had full sets of masts and sails as well as steam propulsion systems. Sail frigates were also then under construction in other navy yards, but those ships conformed to a design approved in 1820. The design of the *Congress* had been worked out in 1838 and incorporated some British advances that led to speedier ships.[3] Construction continued and the *Congress* was launched on August 16, 1841, two years after laying the keel. Work had been suspended from September 1839 until the following April, but there was no pause during the subsequent winter. Sloat reported to the secretary that the launch took place in "fine style" and the ship was then anchored in the Piscataqua River. A local newspaper took an almost exuberant tone in reporting the launch. It said that the *Congress* was one of the most beautiful ships in the navy. The ship slid down the ways without any difficulty, and the ceremony was perfectly arranged and executed. The whole affair must have reflected positively on the United States Navy, on Captain Sloat, on naval constructor Samuel Pook, and on every sailor and civilian employee at the Portsmouth Navy Yard. The paper went on to remind its readers of the economic contribution to the community that the *Congress* represented. Over each of 522 actual working days, an average of eighty-six tradesmen were employed

Figure 12.1. *View of the United States Navy Yard at Portsmouth, N.H.*, unknown artist, 1853. (From Wikimedia Commons.)

as follows: forty-two carpenters, eight blacksmiths, ten joiners, six sawyers, five caulkers, and fifteen laborers, with an average daily wage of $1.43.[4]

The newspaper article did not mention work done by contractors in addition to that by tradesmen on the navy yard payroll, but that work also did take place. A significant example is the contract apparently awarded to Messrs. Garrick and Sons to install the lead sheathing on the frigate's hull. Sloat had reviewed the proposals and Garrick's was the lowest bid. He forwarded the documents to the navy agent in Portsmouth, one John Leighton, saying that Garrick should get the job as long as his was a responsible firm.[5] As the commandant of the Portsmouth yard, Captain Sloat held responsibility for all navy activity in his area. Besides the subordinate officers, sailors, and marines assigned to the yard, two important civilian officials played major roles in contracting and supply. These were Navy Agent Leighton and Naval Storekeeper Charles Cutter. They performed functions that in the modern navy fall to commissioned officers of the Supply Corps, the successors to the pursers. As civilians, these two persons were not subject to naval discipline, but they did receive their appointments from the secretary of the navy. No record of difficulty between Sloat and them appears in the archives, but another yard commandant recommended that the agents and storekeepers should be made warrant officers like the pursers, which would bring them under better control.[6]

A complex and costly undertaking such as building a large warship required a large amount of skilled labor and consumed a large amount of material resources. Coordination of those efforts was essential to keeping the project moving forward, and that responsibility lay ultimately with the navy yard commandant. The record contains documents about many matters that may seem trivial, but when taken together, they show what a commandant did from day to day. Not only did he exercise command over the people at Portsmouth, but Captain Sloat also had to deal with commercial suppliers and also other navy yards so that the *Congress* would be ready as soon as possible.

A few months before the *Congress* first slid into the water, Sloat requested that Commodore James Renshaw, commandant of the New York Navy Yard, send a cylindrical tube for a frigate's air port, like the ones Sloat said that he had seen on the steam frigate *Missouri*. If one was not available from the yard's stores, Sloat asked Renshaw then to advise where he got them and how much they cost. A request to the yard in Brooklyn to support the Portsmouth yard was a fairly unusual one, but Sloat directed many requests to Commodore John W. Downes at the Charlestown Navy Yard in Boston. It appears that some manufacturing capabilities existed there that did not exist at the Portsmouth yard, and also that Boston's commercial ship chandlers could supply items not available in smaller ports like Portsmouth or Kittery. Rigging, standing gear, anchors, and sails for the *Congress* all came via the Boston yard. Sloat asked Downes about the availability of a signal lantern design that he had seen in Boston and thought was particularly good.[7] These letters suggest that Captain Sloat played an active role and showed initiative as yard commandant.

Sometimes problems arose. Sloat had received permission to construct masting shears at the Portsmouth Navy Yard. These are special cranes used to emplace masts, or to "step" them in nautical parlance, on ships moored alongside a wharf. The shears were used to remove masts as well, and the new capability would save the navy money because it would no longer have to hire one of the Portsmouth are shipbuilders for that function. The Charlestown yard sent a nine-hundred-foot length of nine-inch-diameter rope, intended to be used as a fall in the masting shears. The rope arrived in two pieces. Sloat requested a replacement because splices in lines that large were unreliable. Sloat assured Downes that he was sure that his colleague did not know that the rope had been sent out as two pieces. It seems to have worked out well, and the new shears were first used to step the masts on the *Congress.*[8]

Several more months were needed to fit out the newly launched frigate and place her in commission. Now that she was in the water, the ship needed a small crew for security and emergencies. Just before the launch, Sloat wrote to Downes and advised him that the Board of Naval Commissioners was about to task him with sending twenty men to Portsmouth for the *Congress.* Portsmouth had no receiving ship and so no navy seamen were available there for assignment. Sloat requested that good men be sent because it was impossible to prevent desertion at the Portsmouth yard. The men chosen should have some pay due to them. Downes sent nineteen sailors whose enlistments were soon to expire. Sloat next wrote to Secretary of the Navy George E. Badger and expressed his need for twenty-five men to guarantee the safety of the *Congress.* He asked the secretary for authority to enlist men specifically for ordinary service in the *Congress.* Sloat believed that he could get local men who would not desert. Presumably, no able seamen would have been needed. This seems an innovative proposal for the specific problem, but apparently Badger did not approve Sloat's request to enlist sailors under such conditional terms. By November 1841, Sloat received an inquiry from Abel P. Upshur, the Tyler administration's new secretary of the navy, about a complaint filed by a seaman. Sloat replied that the men sent to Portsmouth were from the *Ohio*, whose commission had finished. The *Ohio* then became the navy receiving ship in Boston harbor. These particular sailors still had remaining time on their enlistments, and their misconduct in Boston led Downes to send them to Portsmouth. For a while, they performed well enough, but after their conduct ashore in Kittery and Portsmouth became bad, Sloat confined them to the yard in order to protect the local citizenry. He felt that the men really should receive punishment, but requested instead simply to discharge them from the navy. Upshur's reply does not survive in the archives, but in the following February, Sloat wrote that he had been authorized to discharge a number of men. He had decided not to discharge one of them, Ordinary Seaman John Davis, because he believed the man "capable of any act of villainy." Sloat feared that if he discharged the sailor, then Davis would remain around Portsmouth and cause trouble. Davis's enlistment would not expire for another twenty-eight months. Sloat wanted to return him, presumably under guard, to the receiving ship *Columbus* from which he could be sent to sea.[9] In the case of Davis, Sloat essentially proposed to keep him in the navy as a form of imprisonment.

Readers familiar with the present-day practices of the United States armed forces may discern a familiar pattern in Sloat's request to discharge the other miscreant sailors from the *Ohio* instead of going to considerable administrative trouble and then inflicting on them the maximum punishment that he could. By discharging Ordinary Seaman Davis, Captain Sloat could have easily washed his hands of anything that the man might have done afterward. Were Davis a private citizen, then his misconduct would fall exclusively under the jurisdiction of civil authorities. But Sloat did not discharge Davis as authorized, acting instead upon his considered judgment of the particular situation.

Navy yard commandants had a great deal of individual leeway in many matters of managing their commands. President Van Buren had issued in April 1840 an order regulating the work hours in navy yards, but the individual commandants appear to have had the power to set the wage scales for civilian tradesmen at their yards, instead of a government-wide civil servant pay scale or the navy pay scale for everyone including captains and ordinary seamen. Captain Matthew Calbraith Perry took command of the New York Navy Yard in 1841. That yard was then building the steam frigate *Missouri*. He soon wrote to ask several questions about how Sloat ran things at Portsmouth. Sloat sent Perry a copy of his current Portsmouth wage rates, a document that no longer remains attached to the letter itself. Sloat added that between October 1 and March 20 of each year, all workmen except for master tradesmen received a 10 percent wage reduction. No explanation was given for the wage cut, but a later document suggests shorter daylight reduced the length of the winter work day. Also, if on any morning the temperature at sunrise was five degrees above zero (Fahrenheit) or lower, then a signal flag would be hoisted and no outside work would be allowed. Any workers who showed up anyway would be sent home.[10] Captain Sloat felt that no productive work would likely get done outside if it were too cold, and therefore did not to want to pay anything at all on such days.

Responding to an inquiry by Secretary Upshur, Sloat compared wages and working hours at the navy yard with private shipyards around the Portsmouth and Kittery area. A tradesman's stint began at dawn and ended at sundown, unless the sun rose before seven o'clock or set before six o'clock. Those times then marked the workday. Ten hours marked the maximum workday in any event. Sloat included a summary of daily wage rates that appears in table 12.1 and added that he had no trouble attracting "the very best men" (underlined in the original) at those rates of pay. The weather restrictions and seasonal deduction that Sloat had described a year earlier to Perry at the New York yard remained in effect because only nine hours of daylight were ever available during the winter.[11]

The yard commandants also had responsibility for procuring the guns themselves for a ship's main battery. The Napoleonic-era cannons used on ships during the War of 1812 fired solid cannonballs at an enemy ship, shotgun-like grapeshot to sweep across decks with exposed personnel, or chain shot meant to dismast the enemy ship. These had come to be supplemented, and would eventually be replaced, by Paixhans guns. Named for the French artillery officer who first developed them,

Table 12.1. Daily Wage Rates at the Portsmouth Navy Yard, November 1842

Trade	Minimum (Dollars)	Maximum (Dollars)
Carpenters	1.25	1.50
Sawyers	1.28	1.42
Caulkers	1.75	2.00
Plumbers	2.00	2.00
Joiners	1.34	1.50
Smiths	1.00	1.625
Spar Makers	1.34	1.50
Boat Builders	1.20	1.50
Sail Makers	1.50	1.75
Coopers	1.25	1.50
Riggers	1.25	1.50
Laborers	0.75	1.00

Source: Letter, Captain John D. Sloat to Secretary of the Navy Abel P. Upshur, Portsmouth Navy Yard, November 2, 1842, Microform M125, roll 295, Letters to the Secretary of the Navy from Captains, Record Group 45, National Archives.

Paixhans guns fired explosive shells and constituted a major development in large guns, both ashore and afloat. The navy's Board of Commissioners decided to put some of them in the *Congress.* Downes informed Sloat that he had just been directed to send to Portsmouth "eight Paixhans guns instead of four previously ordered" for the *Congress.* Downes also asked Sloat if he already had any Paixhans guns and, if so, requested to know from where he had got them. Sloat immediately answered that no Paixhans guns had been received at the Portsmouth yard, and that none had been ordered except for the eight that the Boston yard was to supply. By 1846, many American warships had been fitted with these shell guns, but it appears that some new ships went into commission without that part of their battery because the foundries simply had not yet cast the guns.[12] No centralized procurement system existed, and so the navy commissioners left yard commandants to their own devices to procure a range of equipment astonishing to a modern day naval person.

Besides Paixhans guns, the Board of Commissioners also ordered Downes to provide sixteen thousand pounds of cannon powder and two thousand pounds of priming powder for the *Congress.* Downes warned the commissioners that when he complied with that order, almost no powder would be left in the Boston yard's magazines. Up in Portsmouth, a different problem existed because the yard there lacked sufficient storage for so much powder. Sloat wrote to Captain Justin Dimick of the U.S. Army, the commanding officer at Fort Constitution, which guarded the entrance to Portsmouth harbor. He explained the situation and asked Dimick to allow the navy temporarily to store the powder at Fort McClary, located on Kittery Point across the Piscataqua from Fort Constitution. This expedient had been used in earlier years.[13] Apparently, Dimick complied with the request without involving higher authorities in either the War or Navy Departments.

Construction and fitting out of the *Congress* had nearly completed when the bulk of the frigate's crew arrived on May 6, 1842, from the Boston receiving ship. This draft of about 160 seaman left the ship still short of eighty crewmen, most of those vacancies being various petty officers and therefore even more important to fill. Charts and navigational instruments had not yet arrived from the depot in Washington. On June 1, Captain John B. Nicolson relieved Downes as yard commandant in Boston. Nicolson had served as one of the lieutenants in the *United States* during the *Macedonian* action, and the tenor of his correspondence suggests the connection between old shipmates made for a more cooperative working relationship than Sloat had with Downes. Nicolson informed Sloat that he could not meet his request for seamen because there were only two or three able seamen at the Boston yard available for transfer, but if ordinary seamen could be substituted, then there were enough good ones to send. Nicolson asked for a list of personnel requirements for the *Congress* crew and the number that the frigate already had. By July 1 the ship lacked only the small arms for the contingent of marines. Captain Sloat performed his final inspection on July 11 and reported to Secretary Upshur that the frigate *Congress* was ready for sea in all respects.[14]

Shipbuilding continued at a steady pace throughout Sloat's tenure in command at Portsmouth. Immediately after the August 1841 launch of the *Congress*, yard workers laid the keel of a new sloop-of-war, to be christened *Saratoga.* Two weeks after the *Congress* made her way down the Piscataqua to join the fleet, the *Saratoga* was ready for launch. With *Saratoga* riding anchors in the river, the yard then laid the keel of the

Portsmouth, a sloop-of-war that would go to California with Sloat in 1846. The *Saratoga* was ready for sea in March 1843, and the *Portsmouth* was launched on October 23, 1843, a few days before Sloat relinquished command of the Portsmouth Navy Yard.[15] Construction and fitting out of the two sloops brought out again many of the same kinds of issues and action items as had the *Congress*.

Although no centralized procurement system as such existed at the time, the officers in the naval establishment do seem to have been very careful in documenting their doings, especially where government-owned items were involved. Downes's correspondence with Sloat might even be taken as testy, but there is certainly an emphasis on order and form. Downes did not do anything that he was not ordered to do. Sloat was also a stickler about things for which he might be called to account. Soon after taking command at Portsmouth, Sloat responded to an inquiry by Downes about books meant for the library of the newly built *Preble*. No library books were at Portsmouth, except for two sets of *Encyclopedia Britannica*. One had been for the yard and the other for the *Preble*. But the ship's commanding officer declined to take the encyclopedia, saying that the ship lacked the storage space. Sloat offered to send that set to Boston by rail immediately. Two weeks later, the encyclopedia left on a train for Boston. Seven weeks after that, Sloat complained to Downes that he had received no acknowledgment that the encyclopedia had arrived, and would Downes be good enough to send a receipt.[16]

A similar incident arose around a two-volume edition of *Webster's Dictionary*. A Treasury Department auditor disallowed a fourteen-dollar expense on Navy Agent Leighton's accounts, saying that the Portsmouth Navy Yard Library did not have authority to include the dictionary in its holdings. Leighton informed Sloat, who wrote to inform the treasury auditor that the dictionary was meant for the commandant's office and was public property. Two months passed with no reply. Sloat wrote to complain about the failure to respond, to reiterate his earlier position, and to add that other navy yards had been allowed to procure dictionaries.[17] The trail vanishes at this point.

During a period when Sloat was visiting in Boston but apparently did not make a personal call on Downes, the officer left in charge at Portsmouth submitted a requisition for composition thimbles for the *Congress*. Thimbles are rings, usually of metal at that time, that are set flush into blocks and pulleys, and eye-spliced lines (loops at the end of wire or fiber rope that are woven back into the rope so that an open loop exists at the end of the line) to protect them from wear due to chafing. "Composition" refers to any one of a variety of treatments applied to metal objects, such as thimbles, to prevent fouling and corrosion. The term can also refer to copper-based alloys.[18] Stating that "composition" had not been approved for use in ships of the United States Navy, Downes rejected the requisition. Sloat replied that he had meant to write Downes when he returned to Portsmouth and was informed of the problem with the requisition, but the matter had slipped his mind. Sloat went on to request that Downes send some iron clew pieces for the *Congress*'s sails if he could, and "*without writing to the Commissioners.*"[19]

As much documentation survives in the Navy Department archives about a set of *Encyclopedia Britannica* and a *Webster's Dictionary* as does about procuring the main battery of the fleet's newest frigate. To claim that yard commandants spent as much time worrying about the books as they did the guns would greatly overstate the case. But nobody can deny that accounting for those books is a far cry from handling the *United States* thirty years earlier in a sea battle against HMS *Macedonian*. So it went in the United States Navy after 1815. Hundreds of documents written in similar veins remain in the National Archives' Navy Department files. They show a great concern among the officer corps for administrative precision, particularly in matters of personal accountability. John Drake Sloat seems to have been quite a stickler in these matters even since his days as a merchant shipmaster. The blurbs in the shipping news about his voyages include narrative details of information that do not typify the usual reports to the newspapers. But Sloat was not at all unique among United States Navy captains in his manner of dealing with the Navy Department bureaucracy of which they were a part. John Downes, Thomas ap Catesby Jones, Jesse Duncan Elliott, Matthew Calbraith Perry, William Branson Shubrick, to name but a few, all did the same.

One surviving letter to a would-be contractor shows that Sloat could take a high-handed tone and certainly would not be bullied. One Benjamin Bartlett of Kittery complained that he had not heard about a bid that he submitted to the Portsmouth Navy Yard. Sloat replied in no uncertain terms and said that the advertisement did not obligate him to accept any bid if he did not like the price or had no confidence in the bidder. No regulation existed that required him to respond to unsuccessful bidders, and he had no practice of doing so. Sloat went on to add that Bartlett would have won the contract, but several bids were considerably lower and so he felt no need to reply.[20]

At times, the yard commandant could find himself dragged into local issues and rivalries. One Nathaniel March was in 1841 the agent of the Portsmouth Bridge that spanned the Piscataqua River. He wrote to Sloat and asked if the officers of the yard felt that the bridge was an important avenue to the yard and whether it improved the security and protection of U.S. government property. Sloat answered back immediately that it was a boon to the yard. The *Portsmouth Journal* published the correspondence and gave the story. The citizens of Dover, just up the river from Portsmouth, had launched a campaign to get the bridge torn down. They argued in their own newspaper, the *Dover Enquirer*, that the ferry crossing at Dover offered a safer and more convenient way across the Piscataqua. The Portsmouth editors added that the ferry fare was six cents, whereas the bridge toll was only three cents. They went on to discuss the trade rivalry between Portsmouth and Dover and linked it to a rivalry in New Hampshire between the Dover Railroad and the Eastern Railroad. A third newspaper joined the fray in favor of maintaining the bridge because of Portsmouth's important commerce with York County, Maine, and also the access that it gave Portsmouth firefighters to the navy yard in Kittery. The first bridge across the Piscataqua from Portsmouth had been built in 1822, before which time yard workers used the navy boat pool to get to the yard from the New Hampshire side of the river.[21] Sloat's earlier tour of duty at Portsmouth while a lieutenant had been before the construction of the Piscataqua bridge.

After the *Saratoga* was ready for sea, Captain Sloat requested leave to visit New York. On the very date of Sloat's request, Secretary Upshur preferred charges in one of the most famous courts-martial in the history of the United States and ordered Sloat to serve as a member of the tribunal. Commodore Downes had been assigned as the president of the court. The trial lasted throughout February and March and took place onboard the receiving ship in New York's East River. The five charges against Commander Alexander Slidell Mackenzie included several specifications each of murder, oppression, illegal punishment, conduct unbecoming an officer, and cruelty. These were serious enough charges for anyone, but especially so when leveled against the commanding officer of a United States Navy warship. Mackenzie had command of the *Somers*, a brig that had been on a training cruise across the Atlantic. The *Somers* affair has generated a great deal of historical literature, and the controversies surrounding Commander Mackenzie continue to the present day, even though the basic sequence of events is well established. What follows is a brief encapsulation of events from a variety of secondary sources.[22]

The *Somers* carried a larger than normal crew because many of them were naval apprentice boys. Recall from a previous chapter that Sloat had addressed recruitment problems years before, when he commanded the New York Naval Rendezvous. He was not alone in his concerns. The Navy Department had worries about the fleet's continued reliance on foreign-born enlistees, and growing concerns about the high rate of alcoholism among fleet sailors reflected Americans' increasing preoccupations with like matters among the general public. The navy established a program of apprenticeships, intended to attract young men born in the United States to service as navy sailors. Captain Matthew C. Perry took a great interest in this reform project. As commandant of the New York Navy Yard, he successfully used his influence to have the *Somers* assigned as a school ship for apprentices. Commander Mackenzie was Perry's brother-in-law. Lieutenant Guert Gansevoort, who as a passed midshipman had served under Sloat's command as sailing master of the *St. Louis*, became first lieutenant of the *Somers*.

Trouble on the *Somers* revolved around another young gentleman. Midshipman Philip Spencer came to the ship with a record of undisciplined conduct in two ships and had been expelled from several universities before that. Mackenzie attempted to have him transferred somewhere else. Captain Perry refused to support his brother-in-law's entreaties, probably because the young man came from no ordinary elite family. John C. Spencer then served as secretary of war in President Tyler's cabinet, and he hoped that the navy would straighten out his wayward son. Secretary Spencer inspired political fear in Perry.[23]

The *Somers* sailed from New York and passed Sandy Hook on September 13, 1842, carrying dispatches for a ship on antislavery patrol off the African coast. The ship visited Madeira, the Canary Islands, and the Cape Verde Islands before arriving at Cape Mesurado and Monrovia. From there, she headed west for home. Spencer did not mix with the other midshipmen and frequently fraternized with a number of the sailors. The insubordinate midshipman had notions of becoming a pirate on the high seas. The purser's steward reported to Lieutenant Gansevoort that Spencer had attempted to enlist him in a plot to kill the officers and turn the brig into a pirate cruiser. Mackenzie initially scoffed when his first lieutenant relayed the report, but he did put Spencer under surveillance. A search of Spencer's personal gear turned up a list of crew members, written in Greek letters, indicating which ones Spencer thought reliable or not so. Mackenzie became increasingly worried as the *Somers* raced through Atlantic waters and had Spencer placed in chains on deck. The miscreant midshipman had been seen on several occasions to speak furtively with Boatswain's Mate Samuel Cromwell and Seaman Elisha Small, both experienced sailors with years of service. Mackenzie had them arrested and also chained on deck, even though Cromwell's name did not appear on the Greek list at all. Although regulations limited to squadron commanders the authority to convene a general court-martial that could order a death sentence, Mackenzie had Lieutenant Gansevoort, sailing master Passed Midshipman Matthew C. Perry, Jr., and the other officers convene a drumhead court. Spencer, Cromwell, and Small were not present at the proceedings and so could not themselves testify, cross-examine witnesses, or call defense witnesses. The "court" recommended death sentences. Mackenzie agreed. On December 1, 1842, with the *Somers* two days' sailing distance from St. Thomas, all hands were summoned to quarters to witness punishment. Midshipman Philip Spencer, Boatswain's Mate Samuel Cromwell, and Seaman Elisha Small were then hanged from the port and starboard yardarms.

The *Somers* took on water in St. Thomas and hurried back to New York. Mackenzie quickly sent Acting Midshipman Oliver Hazard Perry II, yet another of his own nephews among the *Somers*'s officers, to Washington with his report to the secretary of the navy. Mackenzie contended that he had no choice but to execute the three men, or else they would have led a mutiny and taken over the ship. Nobody stood up for Cromwell or Small, but the incensed secretary of war John C. Spencer set out to take revenge against Mackenzie. Upshur placated Spencer by convening a court of inquiry, an investigatory body that could recommend a trial by court-martial. The court of inquiry found Mackenzie blameless because of exigent circumstances and recommended no further action. Mackenzie recognized that he could be vulnerable to a civilian murder trial and so requested that Upshur convene a general court-martial anyway.

The two-month trial captivated the public's attention and received daily newspaper coverage. James Fenimore Cooper published a verbatim trial transcript and added his own commentary, none of it favorable to Mackenzie. The transcript shows that Captain Sloat asked six questions of different witnesses. Each one was to clarify something that a witness had said. Three other officers had, at different points, launched into extended lines of questioning of the witnesses. This was in addition to the questions posed by the judge advocate chosen as prosecutor and those posed by Commander Mackenzie, who conducted most of his own defense.

Two charges against Mackenzie were dismissed during the trial, leaving three more for the court to decide. The court found the charges were "not proven" and so voted to acquit Mackenzie. The vote had not been a unanimous one. Three of the twelve members had voted for conviction on the murder charge, and four voted to convict Mackenzie of oppression. Their identities remain unknown. The court unanimously voted that that the charge of illegal punishment remained "not proved." Commander Mackenzie thus stood "acquitted." But significantly, only three members of the court voted to acquit Mackenzie with honor, and so the defendant did not receive the vote of approbation from his brother naval officers for which he had hoped.

Commander Mackenzie thus went free and kept his commission. But he did not escape public disgrace and found his reputation as a leader tarnished. Captain William B. Shubrick wrote to his friend James Fenimore Cooper while the trial still progressed that he found the *Somers* affair "extraordinary and perplexing." Commanding officers needed a great deal of leeway, but Mackenzie's crew must have been very different than most if he did not think he could control the crew after the ringleaders of the mutiny plot had been identified. Shubrick went on to the heart of one side of the matter. Whatever the outcome, Mackenzie stood to be ruined and Secretary of War Spencer would make sure of that. Cooper replied that the "miserable business" of the *Somers* would result in acquittal of Mackenzie even though he deserved conviction on every charge and specification. Cooper fulminated that four (unnamed) officers on the court would vote to acquit Mackenzie even if he outright confessed and went on to argue that Mackenzie's acquittal stemmed from commercial interests because shipowners and insurers benefited from the power to send a sailor to the gallows without a fair trial. Most lamentable of all was the diminution of public confidence in the entire navy that resulted from the *Somers* affair.[24] Three navy captains had avoided serving on the Mackenzie court. John H. Aulick and Bladen Dulany wriggled out for unrecorded reasons, but Robert F. Stockton told Secretary Upshur point-blank that he could not serve because he had already read enough to believe that Mackenzie was a murderer and should be hanged forthwith.[25] Sloat's votes remain secret, but one should note here that no sooner had Sloat been notified in 1844 that he was to command the Pacific Squadron did he then request that Mackenzie also be ordered to duty there. The only justification in the letter is that Mackenzie's command of the Spanish language would be very useful. That would have been true enough, but it seems a flimsy justification. Sloat must have intended to help Mackenzie, who languished ashore under a cloud, waiting for orders.[26] No reply to Sloat's request survives in the record, but Mackenzie did not get orders to the Pacific.

Mackenzie suffered in the public view despite his legal escape. Whatever leeway he deserved as a navy commanding officer at sea, Mackenzie's disgrace could be taken as the result of a quick and ill-considered decision that could not be undone once the three men were dead.

While in New York for the Mackenzie court-martial, Sloat began to press claims for his next assignment. He applied to command the Africa Squadron that was about to deploy but shortly learned that Matthew C. Perry would be sailing in that command. Perhaps rankling Sloat a little more, the *New York Tribune* announced Perry's appointment and declared in print that the editors could not imagine a "more discreet or fitting officer for such a delicate post." Sloat assured Secretary Upshur that he understood there were doubtless good reasons for the choice, but those posts before had gone to the senior applicant. Recall that Sloat was one number senior to Perry on the navy list. Sloat continued to pressure Upshur. In a possibly accusatory tone, he asked if there were any negative reports about him on file, because he had always received approbation and had never been censured for his performance of duty. He was therefore deeply concerned about the "apparent degradation." Upshur reassured Sloat, who then renewed his request for any service afloat, confident that justice would be done him. Interestingly, Perry also complained that people in Washington had been conspiring to deprive him of the Africa Squadron command. This likely referred to Secretary of War Spencer and perhaps some navy persons who were not part of the Perry circle of influence.

The matter of the Africa Squadron command was probably not the first time that Sloat felt nettled by preferential consideration of Perry, who still remained his friend. Soon after Perry took command of the navy yard in Brooklyn, he hoisted the broad pennant of a commodore and began to use that title. As commandant, Perry had authority over all navy ships in New York. That included a number of ships in commission as well as the ones laid up in ordinary. Portsmouth, however, was only a shipyard and not a fleet base. Even so, Sloat wrote to Upshur to ask for authority to hoist a commodore's pennant because yard commandants junior to him had received that privilege. Sloat declared that nobody cared about outward displays less than he did, and he would never do it without proper authorization.[27] Declarations aside, John Drake Sloat obviously cared a great deal about outward displays of rank and circumstance.

Captain Sloat returned to Portsmouth in time for the commissioning of the *Saratoga* and her departure for active service. In July he asked again for a squadron command, having heard that Commodore Morris would be returning from the Mediterranean. He hoped that officers who had declined commands would not get preference for that assignment. Sloat did not get the job. David Henshaw received a recess appointment as secretary of the navy when Upshur succeeded Daniel Webster as secretary of state. Sloat lost no time in complaining to Henshaw that someone junior to him got a command for which he had also applied. Sloat asked why he had been placed in such a "mortifying" position in front of the navy and the nation and insisted that "the rank and just rights of an honorable officer are dearer to him than life." Henshaw's reply implied that Sloat was to remain at Portsmouth, even though his three-year tour of duty was almost done. Sloat wanted to know for certain, because he would need to move his household effects to New York before the packet ships stopped running for the winter. Less than two weeks later, Henshaw notified Sloat that he would be relieved at Portsmouth by Captain George W. Storer, effective November 1, 1843. The sloop *Portsmouth* was launched into the river on October 23, and

Figure 12.2. John and Abby Sloat. Daguerreotype likely made in 1843 or 1844. (Permission of Braun Research Library Collection, National Autry Center, Los Angeles; 92.140.1)

Sloat left for Staten Island after Storer took command as scheduled. At home in New Brighton, he would again wait for orders.

In early 1844, Captain Sloat and other senior naval officers received another object lesson on what they could expect if what they thought were their well-intentioned initiatives and decisive actions somehow went awry. Commodore Thomas ap Catesby Jones arrived in Washington after being recalled from command of the Pacific Squadron. A fuller treatment of the affair will appear in a subsequent chapter, but suffice it here to say that in late 1842, Jones reacted to rumors in Peru that the United States and Mexico had gone to war. After consulting with experienced officers under his command, Jones decided to invade the Mexican province of

California. The commodore chose the capital pueblo (town) of Monterey as his point of attack. The Pacific Squadron sailed north from Callao. The *United States* and *Cyane* proceeded to Monterey, while the *Dale* diverted to Panama carrying dispatches for forwarding to Washington. The *United States* and *Cyane* arrived off the remote and rather sleepy pueblo on October 19, 1842. Jones demanded that Governor Juan Bautista Alvarado surrender the province to him. The astonished Alvarado complied, although he protested that he knew nothing of any war. Soon after, a stack of recent Mexican newspapers was found and those indicated that no state of war existed. Jones then restored Mexican rule, hoisted the Mexican flag, and fired a salute. The squadron sailed south in January 1843.

The Mexican government protested furiously in Washington. Jones was recalled and Captain Alexander J. Dallas was ordered out to relieve him. President John Tyler and Secretary of State Daniel Webster were incensed because Jones's actions had upset Mexico to the point where negotiations for the purchase of some or all of California became impossible. Secretary of the Navy Abel Upshur stood up for Jones. By the time Jones actually arrived in Washington, Upshur had become secretary of state and then died in an explosion during a gun demonstration aboard the screw-powered, steam sloop-of-war *Princeton*, but Secretary of the Navy John Mason informed Jones that President Tyler approved of his zealous service to his country. No official punishment would be meted out to Jones. But as Jones biographer Gene A. Smith notes, officers in the navy held a different perception about what constituted "punishment." Jones may not have been tried by a court-martial, but relieving him of his command was indeed punishment. Furthermore, no public statement of support for Jones had appeared from the White House or the Navy Department. In Jones's own eyes and those of his peers, he had indeed been publicly humiliated, and to an antebellum naval officer, that was indeed punishment.[28]

That year saw another navy captain harshly punished for actions swift and decisive, if not rash and ill considered. Captain Philip Voorhees commanded the newly built frigate *Congress*, then serving in the Brazil Squadron under Commodore Daniel Turner. Voorhees had been a midshipman in the *United States* during the capture of the *Macedonian*. Commodore Turner sent the *Congress* to the Rio de la Plata to represent United States interests. Struggles had continued for years against the rule of Buenos Aires governor Juan Manuel de Rosas, a dictator strongman who held sway over most of the United Provinces of Argentina. Another facet of the complicated situation was the ongoing issue of Uruguay's status, which had been part of Spain's Viceroyalty of the Rio de la Plata and then, for some years, the Cisplatina province of Brazil. Uruguay emerged as a buffer state between the former Spanish and Portuguese colonies. A Blanco (white) party within Uruguay was allied with Rosas and the conservative side of Argentine politics, and the opposing Colorado (red) party had ties to both liberal Argentine opponents of Rosas and to Brazilian interests as well. Rosas had declared a blockade of Montevideo in support of his Blanco ally Manuel Oribe, the deposed and exiled president of Uruguay. Argentine troops also laid siege to Montevideo. The commercial interests of the United States, Britain, and France had been severely affected not only in the Rio de la Plata but also up the Paraná River into Brazil. On September 29, 1844, Oribe's schooner *Sancala* sailed from Buenos Aires, under the Uruguayan flag, with dispatches for the Argentine blockade commander. The *Sancala* commanding officer decided to pursue a fishing boat then sailing near the *Congress.* The fishermen tried to escape to a United States–flagged merchant ship anchored nearby, and shots were fired in the American ship's direction. Captain Voorhees then seized the *Sancala*, and the *Congress* continued on to force the surrender of three small blockading warships that flew the Argentine flag. Voorhees soon released the Argentine ships but held the *Sancala*, claiming the latter was a pirate. Upon hearing of the fracas, Commodore Turner left Rio de Janeiro and arrived the following month. Turner smoothed matters over with Rosas, who at the time hoped for American support to counter Brazilian, British, and French support of his opponents in neighboring Uruguay and at home in Argentina. Secretary of State John C. Calhoun expressed official regrets to Rosas, and Secretary of the Navy John Mason ordered Voorhees home to face trial by court-martial. The court convicted Voorhees and sentenced him to dismissal from the service. Newly inaugurated President James K. Polk reduced the sentence to suspension for three years, and even that term was later shortened.[29] Both of those sentences were severe. Sloat had left for the Pacific just as the *Sancala* affair began to unfold, but the word had plenty of time to catch up. Captain Voorhees had reacted as he thought best to a fast-unfolding situation that he had watched develop firsthand. How well Voorhees understood the complex politics and diplomacy of the Rio de la Plata region is impossible to say with any certainty, but he had not been on station in South America for very long. His ill-considered but swift and decisive actions brought embarrassment to his country and to its navy, as well as official punishment and personal humiliation to himself. But one can also easily see how some might see Voorhees as having been second-guessed by a squadron commander and by cabinet officials after doing what seemed right to him at the moment.

In April 1844, Sloat once again served on the Board of Examiners of Midshipmen at the Naval Asylum in Philadelphia. His friend Commodore James Biddle once again presided over the board. The examination procedures had changed since Sloat had last served on the board. Besides the seamanship and navigation examinations by the officers of the board and a mathematics examination by Professor William Chauvenet, midshipmen now faced examinations in foreign languages from Professor Julius Mease. Forty-four midshipmen presented themselves for examination. Four of those withdrew from the process soon after the examinations began so they could try again the following year. Another four failed and were recommended for dismissal from the navy, including one whose reexamination had been denied by the board but who had won another chance by appealing to the brand-new secretary of the navy. That candidate withdrew from the mathematics reexamination after just a few minutes and left the room. Perhaps resenting being overruled, Biddle's letter on behalf of the board seemed to exult triumphantly in reporting that particular debacle and also added that the midshipman, one William Webb, never went to French class and was at the bottom of the class in Spanish.[30]

Sloat also visited Washington that spring and paid a call upon John Y. Mason, who had then just succeeded David Henshaw as secretary of the navy. No repercussions appear to have resulted to anyone over the Midshipman Webb debacle. Sloat learned in Washington that Commodore Alexander J. Dallas had become seriously ill and might need to be replaced in command of the Pacific Squadron. Sloat asked Mason for the job if Dallas required a relief. Dallas died in Callao on June 3, and Sloat received orders in August to command United States naval forces in the Pacific Ocean.[31] After placing his affairs in order, John Drake Sloat headed once again to Peru, taking with him to serve as commodore's clerk his twenty-eight-year-old son Lewis. They sailed on September 21, 1844, from Norfolk as passengers aboard the brig *Oregon*, bound for Chagres on the Caribbean coast of the Panamanian isthmus.[32] The squadron command that represented the very pinnacle in the pre–Civil War United States Navy was finally to be his.

CHAPTER THIRTEEN

Mexican California

Commodore John Drake Sloat continued on to Peru from Panama in the schooner *Shark* and arrived in Callao by early January 1845. James K. Polk won the presidential election that took place a few weeks after Sloat left to assume command of the Pacific Squadron. Polk would take more aggressive action than had his predecessor John Tyler to acquire what has become the southwestern United States.[1] The United States had finally annexed Texas just before Tyler left office, but Mexico had also felt pressure on its department of California for many years.

Sloat had last been to Mexico in 1830, when the *St. Louis* spent several weeks in Mazatlán and San Blas on the Pacific coast. In 1824, he took the *Grampus* to the Gulf of Mexico ports of Campeche, Veracruz, and Tampico, and he had also called as a merchant skipper at least once at Campeche before Mexico's independence wars began. He had never been to California. At this point, it is useful to interrupt the narrative biographical sequence for a consideration of cultural, economic, and political aspects of the California society that Sloat would encounter upon his arrival in Monterey. This chapter will first draw upon the substantial body of scholarship that shapes today's understanding of Californios and their world, and then consider the lenses and notions through which Sloat and his colleagues created their own ideas of what and whom they were dealing with.

Spanish claims in western North America went back for several centuries, but the area north of about thirty-two degrees North latitude had been only occasionally traversed by explorers serving the kings of Spain. The treaty that ended the Seven Years' War in 1763 extended Spanish sovereignty over French North American territory lying west of the Mississippi River. Written in a far-off European capital by diplomats looking at maps on walls, this treaty had little meaning to peoples such as the Miwoks, the Yokuts, or the Chumash who actually lived on present-day California lands and believed them to be their own. Their lives would soon change as forces began to converge upon them.

The viceroyalty of New Spain, the pre-independence antecedent of Mexico, included today's Mexican republic, the Central American republics except for Panama, and western North America with a very vaguely defined boundary on its north. From his seat in México, the capital city and vital center of the kingdom of New Spain, the Spanish viceroy served as a surrogate for the king in Madrid. In the latter part of the eighteenth century, King Charles III (r. 1759–1789) began a series of changes to strengthen government in Spain and in its empire that are collectively known as the Bourbon reforms. One concern was protecting Mexican silver mines from capture by the British. In an eerily prophetic report, a Spanish military commission reported to the viceroy in 1774 that the only realistic British threat at that time was through Veracruz, but given the well-known nature of the North American colonists, one might materialize on the northern frontier perhaps fifty years later. Another concern was the small but growing presence in upper California, or Alta California, of Russian traders and voyagers based on the Siberian Pacific coast and in Alaska. The possibility that the Protestant English would discover a northwest passage to the North American coast also played in the minds of Spanish colonial policy makers.[2]

Spain decided to strengthen its presence in far-off Alta California by establishing a series of missions to convert the indigenous peoples to Christianity and to encourage soldiers and settlers to accompany the missionaries and found pueblos, or townships, the smallest of the three types of political settlements established under Spanish law. In principle, regular clergy established missions and converted the nonbelievers. Outside funding supported these efforts. Upon completion of the conversion process and once Spanish society had been replicated among an assimilated populace, the mission would be closed. Secular priests under the supervision of a bishop would take over the tending of the Christians, whose tithes would support the new parishes and the diocese that supervised them. This, at least, was the plan.

Things did not quite work out that way in Alta California. Church authorities first tapped the Jesuit order to proselytize in Baja California and Sonora, but the Bourbon reforms included a royal decree to expel the Jesuits from the entire empire in 1767. So creating the Alta California mission system fell to the priests of the Franciscan order instead, and Friar Junípero Serra founded the first of the famous chain of missions in San Diego in 1769. Others were founded in following years in the coastal region as far north as present-day Sonoma. Each mission became the nucleus of a small settlement, and each had its own territory, although sometimes defined in rather vague terms that led to disputes with military or civil towns. The missions raised crops and tended herds of cattle, sheep, and horses. They also produced crafts to support themselves and for trade outside the mission. Some historians contend that these economic aspects of the missions even became more important than religious concerns to the missionary friars around the turn of the nineteenth century, and one must always keep in mind that, at bottom, this system of production depended on the labor of indigenous Californians who often suffered greatly from disease, abuse, and alcoholism as the priests attempted to transform them culturally into good subjects of the Spanish king.[3]

Spanish soldiers, many from a Catalonian regiment, accompanied the first evangelical friars and added a military muscle component to the northward extension of the mission chain. Towns then grew up around each of the four *presidios*, or military forts, that were subsequently established and garrisoned to protect the missions from attack by native Californians who had not been converted, and to protect Alta California itself from foreign aggression. These were located at San Diego, Santa Barbara, Monterey, and San Francisco. Some presidio soldiers married convert women and mustered out of the army. Spanish regulations authorized those men to receive land grants and cash bonuses. Missionary friars and mission Indians frequently found themselves at odds with residents of presidio towns and the soldiers themselves. Additionally, civil towns were established at Los Angeles, Branciforte (near present-day Santa Cruz), and San José. In 1792, these towns held very small populations. Santa Barbara was the largest with 230 inhabitants, while Monterey had 202. Los Angeles had only 131, and tiny San José tipped in with seventy-eight.

Reflecting his concern about the British presence on the coast after the Nootka Sound controversy of 1790, Viceroy the Marquis of Branciforte ordered the establishment of the town that also bore his name. Optimistically, Branciforte had been established as a *villa*, a polity ranking between a *ciudad* (city) and the ubiquitous pueblo. By the end of 1797, however, the population of Branciforte had only increased to a mere forty souls, and like the civil settlers in other towns, a number of these were convicts sent from cities like Guadalajara in central New Spain. This network of settlements did not extend east into the San Joaquín or Sacramento valleys, although the Catalonian soldiers did mount an exploratory foray into them, and punitive expeditions against indigenous peoples would follow in later years. Trappers and traders also passed through the valleys, bringing with them diseases that wrought demographic destruction among the native populations.[4]

Because of their sparse populations, the area that is today the southwest United States did not become intendancies under the major administrative reforms in Mexico of 1786. They were labeled as "interior provinces," and a commandant general exercised military and political control, in perhaps a nominal sense given the distance between his seat in Chihuahua and Monterey or Los Angeles. The boundaries of the interior provinces would change a few times in the years preceding Mexican independence, but Alta California remained a far-off province isolated by distance from higher levels of government. Town governments included a *cabildo*, or town council, whose members elected replacements when individual terms expired. They also chose men to serve as *alcalde ordinario*, and one as *alcalde mayor*, who combined judicial functions as chief magistrate with executive power as town mayor. Incumbents were not to succeed themselves in office, but in practice cabildo seats became the de facto property of individual families. Other important posts were handed back and forth between them in a system of mutual alliances and reciprocity. Practices such as these were the norm throughout the Spanish empire.[5] Perhaps the small Mexican settler population in Alta California made them particularly evident there. Personal relationships in an extended network of social and familial ties characterized Californio society.[6]

Social power centered on the family and the extended clan. Patriarchal hierarchy characterized ranchero families. The patriarch held authority not only over his blood relatives but also the servants, tenant settlers,

Figure 13.1. *A California Wedding Party in 1845*, by Emmanuel Wyttenbach. (In Davis, *Seventy-Five Years in California*. Courtesy of the California State Library.)

ranch laborers, and also soldiers if he held a commission as a militia officer. With patriarchy also came obligations to each of these groups of people, in a complex web that one historian has characterized as seigneurial in nature. Family honor was crucial, and that honor depended on many things, including in particular the protection of its women's chastity and purity. Catholic Church rules from the Councils of Trent, as well as tradition itself, demanded that a father take his daughter's marriage wishes into account, but a royal decree in the late eighteenth century asserted patriarchal rights in marriage matters. Arranged marriages were common in Alta California as elsewhere in the Spanish world, and these often played a crucial role in maintaining a family's wealth from one generation to the next.

Spanish inheritance laws derived from the ancient Visigoths and did not allow for primogeniture. Each son and each daughter was entitled to an equal share of the estate. The laws did allow one or two heirs to receive a somewhat larger portion, but not to the point that would maintain an estate virtually intact. Laws did not, however, restrict the dowry that could be given to a bride by her father. That dowry remained her prior property, and dowries became a means around the partible inheritance requirements. One daughter often received a very large part of the estate as her dowry, usually when she married a man being brought into the family business. The groom may have been a distant relative from some poorer branch of the family, but in the case of early nineteenth-century Alta California, he was frequently an American. The groom assumed a role in the business and freed up the bride's brothers for more prestigious careers in government service, the army, or the church.[7] The strong presence of the Franciscan missions in Alta California meant that opportunities in the secular clergy did not exist on as large a scale as they did in central Mexico. Although those priests figure greatly in works dealing with other places in Spanish America, the literature on pre-1846 Alta California hardly mentions diocesan clergymen.

Another aspect of family honor hinged on ancestry. European ancestry equated to high status. Many people in the Spanish colonial empire had ancestral roots in three continents: Africa, the Americas, and Europe. By the late eighteenth century, a formal *sistema de castas* had been codified in law to define people's places in the racial hierarchy of society. In the Mexican version, eighteen categories of *calidad* (quality) delineated various mixtures of ancestry. At the top was the *español*, the (white) Spaniard. Its intended rigidity notwithstanding, the system was actually quite porous, and considerable fluidity existed in the social construction of an individual's racial identity.[8] One must remember the desirability of a "white" husband in Californios' minds when considering the marriages of Anglo-Americans into Californio families during the early nineteenth century that some modern historians seem to consider a form of cultural treason. The liberal Mexican Constitution of 1824 formally abolished the *sistema de castas*, but the ideas behind it lingered on.

The armed struggle for Mexican independence erupted on September 16, 1810, when Father Miguel Hidalgo y Costilla uttered the *Grito de Dolores* and called for the overthrow of Spanish colonial rule. The independence wars ravaged Mexico for the next decade, but distance and isolation spared Californios from the sufferings of their countrymen to the south. In November 1818, two privateer ships in the service of the independent government in Buenos Aires arrived off Monterey. The ships were commanded by one Hipólito Bouchard. Governor Pablo Vicente de Solá found himself forced to retreat to present-day Salinas. Bouchard's crews sacked Monterey and then sailed south, attacking several mission towns before departing the area altogether.[9]

Alta California resumed its peaceful existence when the independence wars ended. Liberal military rebels marched on Madrid and forced King Ferdinand VII of Spain to repromulgate the Constitution of 1812, a document that promised considerable political liberalization throughout Spain's empire as well as on the Iberian Peninsula. Royalist conservatives in Mexico reacted to news from Madrid by striking a deal with insurgents that ended the long independence war. Agustín Iturbide turned against his king, led the Army of the Three Guarantees into Mexico City, and began to establish a conservative regime aimed at maintaining the essence of the colonial order under a Mexican banner. First, a constitutional monarchy would be established. Second, white men born in the Americas would be the equals in all respects of those born in Europe. Third, the Catholic Church would remain the only church in the country and the clergy would retain all existing rights and privileges. Perhaps unsurprisingly, the search for a European prince quickly proved fruitless, and Iturbide had himself crowned Emperor Agustín I of Mexico. In Alta California, the news that a Mexican sovereign had replaced the Spanish one caused hardly a ripple. Politically chaotic from its beginning, the Iturbide regime soon drove the nation toward bankruptcy. Another former royalist officer, Antonio López de Santa Anna, led an uprising against the new emperor who abdicated in early 1823.[10]

A new Constitution of 1824 established a federal republic, modeled very much on the United States with nineteen individual states sharing power with the national government in Mexico City. Alta California remained a territory because of its small population of citizens. California-born Luis Argüello had succeeded Solá as governor, and he remained in office during the imperial period and the first years of the new republic. The missions retained their power, however, and military rule was the actual reality on California ground.

The government in Mexico City remained concerned about its northern half not being populated with acculturated citizens. The Colonization Law of 1824 meant to effect a quick solution. Mexicans could not be persuaded to move north on their own accord, and so Mexico looked for western foreigners to immigrate and create the society they wanted. An immigrant of good character could purchase land at about one-tenth of its price in the United States. He could buy 640 acres for himself, 320 for his wife, 160 for each of his children, and eighty for each slave that accompanied him. The colonizers were to convert to Roman Catholicism and to become naturalized citizens of Mexico. Large numbers of Americans quickly moved into Texas from the southern United States.[11] California became open to foreign settlement under these terms but never saw the numbers that Texas did in the 1820s. But the law did open a door that had formerly been closed.

Significantly for California, Mexico established free international trade upon independence. Spanish imperial law had mercantilist restrictions on foreign traders, although these had been relaxed for the Americas during the Napoleonic wars. After 1821, traders could enter California ports freely. A brisk trade in otter and seal skins quickly emerged. The ranchos and missions sold cattle hides, sheepskins, and tallow to ships ranging the coasts. Shipping agents took up residence in the various towns, as did some seamen who "swallowed the anchor" in favor of life ashore. As discussed earlier, a number of these men married the daughters of Californio families. Abel Stearns in Los Angeles and John B. R. Cooper in Monterey are two such examples. Each of them converted to Catholicism and became Mexican citizens. Cooper's half-brother, Thomas O. Larkin, also came to Monterey, but the latter married an American widow and neither converted nor naturalized.[12]

After Argüello, a number of governors would rule California, some of them for very short periods of time. A major issue from the period preceding 1836 is the secularization of the missions. Liberal-minded Mexicans held that the missions were backward, feudalist institutions that were by their nature oppressive and therefore not as productive as they should be. Some Californios felt otherwise, contending that the friars and the mission communities represented the only viable way, in the existing society, to keep the Indians subdued and working on the land. Local governors attempted intermittently to secularize the California missions, which were by the early 1830s in a general state of decline. In 1833, the national legislature in Mexico City took the matter into its own hands and passed a secularization act. The friars' authority was transferred to secular priests, and the mission lands became available for settlement. A very few Indians did become freeholders in the aftermath, but those were the exception. Mission Indians had lost many of their own cultural ways and, through secularization, lost some of their new ways as well. A flurry of land grants ensued over the next several years, and some went to men who joined the ranks of the rancheros. But the bulk of the mission lands ended up in the hands of the Californio ranchero families who were already established landowners.[13]

The year 1836 would turn out a fateful one. President Santa Anna and his supporters had decided that years of turmoil had proven that the liberal, federalist 1824 Constitution could not work in Mexico. Santa Anna eventually abrogated the 1824 Constitution and replaced it with the Constitution of 1836, known as the Siete Leyes (Seven Laws). The new government of the Siete Leyes very much resembled the centralized, colonial regime of the late eighteenth century. In particular, the individual states were abolished and replaced by departments with governors

Figure 13.2. Mission San Juan Bautista. Following secularization of this mission, José Castro received one of its ranches as a grant and then resided by this central plaza. (Photo by author.)

picked in Mexico City. Efforts to recentralize power caused revolts in some places, including in Texas. Santa Anna took personal command of the army and marched north to put down the rebellions. He was initially successful when he got to Texas but then suffered defeat at the hands of the Texas rebels who had declared independence from Mexico and would lose no time starting a campaign for annexation by the United States.[14]

In the new department of California, the governor who was sent to formally establish the Siete Leyes government was overthrown after just three months. The same thing happened to his interim successor after another three months when a force of Californios led by José Castro

Figure 13.3. Juan Bautista Alvarado. (Courtesy of the California State Library.)

Figure 13.4. *José Castro*. (Courtesy of the California State Library.)

and supported by a group of American frontiersmen led by one Isaac Graham captured Monterey. A committee led by Juan Bautista Alvarado, Mariano Guadalupe Vallejo, and Castro issued a declaration that California had seceded from Mexico and would remain so until the liberal Constitution of 1824 was reestablished. The twenty-seven-year-old Alvarado then became civil governor of California, and Vallejo, the young governor's twenty-nine-year-old uncle, became military commandant.[15] The independence declaration went nowhere, and the government in Mexico City confirmed Alvarado as governor, even though he had opposed the constitution that underpinned his office. Serving from 1836 to 1842, he became the only Mexican period governor in California to serve a full term in office. The department of California continued very much on its own way throughout the years of political turmoil that followed. The Pastry War of 1839, the rotations of Antonio de Santa Anna, Nicolás Bravo, and others in and out of the Mexican presidency, and other political events in central Mexico had no practical effect in faraway Monterey or Los Angeles. Californios had begun to develop a separate identity.

The nature and extent of the Californio identity has been a subject of debate. Many Californios later recalled a general sense of abandonment by Mexico City when remembering the years before 1846. A triumphalist and ethnocentric school of thought folded that idea into its justification for the United States invasion of California, simplistically holding that Californios happily welcomed the new American regime. Indeed, more than a few rancheros did exactly that, Mariano Guadalupe Vallejo most prominent among them. Another position sees those Californios as gringo collaborators and traitors to Mexico, an understandable position but a simplistic one that projects a consensus about Mexican identity that would not exist until liberals and conservatives emerged from the crucible of the War of Reform (1857–1859) and the French intervention (1861–1867). A more complex and nuanced understanding is needed here. Historian Louise Pubols reminds us that residents of California felt loyalty to Spain, to Mexico, and to California at different times and in different ways.[16] To be Californio or Mexican might not be mutually exclusive for any person, even when the two ideas seem diametrically opposed. It might simply depend on that person's situation and surroundings at any particular time.

Foreign immigration into California increased steadily after 1830. For the first several years, they arrived by sea, either as passengers or crewmen who jumped ship. A few trappers had come by land, but by about 1840 settlers began to arrive in increasing numbers via transcontinental trails. Many came via the Oregon Trail and then south along the Sacramento River valley. Some used the shorter route across the deserts of present-day Nevada and Utah.

After abandoning his wife, his children, and his debts in Switzerland, Johann Augustus Sutter ended up settling by the confluence of the Sacramento and American rivers. There he established Sutter's Fort, from which sprang today's state capital city. This area in the central valley had not been settled by Californios, and Alvarado granted Sutter naturalized Mexican citizenship. The fort became a mecca for overland immigrants, and Sutter upset Californio leaders such as José Castro by granting large numbers of permanent entry visas. Most of these settlers came from the United States, and they numbered in the hundreds instead of in the dozens as had been the case in earlier years. Furthermore, these new overland travelers included many families instead of just single men. The families frequently preferred to settle in areas that had few if any Californios.[17] Those numbers were significant, given the population and demography of California in the 1840s.

Not only did immigrants from the United States establish a growing presence in California, but their government in Washington also cast covetous eyes on the Pacific coast. President Andrew Jackson attempted without success to purchase the area south of the Oregon border including down past San Francisco Bay. John Tyler later attempted to divide the Oregon territory at the Columbia River if Great Britain would bring pressure on Mexico to sell to the United States, but the confidential overtures leaked into the Mexican press where they caused a public furor. Secretary of State Daniel Webster favored acquiring California, but his opposition to annexation of Texas led Tyler to replace him.[18] United States interest in California was certainly no secret, even before the Jones debacle at Monterey.

As the end of his term neared in 1842, Juan Alvarado expressed his concerns to Mexico City about the future of California. He worried about the inability to stem the flow of foreign immigrants and pointed out that the Californios would be unable to mount an effective military defense against an invasion. Alvarado feared that what had happened in Texas could happen in California. Santa Anna sent Brigadier General Manuel Micheltorena to Monterey to serve as both civil governor and military commander. Accompanying him were some three hundred troops, many of whom were convicted felons who had been impressed from prisons in central Mexico.[19]

Micheltorena had reached Los Angeles with his troops but had not proceeded farther north when Commodore Thomas ap Catesby Jones arrived in Monterey on October 19, 1842, as briefly mentioned in the preceding chapter. Mistakenly believing that war had broken out between Mexico and the United States, Jones demanded the surrender of California. Bringing local officials together for an emergency meeting, Alvarado argued that even though Micheltorena had yet to arrive at the capital, the latter was then the governor. Alvarado claimed that he lacked authority to act. The group forced Alvarado to remain in authority, and on the next day the Americans entered the town. Led by Captain James Armstrong, commanding officer of the frigate *United States*, 150 sailors and marines occupied the presidio and paraded in the town. The Mexican tricolor was lowered and the United States flag hoisted in its place. After still another day, Commodore Jones came ashore. Monterey merchant Thomas O. Larkin told Jones that he was unaware of any state of war, and that recent newspapers said nothing about one. A search of government records yielded recent newspapers from Mexico City that convinced Jones of his error. He issued apologies, restored the Mexican flag to its proper place, and formally saluted it with twenty-one guns. Jones sailed south to Los Angeles and made additional apologies directly to Micheltorena. A ball was held that both Micheltorena and Jones attended, and then the United States squadron sailed away in January 1843.[20] Later that year, Lieutenant John C. Frémont of the U.S. Army Corps of Topographical Engineers entered Mexican territory on the second of his surveying expeditions into what would become the American West. By February 1844, Frémont's party had arrived at Sutter's Fort. He later proceeded south through the San Joaquín Valley and then turned east. Frémont's 1886 memoir reports that he had extensive contact with Sutter but makes no mention of any other Mexican government official.[21] As will be seen in the following chapter, Frémont's third expedition into California would make a bigger splash. Lieutenant Zebulon Pike's 1807 entry into present-day Colorado caused diplomatic trouble between the United States and Spain. The United States government expected commercial, diplomatic, or political benefits from expeditions such as Frémont's.[22] But in 1843–1844, President Santa Anna in Mexico City and Governor Micheltorena in Monterey faced problems that overshadowed Frémont's relatively uneventful exploration.

Micheltorena proceeded to Monterey with his troops. They had not been paid and there was no money to pay them. Not surprisingly given the number of criminals in their ranks, the soldiers quickly gained a reputation for pillage and rape among the Californio populace, and Micheltorena proved unable to control them. Juan Alvarado and José

Castro gathered support and rose up against Micheltorena in November 1844. Alvarado wrote to his kinsman Vallejo and asked for support. Vallejo did not join directly but disbanded his own command that he had been paying out of his own money. Vallejo recommended that Micheltorena ship his troops out of California in order to restore the peace. (One cannot help but speculate how later events might have turned out had the American sailors and marines faced a properly disciplined and trained regiment of dragoons.) Alvarado and Castro moved south with their force, followed by Micheltorena and his supporters, who included Sutter. In February 1845, the two sides faced each other in the Cahuenga Pass near Los Angeles along the present-day Hollywood Freeway. After an exchange of artillery fire that resulted in no casualties, Micheltorena capitulated and returned south to central Mexico. Pío Pico of Los Angeles assumed the civil governorship, but José Castro of Monterey once again became military commandant of the department. To Pico's chagrin, the customs house and its treasury remained in Monterey, and Pico placed Alvarado in charge of it.[23]

Commodore John Drake Sloat received reports about the overthrow of Governor Micheltorena and understood that the Alvarado and Pico uprising was not an independence movement against the Mexican government.[24] Recall from earlier chapters that he had considerable experience in the Spanish-speaking world as a merchant skipper before the War of 1812, while serving as a lieutenant on the *Franklin* and later the *Congress*, campaigning against pirates off Puerto Rico, as well as during his three-year cruise in the Pacific in command of the *St. Louis.* Recall also that Sloat requested that Commander Alexander Slidell Mackenzie be assigned to the Pacific Squadron, using the latter's fluency in Spanish as justification, and that nothing came of that request. Sloat may have acquired some command of Spanish along the way, but nothing in the documentary record suggests that he had any substantial fluency. When Sloat got to the Pacific Squadron, he inherited Commodore Dallas's aide, one Midshipman William P. Toler, who had also served Commodore Jones in the same capacity. Born in Caracas to the United States consul and his Venezuelan wife, Toler was completely fluent in Spanish. It was Toler who discovered the papers that convinced Jones of his mistake in Monterey, and after leaving the navy, he married Maria Antonia Peralta, whose father had a large land grant in what is now Oakland.[25]

No papers survive from which to glean how John Drake Sloat actually perceived the peoples of the Hispanic world. But he was raised in New York and descended from Dutch Protestants. It would have been truly exceptional had he not shared the general disdain for Catholics and Hispanic persons that most white American Protestants expressed. An officer on a Pacific Squadron ship, Lieutenant Joseph W. Revere, left a forthright expression of such views in his memoir of service in California. Those cultural and racial prejudices have deep roots, going back to the days of the Reformation, the sixteenth-century conflicts between England and Spain, and the anti-Spanish Black Legend.[26] On the other hand, Sloat's daughter Jeanette would convert and marry a prominent Irish Catholic politician after losing her first husband. But that had not yet happened in 1846. Whatever prejudices and notions Sloat may have harbored in his mind, he did have specific orders to do his utmost to establish good relations with the Californios if war broke out and he occupied Monterey and San Francisco Bay.

CHAPTER FOURTEEN

Squadron Command

The Navy brig *Oregon* arrived in Chagres on the Caribbean side of the Panamanian isthmus on October 18, 1844, after a twenty-seven-day voyage and discharged its two passengers. Commodore John Drake Sloat and his secretary and son, Lewis W. Sloat, then crossed to the Pacific side, probably by boat up the Chagres River and then by mule train down to Panama City. The two then found themselves stuck in Panama long enough that Commodore Sloat felt the need to inform Secretary of the Navy John Young Mason that they had yet to join the Pacific Squadron because they still awaited transportation. On November 21, the schooner *Shark* finally arrived in Panama and carried the new squadron commander to Callao, where he arrived on January 3, 1845.[1] A full seven months had passed since Commodore Alexander J. Dallas died there.

The particular timing here is important to what follows. Sloat was sent to command the Pacific Squadron by the Tyler administration during that president's last year in office. The presidential campaign between Whig Henry Clay and Democrat James K. Polk was then in full swing. Issues of westward expansion figured large in that campaign. The occupation of Monterey in 1842 had brought to a standstill the efforts of President Tyler and Secretary of State Webster to acquire California from Mexico. In any event, California came to be overshadowed as a campaign issue by the Oregon Territory dispute with Great Britain and by the annexation of Texas, controversies which led to confrontation with Mexico.[2] The 1844 election had not taken place when Sloat left the United States, and James K. Polk still had not taken office when Sloat took command of the squadron.

The new commodore quickly wrote to the secretary of the navy to pass along his concerns about the manning levels in his command. Only ten commissioned lieutenants were assigned to the various ships of the Pacific Squadron. By the 1840s, passed midshipmen of considerable experience frequently served as sailing masters of warships, and that was the situation in Sloat's command as well. Some passed midshipmen held billets aboard ship that rightfully should have been held by lieutenants, and that worried Sloat.[3] No stated reason for Sloat's concern appears, but by 1846, many midshipmen were veteran officers with years of sea duty under their belts. Inexperience was not likely one of Sloat's worries.

Figure 14.1. *Commodore John Drake Sloat*, unknown artist, 1846. The lithograph is from an original painting that was probably destroyed in the 1906 earthquake and fire in San Francisco. (Courtesy of the Navy Art Collection, Naval History and Heritage Command.)

More likely, his concerns were legal ones. Midshipmen held their office by warrants, whereas lieutenants held commissions from the president of the United States and had been confirmed by the Senate. With their higher status, commissioned officers can be held to a higher standard of accountability, and they can represent their country with a degree of authority and gravitas that warrant officers simply did not have.

The ships of the Pacific Squadron had dispersed during the months since the death of Commodore Dallas. The frigate *Savannah*, then commanded by Captain James Armstrong, had been at Monterey in December 1844 but did not show up at Callao until the end of the following March. In the meantime, Commodore Sloat flew his pennant in the sloop *Levant*. That ship being rather small, Sloat actually stayed aboard the store ship *Relief*. Concerns about the paucity of commissioned officers on station notwithstanding, Sloat took command of the *Savannah* so Armstrong could return home after many years of being away.[4] Perhaps Armstrong did not wish to remain there under another's command after having been the senior officer present for several months after Commodore Dallas's death.

The United States had concerns about possible British or French designs on California, and those countries also had a naval presence at Callao. France did have an interest in California and the Pacific, but the United States and Great Britain far overshadowed the French presence in California. Rear Admiral Sir George Seymour and two Royal Navy ships of the line rode at anchor in Callao. Sloat mentioned a French presence when reporting to Mason that the *Portsmouth* had reported on station and that both British and French officers had admired the new arrival. Sloat gave himself a small pat on the back by remarking upon his personal pride at having had a role in building that fine sloop.[5] In command of the *Portsmouth* was Commander John B. Montgomery, who had served as a lieutenant under Sloat at the New York Naval Rendezvous a decade earlier.

On March 4, 1845, James K. Polk assumed the presidency in Washington. One week later, George Bancroft joined the cabinet as secretary of the navy and John Y. Mason became the new attorney general. The senior American naval officer in the Pacific had not had the benefit of personal consultation with Polk or Bancroft before assuming command. He could not receive any information that they might wish not to commit to paper, and the delay time in communications with a commander so far away was very long. In late July, Commodore Sloat received a warning of impending war with Mexico that Bancroft penned on March 21, less than three weeks after the Polk administration took office. Bancroft directed Sloat to concentrate his forces in Mexican waters.[6]

Even before receiving Bancroft's letter, Sloat had grown increasingly concerned about the deterioration of relations between the United States and Mexico. He sent ships north to Mazatlán at least twice to report back to him about that crucial situation. Highlighting his concerns about slow communications with the Navy Department, Sloat told Bancroft that the British admiral in Callao had received official notification all the way from England that the United States had annexed Texas before he learned anything of it, and that he had only newspapers as a source of information. Sloat added that slow communications were not the only problems that he faced in the Pacific. If trouble emerged between the United States and a superior force, then Valparaiso (Chile) and Callao (Peru) were the only sources of supply that would be available. Reiterating the concern he had expressed earlier to Mason, Sloat pointed out to Bancroft that he was the only captain out there, and that were something to happen to him, then one of the commanders would have to take charge and one of the lieutenants would have to take command of a sloop-of-war.[7] The contents of these letters show Commodore Sloat's great concern about British intentions and actions in the Pacific theater. By "superior force," Sloat can only have meant the British squadron. The Mexican naval presence on its Pacific coast consisted of only two schooners.[8] He would carry those concerns with him to Monterey. Sloat decided to move to Mexico in two steps. He would first sail to Hawaii and then move on to Mexico.

By mid-September 1845, Sloat had arrived in Honolulu. He found himself embroiled in an ongoing diplomatic squabble involving United States Commissioner George Brown, who represented American interests in the Hawaiian kingdom. Brown had engendered resentment with a generally high-handed approach. The particular issue centered around one John Wiley, an American in Honolulu facing a series of legal difficulties. Sloat petitioned for an audience with King Kamehameha III, which was immediately granted and took place on September 29. Sloat complained that Wiley had been denied a trial by jury. Even though the United

States had no treaty with the kingdom of Hawaii, it could not stand idle in Wiley's case when the kingdom afforded the right of trial by jury to British subjects and French citizens. Following the audience, the foreign minister of Hawaii, the Scotsman Robert C. Wyllie, explained that Sloat had been misinformed and that Wiley did get the same privileges as did Britishers or Frenchmen. Wiley had demanded even more than that, and Commissioner Brown had backed him. On October 11, Sloat filed another complaint with Foreign Minister Wyllie, expressing regret that the king had thought it inadvisable to reestablish relations with Commissioner Brown.[9] Commissioner Brown wanted Commodore Sloat to punish Hawaii with punitive military action. In his letter to Bancroft about the Honolulu affair, Sloat emphasized that American agents and the Hawaiian government seemed to misunderstand each other on a host of issues, and that he attempted to smooth things over. Foreign Minister Wyllie's records contain many references to the actions of the British consul general, who attempted to counter the influence of Americans by emphasizing to Hawaiians the pervasiveness of racism in the United States and its continued practice of chattel slavery.[10] Her Majesty's consul general in Honolulu was none other than the same William Miller whom Sloat had met in Callao when that English general in the Peruvian Army sought protection from forces loyal to La Mariscala and president of Peru Antonio Gamarra. Miller made a formal call on Sloat aboard the *Savannah*, where he received a formal gun salute upon boarding.[11] The two doubtless enjoyed the comparison between the formality of the visit in Honolulu in 1845 and the urgency of Miller's escape from Peru in 1831.

The ships would depart shortly after for Mazatlán on Mexico's Pacific coast. Sloat left behind in Honolulu a letter for Captain John P. "Mad Jack" Percival, the commanding officer of the frigate *Constitution*. Then circumnavigating the world, "Old Ironsides" arrived in Honolulu from Manila in November, and Percival received Sloat's instructions. Sloat marked the letter "Private and Confidential," and its contents show the commodore's view of the situation then developing.

Sloat told Percival that deteriorating relations with Mexico necessitated holding the *Constitution* in the Pacific instead of allowing the frigate to proceed homeward. He directed Percival to replenish rapidly in Hawaii and then to sail for Monterey to look for the Pacific Squadron. If the ships were not there, then the *Constitution* should next look for them in San Blas and in Mazatlán. Sloat informed Percival that President Polk earnestly desired to preserve the peace. If Percival found beyond a doubt that the United States and Mexico had gone to war, then he was "to annoy the enemy to the utmost." Otherwise, he must act to preserve harmony between the nations and to maintain friendly relations with any local inhabitants. In the event of hostilities, Percival would find further instructions from Sloat at San Blas or Mazatlán. Sloat added that he had not yet been to the Mexican coast himself and reminded Percival to act with due discretion because he would bear responsibility for the honor and the interests of the United States. The *Constitution* arrived in Monterey on December 31 but found no American warships there and so proceeded to Mazatlán. "Old Ironsides" anchored there on January 14, 1846. There, Percival found not only more of Sloat's instructions but the Commodore himself and the Pacific Squadron as well.[12]

Sloat had sailed from Honolulu in the *Savannah* on October 13, scouted the coast of California, and then proceeded south. The flagship arrived in Mazatlán on November 17, 1845, and found the sloop *Portsmouth* already there. The sloops *Warren* and *Levant* each arrived within three days.[13] Mazatlán's good harbor made it a viable base for the Pacific Squadron before the outbreak of war with Mexico. Overland communications routes to Veracruz and Tampico and thence to Washington did exist, but the precarious international situation made their use risky. The safer route via Panama meant correspondence took four months to travel between the commodore in the Pacific and the secretary in Washington.

Two days after the *Savannah* anchored off Mazatlán, Sloat received "secret and confidential" instructions from Bancroft that had been written five months earlier, on June 24, 1845. Because the phrasing of this and subsequent directives from Bancroft weigh heavily in the subsequent evaluation of Sloat's actions when the United States went to war with Mexico, the text of the letter follows.[14]

> SIR: Your attention is still particularly directed to the present aspect of the relations between this country and Mexico. It is the earnest desire of the President to pursue the policy of peace, and he is anxious that you and every part of your Squadron should be assiduously careful to avoid any act which could be construed as an act of aggression.

Should Mexico, however, be resolutely bent on hostilities, you will be mindful to protect the persons and interests of citizens of the United States near your station; and should you ascertain beyond a doubt, that the Mexican government has declared war against us, you will at once employ the force under your command to the best advantage. The Mexican ports on the Pacific are said to be open and defenseless. If you ascertain with certainty that Mexico has declared war against the United States, you will at once possess yourself of the port of San Francisco and blockade or occupy such other ports as your force may permit.

Yet, even if you should find yourself called upon by the certainty of an express declaration of war against the United States to occupy San Francisco and other Mexican ports, you will be careful to preserve, if possible, the most friendly relations with the inhabitants, and where you can do so, you will encourage them to adopt a course of neutrality.

Should you fall in with the Squadron under Commodore Parker, you will signify to him the wish of the Department that, if the state of his vessels will admit of it, he should remain off the coast of Mexico until our relations with that power are more definitely adjusted, and you will take directions from him as senior officer, communicating to him these instructions.

The great distance of your Squadron and the difficulty of communicating with you, are the causes for issuing this order. The President hopes most earnestly that the peace of the two countries may not be disturbed. The object of these instructions is to possess you of the desire of the Government in the event of a declaration of war on the part of Mexico against the United States—an event which you are enjoined to do everything, consistent with the national honor on your part to avoid.

Should Commodore Parker prefer to return to the United States, he has permission from the Department to do so. In that event you will command the united Squadron.

Very respectfully, your obedient servant,
GEORGE BANCROFT

Sloat's letter acknowledging receipt of the directive from Bancroft is the same one in which he commented upon the overthrow of Manuel Micheltorena as governor of California as described earlier. Sloat added that Mexican ports did have poor defenses, with the possible exception of Acapulco, and that California was, for all intents and purposes, independent even though no such declaration had been made. The commodore also worried about the reliability of communicating with Washington through Mexico.[15] Mexico broke off diplomatic relations with the United States after the Texas annexation, but American consulates still remained open and in communication with each other at Veracruz, Mexico City, and Mazatlán. Consul Thomas O. Larkin continued to function at Monterey.

Figure 14.2. *Thomas O. Larkin*. (Courtesy of the California State Library.)

The Pacific Squadron remained in Mazatlán in early 1846 during the run-up to the war. In the meantime, reinforcements sailed from the East Coast for the Pacific theater. The sloop-of-war *Cyane* under the command of Captain William Mervine sailed in August 1845 and arrived in January. The frigate *Congress* sailed at the end of October but would not join the squadron until the middle of 1846, after the war began. The *Congress* carried Captain Robert F. Stockton, who was ordered to serve as Sloat's second in command and to relieve him if the commodore's health deteriorated to the point where he could no longer fulfill his responsibilities.

Upon arriving in Mazatlán in December 1845, Sloat found an increasingly tense diplomatic and political situation. By that point in time, Santa Anna had been exiled to Havana. Another army officer, José Joaquín de Herrera, held the presidency. Herrera took a moderate position on the Texas issue and even managed to get the Mexican Congress to allow negotiations with the Texans about recognition of their independence. But the United States annexation of Texas led not only to the rupture of diplomatic relations, but the public outcry in Mexico forced Herrera to take a more confrontational stance with the northern neighbor. Polk made another attempt to deal with Herrera. He requested to send a commissioner to discuss the Texas matter. The foreign minister agreed, and Polk sent John Slidell on his way. The Home Squadron under Commodore David Conner had been anchored off Veracruz but withdrew. But Polk raised the stakes by appointing Slidell as minister plenipotentiary, which today would carry the title of ambassador. Receiving a minister instead of a commissioner would have amounted to reestablishment of diplomatic relations. Slidell reached Mexico City on December 6. He had secret instructions from Polk to discuss not only Texas and issues of monetary claims against Mexico but also the purchase of California and New Mexico. Slidell's true intentions quickly leaked out and caused another public uproar. A plot to overthrow Herrera had already been brewing for some time, and it then moved into action as suspicions intensified that the president intended to compromise Mexican national honor by selling territory. Instead of following Herrera's orders to march north to the Rio Grande, General Mariano Paredes y Arrillaga led his division toward Mexico City. Other commanders joined the uprising and forced Herrera to resign. On January 2, Paredes entered Mexico City and was soon elected interim president. Although a hardliner, Paredes preferred to avoid a war with the United States, but the British foreign secretary had repeatedly made it clear that Mexico could not expect any help from that quarter. Throughout the early months of 1846, Paredes continued to refuse to receive Slidell.

The Home Squadron had been ordered back into position off Veracruz in January, and Polk also ordered Brigadier General Zachary Taylor to move with two thousand troops across the Nueces River and then down to the Rio Grande. Texas had claimed the area between the two rivers before annexation. Mexico rejected that claim about the boundary between Texas and Coahuila, but one should remember that Mexico still refused to recognize that any part of Texas was not Mexican territory. By the time Taylor's force took up its forward positions at the end of March, John Slidell had given up on his diplomatic mission and started his return journey to Washington.[16]

Commodore Sloat would have become aware of happenings in Mexico City and perhaps even on the Gulf coast of Mexico in comparatively short order. About a week was needed to go from Veracruz to the capital by stagecoach, and another week to get to the Pacific coast. On February 9, 1846, a special agent arrived in Mazatlán bearing messages from President Polk and Secretary Bancroft. Posing as a British business traveler, First Lieutenant Archibald H. Gillespie, U.S. Marine Corps, journeyed incognito across Mexico. He had been present in Mexico City when General Paredes took power, and that situation prevented him from leaving the capital for a while. Gillespie carried orders for Sloat, for Thomas O. Larkin, the American consul in Monterey, and for Captain John C. Frémont, the army engineer officer then leading what was billed as another mapping exploration into California.[17] The letters for Frémont included letters from his wife and also his prominent father-in-law, Senator Thomas Hart Benton of Missouri. Those letters have been the subject of historians' speculation for many years. Their contents have never been revealed, but the consensus view today holds that President Polk sent no secret instructions to Captain Frémont via Lieutenant Gillespie. Before his arrival in Veracruz, Gillespie became concerned for the security of the official correspondence. He committed the texts to memory and destroyed the papers before disembarking in the Mexican port. Larkin had been appointed a confidential agent, in addition to his consular duties. Through Secretary of State James Buchanan, Polk directed Larkin to encourage any effort by Californios to achieve independence from Mexico. Reflecting concern in Washington about British intentions on the west coast of North America, Polk also directed Larkin to counter any attempts by foreign countries to get control of California. Gillespie was to assist Larkin in those efforts. Sloat assigned the sloop-of-war *Cyane* to transport Gillespie to Monterey, and the ship left Mazatlán on February 23. As a deception, the *Cyane* sailed by way of Hawaii in order to deflect any suspicion that the warship might actually be headed for California. Gillespie maintained his cover story when the *Cyane* arrived in Monterey on April 17. He delivered the instructions to Larkin and then moved on to look for Frémont in the central valley. But at least one Mexican official recognized Gillespie as the marine officer aboard the frigate *Brandywine* during an 1844 visit to Monterey, and someone on the *Cyane* may have leaked the lieutenant's true identity. So the Californios knew that something was up.[18]

Revised directions for Commodore Sloat came from Secretary Bancroft, in a letter dated October 17, 1845. Another copy of the letter was on its way around Cape Horn in the custody of Captain Robert Stockton. The letter contained some amplifying orders for Sloat about what to do if no war broke out.[19] Significantly, it also contained the following paragraphs:

> In the event of actual hostilities between the Mexican Government and our own, you will so dispose of your whole force as to carry out most effectually the objects specified in the instructions forwarded to you from the Department in view of such a contingency. Should peace continue, you will still retain your squadron off the coast of Mexico and Oregon.
>
> You will communicate frequently with our Consul at Monterey, and will ascertain as exactly as you can, the designs of the English and the French in that region, the temper of the inhabitants, their disposition towards the United States, and their relations towards the central governments of Mexico. You will do everything that is proper to conciliate towards our country the most friendly regard of the people of California.

The difference in wording between "in the event of actual hostilities between the Mexican Government and our own" and the earlier "should you ascertain beyond a doubt, that the Mexican government has declared war against us" probably created some confusion in Sloat's mind. In particular, this October 17 letter did not state that it superseded any of the instructions in the June 24 letter. After the *Cyane* sailed, Sloat reported to Bancroft that Gillespie had arrived a few days earlier, and that he had sent the lieutenant onward as directed by the *verbal* (emphasis added) orders of the president and the secretary of the navy. The Pacific Squadron commander reported that they were getting on well with the people of Mazatlán, and that his squadron was fully ready for any service. Echoing a concern of Gillespie's for security of the dispatches, he felt safest to send that letter to Mrs. Sloat in New York so she could forward it to the secretary. Shortly afterward, Sloat again acknowledged the October 17 instructions and also advised Bancroft that rheumatism, neuralgia, and liver problems were taking an increasing toll on him.[20]

The confrontation on the Rio Grande between Mexico and the United States continued to worsen, but the news had not reached Mazatlán by April 1846. Commodore Sloat did, however, learn that a U.S. Army officer had caused difficulties in Monterey. The erstwhile Captain John C. Frémont crossed the Sierra Nevada and reached Sutter's Fort in December 1845. He soon left and moved south through the valley in an unsuccessful attempt to locate a part of his exploratory expedition that he had sent to cross the Sierra Nevada by another pass, and Frémont then returned to Sutter's Fort. Leaving most of his people there, he and a small party set out to meet with Consul Thomas O. Larkin in Monterey after first passing through the pueblo of Yerba Buena, present-day San Francisco. Frémont briefed Larkin, and the two then called on local officials, including military commander José Castro and ex-governor Juan Alvarado. The two Californios acquiesced to Frémont's request to spend the winter in California. Writing from Los Angeles, civil governor Pío Pico concurred in Alvarado and Castro's concession but urged that Castro monitor Frémont closely to ensure that he actually headed north to Oregon as soon as feasible. Frémont rejoined his men, and by March 1846 they had moved into the Salinas valley near Monterey itself instead of remaining in the more remote San Joaquín valley. With a copy to Larkin, José Castro sent a written order to Frémont directing him to leave the department of California immediately, or else Castro would take steps to force him out. Frémont refused to send a written reply but told Castro's courier that he was offended and would not leave. Frémont then moved his camp a few miles to the top of Gavilan Peak. From that vantage point near San Juan Bautista, Frémont had a commanding view of the bay from Monterey all the way around past Santa Cruz. Once there, he built some temporary fortifications and raised the United States flag. José Castro sent a mounted column to the foot of the mountain. Manuel Castro, the civil prefect in Monterey, confronted Larkin about Frémont's actions, and the consul immediately sent a letter that urged the captain to withdraw and to head to Oregon as he had promised. Frémont and his men quietly left their Gavilan Peak redoubt on the night of March 9.

Figure 14.3. *John C. Frémont*. (Courtesy of the California State Library.)

Larkin reported the affair to the secretary of state in Washington and to Sloat in Mazatlán. The consul recommended that the commodore send an American warship to Monterey. Lieutenant Gillespie and the *Cyane* had not yet arrived when Larkin sent his request. The sloop *Portsmouth* sailed from Mazatlán and arrived off Monterey on April 23, only six days after the *Cyane* finally arrived via Honolulu. Sloat duly informed Bancroft about the troubling reports he had received concerning Frémont. Finally bowing to repeated complaints from Captain Percival that his ship was in poor condition and that many enlistments among his sailors would soon expire, Sloat permitted the *Constitution* to sail for the United States on April 23.[21]

Aboard the *Savannah*, Sloat continued to monitor the situation and to look for news of war. The *Cyane* returned from Monterey. The sloops *Levant* and *Warren* also remained at anchor in the Mexican port along with the store ship *Erie*. On May 17, Sloat received an urgent letter from Surgeon William Maxwell Wood, who had been detached and transferred back to the United States. Wood had traveled across Mexico in company with John Parrott, the outgoing United States consul in Mazatlán. The pair had arrived in Guadalajara and heard that fighting had broken out along the Rio Grande between Mexican and United States forces. When Sloat received Wood's message, he sent Captain William Mervine and the *Cyane* back to Monterey on May 19 to inform Larkin of the developments. The *Erie* left for Hawaii, presumably to replenish stores and provisions for what might lie ahead. On May 25, Admiral Seymour and HMS *Collingwood* also left Mazatlán for an undisclosed destination.

The *Savannah* sailed from Mazatlán on June 1, headed for Monterey. After two days at sea, Sloat headed back to Mazatlán and arrived there on June 5. He wrote to Bancroft that "upon more mature reflection," he concluded that the conditions laid out by the secretary in his original letter of June 24, 1845, had not been met and the Pacific Squadron therefore could not seize California ports. On the day after his letter to Bancroft began to wend its way to Washington, Sloat received another report from Wood and Parrott, who had continued from Guadalajara to Mexico City. This second letter from Wood confirmed the earlier reports about the battles at Palo Alto and at Resaca de la Palma along the Rio Grande. On June 7, word reached Mazatlán that the Home Squadron under Commodore David Conner had established a blockade of Veracruz and other ports on the Gulf of Mexico. Leaving the *Warren* behind to await any additional dispatches, Commodore Sloat now concluded that Secretary Bancroft's requirements had in fact been met and that he finally had authority to act. He sailed for Monterey in the *Savannah* on June 9 and anchored there on July 2. The *Cyane* and the *Levant* were already there, and Commander Montgomery had taken the *Portsmouth* to San Francisco Bay at Consul Larkin's request.

As earlier reports had indicated, the California ports were essentially defenseless. But Sloat learned from Commander Montgomery in Yerba Buena and from Consul Larkin there in Monterey about a totally unexpected development. American settlers had risen in armed rebellion against the California government, and Captain Frémont of the United States Army appeared to be deeply involved in what would come to be known as the Bear Flag revolt.

Lieutenant Gillespie had caught up with Frémont near Klamath Lake, just across the border in Oregon country. The marine officer delivered the packet of letters and conferred with Frémont. What was said remains obscure to this day, but Frémont moved south again and set up

Figure 14.4. Monterey customs house, mid-nineteenth century. (Courtesy of the Library of Congress.)

camp, almost fifty miles north of Sutter's Fort near the Sutter Buttes, volcanic lava crags that rise up out of the valley floor. Rumors swirled among American settlers in the Sacramento valley that José Castro meant to expel them because their presence in Mexican territory was illegal. Frémont's earlier confrontation doubtless fanned those flames. In his role as military commander in California, Castro had just acquired from Mariano Guadalupe Vallejo a large number of horses. The horses were being driven from Vallejo's ranch in Sonoma toward San José, which route in those days took them through the Sacramento valley and the delta. The settlers decided that Castro really meant to use the horses in a move to expel them. A group of them stole the horses on June 10 and drove them to the Sutter Buttes. They then marched on Sonoma, and their number had swelled to about thirty when they arrived at Vallejo's house on Sunday morning, June 14. Despite the fact that Vallejo was a leader among the Californio faction that favored annexation of California by the United States, the rebels burst into Vallejo's house and rousted him out of bed. Vallejo donned his Mexican Army officer's uniform and went out to face the mob of raggedly dressed but fully armed settlers. Vallejo's brother-in-law, Sonoma merchant Jacob Leese, soon arrived to translate. The rebels demanded animals for military supplies as well as the arms and ammunition that Vallejo stored as a militia officer. Vallejo broke out his brandy to share during the talks, and the rebel leaders partook extensively while their followers impatiently waited outside. Vallejo had negotiated a parole but the rabble outside would have none of it. General Mariano Vallejo, his brother Captain Salvador Vallejo, and Lieutenant Colonel Victor Prudón all ended up as prisoners of the rebels who took them to Sutter's Fort.

William B. Ide of Red Bluff then assumed leadership of the Bear Flag rebels. They fought an inconclusive skirmish with Californios near San Rafael and retired toward Sonoma. Ide sent a message to Commander Montgomery in San Francisco requesting arms and ammunition. Montgomery rebuffed the request, saying that he could not support rebels in a country that to his knowledge was at peace with the United States, even if he personally sympathized with their cause.[22] Gillespie had told Montgomery that Frémont had no direct involvement with the Bear Flaggers, and he reiterated the denial when José Castro sent a complaint to the marine on board the *Portsmouth* about the conduct of his country-

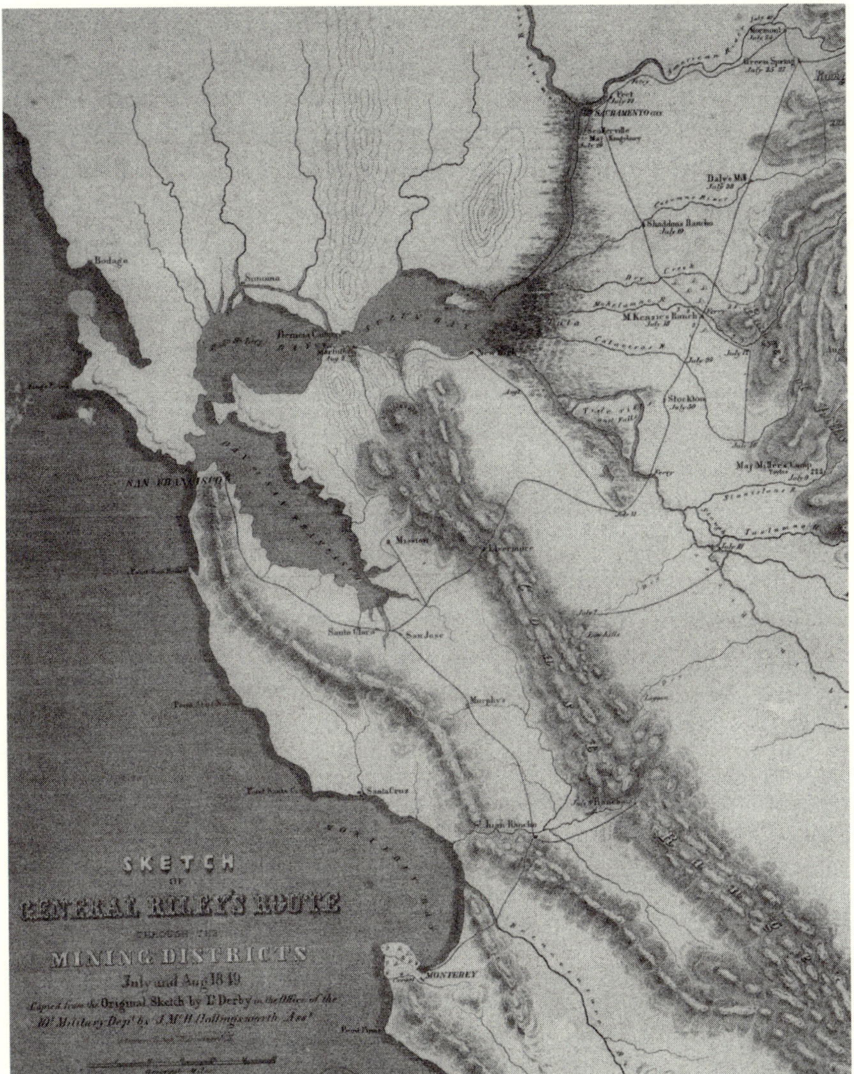

Figure 14.5. Map of Northern California, 1849, showing Monterey, San Francisco Bay, and Sutter's Fort at New Helvetia. (Courtesy of the Library of Congress.)

men. Castro was equally unaware that his country was at war the United States, and it appeared to him that Larkin, Montgomery, and Frémont had acted in concert to overthrow Mexican rule in California.

By June 28, Frémont had taken de facto command of the Bear Flag rebels. Near San Rafael, a boat landed and José de los Reyes Berreyessa disembarked accompanied by his twenty-year-old twin nephews, Francisco and Ramón De Haro. Having no room for prisoners, civilian scout Christopher "Kit" Carson simply killed the three of them, apparently with Frémont's tacit concurrence if not his direct orders. By July 2, Frémont had spiked the guns in the presidio at San Francisco and returned to Sonoma. The Bear Flag rebels remained active, having declared an independent republic as the Texans had done in 1836. Here stood matters when the Pacific Squadron arrived in Monterey and Commodore John Drake Sloat took stock of the situation ashore.

Captain William Mervine of the *Cyane* wrote a summary of the situation as soon as the *Savannah* was sighted and had it delivered immediately to the commodore. After leaving Mazatlán, the *Cyane* had been followed for a while by two warships that eventually broke off contact. Mervine believed them to be British. He also advised Sloat that people in Monterey generally thought that Frémont's presence in California, Gillespie's arrival in Monterey, and the continued presence of the *Portsmouth* in San Francisco Bay all indicated that the Bear Flag rebels had the support of the United States.[23]

Sloat received reports from Commander Montgomery in San Francisco Bay and met with Consul Larkin immediately after arriving in Monterey. The preceding summary stems from present-day historical literature, and we are left to speculate which parts became immediately known to the commodore and which parts were revealed as news arrived over the course of the subsequent few weeks. But he did know from the moment of his arrival in Monterey about some of the Bear Flag rebels' doings, and about some things that Captain Frémont had done up to that point. Those aspects of the situation on the ground in California differed greatly from what Sloat expected to find. Bancroft's directions included an order to maintain friendly and conciliatory relations with the Californios as much as possible. President Polk wanted a peaceful annexation of California if he could get one. The Bear Flag rebellion's mere existence made that more complicated.

On the day the *Savannah* arrived in Monterey, Commodore Sloat proposed a formal salute to the Mexican flag. Officials in Monterey declined the proposal because they did not have the gunpowder to return it. Obviously then, they also lacked the means to use artillery in a defense of their town. Sloat went ashore and toured Monterey on July 3 in company with Larkin. Montgomery sent another letter from San Francisco by one of the *Portsmouth*'s boats informing Sloat about Frémont's increased personal involvement with the Bear Flag rebellion and their spiking of the guns at the presidio of San Francisco. The army officer's political connections were well known to the general public after stories of his earlier explorations were published. Commodore Sloat believed that Frémont must have been acting on some kind of official orders. He summoned Consul Larkin to the *Savannah* on July 6 and made plans to occupy Monterey the next day. The *Portsmouth*'s boat carried back a directive for Montgomery to occupy Yerba Buena and raise the United States flag there.

Two contradictory accounts deserve note here, although most histories of the events in Monterey omit them. Purser Rodman M. Price served in the *Cyane* under Captain Mervine. Years afterward, Price wrote to Frémont that he had paid a call on Commodore Sloat the night before the flag raising at Monterey. Price had been at the White House just before the *Cyane* sailed to join the Pacific Squadron. He declared that he had spoken personally with President Polk and understood the chief executive's wishes to occupy California. After Mervine returned from a call on Sloat, the former shared with *Cyane* officers his frustration at Sloat's cautious approach to the situation in California. Reminding Mervine of his having met Polk and discussed California with him, Price requested permission to call on Sloat. Mervine initially refused. He soon decided to allow Purser Price to use a *Cyane* boat to go to the *Savannah* but emphasized that Price was going on his own and in no way spoke for Mervine. Price called on Sloat, who shared his concerns about repeating Commodore Jones's debacle. Price claimed that he convinced Sloat that the situation in 1846 had changed and that the president wanted him to invade and occupy California. Immediately afterward, according to Price, Sloat issued the occupation orders to be carried out the next day and turned in for the night. Price returned to the *Cyane* where he received congratulations from his fellow officers and Captain Mervine. Price's account does not comport exactly with the chronology developed in later histories, and he wrote it many years after the events for Frémont, who spent decades trying to clear his reputation of the controversies that he created and attracted to himself in California, as a candidate for president, and as a general officer during the Civil War. The very idea that a purser, an officer in charge of supplies and accounts, would make a personal call on the senior line officer present and influence the latter's decisions seems so bizarre that there might well be some truth to it. Even more so because Mervine seems to have been afraid of Sloat, and Sloat seems to have kept his own counsel and made his own decisions. Exactly when Price went to the *Savannah*, and just what influence he did manage to exert upon Sloat, are questionable in view of the decades that elapsed between the events and the memoir. Perhaps Purser Price did speak with Commodore Sloat there in Monterey before the occupation and flag raising. Price served as alcalde of Monterey during the occupation. He later served two years in the U.S. House of Representatives and also a term as governor of New Jersey. The historian Allan Nevins finds Price to be a credible individual.[24]

William Heath Davis, a Pacific coast merchant in 1846, relayed a different story from Captain Mervine. Davis arrived in Monterey shortly after the customs house flag raising. He soon presented himself to Sloat and Larkin and sold some provisions to the ships of the squadron. Davis's memoirs were first published in 1889, more than forty years after the events. He remembered Sloat as an "agile, nervous little man," but one who was very satisfied with the steps he had taken after arriving in Monterey. Somewhat later, Mervine told Davis that Sloat had convened a "council of war" (Davis's term) aboard the *Savannah* on the evening of July 6. Commander Samuel Du Pont and some other officers were in attendance. As Mervine told it to Davis, it was he whose forceful arguments convinced Sloat to proclaim annexation on the next morning. Davis recalled Captain Mervine as a bluff, forceful individual and considered him a much better naval officer than was Commodore Sloat. Purser Rodman Price appears nowhere in Davis's story.[25]

Obviously, Davis and Price cannot both have told a historically accurate story, and each memoir was written decades after the events themselves. Price champions himself, but Davis's applause of Mervine does not derive from a wish to advance his own reputation. Neither is complimentary to Sloat. They do agree, however, that Mervine attended some kind of meeting on board the *Savannah* and that the naval landing party occupied Monterey the next day. They both say Sloat's instructions were immediately sent by boat to Montgomery in Yerba Buena.

On the morning of July 7, 1846, Captain Mervine and a small escort party went ashore in Monterey and demanded the surrender of the town. Captain Mariano Silva replied that he had no authority to surrender it, that he had no means to resist, and that he would forward the demand to José Castro, the Mexican military commandant. In the meantime, a landing party of more than two hundred marines and sailors assembled from the *Savannah*, *Cyane*, and *Levant*. The commodore's general order was read to the entire crew of each of the three warships. It prescribed much different standards of conduct than those followed by Frémont and his men in the murder of Berreyessa and the De Haro twins. Sloat threatened the severest punishment to anyone who misbehaved ashore, who plundered any article, who insulted any local person, or who offended any woman with any indignity (see appendix A). The landing party embarked in six boats and then proceeded ashore in two columns behind the *Cyane*'s gig, which carried Captain Mervine.

Once ashore, two midshipmen raised the United States flag at the customs house. In a proclamation read aloud in both English and Spanish, Sloat formally proclaimed that California was no longer Mexican territory and annexed henceforth to the United States. Consul Thomas Larkin consulted extensively with Sloat in drafting the proclamation.[26] Among other things, the proclamation promised elections and good government, protection of personal property, reduction of tariffs to the levels in the United States, and the protection of churches and church property. Sloat invited civil officials to continue in their same capacities until the government was restructured at some later time (see appendix B). They refused, so Sloat appointed Purser Rodman Price and Surgeon Edward Gilchrist to serve as alcaldes in their place. To patrol the area, Purser Daingerfield Fauntleroy of the *Savannah* organized a platoon of thirty-five mounted personnel, labeled somewhat optimistically as "dragoons." Some marines took up quarters in the Monterey customs house as an additional security force.

Commander Montgomery read the proclamation and raised the flag in Yerba Buena on July 9 as soon as he received Sloat's orders. Both Montgomery and Sloat sent messengers to Sonoma to inform Frémont of the occupation and to advise the soldier that the commodore wished to consult with him. As soon as the messages arrived, the Bear Flag came down and the Stars and Stripes went up. Montgomery also sent a flag to be raised at Sutter's Fort.[27] Frémont sent Gillespie to Monterey without delay and then set out himself at a slower pace to meet with the commodore. The Vallejo brothers and Prudón remained imprisoned at Sutter's Fort. Thus ended the Bear Flag revolt. It would later be celebrated by some as a triumph for Manifest Destiny, and derided by others as a comic opera farce. It was no farce to the Californios, for whom it was one in a series of tragedies. As for indigenous Californians who had suffered at the hands of the Californios, they would continue to suffer in the years after the Stars and Stripes replaced the Mexican tricolor.[28]

Sloat sent a demand for surrender of all Mexican forces to General José Castro, who was then inland at San Juan Bautista, with a copy to civil governor Pío Pico in Los Angeles. Castro refused to surrender or even to come to Monterey at all.[29] Instead, he moved south and met with Pico on July 12 near San Luis Obispo. As civil governor, Pico also categorically refused Sloat's surrender demand. Castro and Pico had been antagonists for a long time, to the point where many had believed a civil war between their factions was in the offing. They agreed to set aside their differences and resist the American invasion. Sloat had his hopes for peaceful cooperation, but he also took precautions and asked Larkin to provide some reliable scouts that could unobtrusively watch the roads leading into Monterey and warn of any approaching force.[30]

The *Congress* arrived on July 15, completing her seven-month journey from the East Coast. The frigate carried Captain Robert F. Stockton, whom Secretary Bancroft had ordered to serve as Sloat's second in command. Recall that Bancroft had also authorized Sloat to turn over command of the Pacific Squadron to Stockton should Sloat's health so dictate. On the following day, HMS *Collingwood* anchored in Monterey, and Rear Admiral Seymour learned of Sloat's annexation proclamation. Americans harbored serious worries about British intentions for California, but British leaders had no wish for a confrontation with the United States, even though they probably preferred that California become independent under British protection. Meetings between Seymour and Sloat were cordial, although some accounts state that Seymour fell into a rage when he first spotted the United States flag flying over the Monterey customs house. Seymour doubted that Sloat had authority under the U.S. Constitution to proclaim annexation.[31] Although unconvinced of its legality or permanence, the British admiral took no action to counter the annexation, dashing the hopes of that faction of Californios that wished for some sort of support from the British against both the United States and the government in Mexico City.

Captain Frémont and his band of adventurers arrived in Monterey on July 19. Lieutenant Gillespie had arrived earlier but, following instructions from Frémont, had provided no information to Commodore Sloat. Frémont and Gillespie called on the commodore aboard the *Savannah*. Inconceivable to him that the soldier could have acted without orders, Sloat asked Frémont by what authority had he acted in California as he did. Frémont replied that he had acted entirely on his own accord, and added that he hoped for support from Sloat. The horrified commodore terminated the interview at that point and abruptly dismissed the two junior officers.

Two days later, Frémont called on Captain Stockton to make his case for a continued land campaign against Castro and Pico. Stockton concurred and persuaded Sloat to assign him control of the *Cyane* and command of the forces ashore. Frémont established the provisional California Battalion, placed himself in command with the rank of major, and appointed Gillespie as his deputy with a promotion to captain. Those accounts of the meeting between Sloat and Frémont that portray the commodore as timid and indecisive usually praise Frémont as an eager man of action. Frémont's subsequent actions in California would lead to conviction by an army court-martial on charges preferred by Brigadier General Stephen W. Kearny: mutiny, disobedience of orders, and conduct prejudicial to the maintenance of good order and discipline. President Polk set aside the sentence of dismissal from the army and the conviction on the mutiny charge, but the undisciplined Frémont resigned his commission in protest anyway.[32]

Commodore John Drake Sloat decided to act on Secretary George Bancroft's earlier authorization and turn over command of the Pacific Squadron to Captain Robert F. Stockton. Why he did not do that when he gave Stockton command of the land forces remains a mystery. He may have decided later that he did not want to deal with the aggressive, arrogant, and politically powerful Stockton. He may have believed that his health was such that he could not effectively command a land campaign and so left it to the younger Stockton. He may have figured that as a sailor, he knew nothing of land warfare and could not do a

Figure 14.6. *Robert Field Stockton*, engraving by H. B. Hall from a painting on ivory by Newton, London, 1840 (Courtesy of the Navy Art Collection, Naval History and Heritage Command.)

soldier's job. He did not yet know that Captain William B. Shubrick had already been ordered out to relieve him. He had been a squadron commander for almost two years and knew he was entitled by custom to hoist a pennant and be addressed as "Commodore" forever more. Or perhaps all of the foregoing, each one in some measure. The evidence permits no more specific conclusion.

Having made his decision, Commodore Sloat turned over command. Commodore Stockton hoisted his broad pennant, and Sloat and his son departed together on July 29 for Panama in the *Levant*. Sloat reported to Secretary Bancroft that Stockton had command of the squadron. His letter stated that on June 7, he had received word that Mexico had attacked the United States, and that he left Mazatlán the next day. The letter included an encapsulation of the events of July in Monterey but omitted any mention of having turned back to Mazatlán after first heading north.[33] The journey home was an eventful one. After crossing the Panamanian isthmus, he took passage in the navy brig *Perry*. Forty miles from Key West, the *Perry* became caught in a hurricane and was wrecked on a reef. The Sloats, father and son, were rescued and taken to Havana. They then traveled to New Orleans and then on to Washington, arriving in the capital on November 2.[34] By that time, George Bancroft had resigned as secretary of the navy to become the United States minister in London, and John Y. Mason had returned to head the Navy Department.[35]

Commodore Sloat had barely arrived home in New York when an article about him appeared in *Hunt's Merchants Magazine*. An anonymous "New York Merchant" authored a ten-page biography of Sloat, portraying him as the hero of the conquest of California. The *New York Daily Tribune* published an encapsulation of the magazine article. The *Merchant's Magazine* article seems to have provided the core of Edwin Sherman's 1902 biography. It contains claims of supposed kinship with Sir Francis Drake, the story of the Quasi-War service, lifelong friendship with Stephen Decatur, Sloat's role in the capture of the *Macedonian*, agreeing to spirit Napoleon Bonaparte out of France, capturing Roberto Cofresí, and the incident involving Vice President Antonio Gutiérrez de la Fuente in Callao. Possibly implying that the commodore supported the abolition of slavery, the article also stated that Sloat manumitted the twelve slaves that he supposedly inherited as a young man. There is no mention of turning back to Mazatlán after having sailed for Monterey.[36] This New York merchant must have known Sloat extremely well to write such a detailed article, but it seems likely that Sloat gave an interview of some sort if he did not actually ghostwrite it himself.

George Bancroft, by that time the former secretary of the navy, did not share the laudatory opinions that appeared in the New York magazine. He sent a number of letters to Sloat during the summer of 1846, none of which reached the commodore while he was on station in California. President Polk signed Congress's declaration of war on Mexico on May 13, and Bancroft immediately directed Sloat to carry out the orders of the June 24, 1845, letter. That shows that even Bancroft himself considered his earlier directive still in effect and not superseded by his October 17 letter that Gillespie had delivered. When he received Sloat's letter saying that, upon mature reflection, he had decided to await a more concrete indication that war had been declared, Bancroft became extremely agitated. He sent Sloat a blistering reprimand on August 13 that recounted each of his letters in the order that he wrote them and the dates that Sloat acknowledged receiving them. Bancroft took Sloat to task for detaching the *Constitution* and sending the frigate home and said that he hoped a valid reason for that would come to light. In closing, Bancroft's letter reads, "The Department ~~does not charge you with disobedience of orders. It~~ [crossed out in original] willingly believes in the purity of your intentions. But your anxiety to do no wrong, has led you into a most unfortunate and unwarranted inactivity." The words were lined out but remained legible for Sloat to read.[37] Bancroft appears to have wanted to express his anger and still be able to claim that he had not put it in official correspondence.

Even allowing for nineteenth-century styles of expression, Bancroft tried to speak out of both sides of his mouth in his directions to Sloat. This is especially true in the October 17, 1845, letter delivered by Gillespie, but is also evident in the earlier letter of which Sloat had received a paper copy from the Navy Department. Orders sent by the secretary of war to General Taylor on the Rio Grande contain similar words about the pacific intentions of the United States and its desire to settle peacefully its disputes with Mexico. The wording of Bancroft's letters must have been approved at some point by President Polk, so any responsibility for lack of clarity must be shared between the president and the secretary. Taylor was not to disturb Mexican forces unless an actual state of war existed.[38] No such quandary existed for Taylor, whose troops were attacked by Mexican forces after the general refused a demand to withdraw north of the Nueces River. Comments by Bancroft afterward indicate that he wanted Sloat to act most aggressively, but the actual wording of his orders left considerable room for hesitation. Bancroft sent the reprimand to Sloat and relieved him of command. Then he ordered Sloat to remain on station and to wait for Captain Shubrick to relieve him. Shubrick had already been ordered out to relieve Sloat, and he ended up taking over from Stockton after arriving on station in February 1847. One month later, Commodore James Biddle arrived in California and took over from Shubrick. Biddle was returning from a failed attempt to end the Tokugawa shogunate's self-isolation of Japan. Bancroft's flurry of letters was moot, of course, because Commodore Sloat was on his way home and did not receive any of them until later. The historian K. Jack Bauer has been sharply critical of both Sloat and Stockton, but he also writes with disdain of George Bancroft's performance as secretary of the navy. Once Polk got John Mason to agree to return to the Navy Department, he accepted Bancroft's resignation and sent him to London. In Bauer's words, Mason restored "stability and sanity of leadership" to the navy.[39]

Commodore John Drake Sloat however, cannot escape criticism. A careful analysis requires a bifurcation of the question. Let us first consider the delay of five days between anchoring in Monterey and demanding its surrender. The situation there was not as expected. Frémont and the Bear Flaggers had complicated the picture. Mexican forces lacked the strength to offer any meaningful resistance to United States invaders, and there was no way to get reinforcements to California even if Mexico City had been inclined to send them. Delaying the occupation on that account mattered not at all. The Pacific Squadron had sufficient forces on hand to occupy California at will. Waiting five days or even five weeks to hoist the United States flag would not have mattered with respect to the Mexican factors in the California situation.

The decision facing Sloat in Monterey thus boiled down to a matter of what to do about the Bear Flaggers, and what the British might do. The Bear Flaggers presented a problem, but they were not going to oppose an American occupation or annexation of California. But for Sloat to have acted without first learning from Commander Montgomery about the situation in San Francisco and Sonoma would have been imprudent. Raising the American flag in California before the British could intervene was important, and, not knowing that the British had no intentions of occupying it themselves, Sloat's decision to act on his fourth day in Monterey was well taken.

British policy aimed to deter the United States from an armed confrontation. The Royal Navy had enough strength in Halifax to threaten havoc by blockading United States port cities on the Atlantic and Gulf of Mexico coasts. The United States Navy would have had a difficult time defending the Atlantic coast against the British, even if its strength was in home waters and not deployed against Mexico. On the Pacific coast, Britain already had what it wanted. A naval base in Esquimalt on Vancouver Island protected the port city of Vancouver on the mainland. The British had the elements of a solid trade connection through Canada and then across the Pacific to China. An extensive commerce between both Great Britain and its Canadian colony continued with the United States just as it had in the preceding years.[40] British power in North America was a fundamental part of the international landscape. Commodore Sloat understood that, and so did President Polk and Secretary Bancroft even though they may have railed against it in public declarations. People in California understood it too. The Californiana (feminine form of Californio) resident Dorotea Váldez thought that while Sloat and Larkin held out hope for an uprising by Californios in favor of United States annexation, the commodore acted when he did out of concern that the British would arrive and wanted to present Admiral Seymour with a fait accompli.[41] In the end, the United States got what it wanted, Great Britain got what it wanted, Mexico got left out in the cold, and the Californios had just begun to suffer.

Now for the second part of the question. Sloat's false start in Mazatlán requires an entirely separate evaluation from his actions in Monterey. After sailing for California, he turned the *Savannah* around and headed back to Mazatlán to wait for more certain word if there was a war or not. It delayed his arrival in Monterey by probably five days: two days to return to Mazatlán, the one day spent there before leaving again, and then two more days to get back to where he had been. The situation probably would not have been much different had he arrived on June 27 instead of July 2. But Commodore Sloat did vacillate at that key juncture in time, and there is no way to escape from that particular accusation. Omitting it from his report suggests that Sloat wished he had not gone back to Mazatlán. Fear of making a mistake must have figured into his decision making. He knew well what consequences he would face for an error of rashness. There were plenty of examples, among them Porter, Mackenzie, Jones, and Voorhees.

Polk and Bancroft's optimistic hopes that the Californios would happily accept United States annexation turned out to have been misplaced. Consul Thomas Larkin earnestly hoped for it, and a Californio faction led by Mariano Guadalupe Vallejo favored it even after the Bear Flag revolt. Sloat and Larkin's attempt to maintain the prewar local government while merely changing the flag over the plaza came to naught. José Castro, in particular, was on the move from the very beginning, as was Pío Pico down in Los Angeles. What Sloat would have done had he remained in California is, of course, a counterfactual speculation best to be avoided. Centered mostly in the south, armed Californio resistance continued into early 1847, but that, too, is beyond the scope of a biography of John Drake Sloat.

CHAPTER FIFTEEN

Norfolk and Retirement

Commodore John Drake Sloat returned to Staten Island to await orders once again. Very soon, Abby's mother, Susan L'Hommedieu Gordon, died at New Brighton where she had been living with the Sloat family after Major James Gordon died in 1837. She was buried in Norwich.[1] Sloat was chosen in the summer of 1847 to sit on the examining board that evaluated midshipmen's readiness for promotion.

The site of the board had moved to Annapolis, Maryland, instead of at the Naval Asylum in Philadelphia. The shock of the hanging of Midshipman Philip Spencer aboard the *Somers* seems to have helped to overcome resistance by tradition-minded senior officers to creation of an academy for the navy like West Point. Even so, Secretary John Y. Mason objected that midshipmen could not be spared from ships to spend long periods at a naval school. Mason's objection corroborates the idea that midshipmen with years of experience were actual assets to their ships, and not merely trainee officers as they later became. After he succeeded Mason as secretary of the navy, George Bancroft's most memorable achievement during his tenure in that office was probably the founding of the Naval School in 1845. The school was located on the grounds of Fort Severn that Bancroft had acquired from the War Department. In these first years, the education and training of midshipmen did not radically change. Midshipmen came to Annapolis from the fleet for a course of study to prepare for their examinations as they had done in Philadelphia. Newly appointed midshipmen spent one year at Annapolis before going to ships of the fleet for three years and returning for a final finishing year and then examinations. Not until 1850 would the school be named the United States Naval Academy and implement a four-year program of instruction for midshipmen. In his discussion of Secretary John Y. Mason's opposition to the sort of school that his successor created, historian William P. Leeman finds that Bancroft chose the 1846 Board of Examiners very carefully to insure that it comprised only officers who supported the establishment of a naval academy.[2] By 1847, Bancroft had left Polk's cabinet and John Y. Mason was once again secretary of the navy. Despite his earlier opposition to creating a naval academy, Mason did not disestablish the school that Bancroft had created. He may not, however, have chosen a Board of Examiners so carefully calculated to support the school as Bancroft had done the year before.

As the senior officer assigned for the year 1847, Commodore Thomas ap Catesby Jones served as president of the board. Jones's biographer Gene A. Smith writes of the proceedings. Besides Sloat and Jones, other board members included Commodore Foxhall A. Parker, Captain Bladen Dulany, and Captain Hiram Paulding. The Naval School faculty administered examinations in gunnery, steam engineering, French, natural philosophy (i.e., science), mathematics, chemistry, and astronomy. The board of captains then reviewed the examination results, examined the midshipmen's cruise journals from their years at sea, and then subjected each young gentleman to an oral examination on practical seamanship. After adding an evaluation of personal character and financial indebtedness, the board recommended who would become passed midshipmen and who would not.[3] The actual examination process in 1847 appears a rather unsmooth one.

Historian Charles Todorich finds that a strong current of anti-intellectualism persisted among the navy officer corps and that led to a struggle over the very nature of the Naval School itself. Commander George Upshur had just replaced Franklin Buchanan as superintendent of the school and quickly found himself at odds with the instructional staff. The faculty included lieutenants, passed midshipmen, and professors. Controversies about the relative importance of different subjects contributed to the tension, but the faculty members also objected to restrictions that Upshur enforced upon them that they viewed as disrespectful. As long as a midshipman got high marks in seamanship and navigation, failures in French or even in mathematics did not result in dismissal. An Academic Board of faculty members had the task of conducting the faculty's portion of the examinations. The Academic Board voted to exclude the new superintendent from the examinations altogether, supposedly in the interests of the midshipmen examinees. The officers of the Board of Examiners retaliated by excluding the Academic Board from the process, again supposedly in the interests of the midshipmen. The Academic Board would ultimately prevail in implementing its reform agenda after Upshur left in 1850 and the Naval School was renamed as the United States Naval Academy. But in 1847, Secretary Mason supported Jones and the other captains on the Board of Examiners.[4] These actions of the examiners suggest that the path of progress did not always run smooth, and one is left with the impression that Thomas ap Catesby Jones, John Drake Sloat, and the other examiners may have been both jealous of officers' prerogatives and doubtful about the idea of creating a naval academy. Persons who have risen to the top often acquire a deep sense of loyalty to the system that validated and promoted them.

The proceedings of the board record that Sloat missed several days due to "indisposition." Captain Dulany also missed a day, and Jones took a day off to visit his family. After issues relating to academic subjects had been resolved, the oral examinations in seamanship began as the final phase of the process. At that point, Sloat attended each day. Each midshipman's seamanship examination seems to have taken about ninety minutes, during which he appeared in a room before the four officers. Fifty midshipmen's names had been presented to the Board of Examiners for 1847. Thirty-seven of them would pass. Twelve midshipmen failed at least one of the academic examinations, including two who failed all six of them. Three who failed the seamanship section were recommended for retention and reexamination the following year, and six others were recommended for outright dismissal. Midshipman James Waddell passed seamanship but failed several academic examinations, and the board recommended suspension of the examination so Waddell could try again in 1848. Waddell later achieved fame during the Civil War as commanding officer of the Confederate commerce raider *Shenandoah*.[5]

After leaving Annapolis, Commodore Sloat again returned to New York and awaited orders. They came a few months later. Secretary of the Navy Mason assigned him as commandant of the navy yard at Gosport. Located next to Portsmouth, Virginia, that installation today is called the Norfolk Naval Shipyard. As at the Portsmouth Navy Yard in Kittery, the Norfolk yard also served the functions of today's naval station, and the commandant held command responsibility over all naval units in the area. The naval station aspect of the New England yard amounted to comparatively little, but the Norfolk yard's position at the Atlantic entrance to Chesapeake Bay made it arguably the most important shore installation in the navy of that time.

Sloat relieved Commodore Lawrence Kearny on January 19, 1848. Kearny returned home to Perth Amboy, New Jersey, and actually served a term as mayor of that town while he waited for orders.[6] The 1850 federal census indicates that Abby Sloat's younger sister, Eliza Gordon, lived with them in the commandant's quarters, but the names of their own three children do not appear on the register. Jeanette lived in New York with her husband, their son, and their infant daughter. John Drake Sloat, Jr., then seventeen years old, may have stayed in the New York City area or perhaps went to school in Connecticut. Lewis Warrington Sloat may have already returned to California. In 1853, Lewis was a real estate broker and notary public in San Francisco. He would become the first corresponding secretary of the California Academy of Sciences and would serve as its curator of conchology.[7]

The Norfolk yard had more personnel assigned for duty than had the yard at Portsmouth. Besides Commodore Sloat in command, the officer staff included Commander Zachary Johnston and Lieutenants John Carter and John Ring, as well as two pursers, one surgeon, one chaplain, two sailing masters, two gunners, one boatswain, one carpenter, and one chaplain. It is interesting to note that no engineering officers or sailmakers appear on the 1848 Norfolk yard roster. Key civilian staff included Navy Agent George Loyall, Naval Storekeeper Merit Jordan, and Naval Constructor Samuel T. Hartt. The number of tradesmen employed varied with the work load as it had done at Portsmouth. In 1848, the Norfolk yard maintained seven ships in ordinary: ship of the line *Delaware*, frigates *Columbia* and *Constellation*, and sloops *Fairfield*, *Vandalia*, *Levant*, and *St. Louis.*[8]

Two other ships rounded out the fleet of hulls at the Norfolk yard. The *New York*, a seventy-four-gun ship of the line, had been laid down in 1820 and remained on the stocks in 1848. The *New York* hull would be burned on those same stocks in 1861 as yard personnel attempted to destroy anything of military value from falling into Confederate hands.

Construction of the steam frigate *Powhatan* was the most significant activity then at the Norfolk yard. *Powhatan* and the *Susquehanna* were then the second pair of United States Navy frigates propelled by steam-powered paddle wheels as well as a full set of square-rigged sails. Although screw-propelled frigates would soon advance steam technology even more, *Powhatan* and *Susquehanna* were the most advanced ships in the navy at that particular time. Addition of a thirty-eight thousand gallon storage tank for fresh water storage improved *Powhatan*'s range under steam over the earlier *Missouri* and *Mississippi*. *Powhatan*'s keel was laid in August 1847, and the yard launched the ship in September 1850. Final fitting out and commissioning did not finish up until September 1852. The engines and boilers came from a contracted supplier and would have been mounted in the ship prior to launch. The long duration of the construction period is not a surprise because installing a steam propulsion plant made constructing the *Powhatan* a considerably more complex task than building a ship with only masts, spars, and sails. The yard's industrial facilities required expansion to match the need for increased technical capabilities. Congress authorized substantial increases in the capacity of the yard, of its piers and wharves, and improvement of shop equipment capabilities that took place during Commodore Sloat's three years in command at Norfolk.[9]

Records from the Norfolk Navy Yard before 1861 were largely destroyed as navy and marine forces withdrew in the face of Confederate troops attacking the yard, so many documents of the sort that were collected during the twentieth century by the National Archives from other navy yards no longer exist in the case of Norfolk.[10] One document that did survive is the journal of daily transactions, which is analogous to a ship's log. The entries are terse and repetitive. The *Powhatan* was under construction. The yard's tradesmen placed ships in ordinary, maintained them for varying lengths of time in that inactivated status, and then prepared them to return to full service. Trades and wage rates are not specified, but the number of wage earners employed each day does appear for most of the time Sloat was in command. The navy yard typically employed about three hundred men, but that number dropped to about two hundred by January 1851. Of those, about fifty were black. At one point, the work of the black employees is identified. They worked in a mud drudge, were wagon drivers and stable keepers throughout the yard, and a small number worked as servants in the officers' quarters. The work week consisted of six days, and work stopped on Christmas, on federal and state election days, and if weather precluded it.[11] Sloat's years at Norfolk probably were very similar to his experiences at Kittery with personnel problems, procurement problems, and so on. Much future research is needed to develop our understanding of the navy yards as industrial enterprises. At the end of the usual three years in command, Sloat was relieved on February 17, 1851, by Captain Silas H. Stringham.[12]

In early 1850, the secretary of the navy in the Zachary Taylor administration, William B. Preston, sent a circular letter to the senior officers of the navy and asked their opinions on the sailors' grog ration and corporal punishment. Calls for social reform had gained increasing public sway in the United States as the nineteenth century progressed. Movements for the abolition of slavery, for equal suffrage and rights for women, and temperance groups stand out in the historical memory of the antebellum United States. Out of the same philosophical roots arose a campaign to abolish the daily grog ration of navy sailors and to prohibit the flogging of sailors as punishment for various crimes and infractions. Such punishments became increasingly seen as barbaric despotism, if not outright sadism. Calls to abolish flogging went hand-in-hand with the ill-fated naval apprentice program and a desire to recruit native-born Americans into warship crews instead of the foreigners that then predominated. But as historian Myra Glenn emphasizes, the campaign against flogging represented just one aspect of a reformed vision of how society ought to work.[13]

Secretary Preston hailed from Virginia and would later draft that state's secession ordnance from the Union. Most likely he was proslavery and in favor of corporal punishment. One might suspect that he meant to arm himself for a political battle over naval flogging with opinions from the officers who had to command navy ships and administer naval discipline. Historian Harold Langley finds that among the eighty-four replies on file, only seven favored abolishing flogging and two of those came from naval surgeons. Three captains wrote in favor of outlawing the colt and the cat-of-nine-tails: David Conner, Isaac McKeever, and Robert Stockton, who resigned his commission later that year and won a seat as a United States senator from New Jersey. Stockton immediately introduced a bill that outlawed flogging and it passed into law.[14]

Sloat wrote to Preston and argued that the navy could not dispense with corporal punishment. Good men had nothing to fear, he contended, because only troublemakers ever felt the lash of the whip. Emphasizing that "[we] cannot reform all mankind," Sloat declared that the navy must accept sailors as they are, with their peculiar dispositions, instead of how one might wish them to be. He declared that he had never known any abuse of corporal punishment under the extant regulations. Sloat argued that stopping the grog ration was an effective punishment, and so abolishing it would be a bad idea. He felt that a money substitute for the spirits ration would get better results.[15]

The logs from the *Grampus* and the *St. Louis* under Sloat's command record just one and four instances, respectively, where sailors were flogged. Those logs cover a period of about five years. Historian Langley finds that Matthew C. Perry resorted to the lash rather frequently while in command of the sloop *Concord*. Samuel Eliot Morison earlier defended Perry on that particular score. Perry had transported John Randolph to St. Petersburg to take up his post as U.S. minister to Russia, and Randolph had decried, in a letter to President Andrew Jackson, Perry's flogging of four sailors during the two months in transit. Morison also notes that while in command of the *Mississippi*, Perry had fifteen men flogged over a period of three months at the end of 1846. One could find far worse than that. Over a twenty-one-month period beginning in 1846, an average of five floggings per week took place on board the frigate *United States.*[16] Possibly floggings went unrecorded in Sloat's log, but it seems unlikely for an officer so punctilious about conforming to regulations and administrative requirements.

One member of the *Savannah* crew remembered it differently. Charles Byrnes was the frigate's sailmaker in 1846. The semi-centennial celebrations of the United States' conquest of California gave occasion to a number of newspaper articles in 1896. Byrnes stated that Commodore Sloat was quick to have a sailor flogged, and without bothering to investigate fully the circumstances. He recalled a botched rendering of honors to a foreign dignitary, although he did not say in which port it happened. The sailor in charge of the saluting gun crew told the first lieutenant that the gun was not yet ready because the tompion (muzzle plug) was still in the muzzle. The first lieutenant heard incorrectly and so gave the order to fire The sailor fired when ordered, and the exploding powder charge propelled the tompion in the direction of the official's boat. Byrnes said that Sloat gave the sailor a choice between apologizing to the lieutenant or receiving twelve lashes. The sailor, a sixty-five-year-old veteran of the Tripolitan campaigns, chose the flogging and afterward berated the lieutenant for the treatment. The sailor was then sent to the brig. Byrnes said that in the navy, sailors followed the commands of officers no matter what.[17] Let us suspend credulity for the moment and assume that a sailor would actually take twelve lashes rather than simply apologize to an officer, even if the sailor thought the officer actually bore all the blame. This author does not condone flogging at all, but the sailor deserved disciplinary action. He must have known that the unsafe action could pose a risk to life and limb, but he went ahead anyway and afterward tried to shift the blame by saying he was only following an officer's orders. Like other "I was there" stories that appeared in the newspaper, Byrnes's recollections elsewhere in that story do not always match the documented records. But something like the events Byrnes described probably did take place, and he was probably not the only one in the ship that disliked the commodore. One can easily imagine Commodore Sloat being in a rage at such a mishap.

Sloat used corporal punishment very infrequently himself, but at the same time he saw it as an essential tool of shipboard discipline. One should keep in mind that he grew up in a slave-owning family. His statement about accepting Jack Tar as he actually was instead of how one might wish him to be is a telling one that comports with his actions during the preceding decades. John Drake Sloat seems profoundly satisfied with the status quo and accepted things as they were without much question. He was not one to "rock the boat."

Commodore Sloat found himself summoned from Norfolk to Washington to serve on yet another important court-martial. Secretary of the Navy William A. Graham brought charges against Commodore Thomas ap Catesby Jones. After the Annapolis examining board had finished its annual business, Jones went back for another tour in command of the Pacific Squadron and relieved Commodore William B. Shubrick in 1848. Jones based most of the squadron in San Francisco throughout the chaotic early months of the California gold rush. Recalled by the secretary of the navy to Washington, Jones faced charges stemming from three issues.

Desertion became a huge problem after the discovery of gold in the American River, and the measures taken to prevent it led to a serious decline in morale among officers and sailors alike. Things came to a head when five sailors from the *Ewing* threw overboard the midshipman in charge of their boat and then headed for the gold fields. The five were recaptured and tried by court-martial. Jones approved death sentences by hanging for two and reduced those of the remaining three to one hundred lashes each. Allegations of mistreatment of junior officers by Jones lay at the heart of another set of accusations. Three lieutenants complained that Jones had falsely maligned them as "tainted by gold fever," and that the commodore had "oppressed" another lieutenant, Fabius Maximus Stanly, by withholding for a time a verdict of acquittal by a court-martial before which that lieutenant had been tried. Furthermore, Jones took personal control from squadron pursers of the Military Contribution Fund. This fund consisted of monies surrendered to the squadron by Mexican customs officials to indemnify claims against Mexico at the end of the recently concluded war. Jones used the cash to buy gold dust at a low price in California that he later sold to the U.S. Mint in Philadelphia and made a profit of eight thousand dollars. Jones also stood accused of submitting bogus statements of accounts to hide from authorities his handling of those funds. Jones faced a total of five charges with several specifications.[18]

Two specifications of the oppression charge related to Lieutenant Stanly and a third that Commodore Jones had illegally convened the court-martial that sentenced two sailors to hang. Jones defended himself against the third specification with a claim that he was on a foreign station because Congress had not made California either a state or a territory. Given the membership of the court, that seems an interesting maneuver since Sloat had formally proclaimed annexation two years before. But the validity of Sloat's proclamation was by then moot. Mexico had ceded sovereignty over California by signing the Treaty of Guadalupe Hidalgo in February 1848. The United States Senate ratified the treaty in March 1848 and the Mexican legislature did so two months later. Jones learned about the terms of the treaty while in Mazatlán in June. California was then administered according to Mexican law as an occupied territory before admission as a state in 1850, but it was not Mexican territory. The change in sovereignty had been completed. However flimsy Jones's argument that he was on a foreign station could have been taken, the court accepted the defense and exonerated Jones on that specification. Article XLI of the Rules and Regulations for the Government of the United States Navy then in effect reads,

> All sentences of courts martial, which shall extend to loss of life, shall require the concurrence of two thirds of the members present, and no such sentence shall be carried into execution, until confirmed by the President of the United States; or if the trial take place out of the United States, until it be confirmed by the commander of the fleet or squadron . . .[19]

Both Sloat and a second member, Commodore John Downes, had sat on the Mackenzie court-martial, which had decided not to convict that defendant on a similar matter. As for the oppression of Lieutenant Stanly, Jones never seems to have addressed those particulars but claimed that he had given the lieutenant a transfer to a better job in the squadron. The court convicted Jones on those two specifications.

Another charge was scandalous conduct that destroyed good morals. One specification was that he had maligned in writing the other three lieutenants mentioned earlier, and the other two specifications related to the handling of the public monies. A charge of neglect of duty consisted of four specifications, all related to those monies: neglectfully removing money from pursers' control and failure to provide proper accounts when requested by the Navy Department. The court convicted Jones of these charges and specifications.

The court found the remaining two charges not proven. Those charges were for fraud, and for attempting a fraud, against the United States. In a careful analysis of the charges and specifications, historian Gene Smith notes that Jones's actions may have been unsavory but they were not actually illegal because no regulations required him to act otherwise. Smith also points out that not only did Secretary Graham issue the charges, but he also acted as prosecutor during the trial. As secretary, he would have to approve the court's verdict. Graham had one of the three accusing lieutenants act as an assistant prosecutor during the trial. Commodore Jones viewed the court-martial as an attack by his enemies. Smith highlights inconsistencies in the verdicts and concludes that "Jones was innocent when considering the letter of the law yet guilty in the eyes of his judges." The historian Robert Erwin Johnson contends that Jones played fast and loose with cash and with the rules. In his study of United States Navy discipline, historian James Valle takes an even more disapproving interpretation and finds outright peculation in Jones's actions.

The court sentenced Jones to suspension from the service for five years, the first two and a half to be without pay.[20]

A different, but still tentative, interpretation of the trial outcome follows: The court-martial that tried Commodore Jones consisted of the following officers, only one of whom does not appear elsewhere in this essay. They were Charles Stewart presiding, Lewis Warrington, John Downes, Henry Ballard, William B. Shubrick, Lawrence Kearny, John D. Sloat, and Matthew C. Perry. They awarded Jones a very harsh sentence indeed, but they could have given him an even harsher one. The issues relating to the four aggrieved lieutenants do not seem to justify suspension from the service, and so the misappropriation of funds seems to have been the true heart of the matter. The court could have easily convicted Commodore Jones of fraud because he took the government's money for personal profit and even admitted that he had done so. But conviction of the fraud and attempted fraud charges was unnecessary since the neglect charges were judged to be proven. Furthermore, conviction of outright fraud against the United States government might have obligated the court to award Jones a sentence of permanent dismissal from the navy instead of "mere" suspension. Recall from an earlier chapter that after the *Franklin* cruise under Commodore Stewart's command, Lieutenant William Weaver had been convicted of financial irregularities and dismissed from the navy. The commodores on the court perhaps gave Jones what they thought he deserved, essentially choosing the crimes to fit the punishment. Historian Ira Dye, who, like this author, served a full career as a U.S. Navy officer and thus could share certain biases, cuts to the core of the matter: in the antebellum navy, courts-martial were not about justice but about maintaining discipline.[21] In 1850, there may not yet have been a specific rule against Jones's appropriating public money for his own profit in commodity transactions, but that was not how the navy wanted its officers to behave. The commodores on the court probably felt that should have been obvious to Jones.

The Jones court-martial verdict was handed down on February 1, 1851, and Sloat returned to the Norfolk yard just in time for the end of his three years in command there. Sloat returned to New York and his Staten Island home to await new orders.[22]

Chosen in January 1852 to preside over a board that evaluated sites for a navy yard on the West Coast, Sloat headed back to California and spent much of the year there. The board ended up consisting of Sloat, Commander William S. Ogden, Lieutenant Simon Blunt, and Engineer William P. S. Sanger. President Fillmore had earlier reserved Mare Island for government purposes. The island lies in northeast San Pablo Bay, just to the north of the Carquinez Strait through which pass the rivers draining the Sacramento and San Joaquín valleys toward the Golden Gate. The board considered Mare Island to be a favorable location for a navy yard and drew up the plans for siting the original docks and buildings before returning east. The land purchase was completed in January 1853, and the Mare Island Navy Yard opened in 1854 under the command of Commander David G. Farragut.[23]

At the outset of Sloat's visit to California, son-in-law James Bayard Whittemore died in New York of erysipelas, an aggressive skin disease usually caused by a streptococcus infection. He left behind widowed Jeanette and their two children, James Bayard Whittemore, Junior (1840–1898), and toddler Jeanette Sloat Whittemore (b. 1849).[24] Two years after Whittemore's death, his widowed mother Jane sued John Drake Sloat. Recall that the Whittemores were a very wealthy family that possessed a wide range of business interests and also a substantial amount of Man-

Figure 15.1. *U.S. Navy Yard at Mare Island, California*, 1855. (Courtesy of the Library of Congress.)

hattan property. When Samuel Whittemore died in 1835, he appears to have left Jane a life interest in his estate. Jane Whittemore would be protected for the rest of her life, but the real estate was encumbered and could not be sold or transferred until she died and it had passed to the heirs named in Samuel's will. Soon thereafter, Jane went to court and got the life estate changed so that the properties could be divided up between herself and her ten children. Jane was guaranteed an annual income of four hundred dollars from each of the land parcels that went to the children. James Bayard Whittemore got two of those parcels of land. James later borrowed money from his father-in-law, using one of the parcels as collateral for the mortgage. When James did not make his payment, Sloat foreclosed on his son-in-law's property and took title to it. He also then designated himself as the insurance beneficiary on that property instead of Jane. After James died, Jane Whittemore sued John Drake Sloat and asserted a life estate interest in the property, which would mean that title could not be transferred. She also claimed back rent on the property. In April 1854, Sloat won before a New York appellate court. Justice James John Roosevelt (granduncle of President Theodore Roosevelt) ruled that Jane could not assert both a life estate and a lien, because those were mutually exclusive. Sloat got the title, Whittemore got her lien, and Roosevelt directed Sloat to restore Whittemore as the insurance beneficiary. Representing Sloat before the court was prominent New York lawyer and politician John McKeon (1801–1883), whom Sloat had once appointed as judge advocate for a court-martial.[25]

One month later Jeanette Eliza Sloat Whittemore married John McKeon. Perhaps displeasure over the impending remarriage of her widowed daughter-in-law precipitated Jane Whittemore's lawsuit. Especially popular among Irish Catholics, McKeon at that time served as the United States Attorney for the Southern District of New York, which obviously did not in those days preclude his taking private cases in state court. He had recently been the district attorney for New York (i.e., Manhattan), a New York state legislator, and served twice in the U.S. House of Representatives during 1835–1837 and 1841–1843. One must exercise great caution in equating in any way the political views of persons who happen to be members of the same family. As a state legislator in Albany, McKeon actively supported two of the most important actions of Andrew Jackson's presidency. He endorsed Jackson's veto of the bill to renew the charter of the Second Bank of the United States, and he supported Jackson's actions against South Carolina during the nullification crisis. Recall that years earlier, Sloat declared himself to be a staunch supporter of Jackson. McKeon was a long-standing antagonist of Fernando Wood, who once accused McKeon of secretly aiding abolitionists when they were both in Congress. McKeon's and Wood's differences with each other perhaps centered more on individual ambition than on political philosophy, as they seem to have scrambled for the same ideological turf. When New York Democrats split into two factions, McKeon remained with the conservative "Hunkers" who refrained from challenging Southerners favoring the expansion of slavery. Hunkers themselves later split into "Hard" and "Soft" factions, with the former opposing readmission to party ranks of antislavery Democrats who bolted to the Free Soil Party in the 1848 presidential election. McKeon sided with the Hards and survived considerable local opposition to Franklin Pierce's choosing him as U.S. Attorney. During the Civil War, Sloat stood with the War Democrats. Son-in-law McKeon led one faction of Peace Democrats, or Copperheads, who doubted Democratic presidential nominee George McLellan's willingness to pursue an immediate armistice and peace negotiations with the Confederacy.[26]

Commodore Sloat returned to Washington from California, where in November 1852 he reported the results of the Mare Island siting board. He stayed in the Willard's Hotel, located then as now one block away from the White House. Also at Willard's just then was old shipmate and friend Matthew C. Perry.[27] "Old Bruin" was in Washington preparing to lead the expedition to open commerce and diplomacy with Japan, and the two doubtless discussed it among themselves. Sloat returned to New York and took over Perry's job as what the official naval register vaguely labels "general superintendence" of U.S. mail steamers operating out of New York and elsewhere. In February 1853, Sloat traveled to Alexandria, Virginia, for the arrival of the mail steamer *Ericson*. He joined a large entourage that included President Pierce, two cabinet members, several members of Congress, and two other navy commodores.[28] Lawrence Kearny had the duty in the 1854 register, and it then passed to Captain Charles H. Bell. Several American shipping lines operated steamships to Panama and European ports, and these companies depended heavily upon the mail revenues for profitability. Congress had authorized subsidies for the construction of paddlewheel steamships for transoceanic service, with the caveat that the ships should be convertible to warships when required. The convertibility requirement for the ships whose construction had been subsidized by Congress brought the navy into the picture. The demands of this "special duty" assignment upon the captains who held it must have been minimal, but it did mean a year at full pay instead of awaiting orders. The Post Office Department administered the actual mail subsidies, and the shipping lines ran their ships themselves. The Navy Department's direct interest extended only to ensuring that the companies were maintaining the ships in a condition from which they could be converted for war service if so demanded.

Transatlantic mail service companies connected Havre, Bremen, and Liverpool with New York. Service to Panama and the isthmus railroad connected with California service on the Pacific side. The mail steamship companies were only marginally profitable even in the best of years and would have failed immediately but for the heavy U.S. government subsidies. The largest was the New York & Liverpool United States Mail Steamship Company, more commonly known as the Collins Line. The Collins Line's SS *Arctic* was lost at sea on September 27, 1854, with considerable loss of life off Newfoundland after colliding with a French steamer, the *Vesta*. Each ship was making more than ten knots speed in a heavy fog. Unlike the French steamer that made port afterward, the *Arctic* did not have watertight compartmentation and so foundered from uncontrollable flooding while the captain made for Newfoundland. The navy's direct role did not extend to supervising the navigation of commercial ships, but the loss of the *Arctic* became a subject of discussion in the maritime world. Perry published a number of public suggestions for improvement of safety at sea after the tragedy. Another Collins Line mail steamer disappeared in the Atlantic a little more than one year later. The line went bankrupt and the mail subsidies to all the shipping lines soon ended.[29]

After his year in the mail steamer assignment, Sloat continued on special duty for two more years, this time in an assignment that perhaps required a little more involvement. He acted as the navy representative superintending the construction of the Stevens battery. His years in command of the Portsmouth and Norfolk navy yards during years of active shipbuilding made him a good choice to inspect the contractor's progress in building a U.S. Navy ship. Never actually completed, the Stevens battery was to have been a steam-powered ironclad gunship also equipped with a ram on the bow below the waterline. The designers conceived of the ship as an augment to New York's harbor defenses and so its comparatively small coal storage capacity limited the range of operation. Fears of war with Britain in 1841 over Canadian boundary questions led to approval of Robert and Edwin Stevens's original design for such a ship, but the project soon languished for lack of funds after that war threat subsided. The ship even as originally envisioned was so much larger and more complex than anything afloat that it required the Stevens brothers first to build the construction facilities before they could get on with the hull itself. Contract disputes with the Navy Department followed. Secretary George Bancroft stopped construction completely in December 1845, but John Y. Mason soon restarted it when he took office. Progress was slow, and Secretary William Preston again halted construction in 1849.

From his seat in the U.S. Senate, Robert F. Stockton took an interest in the project and pushed an appropriation through Congress. In 1854, the Stevens brothers designed an even larger version of the battery and

THE STEVENS BOMB-PROOF BATTERY AS IT WILL APPEAR WHEN COMPLETED.

Figure 15.2 The Stevens Battery as conceived in 1861. (Courtesy of the Photo Collection, Naval History and Heritage Command.)

construction began at the dock they had built in Hoboken, New Jersey. Advances in artillery beyond the Paixhans guns necessitated greater armor protection for the ship than had been required ten years before. The increased weight in turn required a hull displacing more water in order to remain afloat. This new design would have resulted in a ship displacing more than four thousand tons and exceeding four hundred feet in length, larger than anything that the navy would have until the end of the nineteenth century. The ship was to have no sails or masts and two propellers at the stern instead of side paddle wheels for propulsion. Construction moved along for two years and as many as five hundred laborers worked on the ship at a time. One of the Stevens brothers died in 1856, and the futuristic but expensive ship languished on the ways for years thereafter.[30] The Stevens battery seems to have been in one way a ship ahead of its time, but at the same time it was a design that had difficulty keeping up with the rapid advances in firepower that were being made. Added to its problems was the limited range for a ship intended essentially as a mobile coast artillery battery for the approaches to New York harbor. Improvements in artillery range extended the coverage of coastal forts and somewhat obviated the need for a ship like the Stevens battery. When the navy did build ships of that size decades later, they were meant for power projection, and harbor defense was left to the army's coast artillery corps.

By the middle of the 1850s, the United States Navy officer corps had become clogged with older officers that blocked the professional advancement and promotion of younger ones. That problem had already developed when John Drake Sloat was promoted to captain in 1837, twenty-two years after James Biddle, whose original midshipman warrant had the same date as Sloat's. The situation got much worse after 1842 when Congress froze the allowed numbers of captains and commanders at the current levels. No system of retirement existed at all. George Bancroft tried in 1845 to implement a board to select officers for promotion based on merit, but its members defied him and the idea went on the shelf. Promotion hopes had become a matter of waiting for someone to die when James C. Dobbin, secretary of the navy in the Franklin Pierce administration, succeeded in getting Congress to pass a solution in 1855. A board would convene to review all of the officers in the navy and then recommend that some of them be removed from the active rolls.

The board had four choices: to continue the officer on the active rolls, to drop the officer from the navy altogether, to place the officer in a reserved status with the pay of one on leave, or to place him in a reserved status at furlough pay, which was half of leave pay.

Commodore William B. Shubrick headed what became known as the Naval Efficiency Board, and Matthew C. Perry was one of the other four captains on it. Of the sixty-three captains in the navy, only twenty-eight would remain on the active list. Seventeen were reserved at leave pay, fifteen more were reserved at furlough pay, and three were dropped. A public hue and cry followed in the press, and the enabling law allowed for an appeals process that many officers used. A fair number of reversals resulted as the procedure dragged on for more than a year, but the results went into effect in early 1857. Of the captains, the final tally came to twenty-one reserved at leave pay, seven at furlough pay, and one remained dropped. For a captain, leave pay amounted to $2,500 per year, which was still more than an active duty commander received.[31] The board placed Sloat on the reserved list. It must have rankled. Antebellum naval officers certainly wore their pride on their sleeves, and like the others, Sloat could be prickly when he perceived a slight. But given his age and the precept of the Efficiency Board, he cannot have been shocked when he learned that he had been placed on the reserved list.

Sloat continued to live on Staten Island and enjoyed continuing recognition as a prominent New Yorker. His comings and goings were sometimes published in the newspapers. He had attended the inauguration in 1853 of the Crystal Palace along with Generals Winfield Scott and John E. Wool, both also of fame in the war against Mexico. President Franklin Pierce had journeyed from Washington to preside at the affair. John and Abby Sloat later numbered among the luminaries attending a gala, grand ball at Manhattan's Metropolitan Hotel. He served on a committee of New Brighton residents hoping for the relocation of New York's quarantine anchorage down to Sandy Hook out of fear of yellow fever breaking out from ships arriving from the West Indies. The funeral for Commodore Matthew C. Perry was a major civic event in New York City. Sloat and Scott both marched on March 6, 1858, as honorary pallbearers for the hero of the Japan expedition.[32]

The outbreak of the Civil War in 1861 found the eighty-year-old Sloat still at home on Staten Island. A few of the younger, but still superannuated, naval officers on the reserved list would serve the Union cause in various temporary capacities, but Sloat was not one of them. Biographer Sherman states that Sloat maintained an active interest in the war's progress and particularly in the actions of officers who had earlier served with him. To blockade the Confederacy required an expansion of the U.S. Navy to a size hitherto unknown, and Congress finally recognized that the incumbents in important and large commands should hold flag rank as rear admirals and commodores. That had been the practice in other navies and had often led to problems on foreign stations for American squadron commanders. But Congress had repeatedly refused from the founding of the United States Navy to create any admiral rank even though the army had generals. Congressmen seemed to believe that the title "Admiral" smacked of nobility and was therefore inappropriate for a democratic republic's institutions. In the summer of 1862, however, reason finally prevailed. Congress authorized rear admirals as equivalent to major generals, and commodores as a rank equal to brigadier generals. Captains were aligned equally with colonels no matter how long they had been in grade, and commanders became equal to lieutenant colonels instead of majors. The rank of lieutenant commander was created and was made equal to major. Congress also provided for the promotion of some officers on the retired list. In recognition of those who had served in the navy but never had a chance for promotion beyond captain, the navy received authorization to nominate nine rear admirals and eighteen commodores from the retired list.[33]

The retired flag officer list appeared almost immediately, with dates of rank fixed at July 16, 1862. John Drake Sloat was on the list of eighteen commodore selectees. When he found out that nine other retired officers had been selected for rear admiral instead of himself, Sloat lost no time in protesting. Bypassing completely Secretary of the Navy Gideon Welles, Sloat penned a five-page letter to President Abraham Lincoln, who as chief executive formally nominated the advisory board's selectees to the Senate for confirmation. The selection list would certainly have passed first through the office of Secretary Welles. Sloat complained that some of the rear admiral selectees were junior to him and then went on to summarize the highlights of his own navy career, which would be supported by the records of the Navy Department. He pointed out that he took possession of California "<u>uninstructed</u>" and claimed that he thereby outfoxed the British admiral. He emphasized his successful cruises in command of the *Grampus* and the *St. Louis*, his actions that prevented the loss of the *Congress*, and, of course, his role and the minor wound that he received in the capture of the *Macedonian*. He also emphasized that he had never been tried by court-martial nor been the subject of any formal discipline at any time in his many years of naval service.[34] That statement, in particular, highlights the very high level of personal concern that Sloat had about facing disciplinary actions.

Interestingly, Sloat stated that "as a proof that I had served faithfully and possessed sufficient capacity for my profession I was retained in Service at the reduction of the Navy in 1801." One wonders how Sloat could make such a claim, since in fact the navy did not retain him as a midshipman when making the reductions required by the Peace Establishment Act. Perhaps he never received a letter formally revoking his midshipman warrant. He may very well have kept his warrant with him when sailing as a merchant shipmaster in the West Indies and to Europe in the years from 1801 to 1812, and it might have served him well against any British impressment demands. He could perhaps claim that until he acknowledged the revocation of his warrant, then he was still a midshipman even though he received no pay and had no duty assignment. But just as it had been with the matter of Simón Bolívar in Guayaquil, for Sloat to claim that he had really been in the navy all those years that he was absent from duty seems at least a major stretch and, at worst, an outright attempt to deceive the president. Any reply from President Lincoln does not survive in the historical record, but Sloat's letter would have arrived in Washington during the first week of August 1862. The Army of the Potomac was repositioning after being defeated at Cedar Mountain, Virginia, and a major squabble of command raged between Generals George McClellan, Henry Halleck, and John Pope.[35] The commander in chief probably had more pressing matters on his mind than the complaints of an affronted octogenarian on the navy retired list.

The reasons behind the board's choices for retired rear admirals remain obscure. Possibly the board members passed over Sloat as a sort of rebuke if they perceived his actions at Mazatlán and Monterey as timid and indecisive. But if that were clearly the case, then they could have just as easily justified to themselves leaving him off the commodore list as well. A detailed analysis of the careers of the nine rear admiral selectees is far beyond the scope of this essay, and several of them are not widely known names today. But a superficial review of them shows accomplishments that could justify the selection of each one of those captains.[36] Had Sloat remained in command in California for a longer period and played a role in vanquishing the Californio resistance that emerged some weeks after he left Monterey, then perhaps he might have been among the nine. Another conceivable explanation lies in the politics of Sloat's prominent son-in-law. Opposition to Lincoln's war policies emerged among "Peace Democrats" who came to be known as "Copperheads" after the poison-

Figure 15.3. Rear Admiral John Drake Sloat, 1866. Albumen print by Tonkin Photo. Sloat is wearing the uniform of a rear admiral following his promotion on the retired list. (Courtesy of the California Historical Society, CHS2015.1988.)

ous snake species. Even by the summer of 1862, John McKeon was a vocal Copperhead and strident critic of President Lincoln and Republican policies throughout the Civil War.[37] Steeped thoroughly in the favoritism and institutional politics of the antebellum United States Navy, the board members may have been reluctant to risk presenting to Welles and Lincoln a selectee with connections to prominent antiwar politicians. The navy officer corps had hoped for decades that flag grades would be authorized, and the board may not have wanted to do anything that might cost the navy that long-sought prize just as it was finally within reach. The senior officers in the navy were a small group of men who had long known each other and Sloat's connection to McKeon would have been known. But once again, the board could just as easily have left Sloat off the commodore list for the Copperhead connection too.

McKeon's Copperhead positions notwithstanding, John D. Sloat's name appears along with George Bancroft's among the Democrat signatories supporting the Lincoln-Johnson presidential ticket in 1864, so perhaps the commodore bore no particular ill will for Lincoln himself. Sloat would have understood that the president acted upon the recommendations of subordinates and would not have played a personal role in the board's deliberations and decisions. After the war ended, Secretary Welles continued in office under President Andrew Johnson and returned to the matter of the retired rear admiral list. Any retired officer who had ever held a squadron command was nominated for promotion to rear admiral. Congress approved, and Sloat was promoted to rear admiral effective August 6, 1866.[38]

Conclusions

Rear Admiral John Drake Sloat's path to the highest rungs of the United States Navy did not follow a "rags-to-riches" trajectory. He did end up as a well-connected, well-to-do, and well-respected New Yorker. He certainly bettered himself over the course of his years through prudent real estate purchases and other investments, where he profited from the rise of New York City during the pre–Civil War decades. But he did not start out on the lowest rung of society. His birth into a minor gentry family gave him an advantageous starting position. John Drake Sloat practically exuded "establishment" from every pore. He did have an Irish Catholic son-in-law, but that congressman and prominent attorney was no poor paddy from the bog.

Contemporary assessments of John Drake Sloat by persons who knew him are few. Charles Wilkes called him a "grandmother[ly]" excuse for a naval officer, but Wilkes's autobiography is tantrum-like in its attacks on dozens of individuals. Samuel Du Pont had served with Sloat aboard the *Congress* as well as in California. Du Pont remembered Sloat as a "fine old gentleman" when writing of his 1846 experiences. Du Pont also spoke highly of officers as different as Commodores Robert F. Stockton, William B. Shubrick, and James Biddle, all of whom commanded the Pacific Squadron during the war with Mexico. Sailmaker Charles Byrnes recalled that the crew of the *Savannah* was happy to see him leave the ship in Monterey. Perhaps the most enlightening observation came from novelist James Fenimore Cooper, who had known Sloat rather well for a long time. Cooper wrote to Captain William B. Shubrick, his friend and shipmate from their own midshipman days on the *Wasp* before the War of 1812:

> As respects the Pacific Squadron, we are of the same mind. In the event of a war with Mexico, it will be the most responsible station afloat, and the most desirable one for a man capable of its high trusts as they should be. How far the present incumbent [Sloat] is that man, you know as well as I do. He will do better than half who have commanded in that remote sea, but one would not send him at a time such as this.[1]

Pleased with the news reports from California, Cooper met Sloat in January 1847 and wrote to Shubrick that Sloat gave a "very sensible account of his proceedings."[2]

In many ways, John Drake Sloat personified the navy's strengths and weaknesses as an institution. First and foremost, Sloat was as good a seaman as any of his fellow officers and probably much better than most of them. That competence, however, probably resulted not so much from navy training but from his early practical experience in the merchant marine.

Given his experiences at sea, Sloat could not have lacked physical courage. Sailing a schooner in a storm-tossed, pirate-infested sea; conning a large frigate in a ship-to-ship duel in the middle of the Atlantic; or saving a ship from foundering during a hurricane, all were crisis tactical situations that called for swift, decisive, and competent action by the officer at the scene. Commanding a widely dispersed squadron in a more slowly developing strategic situation fraught with diplomatic peril required a much different set of skills. Sloat had been in that kind of situation as well. As the senior American officer in Callao, he handled delicate diplomatic situations, coordinated carefully with American diplomats, and earned official praise for his actions. His success in capturing the pirate Roberto Cofresí also stemmed in part from cooperation with authorities ashore in Puerto Rico and in St. Thomas. Unless an urgent situation required immediate action, one would expect him to consult and to coordinate with Consul Thomas O. Larkin in Monterey. Those consultations would take some time.

But within the navy, Sloat tended to keep his own counsel and tried to avoid situations where he worked for others. He turned down a frigate command for that very reason and took a shore command instead. He could be officious, and he seems to have been rather hard-nosed. As navy yard commandant, his letters replying to complaints from civilian contractors could be brusque to the point of dismissiveness. He wrote to Consul Larkin in 1846 that none of the officers in the Pacific Squadron knew what their commodore intended to do, and not until the final day before the landing did he consult with the subordinate officers in his squadron.[3] In today's vernacular, the term "control freak" seems to fit Sloat. On the other hand, he did get along with opposing factions among his peers. Sloat maintained good relations with both Matthew Calbraith Perry and James Fenimore Cooper during the years of their intense and public feud over Jesse Duncan Elliott's actions in the Battle of Lake Erie.

The navy encouraged the prickly sense of personal honor that its officers so frequently exhibited. Sloat was no exception on that account. He complained loud and quickly when he felt slighted in duty assignments. He must have felt pangs of jealousy when he saw his friend Matthew Calbraith Perry get assignments ahead of himself, but he always did get his turn in the end: commandant of a navy yard, command of a major squadron, and then as commandant of a bigger navy yard. John Drake Sloat was very much a stickler on matters of status and precedence, which comes as no surprise given the hierarchical structure of any navy.

Time and again, Sloat had seen senior naval officers tried by courts-martial for rash actions. Commodore Thomas ap Catesby Jones escaped court-martial after his blunder at Monterey in 1842, but he suffered disgrace nonetheless. Commodore David Porter was court-martialed and dismissed from the navy after his actions in Fajardo. Commander Alexander Slidell Mackenzie may not have been convicted by his court-martial, but he did not escape with an unsullied reputation. Captain Philip Voorhees acted on his own to suppress what he thought were acts of piracy and ended up dismissed from the navy. Fear of a trial by court-martial played an important part in maintaining discipline among the navy's officer corps, just as fear of the cat-of-nine-tails maintained discipline among the navy's sailors. Recall Sloat's pride in never having been tried when he wrote to President Lincoln to protest having been chosen for advancement to commodore instead of rear admiral on the retired list.

John Drake Sloat was also a stickler on administrative matters and a "by the book" officer. He was careful with paperwork. Looking through reel after reel of microfilmed Navy Department correspondence, one senses that Sloat was a bit more so than most of his peers. Some officers are like that. That tendency also appears clearly in the shipping reports that appeared in newspapers during Sloat's years in the merchant marine. Those reports frequently published information that he gave the newspapers about voyage conditions, and Sloat seems to have been an exception among merchant skippers on that score. He certainly did couch his official letters in terms most favorable to himself and sometimes conveniently omitted a thing or two when it seemed to his advantage.

Commodore John Drake Sloat was prudent by nature and the navy rewarded him for it. He was not one to "rock the boat." This is evident in many records consulted in the research for this biography, but it is perhaps most clearly shown in his response to the flogging circular of 1850. Deck logs indicate that he seldom resorted to corporal punishment, but he staunchly opposed the abolition of flogging.

Sloat did not always oppose change or reform, but he did not go out of his way to initiate it. He joined the Naval Lyceum, but it is difficult to imagine him having started such an organization. Although trained in sail, he did not resist the advent of steam propulsion or other technologies. The futuristic Stevens battery project appears to have made some actual progress in construction during the two years that Sloat acted as the navy representative. The Stevens battery seems visionary in many ways. But the existing historical and biographical literature does not suggest that the antebellum naval officer corps was a visionary group of people, nor did the "system" encourage them to be. Many of them could envision a bigger "box," but with the possible exception of Robert F. Stockton, they did not think "outside the box." Future research will continue to enhance our understanding of these issues, but, for better or worse, Sloat strikes one as typical a senior officer of the time.

John Drake Sloat passed away on November 28, 1867, at his home in New Brighton. His funeral received prominent coverage in New York newspapers. His body was dressed in the full uniform of a rear admiral and placed in a rosewood coffin. A local Episcopal clergyman performed the service for the dead, and the cortege then crossed by boat to Brooklyn, where four companies of marines joined the procession and escorted the admiral to his final rest in Green-Wood Cemetery.[4]

Admiral Sloat left behind an estate valued at around fifty thousand dollars and the New Brighton property. Abby Sloat received a life interest in the estate, but she also held some separate assets in her own name.

She died on November 15, 1878, and was buried next to her husband. A major feud between surviving children would make headlines in 1883 between Lewis Warrington Sloat on one side and Jeanette and John McKeon on the other, but that is another story.[5]

Throughout his long life and years of service, John Drake Sloat never disgraced his country or its navy, and he deftly handled potentially embarrassing incidents when they arose. His performance of duty during the War of 1812 and against Caribbean pirates was outstanding, just as it was during years in important but less exciting assignments. Sloat's accomplishments in command after the United States went to war with Mexico also reflect great credit upon him. He first joined the United States Navy just after its founding and his passing coincided with the passing of the age of sail. John Drake Sloat's life course personifies as much as anyone's the life course of that navy itself.

APPENDIX A

General Order to Men Landing at Monterey

General Order

Flag Ship Savannah
7th July 1846

We are about to land on the territory of Mexico, with whom the United States is at war. To strike her Flag and to raise our own in the place of it is our duty.

It is not only our duty to take California but to preserve it afterwards, as a part of the United States, at all hazards: to accomplish this is of the first importance to cultivate the good opinion of the inhabitants, whom we must reconcile.

I scarcely consider it necessary for me to caution American Seamen & Marines against the detestable crime of plundering and maltreating unoffending inhabitants.

That no one may misunderstand his duty the following regulations must be strictly adhered to, as no violation can hope to escape the severest punishments.

1st. On landing no man is to leave the shore, until the commanding officer gives the order to march.

2d. No gun is to be fired, or other act of hostility committed, without express orders from the officer commanding the party.

3d. The officers and boat keepers will keep the respective boats as close to the shore as they will safely float, taking care they do not lay aground, and <u>remain</u> in them prepared to defend themselves against attack and attentively watch for signals from the Ships as well as from the party on shore.

4th. No man is to quit the ranks or to enter any house for any pretext whatever without express orders from an officer. Let every man avoid insult or offense to any unoffending inhabitants, and especially avoid the eternal disgrace, which would be attached to our names and country name, by indignity offered to a single female, even let her standing be how low it may.

5th. Plunder of every kind is strictly forbidden, for the plundering of the smallest article forfeits all claim to prize money, and the offender must expect to be severely punished.

6th. Finally, let me entreat you one and all, not to tarnish our brightest hopes of success, by any act that we shall be ashamed to acknowledge before God and our Country

(signed) JOHN D. SLOAT
Commander-in-Chief of the
U. States Naval Forces in the Pacific Ocean.

APPENDIX B

Proclamation of the Annexation of California to the United States

To The Inhabitants of California

The central government of Mexico having commenced hostilities against the United States of America, by invading its territory and attacking the troops of the United States stationed on the north side of the Rio Grande, and with a force of seven thousand men, under the command of General Arista, which army was totally destroyed and all their artillery, baggage, &c., captured on the 8th and 9th of May last, by a force of two thousand three hundred men, under the command of General Taylor, and the city of Matamoras taken and occupied by the forces of the United States; and the two nations being actually at war by this transaction, I shall hoist the standard of the United States at Monterey immediately, and shall carry it throughout California.

I declare to the inhabitants of California, that although I come in arms with a powerful force, I do not come among them as an enemy to California; on the contrary, I come as their best friend—as henceforward California will be a portion of the United States, and its peaceable inhabitants will enjoy the same rights and privileges they now enjoy; together with the privileges of choosing their own magistrates and other officers for the administration of justice among themselves, and the same protection will be extended to them as to any other State in the Union. They will also enjoy a permanent government under which life, property and the constitutional right and lawful security to worship the Creator in the way most congenial to each one's sense of duty will be secured, which unfortunately the central government of Mexico cannot afford them, destroyed as her resources are by internal factions and corrupt officers, who create constant revolutions to promote their own interests and to oppress the people. Under the flag of the United States California will be free from all such troubles and expense, consequently the country will rapidly advance and improve both in agriculture and commerce; as of course the revenue laws will be the same in California as in all other parts of the United States, affording them all manufactures and produce of the United States, free of any duty, and all foreign goods at one quarter of the duty they now pay, a great increase in the value of real estate and the products of California may also be anticipated.

With the great interest and kind feelings I know the government and people of the United States possess towards the citizens of California, the country cannot but improve more rapidly than any other on the continent of America. Such of the inhabitants of California, whether natives or foreigners, as may not be disposed to accept the high privileges of citizenship, and to live peaceably under the government of the United States, will be allowed time to dispose of their property and to remove out of the country, if they choose, without any restriction, or remain in it, observing strict neutrality.

With full confidence in the honor and integrity of the inhabitants of the country, I invite the judges, alcaldes, and other civil officers, to retain their offices and to execute their functions as heretofore, that the public tranquility may not be disturbed; at least, until the government of the territory can be more definitely arranged.

All persons holding titles to real estate, or in quiet possession of lands under a color of right, shall have those titles and rights guarantied [*sic*] to them.

All churches, and the property they contain, in possession of the clergy of California, shall continue in the same rights and possessions they now enjoy.

All provisions and supplies of every kind, furnished by the inhabitants for the use of United States ships and soldiers, will be paid for at fair rates, and no private property will be taken for public use without just compensation at the moment.

JOHN D. SLOAT,
Commander-in-chief of the United States
naval forces in the Pacific ocean.
United States Flag-ship Savannah,
Harbor of Monterey, July 7, 1846

Notes

Chapter 1. Indecision at Monterey?

1. As the commander of the Pacific Squadron, Captain Sloat used the title "Commodore." After 1862, commodore became an official rank and pay grade, but captains who commanded squadrons were still referred to as commodores. In the antebellum navy, once an officer held a commodore billet, he continued to use the title even though he continued to appear on the list of navy captains. I will use the title "Commodore" in this work as was done at the time. Other officers will be identified by their actual naval ranks, even though masters commandant were orally addressed as "Captain," as were lieutenants in command of ships. Contemporaneous documents frequently identify the latter as lieutenants commandant, which was not an official rank, although lieutenants in command of ships did receive a salary increase. Ships of today's United States Navy are always identified as United States Ship and the name, for example, USS *California*. Such was not the case during Sloat's career and is not the case here. For clarity, British naval ships are identified as His Majesty's Ship, as in HMS *Little Belt*.

2. Theodore Henry Hittell, *History of California, Vol. II* (San Francisco: N. J. Stone and Co., 1885), 457–462; Josiah Royce, *California: A Study of American Character* (1886, reprint, Santa Clara and Berkeley: Santa Clara University and Heyday Books, 2002), 124–125; Hubert H. Bancroft, *History of California, Vol. V, 1846–1848* (San Francisco: History Co., 1886), 204–205, 213, 249.

3. Among an extensive historiography, see K. Jack Bauer, *Surfboats and Horse Marines: U. S. Naval Operations in the Mexican War, 1846–48* (Annapolis: Naval Institute Press, 1969), 144–145, 150, 162–163; Bauer, *The Mexican War, 1846–1848* (New York: Macmillan, 1974; Lincoln and London: University of Nebraska Press, 1992), 164–173; Bauer, "George Bancroft, 11 March 1845–9 September 1846," in *American Secretaries of the Navy, Volume I: 1775–1913*, ed.

Paolo E. Coletta (Annapolis: Naval Institute Press, 1980), 224–225; Bernard DeVoto, *The Year of Decision, 1846* (Boston: Little, Brown, and Co., 1943), 255; Robert S. Henry, *The Story of the Mexican War* (Indianapolis: Bobbs-Merrill Co., 1950), 107–117; John S. D. Eisenhower, *So Far from God: The U.S. War with Mexico, 1846–1848* (New York: Random House, 1989; Norman: University of Oklahoma Press, 2000), 214–225; Dale F. Walker, *Bear Flag Rising: The Conquest of California, 1846* (New York: Tom Doherty Associates, 1999), 141–143; David A. Clary, *Eagles and Empire: The United States, Mexico, and the Struggle for a Continent* (New York: Bantam Books, 2009), 88–89, 92; Winston Groom, *Kearny's March: The Epic Creation of the American West, 1846–1847* (New York: A. A. Knopf, 2011), 102–103. On Jones's seizure of Monterey, see James High, "Jones at Monterey, 1842," *Journal of the West* 5:2 (April 1966): 173–186; Gene A. Smith, "The War That Wasn't: Thomas ap Catesby Jones and the Seizure of Monterey," *California History* 66 (June 1987): 104–113, 155–156; and Smith, *Thomas ap Catesby Jones: Commodore of Manifest Destiny* (Annapolis: Naval Institute Press, 2000), 106–121.

4. Citations of most of those historical and biographical works appear in the chapters that follow and in the bibliography.

5. Edwin A. Sherman, *The Life of the Late Rear Admiral John Drake Sloat, of the United States Navy, who took possession of California and raised the American Flag at Monterey on July 7th, 1846* (Oakland: Carruth & Carruth, 1902).

6. For an insightful discussion of this approach to biography, see Alice Kessler-Harris, "Why Biography?" *American Historical Review* 114:3 (June 2009): 625–630, as well as the other related articles in that issue of the *AHR*.

Chapter 2. Upstate Knickerbocker

1. Sherman, *Life of Sloat*, 20–21; http://worldconnect.rootsweb.com/, accessed January 23, 2013; and http://ancestrylibrary.com/, accessed January 23, 2013; http://sloatsburgny.com/, accessed January 23, 2013.

2. Sherman, *Life of Sloat*, 20, and *Dictionary of American Biography*, Vol. 18 (New York: Charles Scribner's Sons, 1958), 214–215.

3. http://rootsweb.ancestry.com/, accessed January 23, 2013; *The Early Records of the First Presbyterian Church at Goshen, New York, from 1767 to 1885*, Charles C. Coleman, compiler (Goshen, NY: n.d., published ms. in the custody of the church secretary).

4. http://rootsweb.ancestry.com/, accessed January 23, 2013, and http://ancestrylibrary.com/, accessed January 23, 2013.

5. David M. Ellis, "Yankee-Dutch Confrontation in the Albany Area," *New England Quarterly* 45:2 (June 1972): 262–270; Thomas S. Wermuth, "The

Central Hudson Valley: Dutchess, Orange, and Ulster Counties," in *The Other New York: The American Revolution beyond New York City, 1763–1787*, ed. Joseph S. Tiedemann and Eugene R. Fingerhut (Albany: State University of New York Press, 2005), 128–129.

6. Irving Mark, *Agrarian Conflicts in Colonial New York, 1711–1775* (Port Washington: Ira J. Friedman, 1965; New York: Columbia University Press, 1940), 50–107; David M. Ellis, "Land Tenure and Tenancy in the Hudson Valley, 1790–1860," *Agricultural History* 18:2 (April 1944): 75–82; Ellis, *Landholders and Farmers in the Mohawk-Hudson Region, 1790–1850* (New York: Octagon Books, 1967; Ithaca: Cornell University Press, 1946), 1–16; Staughton Lynd, "Who Shall Rule at Home? Dutchess County, New York, in the American Revolution," *William and Mary Quarterly, 3rd ser.* 20:2 (July 1961): 330–359; Sung Bok Kim, *Landlord and Tenant in Colonial New York: Manorial Society, 1664–1775* (Chapel Hill: University of North Carolina Press for the Institute of Early American History and Culture, 1978), 17, 234, 256; Thomas S. Wermuth, *Rip Van Winkle's Neighbors: The Transformation of Rural Society in the Hudson River Valley, 1720–1850* (Albany: State University of New York Press, 2001), 91–113.

7. Frank Bertangue Green, *History of Rockland County* (New York: A. S. Barnes and Co., 1887), 156, 397.

8. Tax Assessment Rolls of Real and Personal Property, Goshen, New York, New York State Archives Roll 15, 1799–1800, copy held at the Goshen Public Library; E. M. Ruttenber and L. H. Clark, et al., compilers, *History of Orange County, New York* (Philadelphia: Everts and Peck, 1881), 536, 614; Reeve Huston, *Land and Freedom: Rural Society, Popular Protest, and Party Politics in Antebellum New York* (New York: Oxford University Press, 2000), 43.

9. Ellis, *Landholders and Farmers*, 66–117.

10. 1790 United States Census, New York, Orange County, 376, 384, Department of Commerce Bureau of the Census, Record Group (RG) 29, National Archives and Record Administration (NARA); and 1800 United States Census, New York, Orange County, 363, and Rockland County, 1021, RG 29, NARA; Wermuth, "Central Hudson Valley," 143, 148.

11. Nell Irvin Painter, *Sojourner Truth: A Life, a Symbol* (New York: W. W. Norton, 1996), 13, 14; Margaret Washington, *Sojourner Truth's America* (Urbana and Chicago: University of Illinois Press, 2009), 18–33; Ellis, *Landholders and Farmers*, 103–104; Edwin Olson, "Social Aspects of Slave Life in New York," *Journal of Negro History* 26:1 (January 1941): 66–77; Eugene D. Genovese, *Roll, Jordan, Roll; The World the Slaves Made* (New York: Pantheon, 1974); Robert W. Fogel, *Without Consent or Contract: The Rise and Fall of American Slavery* (New York: W.W. Norton, 1989). For the conversion rate from New York pound to dollars, see John J. McCusker, *How Much Is That in Real Money? A Historical Commodity Price*

Index for Use as a Deflator of Money Values in the Economy of the United States, 2nd ed., revised and enlarged (Worcester: American Antiquarian Society, 2001), 34.

12. Letter, Tom McCutchon, Columbia University Rare Book and Manuscript Library to author, November 16, 2012; Letter, Stephen Ross, Yale University Library, to author, January 24, 2013, Frederick Rudolph, "Introduction," *Essays on Education in the Early Republic*, ed. Rudolph (Cambridge: Belknap Press of the Harvard University Press, 1965), vii–xxi; Rena L. Vassar, editor's comments, *A Social History of American Education, Vol. I: Colonial Times to 1860*, ed. Vassar (Chicago: Rand McNally and Co., 1965), 3, 49; E. Jennifer Monaghan, *A Common Heritage: Noah Webster's Blue-Back Speller* (Hamden: Archon Books, 1983), 13–25; Richard J. Moss, *Noah Webster* (Boston: Twayne, 1984), ix–x, 6–7; Richard M. Rollins, *The Long Journey of Noah Webster* (Philadelphia: University of Pennsylvania Press, 1980), 22, 35.

13. Deed, September 23, 1795, Orange County (New York) Deeds 1788–1799, Vol. E, p. 460, https://familysearch.org/, accessed January 23, 2013.

Chapter 3. Mr. Midshipman Sloat

1. Michael A. Palmer, *Stoddert's War: Naval Operations during the Quasi-War with France, 1798–1801* (Columbia: University of South Carolina Press, 1987), 10–30; Alexander de Conde, *The Quasi-War: The Politics and Diplomacy of the Undeclared War with France, 1797–1801* (New York: Charles Scribner's Sons, 1966), 36–73; William G. Anderson, "John Adams, the Navy, and the Quasi-War with France," *American Neptune* 30:2 (April 1970): 117–120; George C. Herring, *From Colony to Superpower: U.S. Foreign Relations since 1776* (New York: Oxford University Press, 2008), 86–90; Gordon S. Wood, *Empire of Liberty: A History of the Early Republic, 1789–1815* (New York: Oxford University Press, 2009), 245–246; Stanley M. Elkins and Eric McKittrick, *The Age of Federalism* (New York and Oxford: Oxford University Press, 1993), 643.

2. Howard I. Chapelle, *The History of the American Sailing Navy: The Ships and Their Development* (New York: W. W. Norton, 1949; New York: Bonanza Books, 1965), 119–176, is the classic treatment of the technical aspects of the design and construction of these ships, but see also more recently, Ian W. Toll, *Six Frigates: The Epic History of the Founding of the U.S. Navy* (New York and London: W. W. Norton, 2006), 48–60.

3. Christopher McKee, *A Gentlemanly and Honorable Profession: The Creation of the U.S. Naval Officer Corps, 1794–1815* (Annapolis: Naval Institute Press, 1991), 40–115. Many of the works cited throughout this essay also address social aspects of the navy's officer corps, but see also William M. Fowler, Jr., *Jack Tars*

and Commodores: The American Navy, 1783–1815 (Boston: Houghton Mifflin Co., 1984), 131–132.

4. "Admiral Sloat's Great Grandson," *San Francisco Call*, July 1, 1896, p. 8.

5. Alan Taylor, *William Cooper's Town: Power and Persuasion on the Frontier of the Early American Republic* (New York: A. A. Knopf, 1996), 342–344.

6. Anderson, "John Adams, the Navy, and the Quasi-War with France," 120, 129; John Ferling, *John Adams: A Life* (Knoxville: University of Tennessee Press, 1992); David McCullough, *John Adams* (New York: Simon and Schuster, 2001); and Page Smith, *John Adams*, 2 vols. (Garden City: Doubleday, 1962).

7. Certificate as Master Mason, dated October 16, 1805, contains the date of appointment as Apprentice Mason. New-York Historical Society, Patricia K. Klingenstein Library, NSC MISC MSS Box 054, Folder 14, John D. Sloat.

8. Letters, Secretary of the Navy Benjamin Stoddert to John Drake Sloat, February 12, 1800, and March 18, 1800, Letters Sent by the Secretary of the Navy to Officers, 1798–1868, (hereafter, Letters to Officers) Microfilm M149, Roll 3, RG45 NARA; McKee, *Gentlemanly and Honorable Profession*, 40–115; Samuel Eliot Morison, *"Old Bruin," Commodore Matthew Calbraith Perry, 1794–1858* (Boston and Toronto: Little, Brown, and Co., 1967), 27.

9. Eugene S. Ferguson, *Truxtun of the Constellation: The Life of Commodore Thomas Truxtun, U.S. Navy, 1755–1822* (Baltimore: Johns Hopkins University Press, 1956, 2000), 188–204.

10. Letter, Captain Thomas Truxtun to Captain John Barry, January 15, 1801, letter, Captain Thomas Truxtun to Lieutenant Andrew Sterrett, St. Christopher Roads, January 21, 1801, letter, Captain Thomas Truxtun to Secretary of the Navy Benjamin Stoddert, February 19, 1801, *Naval Documents Related to the Quasi-War between the United States and France, Operations: December 1800–December 1801*, Vol. 7 (Washington, DC: U.S. Government Printing Office, 1938), 90–91, 104, 126 (hereafter cited as *NDQW*); Ferguson, *Truxtun*, 206–212, De Conde, *Quasi-War*, 351–373; Palmer, *Stoddert's War*, 214–215, 220–221.

11. Ferguson, *Truxtun*, 210, 211; David F. Long, *Sailor-Diplomat: A Biography of Commodore James Biddle, 1782–1848* (Boston: Northeastern University Press, 1983), 13–15.

12. Palmer, *Stoddert's War*, 214–239; De Conde, *The Quasi-War*, 237–243, 254–256; Elkins and McKittrick, *The Age of Federalism*, 643–661; Herring, *From Colony to Superpower*, 90.

13. Chapelle, *American Sailing Navy*, 504.

14. *Reef Points 1970–71: The Annual Handbook of the Brigade of Midshipmen* (Annapolis: United States Naval Academy, 1970), 25.

15. "Officers of the U.S. Navy and Marine Corps, and in Ships under the Jurisdiction of the Navy, during the Quasi-War with France, 1797–1801," *NDQW*, Vol. 7, 315–63.

16. Wood, *Empire of Liberty*, 246; McKee, *Gentlemanly and Honorable Profession*, 155–177; Fowler, *Jack Tars and Commodores*, 131–132; Toll, *Six Frigates*, 105–106.

17. Charles Morris, *The Autobiography of Commodore Charles Morris, U.S. Navy* (1880; reprint, with introduction and additional notes by Frederick C. Leiner, Annapolis: Naval Institute Press, 2002), 8.

18. McKee, *Gentlemanly and Honorable Profession*, 413–418; Fowler, *Jack Tars and Commodores*, 61–62; Donald Chisholm, *Waiting for Dead Men's Shoes: Origins and Development of the U.S. Navy's Officer Personnel System, 1793–1941* (Stanford: Stanford University Press, 2001), 71–74; Craig L. Symonds, *Navalists and Antinavalists: The Naval Policy Debate in the United States, 1785–1827* (Newark: University of Delaware Press, 1980), 82–90.

19. Letter, Truxtun to Secretary of the Navy Robert Smith, Norfolk, May 12, 1801, Thomas Truxtun Records 1797–1801, Historical Society of Pennsylvania; "Officers of the U.S. Navy . . . during the Quasi-War with France," *NDQW*, Vol. 7, 350; Ferguson, *Truxtun of the Constellation*, 217; Morison, *"Old Bruin,"* 24; Fowler, *Jack Tars and Commodores*, chapter 4.

Chapter 4. Schooner Skipper

1. McKee, *Gentlemanly and Honorable Profession*, 159–164; Long, *Sailor-Diplomat*, 31–32; Smith, *Commodore of Manifest Destiny*, 10.

2. "Shipping News," *New-York Evening Post*, March 30, 1802, p. 3. Many of the newspaper articles cited were accessed through "America's Historical Newspapers" at www.newsbank.com/.

3. Sherman, *Life of Sloat*, 21.

4. Samuel Eliot Morison, *The Maritime History of Massachusetts, 1783–1860* (Boston and New York: Houghton Mifflin, 1921), 106.

5. Geoffrey Gilbert, "Maritime Enterprise in the New Republic: Investment in Baltimore Shipping, 1789–1793," *Business History Review* 58:1 (Spring 1984): 114–129; Robert G. Albion, "Early Nineteenth-Century Shipowning—A Chapter in Business Enterprise," *Journal of Economic History* 1:1 (May 1941): 1–11; John G. B. Hutchins, *The American Maritime Industries and Public Policy, 1789–1914* (Cambridge: Harvard University Press, 1941), 239; Robert G. Albion, William A. Baker, and Benjamin W. Labaree, *New England and the Sea* (Middletown: Wesleyan University Press, 1972), 33–34.

6. "Shipping News," *Commercial Advertiser* (New York), July 20, 1803, p. 1; "Shipping News," *Daily Advertiser* (New York), August 23, 1803, p. 3.

7. "Shipping News," *Commercial Advertiser*, December 19, 1803, p. 3, "Shipping News," *Commercial Advertiser*, March 26, 1804, p. 3; Winthrop L. Marvin, *The American Merchant Marine: Its History and Roman from 1620 to 1902* (New York: Charles Scribner's Sons, 1902), 108; Thomas A. Bailey, *A Diplomatic History of the American People, 6th edition* (New York: Appleton-Century Crofts, 1958), 118; Albion, Baker, and Labaree, *New England and the Sea*, 75. Most shipping news reports contain only a minimum of information, but the ones from Sloat tended to be more fulsome. On the importance of merchant mariners as conduits of information in the period, see Brian Rouleau, *With Sails Whitening Every Sea: Mariners and the Making of an American Maritime Empire* (Ithaca: Cornell University Press, 2014).

8. "Shipping News," *Morning Chronicle* (New York), May 9, 1804, p. 2; "Shipping News," *Daily Advertiser* (New York), August 7, 1804, p. 3. A Philadelphia newspaper, the *Aurora General Advertiser*, on July 28, 1804, listed the *Clarissa* as a brig.

9. "Shipping News," *Commercial Advertiser*, February 4, 1805, p. 3; Clearance document, February 1, 1805, Records of Foreign Clearance, Department of the Treasury, Records of the U.S. Customs Service, RG36, NARA; "Shipping News," *Daily Advertiser*, April 29, 1805, p. 2; Albion, Baker, and Labaree, *New England and the Sea*, 62.

10. Herring, *From Colony to Superpower*, 116, Wood, *Empire of Liberty*, 624; K. Jack Bauer, *A Maritime History of the United States: The Role of America's Seas and Waterways* (Columbia: University of South Carolina Press, 1988), 61–63.

11. "Shipping News," *New-York Gazette*, October 9, 1805, p. 3.

12. Baltimore, Record of Entrances and Clearances, 1780–1939, Vol. 15 and Vol. 16, Records of the U.S. Customs Service, RG36, NARA.

13. "Shipping News," *Baltimore Price-Current*, August 7, 1806, p. 4; Baltimore, Record of Entrances and Clearances, 1780–1939, Vol. 22, RG36, NARA.

14. Will of Steven Slot, August 20, 1792, probated October 18, 1806. Rockland County, New York. Surrogate's Court Book of Wills, Liber A, pp. 150–153; James A. Henretta, "Families and Farms: *Mentalité* in Pre-Industrial America," *William and Mary Quarterly*, 3rd ser. 35 (1978): 29.

15. Will of Joseph Drake, February 12, 1807, with codicil, June 11, 1807. Orange County, New York. Surrogate's Court Book of Wills, Liber D, p. 27.

16. Sherman, *Life of Sloat*, 21.

17. Michael Groth, "Slaveholders and Manumission in Dutchess County, New York," *New York History* 78:1 (January 1997): 45–46.

18. Gary Lawson Brown, *Baltimore in the Nation, 1789–1861* (Chapel Hill: University of North Carolina Press, 1980), 27–29, 52.

19. Howard I. Chapelle, *The History of American Sailing Ships* (New York: W. W. Norton, 1935; Bonanza Books, 1988), 76–77; 219–239, 273–286; Kurt Richter and Nghiem Ta, "Pirates, Prizes, and Profits: Cocoa and the Early American East Coast Trade," in *Chocolate: History, Culture, and Heritage*, ed. Lewis Evan Grivetti and Howard-Yana Shapiro (Hoboken: John Wiley and Sons, 2009), 211–218.

20. Certificate of the U.S. Consul at Bordeaux, William Lee, April 16, 1807, and Certificate of the U.S. Consul at La Rochelle, J. J. Deberoe, December 4, 1835, Marine Documents and Reports, 1802–1862, Records of the U.S. Customs Service, RG36, NARA.

21. Ira Dye, "Early American Merchant Seafarers," *Proceedings of the American Philosophical Society* 120:5 (October 15, 1976): 353.

22. Chapelle, *American Sailing Ships*, 76–77; "Officers of the U.S. Navy and Marine Corps, and in Ships under the Jurisdiction of the Navy, during the Quasi-War with France, 1797–1801," *NDQW*, Vol. 7, 315–363; Fowler, *Jack Tars and Commodores*, 29.

23. Dye, "Early American Merchant Seafarers," 338–351; Ira Dye, "Physical and Social Profiles of Early American Seafarers, 1812–1815," in *Jack Tar in History: Essays in the History of Maritime Life and Labour*, ed. Colin Howell and Richard Twomey (Fredericton: Acadiensis Press, 1991), 225; W. Jeffrey Bolster, *Black Jacks: African American Seamen in the Age of Sail* (Cambridge and London: Harvard University Press, 1997), 225; Harold D. Langley, "The Negro in the Navy and Merchant Service, 1798–1860," *Journal of Negro History* 52:4 (October 1967): 274–276.

24. Donald R. Adams, Jr., "Wage Patterns in the National Period: Philadelphia, 1785–1830," *Journal of Economic History* 28:3 (September 1968): 415–416, 422; Paul A. Gilje, *The Road to Mobocracy: Popular Disorder in New York City, 1763–1834* (Chapel Hill: University of North Carolina Press for the Institute of Early American History and Culture, 1987), 181, and see in general, Sean Wilentz, *Chants Democratic: New York City and the Rise of the American Working Class, 1788–1850* (New York: Oxford University Press, 1984).

25. Fowler, *Jack Tars and Commodores*, 29.

26. Hutchins, *American Maritime Industries and Public Policy*, 221–227; Robert G. Albion, *The Rise of New York Port, 1815–1860* (New York and London: Charles Scribner's Sons, 1939), 7.

27. Many accounts of the Chesapeake and Leopard matter exist, but see most recently Stephen Budiansky, *Perilous Fight: America's Intrepid War with Britain on the High Seas, 1812–1815* (New York: Alfred A. Knopf, 2010), 61–71, Fowler, *Jack Tars and Commodores*, 152–155; and Toll, *Six Frigates*, 289–298. On impressment of American seamen, see in particular Paul A. Gilje, *Free Trade and*

Sailors' Rights in the War of 1812 (Cambridge: Cambridge University Press, 2013), 99–109 and 179–189.

28. Alex Roland, W. Jeffrey Bolster, and Alexander Keyssar, *The Way of the Ship: America's Maritime History Reenvisioned, 1600–2000* (Hoboken: John Wiley and Sons, 2008), 125–127; Wood, *Empire of Liberty*, 650–652; Bauer, *Maritime History of the United States*, 61–66; Albion, *Rise of New York Port*, shows dollar values of exports during 1792–1807.

29. Bradford Perkins, *Prologue to War: England and the United States, 1805–1812* (Berkeley and Los Angeles: University of California Press, 1968), 140–183.

30. "Shipping News," *Baltimore Price-Current*, January 7, 1809, p. 4; "Shipping News," *Paulson's Daily Advertiser*, March 29, 1809, p. 4; "Shipping News," *New-England Palladium*, May 23, 1809, p. 1; "Shipping News," *Federal Republican* (Baltimore), July 27, 1809, p. 3; "Shipping News," *Baltimore Price-Current*, September 23, 1809, p. 4; "Shipping News," *Federal Republican*, November 2, 1809, p. 4; Vol. 24 and Vol. 25, Baltimore, Record of Entrances and Clearances, 1780–1939, RG36, NARA.

31. Wood, *Empire of Liberty*, 665; Toll, *Six Frigates*, 320–321.

32. *Boston Commercial Gazette*, September 10, 1810, p. 2.

33. "Shipping News," *New-York Gazette*, August 28, 1810, p. 3; "Shipping News," *Mercantile Advertiser*, September 26, 1810, p. 2; "Shipping News," *New-York Gazette*, January 11, 1811, p. 3; "Shipping News," *Commercial Advertiser*, January 21, 1811, p. 3.

34. Alan Taylor, *The Civil War of 1812: American Citizens, British Subjects, Irish Rebels, and Indian Allies* (New York: A. A. Knopf, 2010), 411; Herring, *From Colony to Superpower*, 121–124; Wood, *Empire of Liberty*, 666. See also Robert P. Watson, *America's First Crisis: The War of 1812* (Albany: State University of New York Press, 2014); Troy Bickham, *The Weight of Vengeance: The United States, the British Empire, and the War of 1812* (New York: Oxford University Press, 2012); and Donald R. Hickey, *The War of 1812: A Forgotten Conflict* (Urbana and Chicago: University of Illinois Press, 1989). For a useful timeline of the changes in commercial relations with Britain and France in the years preceding the War of 1812, see Bailey, *Diplomatic History*, 134.

35. Budiansky, *Perilous Fight*, 88; Toll, *Six Frigates*, 321–324; and Morison, *"Old Bruin,"* 31–32.

Chapter 5. Sailing Master

1. McKee, *Gentlemanly and Honorable Profession*, 325.

2. Letter, Secretary of the Navy Paul Hamilton to John D. Sloat, Norfolk, January 10, 1812, Letters to Officers, M149, Roll 9, RG45, NARA.

3. Entry dated February 21, 1812, Deck Log, USS *United States*, May 1, 1810 to February 21, 1812, Logs of U.S. Naval Ships, 1801–1915, Department of the Navy, Records of the Bureau of Naval Personnel, RG 24, NARA.

4. McKee, *Gentlemanly and Honorable Profession*, 309–325.

5. Fowler, *Jack Tars and Commodores*, 139.

6. Fowler, *Jack Tars and Commodores*, 29.

7. Chapelle, *American Sailing Navy*, 120–121, 130–131; Chapelle, *American Sailing Ships*, 86–86; John H. Schroeder, "Stephen Decatur: Heroic Ideal of the Young Navy," in *Command under Sail: Makers of the American Naval Tradition 1775–1850*, ed. James C. Bradford (Annapolis: Naval Institute Press, 1985), 207–208, 214; and Robert J. Allison, *Stephen Decatur: American Naval Hero, 1779–1820* (Amherst and Boston: University of Massachusetts Press, 2005), 110–111.

8. Allison, *Stephen Decatur*, 114–115; Budiansky, *Perilous Fight*, 150; Fowler, *Jack Tars and Commodores*, 164–169.

9. James M. Merrill, *Du Pont, the Making of an Admiral: A Biography of Samuel Francis Du Pont* (New York: Dodd, Mead, and Co., 1986), 178; "Admiral Sloat's Great Grandson," *San Francisco Call*, July 1, 1896, p. 8.

10. Each of the biographies of Stephen Decatur, and every history of the naval aspects of the War of 1812, contains an account of the battle between USS *United States* and HMS *Macedonian*. I have relied particularly on Budiansky, *Perilous Fight*, 166–173, which contains a good diagram of the battle; James Tertius deKay, *A Rage for Glory: The Life of Commodore Stephen Decatur, USN* (New York: Free Press, 2004), 114–128; Allison, *Stephen Decatur*, chapter 12; Kevin D. McCranie, *Utmost Gallantry: The U.S. and Royal Navies at Sea in the War of 1812* (Annapolis: Naval Institute Press, 2011), 63–66; Spencer C. Tucker, *Stephen Decatur: A Life Most Bold and Daring* (Annapolis: Naval Institute Press, 2005), 114–120; Toll, *Six Frigates*, 360–367; Schroeder, "Stephen Decatur," 206–207; and Fowler, *Jack Tars and Commodores*, 126–127.

11. Ira Dye, *The Fatal Cruise of the* Argus*: Two Captains in the War of 1812* (Annapolis: Naval Institute Press, 1994), 88; deKay, *Rage for Glory*, 114; Leonard F. Guttridge, *Our Country, Right or Wrong: The Life of Stephen Decatur, the U.S. Navy's Most Illustrious Commander* (New York: Tom Doherty Associates, 2006), 135; Allison, *Stephen Decatur*, 165; S. Putnam Waldo, *The Life and Character of Stephen Decatur* (Hartford. P. S. Goodsell, 1821), 170–175; Schroeder, "Stephen Decatur," 214; and, generally, Cyrus T. Brady, *Stephen Decatur* (Boston: Small, Maynard, and Co., 1900).

12. R. S. Guernsey, *New York City and Vicinity during the War of 1812–1815*, Vol. 1 (New York: C. L. Woodward, 1889), 158–162; Allison, *Stephen Decatur*, 121–128; Bolster, *Black Jacks*, 91; Dye, *Fatal Cruise*, 95–98.

13. Dye, *Fatal Cruise*, 84–85, 98–99; Allison, *Stephen Decatur*, 127.

14. McKee, *Gentlemanly and Honorable Profession*, 342, 495.

15. McKee, *Gentlemanly and Honorable Profession*, 299–301.

16. Dye, *Fatal Cruise*, 100.

17. Letter, Sloat to Secretary of the Navy William Jones, New London, March 20, 1812, Letters Received by the Secretary of the Navy from Commissioned Officers below the Rank of Commander and from Warrant Officers, 1802–1844 (hereafter, Officers Letters) M148, Roll 11, RG45, NARA; Abstract of Service, John Drake Sloat, Abstracts of Service Records of Naval Officers, M1328, Roll 19, RG24, NARA.

18. Ferguson, *Truxtun*, 256–157.

19. Letter, Sloat to Nathaniel Maxwell, New London, May 25, 1813, Officers Letters, M148, Roll 11, Officers Letters, RG4,5 NARA.

20. McKee, *Gentlemanly and Honorable Profession*, 319, 324–325.

21. John H. Schroeder, *Matthew Calbraith Perry: Antebellum Sailor and Diplomat* (Annapolis: Naval Institute Press, 2001), 12–17; Long, *Sailor-Diplomat*, 47.

Chapter 6. Blockaded Lieutenant

1. Burdick H. Brittin and Liselotte B. Watson, *International Law for Seagoing Officers,* 2nd ed. (Annapolis: Naval Institute Press, 1956, 1960), 144.

2. Tucker, *Stephen Decatur*, 132.

3. Morison, *"Old Bruin,"* 49.

4. "Traitors," *Boston Patriot*, December 18, 1813, p. 2; Joseph Goldenberg, "Blue Lights and Infernal Machines: The British Blockade of New London," *The Mariner's Mirror* 61:4 (November 1975): 388.

5. Entries dated December 13 and December 16, 1813, Deck Log, USS *United States*, August 7, 1812, to September 4, 1814, National Archives RG 24; "Officers of the *United States* in action with the *Macedonian*," *A General Register of the Navy and Marine Corps of the United States* (Washington, DC: C. Alexander, Printer, 1848), 511.

6. "Blue Lights again Exhibited!" *Boston Patriot*, January 15, 1814, p. 2; "Blue Lights again!" *Boston Patriot*, March 23, 1814, p. 4; Goldenberg, "Blue Lights and Infernal Machines," 388; Allison, *Stephen Decatur*, 132–133; Letter, Commodore Stephen Decatur to Secretary of the Navy William Jones, December 20, 1813, quoted in Douglas S. Jordan, "Stephen Decatur at New London: A Study in Strategic Frustration," *U.S. Naval Institute Proceedings* 93:10 (October 1967): 64; James Tertius deKay, *The Battle of Stonington: Torpedoes, Submarine, and Rockets in the War of 1812* (Annapolis: Naval Institute Press, 1990), 83–88. Writing in 1860, Frances Manwaring Caulkins concluded that the issue of treason by New Londoners was unresolvable. Caulkins, *History of New London, Connecticut,*

from the First Survey of the Coast in 1612 to 1860 (New London: New London County Historical Society, 2007, 1860), 635.

7. Untitled article, *Connecticut Gazette*, January 5, 1815, p. 1; "The Blue Lights," *Connecticut Gazette*, February 2, 1814, p. 1.

8. Lawrence A. Peskin, "Conspiratorial Anglophobia and the War of 1812," *Journal of American History* 98:3 (December 2011): 647–669.

9. Long, *Sailor-Diplomat*, 47; Allison, *Stephen Decatur*, 134.

10. DeKay, *Battle of Stonington*, 81–83; Andrew W. German, "Mrs. Stewart's Situation," New London County Historical Society, 2012, accessed March 12, 2014, http://warof1812ct.org/?p=733/; Allison, *Stephen Decatur*, 132.

11. Jerry Roberts, *The British Raid on Essex: The Forgotten Battle of the War of 1812* (Middletown: Wesleyan University Press, 2014).

12. Entry dated April 20, 1814, Deck Log, USS *United States*; Allison, *Stephen Decatur*, 137, 143–144; deKay, *Rage for Glory*, 135.

13. "A Court-Martial," *Norwich Courier*, April 20, 1814, p. 3; untitled article, *Federal Republican for the Country* (Georgetown, District of Columbia), April 29, 1814, p. 3; "Naval Court Martial," *New-York Gazette*, June 21, 1814, p. 3; James E. Valle, "The Navy's Battle Doctrine in the War of 1812," *American Neptune* 44:3 (Summer 1984), 172–173; James E. Valle, *Rocks and Shoals: Order and Discipline in the Old Navy, 1800–1861* (Annapolis: Naval Institute Press, 1980), 148–152; Allison, *Stephen Decatur*, 141; deKay, *Rage for Glory*, 140–141.

14. Entry dated May 7, 1814, Deck Log, USS *United States*; Goldenberg, "Blue Lights and Infernal Machines," 388–392; Letter, Sloat to Jones, New London, May 18, 1814, Officers Letters, M148, Roll 13, RG45, NARA.

15. Hickey, *The War of 1812*, 199–200; Reginald Horsman, *The War of 1812* (New York: A. A. Knopf, 1969), 158.

16. Entry dated October 19, 1814, Deck Log, USS *United States*; Goldenberg, "Blue Lights and Infernal Machines," 388–392; deKay, *Battle of Stonington*, 193–194; Joseph A. Goldenberg, "The Royal Navy's Blockade in New England Waters, 1812–1815," *The International History Review* 6:3 (August 1984): 437–438; Andrew J. B. Fagal, "Terror Weapons in the Naval War of 1812," *New York History* 94:3/4 (Summer/Fall 2013): 221–240.

17. Letter, Sloat to Captain David Porter, New York, January 17, 1815, Simon Gratz Collection [250A] Case 5, Box 35, Historical Society of Pennsylvania.

18. Wade G. Dudley, *Splintering the Wooden Wall: The British Blockade of the United States, 1812–1815* (Annapolis: Naval Institute Press, 2003); Hickey, *The War of 1812*, 169–171, 199–200; Horsman, *The War of 1812*, 142–143; Goldenberg, "Blockade in New England's Waters," 438.

19. Troy O. Bickham, *Weight of Vengeance: The United States, the British Empire, and the War of 1812* (Oxford and New York: Oxford University Press, 2012), 177.

20. Allison, *Stephen Decatur,* 133.

21. Untitled article, *Norwich Courier,* June 9, 1813, p. 3.

22. "Married," *Norwich Courier,* November 30, 1814, p. 3.

23. Nancy F. Cott, *The Bonds of Womanhood: "Women's Sphere" in New England, 1780–1835,* 2nd ed. (New Haven: Yale University Press, 1997).

24. Morison, *"Old Bruin,"* 50–53.

25. Untitled article, *Norwich Courier,* July 29, 1812, p. 3.

26. www.ancestrylibrary.com/, accessed March 7, 2013.

27. Norwich, Connecticut, Land Records, General Index, Grantors 1727–1849, Vol. 1, p. 579.

28. Goldenberg, "Blue Lights and Infernal Machines," 396; Allison, *Stephen Decatur,* 159.

29. Chisholm, *Waiting for Dead Men's Shoes,* 84.

30. Letter, Sloat to Crowninshield, New London, March 16, 1815, M148, Roll 14, Officers Letters, RG45, NARA.

31. Chapelle, *American Sailing Ships,* 236–238.

32. Shipping News, *Mercantile Advertiser,* May 23, 1815, p. 1; Letter, Sloat to Crowninshield, New London, May 23, 1815, Officers Letters, RG45, NARA; on the Griswolds, see Hutchins, *American Maritime Industries and Public Policy,* 240.

33. Shipping News, *Columbian* (New York), June 3, 1815, p. 3.

34. "Commodore John Drake Sloat," *Merchant's Magazine and Commercial Review* 15 (November 1846): 446; Sherman, *Life of Sloat,* 24.

35. Baron Pierre Fleury de Chaubulon, *Memoirs of the Private Life, Return, and Reign of Napoleon I in 1815,* Vol. 2 (London: John Murray, Albemarle Street, 1820), 423; Louis Antoine Fauvelet de Bourrienne, *Memoirs of Napoleon Bonaparte,* Vol. 4, ed. R. W. Phipps (New York: Charles Scribner's Sons, 1906), 234–236, corroborates Fleury de Chaubulon's statements about the American merchant captain.

36. Rear Admiral Sir Frederick Maitland, KCB, *The Surrender of Napoleon* (Edinburgh and London: Blackwood and Sons, 1904), 27–30.

37. Shipping News, *Columbian,* November 9, 1815, p. 3.

38. The records here appear to conflict. Midshipman Warrington had been assigned to the *Chesapeake* in 1800 and then transferred to the *President* some time in 1801. Official records do not reveal where else their paths would have crossed prior to 1815, although they did so regularly in subsequent years. *NDQW,* Vol. 7, 315–565, and the Naval History and Heritage Command, *Dictionary of American Naval Fighting Ships,* http://www.history.navy.mil/danfs/w3/warrington-iii.htm/, accessed May 5, 2013.

39. Norwich, Connecticut, Land Records, General Index, Grantors 1727–1849, Vol. 1, p. 579.

40. Shipping News, *Baltimore Patriot,* June 26, 1816, p. 2.

Chapter 7. The First Luff

1. Letter to the editor, *Niles Weekly Register*, December 30, 1815, Vol. 9, 304–306.

2. Morison, *"Old Bruin,"* 63.

3. Letter, Sloat to Secretary of the Navy Benjamin W. Crowninshield, New York, June 7, 1818, Officers Letters, M148, Roll 20, RG45, NARA.

4. Letter, Crowninshield to Lieutenant Matthew C. Perry, October 30, 1817, Letters to Officers, M149, Roll 13, RG45, NARA.

5. Norwich, Connecticut, Land Records, Grant Deeds, Book 38, p. 39.

6. Letter, Sloat to Secretary of the Navy Smith Thompson, Portsmouth, NH, March 2, 1820, Officers Letters, M148, Roll 23; Letter, Sloat to Thompson, Portsmouth, June 22, 1820, Officers Letters, M148, Roll 24, RG45, NARA.

7. Parish Records, St. John's Episcopal Church, Portsmouth, NH, 1795–1884, Vol. 1, p. 39, Typescript at Portsmouth Atheneum, Portsmouth, NH.

8. David F. Long, *Nothing Too Daring: A Biography of Commodore David Porter, 1780–1843* (Annapolis: Naval Institute Press, 1970), 209.

9. George Henry Preble, *History of the United States Navy-Yard, Portsmouth, N.H.* (Washington, DC: U.S. Government Printing Office, 1892), 24, 44, 46.

10. Morris, *Autobiography*, 96.

11. Registers of Naval Officers 1820 and 1821, in *American State Papers, Naval Affairs,* Vol. 6, pp. 636–638 and 708–709.

12. Letter, Sloat to Thompson, New London, January 12, 1821, Officers Letters, M148, Roll 25, RG45, NARA.

13. *Register of the Commision [sic] and Warrant Officers of the Navy of the United States, Including Officers of the Marine Corps* (np: Jacob Gideon, 1822), 6.

14. *Naval Register*, 1822, p. 7; Letter, Thompson to Commodore Charles Morris, Washington, January 6, 1821, Letters Sent by the Secretary of the Navy to Commandants and Navy Agents, M441, Roll 2, RG45, NARA.

15. *Longworth's City Directory of New York*, 1821/1822; "Marine News," *New-York Evening Post*, April 10, 1821, p. 2.

16. Letters, Sloat to Thompson, Portsmouth, NH, May 15, 1821, and June 9, 1821, Officers Letters, M148, Roll 26; Letter, Thompson to Sloat, Washington, May 21, 1821, Letters to Officers, M149, Roll 14, RG45, NARA.

17. Abstract of Service Record of John Drake Sloat, Abstracts of Service Records of Naval Officers, M1328, Roll 19, RG24, NARA; Deck Log, USS *Franklin*, July 21, 1821, to July 31, 1822, Vol. 2 of 98; Logs of U.S. Naval Ships, 1801–1915, RG24, NARA.

18. Claude G. Berube and John A. Rodgaard, *A Call to the Sea: Captain Charles Stewart of the USS* Constitution (Washington, DC: Potomac Books, 2005), 133–156.

19. *Naval Register*, 1822, 5–7.

20. Charles Wilkes, *An Autobiography of Rear Admiral Charles Wilkes, U.S. Navy 1798–1877*, ed. William James Morgan, David B. Tyler, Joye L. Leonhart, and Mary F. Loughin (Washington, DC: Naval History Division, Department of the Navy, 1978), 118–120.

21. Geoffrey S. Smith, "An Uncertain Passage: The Bureaus Run the Navy, 1842–1861," in *In Peace and War: Interpretations of American Naval History, 1775–1994*, 2nd ed., ed. Kenneth A. Hagan (Westport: Greenwood Press, 1984), 92.

22. Leiner, "Notes," in Morris, *Autobiography*, 133; Bruce A. Castleman, "Navigators in the 1490s," *U.S. Naval Institute Proceedings* 118/12/1,078 (December 1992): 39–43.

23. Berube and Rodgaard, *Call to the Sea*, 144–145.

24. Gabriel Paquette, *Imperial Portugal in the Age of Atlantic Revolutions* (Cambridge: Cambridge University Press, 2013), 140–155; Thomas E. Skidmore, *Brazil: Five Centuries of Change* (New York: Oxford University Press, 2009), 36–37, and E. Bradford Burns, *A History of Brazil*, 3rd ed. (New York: Columbia University Press, 1993), 116–133, are good treatments in English of this matter. Berube and Rodgaard's statements that Rio de Janeiro was "liberated" from Portugal and that Emperor Dom Pedro sat on a Brazilian throne at the time of the *Franklin*'s visit are in error.

25. Berube and Rodgaard, *Call to the Sea*, 148–159; Deck Log, USS *Franklin*, July 21, 1821, to July 31, 1822; Wilkes, *Autobiography*, 147.

26. David F. Long, *Gold Braid and Foreign Relations: Diplomatic Activities of U.S. Naval Officers, 1798–1883* (Annapolis: Naval Institute Press, 1988), 83. On the general situation in Chile, see, in English, Simon Collier and William F. Sater, *A History of Chile, 1808–2002*, 2nd ed. (New York: Cambridge University Press, 2004), and Brian Loveman, *Chile: The Legacy of Hispanic Capitalism*, 3rd ed. (New York: Oxford University Press, 2001).

27. Deck Log, USS *Franklin*, July 21, 1821, to July 31, 1822; Allison, *Stephen Decatur*, 115–116, 119, Berube and Rodgaard, *Call to the Sea*, 148–150. Creamer's name appears as Cramer or Cremer in some documents.

28. Berube and Rodgaard, *Call to the Sea*, 179–198; Long, *Gold Braid and Foreign Relations*, 82–83; and see especially Edward Baxter Billingsley, *In Defense of Neutral Rights: The United States Navy and the Wars of Independence in Chile and Peru* (Chapel Hill: University of North Carolina Press, 1967).

29. Sentence of Court-Martial of Lieutenant William A. Weaver, USN, November 23, 1824, American State Papers, Naval Affairs 1: 1058.

30. Naval Register, 1821; Naval Register, 1822.

31. McKee, *Gentlemanly and Honorable Profession*, 133–135, provides a good summary of the first lieutenant's role. But the current author also speaks from his own experience as executive officer of a United States Navy cruiser.

32. Long, *Sailor-Diplomat*, 107–111; Nicholas B. Wainwright, "Commodore James Biddle and his Sketchbook," *Pennsylvania Magazine of History and Biography* 90:1 (January 1966): 20. Sherman, *Life of Sloat*, 25, contains the full text of Daniel Winton's remembrance of the La Guaira hurricane.

33. Letter, Sloat to Thompson, Norfolk, April 12, 1823, M148, Roll 30, Officers Letters, RG45, NARA; Nicholas B. Wainwright, "Voyage of the Frigate *Congress*, 1823," *Pennsylvania Magazine of History and Biography* 75:2 (April 1951): 170–188.

Chapter 8. Pirates in the Caribbean

1. Letter, Sloat to Secretary of the Navy Thompson, New York, July 11, 1823, M148, Roll 31, Officers Letters, RG45, NARA; Morison, *"Old Bruin,"* 82.

2. Chapelle, *American Sailing Ships*, 114–115, 239–240; Chapelle, *American Sailing Navy*, 332–334, 504; see also Robert J. Cressman, "Historic Fleets: 'For the Purpose of Repressing Piracy,'" *Naval History* 28:5 (October 2014): 64–65.

3. Long, *Gold Braid and Foreign Relations*, 60–63; Morison, *"Old Bruin,"* 77–80.

4. Letter, Sloat to Secretary of the Navy Samuel L. Southard, New York, November 3, 1823, Officers Letters, M148, Roll 33, RG45, NARA; Letter, Southard to Sloat, Washington, November 25, 1823, Letters to Officers, M149, Roll 15, RG45, NARA.

5. Abstract of Service, John Drake Sloat, M1328, Roll 19, Abstracts of Service Records of Naval Officers, RG24, NARA.

6. Letter, Sloat to Southard, off Cape Henry, February 29, 1824, Officers Letters, M148, Roll 34, RG45, NARA; entry dated April 11, 1824, Deck Log, USS *Grampus*, 3-14-1824 to 1-17-1828, Logs of U.S. Naval Ships, 1801–1915, RG24, NARA; Letter, Sloat to Commodore David Porter, Matanzas, Cuba, May 29, 1824, American State Papers, Naval Affairs 2: 252.

7. Claude A. Clegg III, *The Price of Liberty: African Americans and the Founding of Liberia* (Chapel Hill: University of North Carolina Press, 2004), 37; Eric Burin, *Slavery and the Peculiar Solution: A History of the American Colonization Society* (Gainesville: University Press of Florida, 2005), 13–21; Douglas R. Egerton, "Its Origin Is Not a Little Curious: A New Look at the American Colonization Society," *Journal of the Early Republic* 5:4 (Winter 1985): 470; Charles I. Foster, "The Colonization of Free Negroes, in Liberia, 1816–1835," *Journal of Negro History* 38:1 (January 1953): 41–50; Daniel Walker Howe, *What Hath God Wrought: The Transformation of America, 1815–1848* (New York: Oxford University Press, 2007), 260–266.

8. Jehudi Ashmun, *History of the American Colony in Liberia from December, 1821 to 1823* (Washington City: Way & Gideon, 1826), 25–36.

9. Burin, *Slavery and the Peculiar Solution*, 17.

10. Letter, Sloat to Southard, New York, September 1, 1824, Officers Letters, M148, Roll 36, RG45, NARA.

11. Letter, Sloat to Porter, May 29, 1824, American State Papers, Naval Affairs 2: 252.

12. Letter, Captain W. B. Finch to Southard, Washington, July 20, 1824, American State Papers, Naval Affairs 2: 686–687.

13. Timothy Anna, "Agustín de Iturbide and the Process of Consensus," in *The Birth of Modern Mexico 1780–1824*, ed. Christon I. Archer (Lanham: Rowman & Littlefield, 2003), 198–201; Josefina Zoraida Vásquez, "Los primeros tropiezos," *Historia General de México*, 4ta ed., Vol. 2, ed. Daniel Cosío Villegas (Mexico City: El Colegio de México, 1997), 747–750.

14. Entries dated April 11, 1824, and September 2, 1824, Deck Log, USS *Grampus*, 3-14-1824 to 1-17-1828, Logs of U.S. Naval Ships, 1801–1915, RG24, NARA; *Longworth's City Directory*, 1824/1825, 387.

15. Testimony of Master Commandant Alexander J. Dallas, July 8, 1825, American State Papers, Naval Affairs 2: 305–307; testimony of Lieutenant Charles J. Platt, July 8, 1825, American State Papers, Naval Affairs 2: 307–311; Long, *Nothing Too Daring*, 228–229; Long, *Gold Braid and Foreign Relations*, 65.

16. Letter, Porter to Southard, Passage Island, November 15, 1824, *American State Papers: Naval Affairs* 1: 1024.

17. Long, *Nothing Too Daring*, 250–253; Long, *Gold Braid and Foreign Relations*, 65.

18. Letter, Sloat to Porter, St. Thomas, February 4, 1825, in Robert Beale, *A Report of the Trial of Commodore David Porter of the Navy of the United States, before a General Court-Martial, Held at Washington in July 1825* (Washington City: 1825) (http://archive.org/, accessed May 31, 2013), 94.

19. Beale, *Report of Trial of Porter*, 11–27, 66; Letter, Captain General of Puerto Rico Miguel de la Torre to Consul General Hilario de Rivas y Salmón, San Juan, November 23, 1824, and the diplomatic exchanges between Secretaries of State John Quincy Adams, Daniel Brent, and Henry Clay and the Spanish legation in Philadelphia are at *American State Papers: Naval Affairs* 2: 663–668.

20. Michael J. Birkner, *Samuel L. Southard: Jeffersonian Whig* (Rutherford: Fairleigh Dickinson University Press, 1984), 96–99.

21. Long, *Gold Braid and Foreign Relations*, 65.

22. Howe, *What Hath God Wrought*, 111–116; Ernest R. May, *The Making of the Monroe Doctrine* (Cambridge: Belknap Press of Harvard University Press, 1975), 12–64, 203–229.

23. David F. Long, "The Navy under the Board of Navy Commissioners, 1815–1842," in *In Peace and War: Interpretations of American Naval History,*

1775–1984, 2nd ed., ed. Kenneth A. Hagan (Westport: Greenwood Press, 1984), 66, 70; Long, *Nothing Too Daring*, 239.

24. Michael J. Birkner, "The 'Foxardo Affair' Revisited: Porter, Pirates, and the Problem of Civilian Authority in the Early Republic," *American Neptune* 42:3 (July 1982): 165–178.

25. Long, *Nothing Too Daring*, 223.

26. Entries dated November 24, 1824, through January 31, 1825, Deck Log, USS *Grampus*.

27. Letter, Sloat to Southard, St. Thomas, January 18, 1825, Officers Letter, M148, Roll 38, RG45, NARA.

28. Letter, Sloat to Southard, St. Thomas, February 6, 1825, Officers Letters, M148, Roll 38, RG45, NARA.

29. Letter, Sloat to Southard, St. Thomas, March 12, 1825, Officers Letters, M148 Roll 38, RG45, NARA.

30. Letter, Sloat to Southard, St. Thomas, March 19, 1825, Officers Letters, M148 Roll 38, RG45, NARA.

31. Roberto Fernández Valledor, *El mito de Cofresí en la narrative antillana* (Mayaguez: Editorial Universitaria, Universidad de Puerto Rico, 1978); Roberto Fernández Valledor, *El Pirata Cofresí mitificado por la tradición oral puertorriqueña* (Ponce: Casa Paoli, 2006), 106–107; Ursula Acosta with David E. Cuesta Camacho, *¿Quien era Cofresí?* (Hormigueros: Dra. Ursula Acosta, 1978); Eric Hobsbawm, *Bandits* (New York: Delacorte Press, 1969); Hobsbawm, "Social Bandits: A Reply," *Comparative Studies in Society and History* 14:4 (September 1972): 503–505; Hobsbawm and Terence Ranger, *The Invention of Tradition* (Cambridge: Cambridge University Press, 1983); Graham Seal, "The Robin Hood Principle: Folklore, History, and the Social Bandit," *Journal of Folklore Research* 46:1 (January–April 2009): 67–89.

32. Morison, *"Old Bruin,"* 82.

33. Letter, Sloat to Southard, St. Thomas, April 5, 1825, Officers Letters, M148, Roll 39, RG45, NARA; Letter, Southard to Sloat, Washington, April 27, 1825, Letters to Officers, M149, Roll 16, RG45, NARA; Letter, Sloat to Southard, Norfolk, August 7, 1825, Officers Letters, M148, Roll 40, RG45, NARA; Letter, Southard to Sloat, Washington, August 13, 1825, Letters to Officers, M149, Roll 16, RG45, NARA; Letter, Sloat to Southard, Norfolk, August 15, 1825, Officers Letters, M148, Roll 40, RG45, NARA; Letter, Southard to Sloat, Washington, Letters to Officers, M148, Roll 40, RG45, NARA; Letter, Sloat to Southard, New York, August 26, 1825, Officers Letters, M148, Roll 40, RG45, NARA; Letter, Sloat to Southard, New York, September 5, 1825, Officers Letters, M148, Roll 40, RG45, NARA.

Chapter 9. New York Interlude

1. Naval Register for 1826, American State Papers, Naval Affairs 2: 443; Morison, *"Old Bruin,"* 83; *Longworth's City Directory for New York*, 1825/1826, 1826/1827, and 1827/1828.

2. Letter, Sloat to Southard, New York, January 4, 1826, Officers Letters, M148, Roll 41, RG45, NARA.

3. Naval Register for 1827, American State Papers, Naval Affairs 2: 782.

4. Naval Register for 1827, American State Papers, Naval Affairs 2: 782; Naval Register for 1828, American State Papers, Naval Affairs 3: 94; Letter, Sloat to Southard, New York, April 25, 1827, Letters Received by the Secretary of the Navy from Commanders, 1804–1886 (hereafter, Commanders Letters) M147, Roll 13, RG45, NARA; Letter, Sloat to Southard, New York, August 4, 1827, Commanders Letters, M147, Roll 13, RG45, NARA.

5. New York County, Land Records, Conveyance Index-Grantee 1654–1866 N-S, Liber 207 p. 227, Liber 214 p. 420, Liber 225 p. 495, Liber 238 p. 67, Liber 234 p. 438; New York County, Land Records, Conveyance Index Grantor 1654–1866 S-Z, Liber 226 p. 225, Liber 234 p. 514, Liber 240 p. 173, http://ancestrylibrary.com/, accessed April 21, 2012.

6. Dorothie Bobbé, *DeWitt Clinton*, rev. ed., with an introduction by Harry Steele Commager (Port Washington: Ira J. Friedman, 1962), 227, 284–285, 294–297.

7. Edwin G. Burrows and Mike Wallace, *Gotham: A History of New York to 1898* (New York: Oxford University Press, 1999), 446–458; Kenneth T. Jackson and David S. Dunbar, "Rise to National Dominance (1782–1860)," in *Empire City: New York through the Centuries*, ed. Jackson and Dunbar (New York: Columbia University Press, 2002), 101–105.

8. Letter, Sloat to Southard, New York, June 3, 1828, Commanders Letters, M147, Roll 14 RG45, NARA; Letter, Sloat to Southard, New York, August 4, 1828, Commanders Letters, M147, Roll 14, RG45, NARA; Letter, Sloat to Southard, New York, August 23, 1828, Commanders Letters, M147, Roll 14, RG45, NARA; *Catalogue of the Trustees, Instructors, and Students, of Plainfield Academy, Plainfield (Con.) August 1828* (Brooklyn: Advertiser Press—John Gray, Jr., 1828), 7, U.S. High School Student Lists, 1821–1923, http://search.ancestrylibrary.com/, accessed January 10, 2013.

9. *Dictionary of American Naval Fighting Ships*, http://www.history.navy.mil/danfs/s17/st_louis_i.htm/, accessed May 2, 2012; Chapelle, *American Sailing Navy*, 365; Chapelle, *American Sailing Ships*, 116; Morison, *"Old Bruin,"* 104; K. Jack Bauer, "Naval Shipbuilding Programs, 1794–1860," *Military Affairs* 29:1 (Spring 1965): 35.

10. Log Book, USS *St. Louis*, 12-7-1828 to 5-3-1831, RG24, NARA.

11. Letter, Sloat to Southard, Washington, December 2, 1828, Commanders Letters, M147, Roll 14, RG45, NARA; Letter, Sloat to Southard, Norfolk, January 16, 1829, Commanders Letters, M147, Roll 15, RG45, NARA; Letter, Sloat to Southard, Norfolk, January 29, 1829, Commanders Letters, M147, Roll 15, RG45, NARA; American State Papers, Naval Affairs 3: 64 includes the personnel allowance for a sloop.

12. Letter, Sloat to Southard, Washington, December 11, 1828, Commanders Letters, M147, Roll 14, RG 45, NARA; untitled article, *Baltimore Patriot*, February 16, 1829, p. 2.

13. Navy Register for 1829, American State Papers, Naval Affairs 3: 271; Letter, Sloat to Secretary of the Navy Levi Woodbury, New York, July 25, 1832, Commanders Letters, M147, Roll 17, RG45, NARA.

14. Letter, Sloat to Southard, Washington, December 6, 1828, Commanders Letters, M147, Roll 14, RG45, NARA; Letter, Sloat to Southard, Norfolk, January 8, 1829, Commanders Letters, M147, Roll 15, RG45, NARA; Letter, Sloat to Southard, Norfolk, January 13, 1829, Commanders Letters, M147, Roll 15, RG45, NARA; Naval Register for 1830, American State Papers, Naval Affairs 3: 402–422.

Chapter 10. South American Cruise

1. Log Book, USS *St. Louis*, 12-7-1828 to 5-3-1831, RG24, NARA.

2. W. Jeffrey Bolster, "'To Feel Like a Man': Black Seamen in the Northern States, 1800–1860," *Journal of American History* 76:4 (March 1990): 1178.

3. Hugh H. Davis, "The American Seamen's Friend Society and the American Sailor, 1828–1838," *American Neptune* 29:1 (January 1979): 45, 57; Harold D. Langley, *Social Reform in the United States Navy, 1798–1862* (Urbana, Chicago, and London: University of Illinois Press, 1967), 65; Spencer C. Tucker, *Andrew Foote: Civil War Admiral in Western Waters* (Annapolis: Naval Institute Press, 2000), 3–17; James Mason Hoppin, *The Life of Andrew Hull Foote, Rear-Admiral, United States Navy* (New York: Harper Brothers, 1874), 33–35; George Sidney Webster, *The Seamen's Friend: A Sketch of the American Seamen's Friend Society* (New York: The American Seamen's Friend Society, 1932).

4. Log Book, USS *St. Louis*.

5. Untitled article, *New Hampshire Gazette* (Portsmouth, NH), June 2, 1829, p. 2.

6. Letter, Sloat to Southard, Valparaíso, June (illegible date), 1829, Commanders Letters, M147, Roll 15, RG45, NARA.

7. Log Book, USS *St. Louis*.

8. John Lynch, *Simón Bolívar: A Life* (New Haven: Yale University Press, 2006), 268–270; Mark J. Van Aken, *King of the Night: Juan José Flores and Ecuador, 1824–1864* (Berkeley, Los Angeles, and London: University of California Press, 1989), 19–20, 32–33.

9. Berube and Rodgaard, *Call to the Sea*, 153–156.

10. Peter Klarén, *Peru: Society and Nationhood in the Andes* (New York: Oxford University Press, 2000), 137–139.

11. Lynch, *Simón Bolivar*, 259–261; Almudena Hernández Ruigómez, *Simón Bolívar* (Madrid: Ediciones Dastín Export, 2004), 206; Charles Walker, *Smoldering Ashes: Cuzco and the Creation of Republican Peru, 1780–1840* (Durham and London: Duke University Press, 1999); Guillermo A. Sherwell, *Simón Bolívar (The Liberator)* (Caracas: The Bolivarian Society of Venezuela, 1951), 198; Van Aken, *King of the Night*, 22.

12. Letter, Sloat to Secretary of State Edward Livingston, Washington, March 29, 1832, American State Papers, Naval Affairs 4:132–133; Log Book, USS *St. Louis*.

13. Letter, Sloat to Livingston, Washington, March 29, 1832; Log Book, USS *St. Louis*.

14. Lynch, *Simón Bolívar*, 259–260, 268–270; Van Aken, *King of the Night*, 30–33; Lester D. Langley, *Simón Bolívar: Venezuelan Rebel, American Revolutionary* (Lanham: Rowman & Littlefield, 2009), 89, 99, 103–104.

15. Sean Wilentz, *The Rise of American Democracy: Jefferson to Lincoln* (New York and London: W.W. Norton and Co., 2005), 359–374.

16. Smith, *Commodore of Manifest Destiny*, 70.

17. Log Book, USS *St. Louis*.

18. Valle, *Rocks and Shoals*, 77–80.

19. Log Book, USS *St. Louis*.

20. Log Book, USS *St. Louis*; untitled article, *Baltimore Patriot*, July 7, 1830, p. 2; untitled article, *Norwich Courier*, August 18, 1830, p. 3; Christon I. Archer, "Fashioning a New Nation," in *The Oxford History of Mexico*, ed. Michael C. Meyer and William H. Beezley (New York: Oxford University Press, 2000), 319–330; Vázquez, "Los primeros tropiezos," 757–759; Van Aken, *King of the Night*, 33.

21. "Claim of a Purser in the Navy. . . . for Reimbursements of Payments Made to Seamen . . ." U.S. Congress, House, 24th Congress, 1st Session, H. Doc 611, March 3, 1836, in American State Papers, Naval Affairs 4: 858.

22. Letter, Sloat to Thompson, Callao, June 24, 1830, Commanders Letters, M147, Roll 15, RG45, NARA; Ship's Log, USS *St. Louis*; Valle, *Rocks and Shoals*, 85–87; for ships' manpower allowances, see American State Papers, Naval Affairs 4: 25, 4: 167.

23. Shipping News, *Baltimore Patriot*, May 6, 1831, p. 2.

24. Natalia Sobrevilla Perea, *The Caudillo of the Andes: Andrés de Santa Cruz* (Cambridge and New York: Cambridge University Press, 2011), 115, 122; Walker, *Smoldering Ashes*, 121–156; Carlos Neuhaus Rizo Patrón, *Pancha Gamarra, La Mariscala* (Lima: F. Moncloa, Editores, 1967), 56–60, 68; and, for a detailed interpretation highly favorable to Gamarra, see also Dante Herrera Alarcón, *Rebeliones que intentaron desmembrar el sur del Perú* (Lima: Imprenta Colegio Militar Leoncio Prado, 1961), 49–90, 95–120.

25. Walker, *Smoldering Ashes*, 160.

26. Margarita Guerra Martiniere, *La República, 1827–1899: Historia General del Perú, Tomo VII* (Lima: Editorial Brasa, 1994), 63–69; Luis Durand Florez, "La República: 1826–1899," in *Compendio Histórico del Perú, Tomo V*, ed. Carlos Milla Batres (Lima: Editorial Milla Batres, 1993), 166–169; Sobrevilla, *Caudillo of the Andes*, 104–105, 123–128; Neuhaus, *Pancha Gamarra*, 59–62; Herrera, *Rebeliones*, 128–132; Letter, U.S. Minister to Peru Samuel Larned to Secretary of State Martin Van Buren, Lima, April 18, 1831, Dispatches from U.S. Ministers to Peru, 1826–1906, General Records of the Department of State, Microfilm T-52, Roll 1, RG 59, NARA; Letter, Sloat to Secretary of State Edward Livingston, Washington, March 29, 1832, *American State Papers: Naval Affairs* 4: 132–133.

27. Letter, Sloat to Larned, Callao Roads, April 18, 1831, American State Papers, Naval Affairs 4: 126; Herrera, *Rebeliones*, 159; Santiago Távara, *Historia de los Partidos*, Jorge Basadre and Félix Denegri Luna, eds. (Lima: Editorial Huascarán, 1951), 82–84; John Miller, *Memoirs of General Miller in the Service of the Republic of Peru*, Vol. 1 (London: Longman, Rees, Orme, Brown, and Green, 1828), 132–134.

28. Letter, Sloat to Larned, April 18, 1831; Letter, Larned to Sloat, Lima, April 19, 1831, American State Papers, Naval Affairs 4:126.

29. Letter, Sloat to Thompson, Callao, April 22, 1831, American State Papers, Naval Affairs 4: 127.

30. Letter, Sloat to Thompson, Callao, April 22, 1831, American State Papers, Naval Affairs 4: 125–126; Letter, Thompson to Larned, Callao, April 23, 1831, American State Papers, Naval Affairs 4: 127; Letter, Larned to Thompson, Lima, American State Papers, Naval Affairs 4: 127–128; Letter, Thompson to Sloat, Callao, American State Papers, Naval Affairs 4: 128.

31. T. Ray Shurbutt, "Chile, Peru, and the U.S. Pacific Squadron," in *New Aspects of Naval History: Selected Papers Presented at the Fourth Naval History Symposium, United States Naval Academy, 25–26 October 1979*, ed. Craig L. Symonds (Annapolis: Naval Institute Press, 1981), 201–203; see also Robert Erwin Johnson, *Thence Round Cape Horn: The Story of United States Naval Forces on Pacific Station, 1818–1923* (Annapolis: Naval Institute Press, 1963).

32. Log Book, USS *St. Louis*.

33. Letter, Sloat to Woodbury, New York, December 10, 1831, Commanders Letters, M147, Roll 16, RG45, NARA; Letter, Sloat to Woodbury, New York, December 24, 1831, Commanders Letters, M147, Roll 16, RG45, NARA.

Chapter 11. Beached in New York

1. Letter, Sloat to Secretary of the Navy Mahlon Dickerson, New York, December 12, 1835, Commanders Letters, M147, Roll 20, RG45, NARA; on the French claims furor, see Bailey, *Diplomatic History*, 195–197.

2. Long, *Sailor-Diplomat*, 148; Howe, *What Hath God Wrought*, 546.

3. Norwich, Connecticut, Land Records, General Index, Grantee, 1727–1849, Vol. 1, p. 579.

4. *Catalogue of the Trustees, Instructors, and Students, of Plainfield Academy, Plainfield, Ct., for the Year Ending August, 1832* (Brooklyn; Advertiser Press, 1832), 2, 6; 1830 United States Census, Connecticut, New London County, p. 100, M19, Roll 100, RG29, NARA.

5. New York, Land Records, Conveyance Index–Grantor 1654–1866 S-Z Liber 297, p. 112; http://ancestrylibrary.com/, accessed April 21, 2012; Norwich, Connecticut, General Index, Grantor 1727–1849; Notice, *Norwich Courier*, February 16, 1825, p. 4; "For Sale," *Norwich Courier*, November 5, 1834, p. 3; Frances Manwaring Caulkins, *History of Norwich, Connecticut from Its Possession by the Indians to the Year 1866* (1866, reprint, New London: New London County Historical Society, 2009), 596.

6. Letter, Secretary of State Edward Livingston to President Andrew Jackson, Washington, April 2, 1832, and Communication, Jackson to House of Representatives, Washington, April 4, 1832, American State Papers, Naval Affairs 4: 125; U.S. Congress, House Committee on Foreign Relations, *On the Expediency of Allowing the Claim of Captain John D. Sloat, of the United States Ship St. Louis, for Giving Refuge to the Vice-President of the Republic of Peru and General Miller During a Revolution in That Country*, 22nd Congress, 1st Session, No. 481, in American State Papers, Naval Affairs 4: 142.

7. Letter, Sloat to Woodbury, New York, March 28, 1833, Commanders Letter, M147, Roll 18, RG45, NARA.

8. Tucker, *Andrew Foote*, 17.

9. Letter, Sloat to Woodbury, New York, March 30, 1832, Commanders Letters, M147, Roll 17, RG45, NARA.

10. Morris, *Autobiography*, 116–117; Remarks of Master Commandant William B. Shubrick to James Fenimore Cooper in Wayne Franklin, *James Fenimore Cooper: The Early Years* (New Haven and London: Yale University Press, 2007), 414–415.

11. Register of Naval Officers, 1832, American State Papers, Naval Affairs 4: 49; Register of Naval Officers, 1833, American State Papers, Naval Affairs 4: 231.

12. Preble, *Navy-Yard, Portsmouth*, 45.

13. David F. Long, *Sailor-Diplomat*, 85. Biddle actually took a higher rate of deposit in 1818 than did Sloat in 1832.

14. Letter, Sloat to Woodbury, Norwich, June 4, 1832, Commanders Letters, M147, Roll 17, RG45, NARA.

15. Naval Registers for 1832 and 1833, American State Papers, Naval Affairs, 4: 234, 445, 446.

16. Paul A. Gilje, *Liberty on the Waterfront: American Maritime Culture in the Age of Revolution* (Philadelphia: University of Pennsylvania Press, 2004), 19–20, 207; Morison, *"Old Bruin,"* 91; 1833 pay rates are at American State Papers, Naval Affairs 4: 167; "Crimp," in *The Oxford Companion to Ships and the Sea*, ed. Peter Kemp (Oxford, New York, and Melbourne: Oxford University Press, 1976), 213.

17. Letter, Sloat to Secretary of the Navy Mahlon Dickerson, New York, December 2, 1836, Commanders Letters, M147, Roll 21, RG45, NARA.

18. Langley, *Social Reform in the Navy*, viii, 74–78; Judith Fingard, "Masters and Friends, Crimps and Abstainers: Agents of Control in 19th Century Sailortown," *Acadiensis* 8:1 (1978): 22–26; Gilje, *Liberty on the Waterfront*, 207–210; Jacob Nagle, *The Nagle Journal: A Diary of the Life of Jacob Nagle, Sailor, from the Year 1775 to 1841*, ed. John C. Dann (New York: Weidenfeld & Nicolson, 1988), 273–274; James Fenimore Cooper, ed., *Ned Myers, or, A Life Before the Mast* (London: Richard Bentley, New Burlington Street, 1843), 274.

19. G. R. Henning, "Fourpenny Dark and Sixpenny Red," *Labour History* 46 (May 1984): 52–56; Denise M. Allborn, "Crimping and Shanghaiing on the Columbia River," *Oregon Historical Quarterly* 93:3 (Fall 1992): 264–275; Lance S. Davidson, "Shanghaied! The Systematic Kidnapping of Sailors in Early San Francisco," *California History* 64:1 (Winter 1985), 10–17; Fingard, "Masters and Friends." For an extensive analysis of changing labor markets, see E. P. Thompson, *The Making of the English Working Class* (New York: Random House, 1963); for the United States generally, see Howe, *What Hath God Wrought*; and for labor in New York in particular, Wilentz, *Chants Democratic*.

20. Letter, Sloat to Commodore Charles G. Ridgely, New York, October 22, 1836, Commanders Letters, M147, Roll 21, RG45, NARA; Wilentz, *Chants Democratic*, 117; "Rules and Regulation, 1833," American State Papers, Naval Affairs 4: 397.

21. Langley, *Social Reform in the Navy*, 79.

22. *The Naval Magazine* 1:1 (January 1836) to 2:2 (March 1837), various pages; Langley, *Social Reform in the Navy*, 26; Steven Lubar, "'To polish

and adorn the mind': The United States Naval Lyceum at the Brooklyn Navy Yard, 1833–1889," *Museum History Journal* 7:1 (January 2014): 84–102; Claude Berube, "The Crucible of Naval Enlightenment," *Naval History* 28:5 (October 2014): 58–63; W. Ray Heitzmann, "In-Service Naval Officer Education in the Nineteenth Century: Voluntary Commitment to Reform," *American Neptune* 39:2 (April 1979): 109–125; Morison, *"Old Bruin,"* 133–134.

23. Register of Naval Officers, American State Papers, Naval Affairs 4: 763–764; List of Members, *The Naval Magazine 1:1* (January 1836): appendix, 39–42; Schroeder, *Matthew Calbraith Perry*, 71.

24. Franklin, *Cooper: The Early Years*, 153–155, 170–172, 290; James Fenimore Cooper, *Letters and Journal*, Vols. 1–6, ed. James Franklin Beard (Cambridge: Belknap Press of Harvard University Press, 1960–1968).

25. Wayne Franklin, Letter to author, July 28, 2013.

26. Lubar, "'To Polish and Adorn the Mind," 84–102; Morison, *"Old Bruin,"* 133–134; Angela G. Ray, *The Lyceum and Public Culture in the Nineteenth-Century United States* (East Lansing: Michigan State University Press, 2005), 1–6, 20, 27–29; Edward Pessen, *Jacksonian America: Society, Personality, and Politics*, rev. ed. (Homewood: Dorsey Press, 1978), 61.

27. "Report of the U.S. Naval Lyceum, Presented to the American Lyceum for Incorporation in the Proceedings of Its 6th Annual Meeting, in May, 1836," *The Naval Magazine* 1: 391–396.

28. Letter, Sloat to Dickerson, New York, March 18, 1837, Commanders Letters, M147, Roll 21, RG45, NARA.

29. Letter, Perry, Sloat et al. to Dickerson, New York, December 1, 1834, Commanders Letters, M147, Roll 19, RG45, NARA; *Register of the Commissioned and Warrant Officers of the Navy of the United States, Including Officers of the Marine Corps, and Others, for the Year 1847* (Washington: C. Alexander, Printer, 1847), 16–24.

30. Letter, Captains Lawrence Kearny, John D. Sloat, and Matthew C. Perry to Dickerson, New York, June 20, 1837, Letters Received by the Secretary of the Navy from Captains, 1805–1861 (hereafter, Captains Letters) M125, Roll 234, RG45, NARA; Letter, Kearny, Sloat, and Perry to Dickerson, New York, December 9, 1837, Captains Letters, M125, Roll 235, RG45, NARA; Morison, *"Old Bruin,"* 136.

31. Smith, *Commodore of Manifest Destiny*, 90–91; Long, "Under the Board of Navy Commissioners," 75.

32. Nathaniel Philbrick, *Sea of Glory: America's Voyage of Discovery, the U.S. Exploring Expedition, 1838–1842* (New York: Viking Press, 2003), 17–42; W. Patrick Strauss, "Preparing the Wilkes Expedition: A Study in Disorganization," *Pacific Historical Review* 28:3 (August 1959): 221–232.

33. St. Thomas Episcopal Church Parish Record, 1831–1865, cited in personal letter, Will Andersen, parish archivist, to author, October 20, 2013.

34. "Court-Martial," *Southern Patriot* (Charleston, SC), January 10, 1839, p. 2.

35. Letter, Sloat to Secretary of the Navy James K. Paulding, New York, November 9, 1839, Captains Letters, M125, Roll 259, RG45, NARA.

36. Stuart M. Blumin, *The Emergence of the Middle Class: Social Experience in the American City, 1760–1900* (New York: Cambridge University Press, 1989), 146; Charles Lockwood, *Manhattan Moves Uptown: An Illustrated History* (Boston: Houghton Mifflin, 1976) 73–75.

37. Ira Dye, *Uriah Levy: Reformer of the Antebellum Navy* (Gainesville: University Press of Florida, 2006), 134, 147–148, 220.

38. Edward Pessen, "The Egalitarian Myth and the American Social Reality: Wealth, Mobility, and Equality in the 'Era of the Common Man,'" *American Historical Review* 76:4 (October 1971): 1022; Pessen, "The Social Configuration of the Antebellum City: An Historical and Theoretical Inquiry," *Journal of Urban History* 2:3 (May 1976): 281; Blumin, *The Emergence of the Middle Class,* 1.

39. Moses Y. Beach, *Wealth and Biography of the Wealthy Citizens of New York City,* 6th ed. (New York: New York Sun Office, 1845), 31; Edward Pessen, "Moses Beach Revisited: A Critical Examination of his *Wealthy Citizens* Pamphlets," *Journal of American History* 58:2 (September 1971): 415–426; Pessen, "Social Structure and Politics in American History," *American Historical Review* 87:5 (December 1982): 1293–1297. Pessen analyzed the tax assessment rolls of New York City and placed Samuel Whittemore among the fifty-nine wealthiest persons in 1828 New York. Pessen, *Riches, Class, and Power before the Civil War* (Lexington: D. C. Heath, 1973), 321.

40. "Remarks Offered to the Board on the Presentation of Portraits of Founders of Early Members of the Board of Trustees of Northern Dispensary," New York State Legislature, Senate, *Documents of the Senate of the State of New York, One Hundred and Thirty-Second Session, 1909,* Vol. 13, No. 35 (Albany: J. B. Lyon Co., State Printers, 1909), 24–33;

41. Pessen, *Riches, Class, and Power before the Civil War,* 206–214.

42. Pessen, "Social Configuration of the Antebellum City," 278.

43. Jerome Mushkat, *Tammany: The Evolution of a Political Machine, 1789–1865* (Syracuse: Syracuse University Press, 1971), 187; Mushkat, *Fernando Wood: A Political Biography* (Kent: Kent State University Press, 1990), 19, 27; M. Regina McEntee, "John McKeon: Catholic Leader and Congressman from New York, 1808–1883" (master's thesis, Catholic University, 1947), 8, 22–23.

44. Douglas T. Miller, *Jacksonian Aristocracy: Class and Democracy in New York, 1830–1860* (New York: Oxford University Press, 1967), 76; on the Searles

painting, see Isaac N. Phelps-Stokes, *The Iconography of Manhattan Island, Vol. 3* (New York: Robert H. Dodd, 1918), plate 91 and p. 577.

45. Burrows and Wallace, *Gotham*, 563–618; Edward K. Spann, *The New Metropolis: New York City, 1840–1857* (New York: Columbia University Press, 1981), 109–112, 187, 433; Lockwood, *Manhattan Moves Uptown*, 75–81.

46. Richmond County, Grantee Index to Deeds, Vol. S1-S2 Liber 7, p. 303; http://en.wikipedia.org/wiki/File:View_of_Brighton,_Staten_Island,_New_York.jpg, accessed November 12, 2013.

47. Letter, Sloat to Paulding, New York, March 25, 1840, Captains Letters, M125, Roll 263, RG45, NARA.

48. *Wisconsin Enquirer*, June 3, 1840, p. 2; "Trial of Commodore Elliott," *Burlington Free Press* (Vermont), May 22, 1840, p. 1.

49. Letter, Sloat to Paulding, New York, April 11, 1840, Captains Letters, M125, Roll 264, RG45, NARA.

50. Valle, *Rocks and Shoals*, 225–226. For the Battle of Lake Erie and the subsequent disputes in the U.S. Navy, see among many David Curtis Skaggs, "Aftermath of Victory: The Perry-Elliott Controversy," *Naval History* 28:1 (February 2014): 38–45; Walter Rybka, "'We have met the enemy and they are ours': The U.S. Navy Brig *Niagara*," in *Coffins of the Brave: Lake Shipwrecks of the War of 1812*, ed. Kevin J. Crisman (College Station: Texas A&M University Press, 2014), 20–24, 37; David Curtis Skaggs, *Oliver Hazard Perry: Honor, Courage, and Patriotism in the Early U.S. Navy* (Annapolis: Naval Institute Press, 2006), 101–142, 218–244; Morison, *"Old Bruin,"* 41–49; Fowler, *Jack Tars and Commodores*, 222–228; George C. Daughan, *1812: The Navy's War* (New York: Basic Books, 2011), 207–219.

51. Allison, *Stephen Decatur*, 209–217.

52. James Fenimore Cooper, *The History of the Navy of the United States, Continued to 1856, from the Author's Notes and Other Authentic Notes* (New York: Stringer and Townsend, 1856); James Grossman, *James Fenimore Cooper* (New York: William Sloan Associates, 1949), 138–140, 188; Morison, *"Old Bruin,"* 140–143.

53. Letter, James Fenimore Cooper to Captain William B. Shubrick, Cooperstown, New York, October 1, 1840, *Letters and Journals* 4: 87–89.

54. Journal of the Board of Examiners of Midshipmen, 1840, Records of the Board of Examiners of Midshipmen, Journals of Proceedings 1836–1850, RG405.6.1, NARA.

55. Letters, Sloat to Paulding, Philadelphia, July 11, 1840, and July 28, 1840, Captains Letters, M125, Roll 267, RG45, NARA; Ralph M. Aderman and Wayne R. Kime, *Advocate for America: The Life of James Kirke Paulding* (Selinsgrove: Susquehanna University Press, 2003), 231–232.

56. Letters, Sloat to Paulding, New York, October 20, 1840, and October 22, 1840, Captains Letters, M125, Roll 270, RG45, NARA.

Chapter 12. Portsmouth Commandant

1. Letter, Sloat to Paulding, New York, October 22, 1840, Captains Letters, M125, Roll 270, RG45 NARA; Letter, Captain William Crane to Paulding, Portsmouth, October 27, 1840, Captains Letters, M125, Roll 271, RG45, NARA; Letter, Sloat to Paulding, Portsmouth, November 9, 1840, Captains Letters, M125, Roll 271, RG45, NARA; Letter, Sloat to Paulding, Portsmouth, December 1, 1840, Captains Letters, M125, Roll 272, RG45, NARA; "Changes at the Portsmouth Navy Yard," *Portsmouth Journal of Literature and Politics* (October 31, 1840): 3; Register of Naval Officers, American State Papers, Naval Affairs 4: 767, 4: 776.

2. Peter Randall, *Portsmouth and the Piscataqua* (Camden: Downeast Books, 1982), 8–9; William G. Saltonstall, *Ports of Piscataqua: Soundings in the Maritime History of the Portsmouth, N.H. Customs District from the Queen Elizabeth and the Planting of Strawberry Banke to the Times of Abraham Lincoln and the Waning of the American Clipper* (Cambridge: Harvard University Press, 1941), 201–202; Chapelle, *American Sailing Ships*, 119.

3. Chapelle, *American Sailing Navy*, 404–405; Chapelle, *American Sailing Ships*, 117.

4. Letter, Sloat to Secretary of the Navy George E. Badger, Portsmouth, August 18, 1841, Captains Letters, M125, Roll 280, RG45, NARA; "Launch of the Frigate Congress," *Portsmouth Journal* (August 21, 1841): 1.

5. Letter, Sloat to Navy Agent John Leighton, Portsmouth, April 19, 1841, Naval Districts and Shore Establishments, Portsmouth Navy Yard, NH, Misc. Letters Sent (Fair Copies), 1823–25, 1828–1867, Vol. 3, RG181, NARA.

6. Letter, Captain J. B. Nicolson to Secretary of the Navy Abel P. Upshur, Boston, November 7, 1842, Naval Districts and Shore Establishments, Boston Navy Yard, Misc. Letters, September 1842–February 1843, RG181, NARA.

7. Letter, Sloat to Commodore James Renshaw, Portsmouth, May 5, 1841, and Letters, Sloat to Commodore John W. Downes, Portsmouth, various dates April to August 1841, Naval Districts and Shore Establishments, Portsmouth Navy Yard, NH, Misc. Letters Sent (Fair Copies), 1823–25, 1828–1867, Vol. 3, RG181, NARA.

8. Letter, Sloat to Downes, Portsmouth, October 16, 1841, Naval Districts and Shore Establishments, Portsmouth Navy Yard, NH, Misc. Letters Sent (Fair Copies), 1823–25, 1828–1867, Vol. 3, RG181, NARA; Preble, *Navy-Yard, Portsmouth*, 68.

9. Letters, Sloat to Downes, Portsmouth, August 9, 1841 and August 20, 1841, Naval Districts and Shore Establishments, Portsmouth Navy Yard, NH, Misc. Letters Sent (Fair Copies), 1823–25, 1828–1867, Vol. 3, RG181, NARA; Letter, Sloat to Badger, Portsmouth, August 17, 1841, Captains Letters, M125, Roll 280, RG45, NARA; Letter, Sloat to Upshur, Portsmouth, November 27, 1841, Captains Letters, M125, Roll 283, RG45, NARA; Letter, Sloat to Upshur, Portsmouth, February 14, 1842, Captains Letters, M125, Roll 286, RG45, NARA.

10. Letter, Sloat to Captain Matthew Calbraith Perry, Portsmouth, February 21, 1842, Naval Districts and Shore Establishments, Portsmouth Navy Yard, NH, Misc. Letters Sent (Fair Copies), 1823–25, 1828–1867, Vol. 3, RG181, NARA; Morison, *"Old Bruin,"* 124; Preble, *Navy-Yard, Portsmouth*, 67.

11. Letter, Sloat to Upshur, Portsmouth, November 2, 1842, Captains Letters, M125, Roll 295, RG45, NARA.

12. Letter, Downes to Sloat, Boston, April 25, 1842, Naval Districts and Shore Establishments, Boston Navy Yard, Misc. Letters, September 1842–February 1843, RG181, NARA (italicized words underlined in original, the file contains numerous documents with dates outside those in the file title); Letter, Sloat to Downes, April 26, 1842, Naval Districts and Shore Establishments, Portsmouth Navy Yard, NH, Misc. Letters Sent (Fair Copies), 1823–25, 1828–1867, Vol. 3, RG181, NARA; Chapelle, *American Sailing Navy*, 438; Spencer C. Tucker, *Arming the Fleet: U.S. Navy Ordnance in the Muzzle-Loading Era* (Annapolis: Naval Institute Press, 1989), 177–190.

13. Letter, Downes to Board of Naval Commissioners, Boston, March 23, 1842, Naval Districts and Shore Establishments, Boston Navy Yard, Misc. Letters, September 1842–February 1843, RG181, NARA; Letter, Sloat to Captain Justin Dimick, Portsmouth, April 4, 1842, Naval Districts and Shore Establishments, Portsmouth Navy Yard, NH, Misc. Letters Sent (Fair Copies), 1823–25, 1828–1867, Vol. 3, RG181, NARA.

14. Letter, Downes to Commander Jacob Crowninshield, Boston, May 2, 1842, Naval Districts and Shore Establishments, Boston Navy Yard, Misc. Letters, September 1842–February 1843, RG181, NARA; Letters Sloat to Upshur, Portsmouth, Captains Letters, May 6 and May 27, 1842, M125, Roll 289, RG45 NARA; Letter, Captain John B. Nicolson to Sloat, Boston, June 13, 1842, Naval Districts and Shore Establishments, Boston Navy Yard, Misc. Letters, September 1842–February 1843, RG181, NARA; Letter, Sloat to Upshur, Portsmouth, July 11, 1842, Captains Letters, M125, Roll 291, RG45, NARA.

15. Letter, Sloat to Upshur, Portsmouth, July 26, 1842, Captains Letters, M125, Roll 291, RG45, NARA; Letter, Sloat to Upshur, Portsmouth, January 5, 1843, Captains Letters, M125, Roll 297, RG45, NARA; Letter, Sloat to Secretary

of the Navy David Henshaw, Portsmouth, October 23, 1843, Captains Letters, M125, Roll 305, RG45, NARA; Preble, *Navy-Yard, Portsmouth*, 69–72.

16. Letters, Sloat to Downes, Portsmouth, December 16, 1840, January 4, 1841, and February 22, 1841, Naval Districts and Shore Establishments, Portsmouth Navy Yard, NH, Misc. Letters Sent (Fair Copies), 1823–25, 1828–1867, Vol. 3, RG181, NARA. On shipboard libraries aboard U.S. Navy ships, see Rouleau, *With Sails Whitening Every Sea*, 26–27.

17. Letters, Sloat to A. O. Dayton, Portsmouth, July 1, 1841, and August 31, 1841, Naval Districts and Shore Establishments, Portsmouth Navy Yard, NH, Misc. Letters Sent (Fair Copies), 1823–25, 1828–1867, Vol. 3, RG181, NARA.

18. "The Fouling of Ships," *The Mechanics' Magazine and Journal of Engineering, Agricultural Machinery, Manufactures and Shipbuilding* (London) 9 (January–June 1863): 287–288. The author expresses his gratitude to David Pelfrey for providing this reference.

19. Letter, Sloat to Downes, Portsmouth, March 21, 1842, Naval Districts and Shore Establishments, Portsmouth Navy Yard, NH, Misc. Letters Sent (Fair Copies), 1823–25, 1828–1867, Vol. 3, RG181, NARA.

20. Letter, Sloat to Benjamin Bartlett, Portsmouth, July 21, 1843, Naval Districts and Shore Establishments, Portsmouth Navy Yard, NH, Misc. Letters Sent (Fair Copies), 1823–25, 1828–1867, Vol. 3, RG181, NARA.

21. "Portsmouth Bridge," *Portsmouth Journal* (June 5, 1841): 2; "Dover Enquirer," *New-Hampshire Gazette*, June 8, 1841, p. 3; http://www.navsea.mil/shipyards/portsmouth, accessed May 6, 2012.

22. Sources consulted for this essay include Valle, *Rocks and Shoals*, 108–110; Leonard F. Guttridge, *Mutiny: A History of Naval Insurrection* (Annapolis: Naval Institute Press, 1992), 87–114; Buckner F. Melton, Jr., *Hanging Offense: The Strange Affair of the Warship* Somers (New York: Free Press, 2003); Philip McFarland, *Sea Dangers: The Affair of the* Somers (New York: Schocken Books, 1985); and by a grandnephew of a *Somers* sailor, Frederic Van de Water, *The Captain Called It Mutiny* (New York: Ives Washburn, 1954). An anthology of selected primary sources is Harrison Hayford, ed., *The* Somers *Mutiny Affair* (Englewood Cliffs: Prentice Hall, 1959). A transcript of the trial is at *Proceedings of the Naval Court Martial in the Case of Alexander Slidell Mackenzie, a Commander in the Navy of the United States, Including the Charges and Specifications Preferred Against Him by the Secretary of the Navy to which Is Annexed an Elaborate Review by James Fennimore* [*sic*] *Cooper* (New York: Harold Langley, 1844). Because of the deep personal involvement of Matthew Calbraith Perry in the *Somers* affair, Samuel Eliot Morison included an entire chapter in *"Old Bruin,"* 144–162, and took such pride in that essay that he included it in the compendium *Sailor Historian: The Best of Samuel Eliot Morison*, ed. Emily Morison Beck (Boston: Houghton Mifflin, 1977),

181–202. As always with the enjoyable but insistently uncritical *"Old Bruin,"* see also Schroeder, *Matthew Calbraith Perry*, 92–95.

23. Schroeder, *Matthew Calbraith Perry*, 92.

24. Letter, Captain William B. Shubrick to James Fenimore Cooper, Norfolk, March 10, 1845, and Letter, Cooper to Shubrick, Cooperstown, March 25, 1843, in *Correspondence of James Fenimore-Cooper*, ed. James Fenimore Cooper (grandson of the novelist) (New Haven: Yale University Press, 1922), 1: 377–382, 2: 496–498; Thomas Philbrick, *James Fenimore Cooper and the Development of American Sea Fiction* (Cambridge: Harvard University Press, 1961), 142–143.

25. Letter, James Fenimore Cooper to Susan Cooper, New York, September 22, 1843, in Cooper, *Letters and Journals*, 4: 412–413.

26. Letter, Sloat to Secretary of the Navy John Y. Mason, New York, August 31, 1844, Captains Letters, M125, Roll 315, RG45, NARA; "Notes," *New York Tribune*, March 8, 1843, p. 2.

27. Letter, Sloat to Upshur, Portsmouth, October 23, 1841, Captains Letters, M125, Roll 282, RG45, NARA; Letter, Sloat to Upshur, New York, February 6, 1843, and February 23, 1843, Captains Letters, M125, Roll 298, RG45, NARA.

28. Smith, *Commodore of Manifest Destiny*, 93–122; Smith, "The War That Wasn't," 104–113, 155; George M. Brooke, Jr., "The Vest Pocket War of Commodore Jones," *Pacific Historical Review* 31:3 (August 1962): 217–233; High, "Jones at Monterey, 1842," 173–186; Lisbeth Haas, "War in California, 1846–1848," *Contested Eden: California before the Gold Rush*, ed. Ramón A. Gutiérrez and Richard J. Orsi (Berkeley and Los Angeles: University of California Press, 1998), 334–336; Robert Ryal Miller, *Juan Alvarado: Governor of California, 1836–1842* (Norman: University of Oklahoma Press, 1998), 93–96; John H. Schroeder, *Shaping a Maritime Empire: The Commercial and Diplomatic Role of the American Navy* (Westport and London: Greenwood Press, 1985), 75–77.

29. K. Jack Bauer, "The *Sancala* Affair: Captain Voorhees Seizes an Argentine Squadron," *American Neptune* 29:2 (1969): 174–186; Schroeder, *Shaping a Maritime Empire*, 71; Long, *Gold Braid and Foreign Relations*, 158–160; David Rock, *Argentina, 1516–1987: From Spanish Colonization to Alfonsín* (Berkeley: University of California Press, 1987), 110–112; Burns, *History of Brazil*, 187; Naval Register for 1848, 511.

30. Journal of the Board of Examiners of Midshipmen, 1844, Records of the Board of Examiners of Midshipmen, Journals of Proceedings 1836–1850, RG405.6.1, NARA.

31. Letter, Sloat to Upshur, Portsmouth, July 3, 1843, Captains Letters, M125, Roll 303, RG45, NARA; Letter, Sloat to Secretary of the Navy David Henshaw, Portsmouth, September 6, 1843, Captains Letters, M125, Roll 304, RG45, NARA; Letters, Sloat to Henshaw, Portsmouth, October 3, October 14,

and October 23, 1843, Captains Letters, M125, Roll 305, RG45, NARA; Letter, Sloat to Mason, New York, April 16, 1844, Captains Letters, M125, Roll 311, RG45, NARA; Letter, Sloat to Mason, New York, June 24, 1844, Captains Letters, M125, Roll 313, RG45, NARA; Letter, Sloat to Mason, New York, August 31, 1844, Captains Letters, M125, Roll 315, RG45, NARA.

32. "By This Morning's Mail," *New York Daily Tribune*, September 25, 1844, p. 2.

Chapter 13. Mexican California

1. Letters, Sloat to Mason, November 14, 1844, Panama, and January 3, 1845, Callao, Letters received by the Secretary of the Navy from Commanding Officers of Squadrons, 1841–1886 (hereafter, Squadron Commanders Letters), M89, Roll 32, RG45, NARA; Robert W. Merry, *A Country of Vast Design: James K. Polk, the Mexican War, and the Conquest of the American Southwest* (New York: Simon and Schuster, 2009), 198–199.

2. Bruce A. Castleman, *Building the King's Highway: Labor, Society, and Family on Mexico's Caminos Reales, 1757–1804* (Tucson: University of Arizona Press, 2005), 12; Joseph P. Sánchez, *Spanish Bluecoats: The Catalonian Volunteers in Northwestern New Spain, 1767–1810* (Albuquerque: University of New Mexico Press, 1990), 32–33.

3. Robert H. Jackson and Edward Castillo, *Indians, Franciscans, and Spanish Colonization: The Impact of the Mission System on California Indians* (Albuquerque: University of New Mexico Press, 1995), 11–17; Michael J. González, "The Child of the Wilderness Weeps for the Father of Our Country: The Indian and the Politics of the Church and State in Provincial California," in Gutiérrez and Orsi, *Contested Eden*, 153–166; James A. Sandos, "Between Crucifix and Lance: Indian-White Relations in California, 1769–1848," in Gutiérrez and Orsi, *Contested Eden*, 201–202.

4. Donald C. Cutter, *California in 1792: A Spanish Naval Visit* (Norman: University of Oklahoma Press, 1990), 28; Florian Guest, "The Establishment of the Villa de Branciforte," *California Historical Quarterly* 41:1 (March 1962), 39; Douglas Monroy, *Thrown Among Strangers: The Making of Mexican Culture in Frontier California* (Berkeley, Los Angeles, and Oxford: University of California Press, 1990), 69–71; Sánchez, *Spanish Bluecoats*, 56, 121.

5. C. H. Haring, *The Spanish Empire in America* (New York: Oxford University Press, 1947), 80, 156–157.

6. Douglas Monroy, "Creation and Re-creation of Californio Society," in Gutiérrez and Orsi, *Contested Eden*, 189–190.

7. Louise Pubols, *The Father of All: The de la Guerra Family, Power, and Patriarchy in Mexican California* (Berkeley and San Marino: University of California Press for the Huntington-USC Institute on California and the West, 2009), 59–64; Monroy, *Thrown Among Strangers*, 140–161; Linda A. Curcio-Nagy, "Faith and Morals in Colonial Mexico," in Meyer and Beezley, *The Oxford History of Mexico*, 180; Patricia Seed, *To Love, Honor, and Obey in Colonial Mexico: Conflicts over Marriage Choice, 1574–1821* (Stanford: Stanford University Press, 1988); Asunción Lavrín and Edith Couturier, "Dowries and Wills: A View of Women's Socioeconomic Role in Colonial Guadalajara and Puebla, 164–1790," *Hispanic American Historical Review* 59:2 (May 1979): 280–304; Susan M. Socolow, "Marriage, Birth, and Inheritance: The Merchants of Eighteenth Century Buenos Aires," *Hispanic American Historical Review* 60:3 (August 1980): 387–406.

8. Pubols, *Father of All*, 21–22, 178; González, "The Child of the Wilderness Weeps," 160; Bruce A. Castleman, "Social Climbers in a Colonial Mexican City: Individual Mobility within the *Sistema de Castas* in Orizaba, 1777–1791," *Colonial Latin American Review* 10:2 (December 2001): 229–250; Ann Twinam, *Public Lives, Private Secrets: Gender, Honor, Sexuality, and Illegitimacy in Colonial Spanish America* (Stanford: Stanford University Press, 1999), 54–55, 289–290.

9. Antonio María Osio, *The History of Alta California: A Memoir of Mexican California*, trans. Rose Marie Beebe and Robert M. Senkewicz (1851; Madison: University of Wisconsin Press, 1996), 44–53; Pubols, *The Father of All*, 52–53.

10. Archer, "Fashioning a New Nation," 304–305; Vásquez, "Los primeros tropiezos," 737–747; Neal Harlow, *California Conquered: The Annexation of a Mexican Province, 1846–1850* (Berkeley, Los Angeles, and London: University of California Press, 1982), 22–24.

11. Monroy, *Thrown Among Strangers*, 122; Josefina Zoraida Vásquez and Lorenzo Meyer, *The United States and Mexico* (Chicago and London: University of Chicago Press, 1985), 30–36; Eric R. Schlereth, "Privileges of Locomotion: Expatriation and the Politics of Southwestern Border Crossing," *Journal of American History* 100:4 (March 2014): 995–1020.

12. Doyce B. Nunis, Jr., "Alta California's Trojan Horse: Foreign Immigration," in Gutiérrez and Orsi, *Contested Eden*, 305–308; Lisbeth Haas, *Conquests and Historical Identities in California, 1769–1936* (Berkeley, Los Angeles, and London: University of California Press, 1995), 64–65; Magdalen Coughlin, "Boston Smugglers on the Coast (1797–1821): An Insight into the American Acquisition of California," *California Historical Society Quarterly* 46:2 (June 1967): 100–102.

13. Monroy, *Thrown Among Strangers*, 133–134.

14. Josefina Zoraida Vásquez, "War and Peace with the United States," trans. Michael R. Brescia in Meyer and Beezley, *Oxford History of Mexico*, 354.

15. Miller, *Juan Alvarado*, 42–52; Alan Rosenus, *General Vallejo and the Advent of the Americans* (Berkeley: Heyday Books/Urion Press, 1995), 18; David J. Weber, *The Mexican Frontier, 1821–1846: The American Southwest under Mexico* (Albuquerque: University of New Mexico Press, 1982), 257–258; Robert Phelps, "On Comic Opera Revolutions: Maneuver Theory and the Art of War in Mexican California, 1821–1845," *California History* 84:1 (Fall 2006): 49–53.

16. Louise Pubols, "Becoming Californios: Jokes, Broadsides, and a Slap in the Face," in *Alta California: Peoples in Motion, Identities in Formation, 1769–1850*, ed. Steven W. Hackel (Berkeley and San Marino: University of California Press for the Huntington-USC Institute on California and the West, 2010), 131.

17. Nunis, "Alta California's Trojan Horse," 308–314; Albert L. Hurtado, *John Sutter: A Life on the North American Frontier* (Norman: University of Oklahoma Press, 2006), 54–56, 125–127; Miller, *Juan Alvarado*, 92; Weber, *Mexican Frontier*, 204.

18. Edward R. Crapol, *John Tyler: The Accidental President* (Chapel Hill: University of North Carolina Press, 2006), 25, 181–182, 232; Vásquez, "War and Peace with the United States," 356–358; Howe, *What Hath God Wrought*, 717; Bailey, *Diplomatic History*, 252–253.

19. Miller, *Juan Alvarado*, 92.

20. Miller, *Juan Alvarado*, 92–94; Pubols, *The Father of All*, 267; Osio, *History of Alta California*, 208; Letter, Jones to Upshur, Monterey, no date given, in Rose Marie Beebe and Robert M. Senkewicz, eds., *Lands of Promise and Despair: Chronicles of Early California, 1535–1846* (Berkeley: Heyday Books, 2001), 454–460.

21. John C. Frémont, *Memoirs of My Life* (1886, reprint, New York: Cooper Square Press, 2001), 346–374.

22. Gene M. Brack, *Mexico Views Manifest Destiny: An Essay on the Origins of the Mexican War* (Albuquerque: University of New Mexico Press, 1975), 22; Clyde A. Milner II, "National Initiatives," in *The Oxford History of the American West*, ed. Milner, Carol A. O'Connor, and Martha A. Sandweiss (New York and Oxford: Oxford University Press, 1994), 159–161; see also William H. Goetzmann, *Army Exploration in the American West* (New Haven: Yale University Press, 1959); Nunis, "Alta California's Trojan Horse," 320.

23. Rosenus, *General Vallejo*, 62–69; Miller, *Juan Alvarado*, 102–110; Monroy, *Thrown Among Strangers*, 175–176; Carlos Manuel Salomon, *Pío Pico: The Last Governor of Mexican California* (Norman: University of Oklahoma Press, 2010), 72–77; Phelps, "Comic Opera Revolutions," 61–63.

24. Letter, Sloat to Bancroft, November 19, 1845, Mazatlán, Squadron Commanders Letters, M89, Roll 32, RG45, NARA.

25. Joseph Eugene Baker, *Past and Present of Alameda County, California*, Vol.

2 (Chicago: S. J. Clarke, 1914), 466–468. Parts of this account appear verbatim in Sherman, *Life of Sloat*, 41. Sherman states that he interviewed Toler before the latter's death in 1899.

26. Joseph Warren Revere, *Naval Duty in California* (1849, reprint, Oakland: Biobooks, 1947), 5–9; Monroy, *Thrown Among Strangers*, 165–169; Kevin Starr, *Americans and the California Dream, 1850–1915* (New York: Oxford University Press, 1973), 16–17.

Chapter 14. Squadron Command

1. Letter, Sloat to Mason, Chagres, October 18, 1844, Squadron Commanders Letters, M89, Roll 32, RG45, NARA; Letters, Sloat to Mason, Panama, November 14, 1844, and November 21, 1844, Squadron Commanders Letters, M89, Roll 32, RG45, NARA; Letter, Sloat to Mason, Callao, January 3, 1845, Squadron Commanders Letters, M89, Roll 32, RG45, NARA.

2. Wilentz, *Rise of American Democracy*, 572–575; Howe, *What Hath God Wrought*, 682–690; Bailey, *Diplomatic History of the American People*, 253–254.

3. Letter, Sloat to Mason, Callao, January 3, 1845, Squadron Commanders Letters, M89, Roll 32, RG45, NARA.

4. Letter, Sloat to Mason, Callao, February 8, 1845, Squadron Commanders Letters, M89, Roll 32, RG45, NARA; Letter, Sloat to Mason, Callao, March 31, 1845, Squadron Commanders Letters, M89, Roll 32, RG45, NARA.

5. Letter, Sloat to Mason, Callao, April 28, 1845, Squadron Commanders Letters, M89, Roll 32, RG45, NARA; Magdalen Coughlin, "California Ports: A Key to Diplomacy for the West Coast, 1820–1845," *Journal of the West* 5 (1966): 155.

6. Bauer, *Surfboats and Horse Marines*, 138. Many accounts of the seizure of California exist in the abundant secondary literature, but the narrative of them in the remaining pages of this chapter is synthesized primarily from Bauer, *Surfboats and Horse Marines*, 135–204, and Harlow, *California Conquered*, and repeated citations to those two sources are omitted from this discussion to avoid needless repetition. Citations to primary sources and to particular secondary sources that supplement Bauer and Harlow continue to appear.

7. Letter, Sloat to Commander Joseph B. Hull, USS *Warren*, Callao, May 17, 1845, Squadron Commanders Letters, M89, Roll 32, RG45, NARA; Letter, Sloat to Bancroft, July 3, 1845, Callao, Squadron Commanders Letters, M89, Roll 32, RG45, NARA; Letter, Sloat to Bancroft, July 29, 1845, Callao, Squadron Commanders Letters, M89, Roll 32, RG45, NARA.

8. Robert L. Scheina, "The Forgotten Fleet: The Mexican Navy on the Eve of War, 1845," *American Neptune* 30:1 (January 1970): 46.

9. Kingdom of Hawaii, Department of Foreign Affairs, *Table of Consular Grievances, 1843–1846,* R. C. Wyllie, compiler (Honolulu: 1846), 22–24; Letter, Sloat to Wyllie, Honolulu, September 27, 1845, Squadron Commanders Letters, M89, Roll 32, RG45, NARA; Letter, Wyllie to Sloat, Honolulu, September 27, 1845, Squadron Commanders Letters, M89, Roll 32, RG45, NARA.

10. Letter, Sloat to Bancroft, Honolulu, October 14, 1845, Squadron Commanders Letters, M89, Roll 32, RG45, NARA; Merze Tate, *The United States and the Hawaiian Kingdom: A Political History* (New Haven and London: Yale University Press, 1965), 19–21.

11. R. C. Duvall, *Journal and Log of U.S. Frigate* Savannah, *1845–1847,* BANC MSS 2011/132, Vol. 2, Bancroft Library, University of California, Berkeley.

12. Letter, Sloat to Captain John P. Percival, Honolulu, October 18, 1845, Squadron Commanders Letters, M89, Roll 32, RG45, NARA; Letter, Sloat to Bancroft, Mazatlán, January 17, 1846, Squadron Commanders Letters, M89, Roll 32, RG45, NARA; David F. Long, *"Mad Jack": The Biography of Captain John Percival, USN, 1779–1862* (Westport: Greenwood Press, 1993), 194.

13. Robert Carson Duvall, "Extracts from the Log of the U.S. Frigate *Savannah* Kept by Robert Carson Duvall," *California Historical Quarterly* 3:2 (July 1924): 108.

14. Letter, Bancroft to Sloat, Washington, June 24, 1845, Sloat Correspondence in Manuscripts, Documents, Letters & Correspondence Relating to the Conquest of California, 1846, North Baker Research Library, California Historical Society, San Francisco (hereafter, referred to as CHS Sloat Correspondence)

15. Letter, Sloat to Bancroft, Mazatlán, November 19, 1845, CHS Sloat Correspondence.

16. Vásquez, "War and Peace with the United States," 357–361; Eisenhower, *So Far From God,* 49–56; Bauer, *Surfboats and Horse Marines,* 11–12; Timothy J. Henderson, *A Glorious Defeat: Mexico and Its War with the United States* (New York: Hill and Wang, 2007), 151–155; David M. Pletcher, *The Diplomacy of Annexation: Texas, Oregon, and the Mexican War* (Columbia: University of Missouri Press, 1973), 352–377.

17. Francis Paul Prucha, *The Sword of the Republic: The United States and the Army on the Frontier, 1783–1846* (New York: Macmillan, 1969), 391, and Goetzmann, *Army Exploration in the American West,* 116–123.

18. Miller, *Juan Alvarado,* 117.

19. Letter, Bancroft to Sloat, Washington, October 17, 1845, CHS Sloat Correspondence.

20. Letters, Sloat to Bancroft, Mazatlán, February 24, 1846, and March 17, 1846, Squadron Commanders Letters, M89, Roll 32, RG45, NARA.

21. Letter, Sloat to Bancroft, Mazatlán, May 5, 1846, Squadron Commanders Letters, M89, Roll 32, RG45, NARA; Tyrone G. Martin, *A Most Fortunate Ship: A Narrative History of "Old Ironsides,"* rev. ed. (Chester: The Globe Pequot Press, 1982), 242–243.

22. In addition to Harlow, see letter, Cmdr. J. B. Montgomery to Capt. J. C. Frémont, USS *Portsmouth*, Sausalito, June 23, 1846, in *The Expeditions of John Charles Frémont, Vol. 2: The Bear Flag Revolt and the Court-Martial*, ed. Donald Jackson and Mary Lee Spence (Urbana: University of Illinois Press, 1973), 155–157.

23. Letter, Captain William M. Mervine to Sloat, Monterey, July 1, 1846, CHS Sloat Correspondence.

24. Statement of Rodman M. Price, in Frémont, *Memoirs of My Life*, 540–542; Allan Nevins, *Frémont: Pathmarker of the West* (New York: Frederick Ungar, 1955), 288n3. In the materials added to the 1905 edition of *Life of Sloat*, Sherman vigorously disputes and disparages Price's account.

25. William Heath Davis, *Sixty Years in California . . .* (San Francisco: A. J. Leary, 1889), 395–396.

26. Harlan Hogue and David J. Langum, *Thomas O. Larkin: A Life of Patriotism and Profit in Old California* (Norman and London: University of Oklahoma Press, 1990), 141.

27. John Sutter, "General Sutter's Diary," in *John Sutter and a Wider West*, ed. Kenneth N. Owens (Lincoln and London: University of Nebraska Press, 1994), 18.

28. Linda Heidenreich, *"This Land Was Mexican Once": Histories of Resistance from Northern California* (Austin: University of Texas Press, 2007), 86–89.

29. Letter, Comandante General José Castro to Sloat, July 9, 1846, San Juan Bautista, CHS Sloat Correspondence.

30. Letter, Sloat to Larkin, Monterey, July 7, 1846, in Thomas O. Larkin, *The Larkin Papers: Personal, Business, and Official Correspondence of Thomas Oliver Larkin, Merchant and United States Consul in California*, Vol. 5, ed. George P. Hammond (Berkeley and Los Angeles: University of California Press, 1955), 113; Salomon, *Pío Pico*, 100–102; Miller, *Juan Alvarado*, 122.

31. Letter, Rear Admiral George F. Seymour, RN, HMS *Collingwood*, to British Vice Consul James Alexander Forbes, Monterey, July 22, 1846, CHS Sloat Correspondence; Abraham P. Nasatir, "International Rivalry for California and the Establishment of the British Consulate," *California Historical Society Quarterly* 46:1 (March 1967): 67.

32. In addition to Harlow's and Bauer's discussions of the meeting, concerning Gillespie see also Werner H. Marti, *Messenger of Destiny: The California Adventures, 1846–1847, of Archibald H. Gillespie, U.S. Marine Corps* (San Francisco:

John Howell Books, 1960), 68–70; and George Walcott Ames, Jr., and Archibald Gillespie, "Gillespie and the Conquest of California: From Letters Dated February 11, 1846, to July 8, 1848, to the Secretary of the Navy," *California Historical Quarterly* 17:2 (June 1938): 123–140, and *California Historical Quarterly* 17:3 (September 1938): 271–284; and concerning Frémont, see Samuel J. Watson, *Peacekeepers and Conquerors: The Army Officer Corps on the American Frontier, 1821–1846* (Lawrence: University Press of Kansas, 2013), 29–30; Ferol Egan, *Frémont: Explorer for a Restless Nation* (Garden City: Doubleday, 1977), 361–365; Nevins, *Pathmarker of the West*, 288–291; Andrew Rolle, *John Charles Fremont: Character as Destiny* (Norman and London: University of Oklahoma Press, 1991) 86–87; Tom Chaffin, *Pathfinder: John Charles Frémont and the Course of American Empire* (New York: Hill and Wang, 2002), 336–344; DeVoto, *Year of Decision*, 464–466; and Groom, *Kearny's March*, 103–106, 248–259. Many of the preceding authors criticize Sloat, and both Watson and Egan condemn many of Frémont's actions during this period.

33. Letter, Sloat to Bancroft, at sea, July 31, 1846, Squadron Commanders Letters, M89, Roll 32, RG45, NARA.

34. "Terrible Storms, the Most Disastrous on Record," *New York Daily Tribune*, October 31, 1846, p. 2; untitled article, *New York Daily Tribune*, November 5, 1846, p. 2; Corey Malcom, "Understanding the Key West Hurricane of 1846," *Florida Keys Sea Heritage Journal* 20:4 (Summer 2010): 1–2.

35. Letter, Sloat to Mason, New Orleans, October 23, 1846, Squadron Commanders Letters, M89, Roll 32, RG45, NARA.

36. "Commodore John Drake Sloat," *Hunt's Merchant's Magazine* (New York) 15:5 (November 1846): 446–456; "Historical Sandwich," *New York Daily Tribune*, December 5, 1846, p. 1.

37. Letter, Bancroft to Sloat, Washington, August 13, 1846, CHS Sloat Correspondence.

38. Merry, *A Country of Vast Design*, 188.

39. K. Jack Bauer, "George Bancroft, 11 March 1845–9 September 1846," and "John Young Mason, 10 September 1846–7 March 1849," in *American Secretaries of the Navy, Volume I 1775–1913*, ed. Paolo E. Coletta (Annapolis: Naval Institute Press, 1980), 224–227, 237; see also Lilian Handlin, *George Bancroft: The Intellectual as Democrat* (New York: Harper and Row, 1984), 204–219.

40. Rebecca Berens Matzke, *Deterrence through Strength: British Naval Power and Foreign Policy under* Pax Britannica (Lincoln and London: University of Nebraska Press, 2011), 65–99.

41. "Reminiscences of Dorotea Váldez," in *Testimonios: Early California through the Eyes of Women, 1815–1848*, trans. Rose Marie Beebe and Robert M. Senkewicz (Berkeley: Heyday Books, 2006), 34–41.

Chapter 15. Norfolk and Retirement

1. *Morning News* (New London, CT), December 12, 1846, p. 2.

2. William P. Leeman, *The Long Road to Annapolis: The Founding of the Naval Academy and the Emerging American Republic* (Chapel Hill: University of North Carolina Press, 2010), 198–227.

3. Smith, *Commodore of Manifest Destiny*, 128–129.

4. Charles Todorich, *The Spirited Years: A History of the Antebellum Naval Academy* (Annapolis: Naval Institute Press, 1984), 48–52, 71; Mark C. Hunter, *A Society of Gentlemen: Midshipmen at the U.S. Naval Academy, 1845–1861* (Annapolis: Naval Institute Press, 2010), 44.

5. Journal of the Board of Examiners of Midshipmen, 1847, Records of the Board of Examiners of Midshipmen, Journals of Proceedings 1836–1850, RG405.6.1, NARA.

6. Carroll Storrs Alden, *Lawrence Kearny: Sailor Diplomat* (Princeton: Princeton University Press, 1936), 220.

7. 1850 United States Census, Virginia, U.S. Navy Yard, Gosport, p. 197, RG29, NARA; 1850 Census, New York, New York County, 18th Ward, p. 248, RG29, NARA; Theodore Henry Hittell, *The California Academy of Sciences, A Narrative History: 1853–1906*, edited, revised, and enlarged by Alan E. Leviton and Michele L. Aldrich (San Francisco: California Academy of Sciences, 1997), 11, 488, 493.

8. *Register of the Commissioned and Warrant Officers of the Navy, 1848*, 115–116, 24–25, 34–35, 104–118.

9. Edward P. Lull, *History of the United States Navy-Yard at Gosport, Virginia (near Norfolk), for the Bureau of Yards and Docks, Navy Department* (Washington, DC: U.S. Government Printing Office, 1874), 5, 40–43.

10. Clare Beverley Whitehead, *History of the Norfolk Navy Yard, Portsmouth, Virginia,* (Portsmouth: Printcraft Press, 1942), 1–12.

11. Log Book, U.S. Navy Yard Gosport [VA] 1844–1851, Journals of Daily Transactions at Navy Yard, Norfolk, Records of the Bureau of Yards and Docks, RG71 NARA.

12. Lull, *Navy-Yard at Gosport*, 43.

13. Myra C. Glenn, "The Naval Reform Campaign against Flogging: A Case Study in Changing Attitudes toward Corporal Punishment, 1830–1850," *American Quarterly* 35:4 (Autumn 1983): 409–410; and generally, Langley, *Social Reform in the Navy*, 131–206.

14. Langley, *Social Reform in the Navy*, 180–181.

15. Letter, Sloat to Secretary of the Navy William B. Preston, Norfolk, February 5, 1850, Corporal Punishment and Spirit Rations, Reports of Officers,

Miscellaneous Records of the U.S. Navy, Microfilm T829, Roll 451, RG45, NARA.

16. Log Books, USS *Grampus* and USS *St. Louis*; Langley, *Social Reform in the Navy*, 149–150; Schroeder, *Matthew Calbraith Perry*, 59–61; Morison, *"Old Bruin,"* 107, 116. Although the catalog says it is there, the log book for the *Savannah* could not be located in the National Archives. Duvall's midshipman journal is otherwise a good substitute, but he did not record punishments.

17. "One of the Savannah's Crew: Charles Byrnes and His Memories of the Unpopular Commander," *San Francisco Call*, July 5, 1896, p. 18.

18. Valle, *Rocks and Shoals*, 226; Smith, *Commodore of Manifest Destiny*, 131, 144–152. To clarify the terminology, if a sailor shot and killed the paymaster officer and his guard and then fled with a case containing the payroll money, that sailor would face one charge of murder with two specifications, and one charge of armed robbery with one specification.

19. Valle, *Rocks and Shoals*, 293.

20. Smith, *Commodore of Manifest Destiny*, 156; Valle, *Rocks and Shoals*, 226; Johnson, *Thence Round Cape Horn*, 100.

21. Dye, *Uriah Levy*, 84.

22. Smith, *Commodore of Manifest Destiny*, 155; Lull, *History of the Navy-Yard at Gosport*, 43.

23. Robert J. Chandler, "An Uncertain Influence: The Role of the Federal Government in California, 1846–1850," in *Taming the Elephant: Politics, Government, and Law in Pioneer California*, ed. John F. Burns and Richard J. Orsi (Berkeley: University of California Press, 2003), 229; Arnold S. Lott, *A Long Line of Ships: Mare Island's Century of Naval Activity in California* (Annapolis: Naval Institute Press, 1954), 7–9; Johnson, *Thence Round Cape Horn*, 104; Sherman, *Life of Sloat*, 104–105.

24. "Died," *New York Daily Times*, February 23, 1852, p. 2.

25. Nathan Howard, Jr., *Practice Reports in the Supreme Court and Court of Appeals of the State of New-York*, Vol. 9 (Albany: William Gould, 1860), 319–325.

26. "A Row in the Wigwam—John McKeon Denounced," *New York Daily Times*, July 14, 1854; Mushkat, *Tammany*, 187, 213, 227, 353–362; Jerome Mushkat, *The Reconstruction of the New York Democracy, 1861–1874* (East Brunswick: Associated University Presses, 1981), 42–51; Mushkat, *Fernando Wood*, 27–34, 126; Joel H. Silbey, *Martin Van Buren and the Emergence of American Popular Politics* (Lanham: Rowman & Littlefield, 2002), 192–193; James M. McPherson, *Battle Cry of Freedom: The Civil War Era* (New York: Oxford University Press, 1988), 771–772; McEntee, "John McKeon," 37–38, 46–48; Leo Hershowitz, "The Irish in the Emerging City: Settlement to 1844," in *The New York Irish*, ed. Ronald H. Bayor and Timothy H. Meagher (Baltimore and London: Johns Hopkins

University Press, 1996), 20, 27; Amy Bridges, *A City in the Republic: Antebellum New York and the Origins of Machine Politics* (Cambridge: Cambridge University Press, 1984), 139.

27. Untitled article, *Brooklyn Daily Eagle*, November 5, 1852, p. 2. On the Japan expedition, see Schroeder, *Matthew Calbraith Perry*; and Morison, *"Old Bruin."*

28. Michael Shiner Diary, entry of February 21, 1853, www.history.mil/research/library/online-reading-room/title-list-alphabetically/d/diary-of-michael-shiner/1850-1859#121/, accessed April 30, 2015.

29. David W. Shaw, *The Sea Shall Embrace Them: The Tragic Story of the Steamship* Arctic (New York: Free Press, 2002); Charles B. Stuart, *Naval and Mail Steamers of the United States* (New York: Charles B. Norton, Irving House, 1853), 115–151, 216; Morison, *"Old Bruin,"* 256–260; Robert J. Chandler and Stephen J. Potash, *Gold, Silk, Pioneers and Mail: The Story of the Pacific Mail Steamship Company* (San Francisco: Friends of the San Francisco Maritime Museum Library, 2007), 1–3; Hutchins, *American Maritime Industries and Public Policy*, 359–362; John Haskell Kemble, *The Panama Route, 1848–1869* (Berkeley: University of California Press, 1943), analyzes the business aspects of the mail service to California.

30. Donald Canney, *The Old Steam Navy, Volume Two: The Ironclads, 1842–1885* (Annapolis: Naval Institute Press, 1993), 2–5; Spencer C. Tucker, "The Stevens Ironclad Battery," *American Neptune* 51 (1991): 15–18; Stephen C. Small, "The Ship That Couldn't Be Built," *Naval History* 22:5 (October 2008): http://www.usni.org/magazines/navalhistory/2008-10/ship-couldnt-be-built, accessed December 7, 2013.

31. Chisholm, *Waiting for Dead Men's Shoes*, 229–237, 264; Morison, *"Old Bruin,"* 416; Howard C. Westwood, "Reform in the United States Navy: The 'Plucking' of Officers in the Later 1850s," *American Neptune* 50:2 (Spring 1990): 107–118; Report of Naval Retiring Board, July 25, 1855, House Ex. Doc.1, 34th Congress, 1st Session, Serial Vol. 841 in *New American State Papers, Naval Affairs, Personnel*, Vol. 7, ed. K. Jack Bauer (Wilmington: Scholarly Resources, 1973), 124–128.

32. "A Gala Day in New York—The President's Reception," *Nashville Union and American*, July 23, 1853, p. 2; 'The Grand Ball at the Metropolitan," *New York Daily Tribune*, January 26, 1854, p. 1; untitled article, *New York Daily Tribune*, September 11, 1856, p. 6; Morison, *"Old Bruin,"* 431.

33. Chisholm, *Waiting for Dead Men's Shoes*, 290–296; McKee, *Gentlemanly and Honorable Profession*, 29.

34. Letter, Sloat to President Abraham Lincoln, New Brighton, NY, July 31, 1862, Abraham Lincoln Papers at Library of Congress, Series 1, General Correspondence 1833–1916, http://memory.loc.gov/, accessed December 11, 2013. Underlined text in original.

35. Letter, Sloat to Lincoln, July 31, 1862; *NDQW Operations* 7: 350; McPherson, *Battle Cry of Freedom*, 526. Sloat's name does not appear in the naval register for 1806, American State Papers, Naval Affairs 1: 158.

36. The nine rear admiral nominees on the retired list were Charles Stewart, George C. Read, William B. Shubrick, Joseph Smith, George W. Storer, Francis Gregory, Elie A. F. Lavallette, Silas H. Stringham, and Hiram Paulding. Chisholm, *Waiting for Dead Men's Shoes*, 292.

37. Jennifer L. Weber, *Copperheads: The Rise and Fall of Lincoln's Opponents in the North* (New York: Oxford University Press, 2006), 68; Edward K. Spann, "Union Green: The Irish Community and the Civil War," in Bayor and Meagher, *The New York Irish*, 208; Mushkat, *Tammany*, 360–362. For a sympathetic analysis of Peace Democrats in the North, see also Frank L. Klement, *Lincoln's Critics: The Copperheads of the North*, ed. Steven K. Rogstad (Shippensburg: White Mane Books, 1999).

38. Journal of the Executive Proceedings of the Senate of the United States of America, February 13, 1866, to July 28, 1866, p. 1055; "Union, Liberty, and Justice," *New York Daily Tribune*, September 24, 1864; Sherman, *Life of Sloat*, 105.

Conclusions

1. Letter, James Fenimore Cooper to Captain William B. Shubrick, Cooperstown, August 18, 1845, *Letters and Journals*, Vol. V, 50–53.

2. Letter, James Fenimore Cooper to Captain William B. Shubrick, Cooperstown, January 17, 1847, *Letters and Journals*, Vol. V, 185–194; Merrill, *Du Pont*, 178, 189; "One of the Savannah's Crew."

3. Letter, Sloat to Larkin, Mazatlán, May 18, 1846, Larkin, *Larkin Papers, Vol. IV*, 378.

4. "Funeral of Rear Admiral John Drake Sloat," *New York Herald*, December 2, 1867, p. 4. Almost verbatim coverage appears in the *New York Daily Tribune* and the *New York Times.*

5. For the legal battles between Jeanette McKeon and Lewis W. Sloat, see *New York Daily Tribune* and *New York Times*, various articles May 26, May 27, June 1, June 9, August 10, October 10, 1883; "Funeral of John McKeon," *New York Times*, November 25, 1883, p. 3. Lewis Warrington Sloat died on March 3, 1886, and Jeanette McKeon died on December 10, 1889.

Bibliography

Documents in the National Archives of the United States

RG24 Records of the Bureau of Naval Personnel, Department of the Navy

RG29 Records of the Bureau of the Census, Department of Commerce

RG36 Records of the U.S. Customs Service, Department of the Treasury

RG45 Naval Records Collection of the Office of Naval Records and Library, Department of the Navy

RG59 General Records of the Department of State

RG71 Records of the Bureau of Yards and Docks

RG181 Records of Naval Districts and Shore Establishments

RG405.6.1 Records of the Board of Examiners of Midshipmen

Other Archival and Manuscript Sources

Abraham Lincoln Papers, Library of Congress.

Duvall, Robert Carson. *Journal and Log of U.S. Frigate* Savannah, *1845–1847.* BANC MSS 2011/132, Vol. 2, Bancroft Library, University of California, Berkeley.

The Early Records of the First Presbyterian Church at Goshen, New York, from 1767 to 1885. Charles C. Coleman, compiler. Goshen, NY, n.d.

Historical Society of Pennsylvania. Simon Gratz Collection [250A].

New York County. Land Records, Conveyance Index—Grantor.

New York County. Surrogate's Court Probate Records.

New-York Historical Society, Patricia K. Klingenstein Library, NSC MISC MSS Box 054, Folder 14, John D. Sloat.

New York State. Tax Assessment Rolls of Real and Personal Property, Goshen, NY, New York State Archives, Roll 15, 1799–1800.

Norwich, Connecticut, Land Records.
Orange County, New York. Deeds 1788–1799.
Orange County, New York. Surrogate's Court Probate Records.
Parish Records. St. John's Episcopal Church, Portsmouth, NH, 1795–1884.
Parish Records. St. Thomas Episcopal Church, New York, 1831–1865.
Richmond County, New York. Grantee Index to Deeds.
Richmond County, New York. Surrogate's Court Probate Records.
Rockland County, New York. Surrogate's Court Probate Records.
Shiner, Michael, diary.

Published Primary Sources

American State Papers, Naval Affairs.

Ames, George Walcott, Jr., and Archibald Gillespie. "Gillespie and the Conquest of California: From Letters Dated February 11, 1846, to July 8, 1848, to the Secretary of the Navy." *California Historical Quarterly* 17:2 (June 1938): 123–140, and *California Historical Quarterly* 17:3 (September 1938): 271–284.

Cooper, James Fenimore. *Correspondence of James Fenimore-Cooper.* Edited by James Fenimore Cooper (grandson). 2 vols. New Haven: Yale University Press, 1922.

———. *Letters and Journals.* Edited by James Franklin Beard. Vols. 1–6. Cambridge: Belknap Press of Harvard University Press, 1960–1968.

Davis, William Heath. *Sixty Years in California: A History of Events and Life in California; Personal, Political, and Military; Under the Mexican Regime; During the Quasi-Military Government of the Territory by the United States; and after the Admission of the State to the Union.* San Francisco: A. J Leary, 1889.

Documents of the Senate of the State of New York, One Hundred and Thirty-Second Session, 1909. Vol. 13, No. 35. Albany: J. B. Lyon Co., State Printers, 1909.

Duvall, Robert Carson. "Extracts from the Log of the U.S. Frigate *Savannah* Kept by Robert Carson Duvall." *California Historical Quarterly* 3:2 (July 1924): 105–125.

Frémont, John C. *Memoirs of My Life.* New introduction by Charles M. Robinson III. 1886. Reprint, New York: Cooper Square Press, 2001.

A General Register of the Navy and Marine Corps of the United States. Washington, DC: C. Alexander, Printer, 1848.

Howard, Nathan, Jr. *Practice Reports in the Supreme Court and Court of Appeals of the State of New-York.* Vol. 9. Albany: William Gould, 1860.

Larkin, Thomas O. *The Larkin Papers: Personal, Business, and Official Correspondence of Thomas Oliver Larkin, Merchant and United States Consul in California.*

Vols. IV and V. Edited by George P. Hammond. Berkeley and Los Angeles: University of California Press, 1953, 1955.

Miller, John. *Memoirs of General Miller in the Service of the Republic of Peru, Volume 1*. London: Longman, Rees, Orme, Brown, and Green, 1828.

Morris, Charles. *The Autobiography of Commodore Charles Morris, U.S. Navy.* 1880. Reprint, with an introduction and additional notes by Frederick C. Leiner. Annapolis: Naval Institute Press, 2002.

Naval Documents Relating to the Quasi-War between the United States and France. 7 vols. Washington, DC: U.S. Government Printing Office, 1935–1938.

New American State Papers, Naval Affairs. Edited by K. Jack Bauer. Wilmington: Scholarly Resources, 1981.

New York State Legislature. Senate. *Documents of the Senate of the State of New York, One Hundred and Thirty-Second Session, 1909*. Vol. 13, No. 35. Albany: J. B. Lyon Co., State Printers, 1909.

Kingdom of Hawaii. *Table of Consular Grievances, 1843–1836*. Compiled by Robert C. Wyllie. Honolulu, 1846.

Longworth's City Directory of New York. Various years.

Register of the Commision [sic] and Warrant Officers of the Navy of the United States, Including Officers of the Marine Corps. Np: Jacob Gideon, 1822.

Register of the Commissioned and Warrant Officers of the Navy of the United States, Including Officers of the Marine Corps, and Others, for the Year 1847. Washington City: C. Alexander, Printer, 1847.

Revere, Joseph Warren. *Naval Duty in California*. 1849. Reprint, Oakland: Biobooks, 1947.

Sutter, John. "General Sutter's Diary." In *John Sutter and a Wider West*. Edited by Kenneth N. Owens. Lincoln and London: University of Nebraska Press, 1994.

Wilkes, Charles. *An Autobiography of Rear Admiral Charles Wilkes, U.S. Navy 1798–1877*. Edited by William James Morgan, David B. Tyler, Joye L. Leonhart, and Mary F. Loughin. Washington, DC; Naval History Division, Department of the Navy, 1978.

Contemporary Publications

Ashmun, Jehudi. *History of the American Colony in Liberia from December, 1821 to 1823*. Washington City: Way & Gideon, 1826.

Beach, Moses Y. *Wealth and Biography of the Wealthy Citizens of New York City*. 6th ed. New York: New York Sun Office, 1845.

Beale, Robert. *A Report of the Trial of Commodore David Porter of the Navy of the United States, before a General Court-Martial, Held at Washington in July 1825*. Washington City: 1825.

Catalog of the Trustees, Instructors, and Students, of Plainfield Academy, Plainfield, Ct. for the Year Ending August 1832. Brooklyn: Advertiser Press, 1832.

Catalogue of the Trustees, Instructors, and Students, of Plainfield Academy, Plainfield (Con.) August 1828. Brooklyn: Advertiser-Press, John Gray, Jr., 1828.

Caulkins, Frances Manwaring. *History of New London, Connecticut from the First Survey of the Coast in 1612 to 1860*. 1860. Reprint, New London: New London County Historical Society, 2007.

———. *History of Norwich, Connecticut from Its Possession by the Indians to the Year 1866*. 1866. Reprint, New London: New London County Historical Society, 2009.

"Commodore John Drake Sloat." *Hunt's Merchant's Magazine* (New York) 15:5 (November 1846): 446–456.

Cooper, James Fenimore. *The History of the Navy of the United States, Continued to 1856, from the Author's Notes and Other Authentic Notes*. New York: Stringer and Townsend, 1856.

Cooper, James Fenimore, ed. *Ned Myers, or, A Life Before the Mast*. London: Richard Bentley, New Burlington Street, 1843.

Énault, Louis. *L'Amerique Centrale et Meridionale*. Paris: F. de P. Mellado et Cie. 1867.

Fleury de Chaubulon, Baron Pierre. *Memoirs of the Private Life, Return, and Reign of Napoleon I in 1815, Vol. II*. London: John Murray, Albemarle Street, 1820.

Osio, Antonio María. *The History of Alta California: A Memoir of Mexican California*. Translated by Rose Marie Beebe and Robert M. Senkewicz. 1851. Reprint, Madison: University of Wisconsin Press, 1996.

Proceedings of the Naval Court Martial in the Case of Alexander Slidell Mackenzie, a Commander in the Navy of the United States Including the Charges and Specifications Preferred against Him by the Secretary of the Navy to Which Is Annexed an Elaborate Review by James Fennimore [*sic*] *Cooper*. New York: Harold Langley, 1844.

Shillibeer, John. *A Narrative of the Briton's Voyage to Pitcairn's Island*. London: Law and Whittaker, 1818.

Newspapers and Periodicals

Aurora General Register (Philadelphia)
Baltimore Patriot
Baltimore Price-Current
Boston Commercial Gazette
Boston Patriot
Brooklyn Daily Eagle

Columbian (New York)
Commercial Advertiser (New York)
Connecticut Gazette
Daily Advertiser (New York)
Federal Republican (Baltimore)
Federal Republican for the Country (Georgetown, District of Columbia)
Hunt's Merchants Magazine and Commercial Review (New York)
Mechanics' Magazine and Journal of Engineering, Agricultural Machinery, Manufactures and Shipbuilding (London)
Mercantile Advertiser (New York)
Morning Chronicle (New York)
Morning News (New London)
Nashville Union and American
The Naval Magazine
New-England Palladium
New-Hampshire Gazette (Portsmouth)
New York Daily Times
New York Daily Tribune
New York Evening Post
New York Herald
New-York Gazette
Niles Weekly Register (New York)
Norwich Courier
Portsmouth [New Hampshire] *Journal of Literature and Politics*
San Francisco Call
Southern Patriot (Charleston, SC)
Wisconsin Enquirer (Milwaukee)

Books, Articles, and Pamphlets

Acosta, Ursula, with David E. Cuesta Camacho. *¿Quien era Cofresí?* Hormigueros: Dra. Ursula Acosta, 1984.

Adams, Donald R., Jr. "Wage Patterns in the National Period: Philadelphia 1785–1830." *Journal of Economic History* 28:3 (September 1968): 404–426.

Aderman, Ralph M., and Wayne R. Kime. *Advocate for America: The Life of James Kirke Paulding.* Selinsgrove: Susquehanna University Press, 2003.

Albion, Robert G. "Early Nineteenth-Century Shipowning—A Chapter in Business Enterprise." *Journal of Economic History* 1:1 (May 1941): 1–11.

———. *The Rise of New York Port, 1815–1860.* New York and London: Charles Scribner's Sons, 1939.

Albion, Robert G., William A. Baker, and Benjamin W. Labaree. *New England and the Sea*. Middletown: Wesleyan University Press, 1972.

Alden, Carroll Storrs. *Lawrence Kearny, Sailor Diplomat*. Princeton: Princeton University Press, 1936.

Allborn, Denise M. "Crimping and Shanghaiing on the Columbia River." *Oregon Historical Quarterly* 93:3 (Fall 1992): 262–291.

Allison, Robert J. *Stephen Decatur: American Naval Hero, 1779–1820*. Amherst and Boston: University of Massachusetts Press, 2005.

Anderson, William G. "John Adams, the Navy, and the Quasi-War with France." *American Neptune* 30:2 (April 1970): 117–132.

Anna, Timothy. "Agustín de Iturbide and the Process of Consensus." In *The Birth of Modern Mexico 1780–1824*, edited by Christon I. Archer, 187–204. Lanham: Rowman & Littlefield, 2003.

Archer, Christon I. "Fashioning a New Nation." In Meyer and Beezley, *The Oxford History of Mexico*, 301–338.

Bailey, Thomas A. *A Diplomatic History of the American People*. 6th ed. New York: Appleton-Century-Crofts, 1958.

Baker, Joseph Eugene. *Past and Present of Alameda County, California, Vol. 2*. Chicago: S. J. Clarke, 1914.

Bancroft, Hubert H. *History of California, Vol. V, 1846–1848*. San Francisco: History Co., 1886.

Bauer, K. Jack. "George Bancroft, 11 March 1845–9 September 1846." In Coletta, *Secretaries of the Navy, Volume I*, 217–229.

———. "John Young Mason, 10 September 1846–7 March 1849." In Coletta, *Secretaries of the Navy, Volume I*, 231–240.

———. "Naval Shipbuilding Programs, 1794–1860." *Military Affairs* 29:1 (Spring 1965): 29–40.

———. *A Maritime History of the United States: The Role of America's Seas and Waterways*. Columbia: University of South Carolina Press, 1988.

———. *The Mexican War, 1846–1848*. New York: Macmillan, 1974. Reprint, Lincoln and London: University of Nebraska Press, 1972.

———. "The *Sancala* Affair: Captain Voorhees Seizes an Argentine Squadron." *American Neptune* 29:2 (1969): 174–186.

———. *Surfboats and Horse Marines: U.S. Naval Operations in the Mexican War, 1846–48*. Annapolis: Naval Institute Press, 1969.

Bayor, Ronald H., and Timothy J. Meagher, eds. *The New York Irish*. Baltimore and London: Johns Hopkins University Press, 1996.

Beebe, Rose Marie, and Robert M. Senkewicz, eds. *Lands of Promise and Despair: Chronicles of Early California, 1535–1846*. Berkeley: Heyday Books, 2001.

Beebe, Rose Marie, and Robert M. Senkewicz, trans. *Testimonios: Early California through the Eyes of Women, 1815–1848.* Berkeley: Heyday Books, 2006.

Berube, Claude G. "The Crucible of Naval Enlightenment." *Naval History* 28:5 (October 2014): 58–63.

Berube, Claude G., and John A. Rodgaard. *A Call to the Sea: Captain Charles Stewart of the USS* Constitution. Washington, DC: Potomac Books, 2005.

Bickham, Troy. *The Weight of Vengeance: The United States, the British Empire, and the War of 1812.* New York: Oxford University Press, 2012.

Billingsley, Edward Baxter. *In Defense of Neutral Rights: The United States Navy and the Wars of Independence in Chile and Peru.* Chapel Hill: University of North Carolina Press, 1967.

Birkner, Michael J. *Samuel L. Southard: Jeffersonian Whig.* Rutherford: Fairleigh Dickinson University Press, 1984.

———. "The 'Foxardo Affair' Revisited: Porter, Pirates, and the Problem of Civilian Authority in the Early Republic." *American Neptune* 42:3 (July 1982): 165–178.

Blumin, Stuart M. *The Emergence of the Middle Class: Social Experience in the American City, 1760–1900.* New York: Cambridge University Press, 1989.

Bobbé, Dorothie. *DeWitt Clinton.* Rev. ed. Introduction by Harry Steele Commager. Port Washington: Ira J. Friedman, 1962.

Bolster, W. Jeffrey. *Black Jacks: African American Seamen in the Age of Sail.* Cambridge and London: Harvard University Press, 1997.

———. "To Feel Like a Man: Black Seamen in the Northern States, 1800–1860." *Journal of American History* 76:4 (March 1990): 1173–1199.

Brack, Gene M. *Mexico Views Manifest Destiny, 1821–1846.* Albuquerque: University of New Mexico Press, 1975.

Brady, Cyrus T. *Stephen Decatur.* Boston: Small, Maynard, and Co., 1900.

Bridges, Amy. *A City in the Republic: Antebellum New York and the Origins of Machine Politics.* Cambridge: Cambridge University Press, 1984.

Brittin, Burdick H., and Liselotte B. Watson. *International Law for Seagoing Officers.* 2nd ed. Annapolis: Naval Institute Press, 1960.

Brooke, George M., Jr. "The Vest Pocket War of Commodore Jones." *Pacific Historical Review* 31:3 (August 1962): 217–233.

Brown, Gary Lawson. *Baltimore in the Nation, 1789–1861.* Chapel Hill: University of North Carolina Press, 1980.

Budiansky, Stephen. *Perilous Fight: America's Intrepid War with Britain on the High Seas, 1812–1815.* New York: Alfred A. Knopf, 2010

Burin, Eric. *Slavery and the Peculiar Solution: A History of the American Colonization Society.* Gainesville: University Press of Florida, 2005.

Burns, E. Bradford. *A History of Brazil.* 3rd ed. New York: Columbia University Press, 1993.

Burrows, Edwin G., and Mike Wallace. *Gotham: A History of New York to 1898.* New York: Oxford University Press, 1999.

Canney, Donald L. *The Old Steam Navy, Volume Two: The Ironclads, 1842–1885.* Annapolis: Naval Institute Press, 1993.

Castleman, Bruce A. *Building the King's Highway: Labor, Society, and Family on Mexico's Caminos Reales, 1757–1804.* Tucson: University of Arizona Press, 2005.

———. "Navigators in the 1490s." *U.S. Naval Institute Proceedings* 118:12 (December 1992): 39–43.

———. "Social Climbers in a Colonial Mexican City: Individual Mobility within the *Sistéma de Castas* in Orizaba, 1777–1791." *Colonial Latin American Review* 10:2 (December 2001): 229–250.

Chaffin, Tom. *Pathfinder: John Charles Frémont and the Course of American Empire.* New York: Hill and Wang, 2002.

Chandler, Robert J. "An Uncertain Influence: The Role of the Federal Government in California, 1846–1850." In *Taming the Elephant: Politics, Government, and Law in Pioneer California*, edited by John F. Burns and Richard J. Orsi, 244–271. Berkeley: University of California Press, 2003. First published as *California History* 81:3/4 (Fall–Winter 2003).

Chandler, Robert J., and Stephen J. Potash. *Gold, Silk, Pioneers and Mail: The Story of the Pacific Mail Steamship Company.* San Francisco: Friends of the San Francisco Maritime Museum Library, 2007.

Chapelle, Howard I. *The History of American Sailing Ships.* New York: W. W. Norton, 1935. Reprint, New York: Bonanza Books, 1988.

———. *The History of the American Sailing Navy: The Ships and Their Development.* New York: W. W. Norton, 1949. Reprint, New York: Bonanza Books, 1965.

Chisholm, Donald. *Waiting for Dead Men's Shoes: Origins and Development of the U. S. Navy's Officer Personnel System, 1793–1941.* Stanford: Stanford University Press, 2001.

Clary, David A. *Eagles and Empire: The United States, Mexico, and the Struggle for a Continent.* New York: Bantam Books, 2009.

Clegg, Claude A., III. *The Price of Liberty: African Americans and the Making of Liberia.* Chapel Hill: University of North Carolina Press, 2004.

Coletta, Paolo, ed. *American Secretaries of the Navy, Volume I, 1775–1913.* Annapolis: Naval Institute Press, 1980.

Collier, Simon, and William F. Sater. *A History of Chile, 1808–2002.* 2nd ed. New York: Cambridge University Press, 2004.

Cott, Nancy F. *The Bonds of Womanhood: "Women's Sphere" in New England, 1780–1835.* 2nd ed. New Haven: Yale University Press, 1997.

Coughlin, Magdalen. "Boston Smugglers on the Coast (1797–1821): An Insight into the American Acquisition of California." *California Historical Society Quarterly* 46:2 (June 1967): 99–120.

———. "California Ports: A Key to Diplomacy for the West Coast, 1820–1845." *Journal of the West* 5 (1966): 153–173.

Crapol, Edward R. *John Tyler: The Accidental President.* Chapel Hill: University of North Carolina Press, 2006.

Cressman, Robert J. "Historic Fleets: 'For the Purpose of Repressing Piracy.'" *Naval History* 28:5 (October 2014): 64–65.

Curcio-Nagy, Linda A. "Faith and Morals in Colonial Mexico." In Meyer and Beezley, *The Oxford History of Mexico*, 151–182.

Cutter, Donald C. *California in 1792: A Spanish Naval Visit.* Norman: University of Oklahoma Press, 1990.

Davidson, Lance S. "Shanghaied! The Systematic Kidnapping of Sailors in Early San Francisco." *California History* 64:1 (Winter 1985): 10–17.

Davis, William Heath. *Seventy-Five Years in California.* San Francisco: J. Howell, 1929.

Daughan, George C. *1812: The Navy's War.* New York: Basic Books, 2011.

Davis, Hugh H. "The American Seamen's Friend Society and the American Sailor, 1828–1838." *American Neptune* 29:1 (January 1979): 45–57.

De Conde, Alexander. *The Quasi-War: The Politics and Diplomacy of the Undeclared War with France, 1797–1801.* New York: Charles Scribner's Sons, 1966.

DeKay, James Tertius. *The Battle of Stonington: Torpedoes, Submarine, and Rockets in the War of 1812.* Annapolis: Naval Institute Press, 1990.

———. *A Rage for Glory: The Life of Commodore Stephen Decatur, USN.* New York: Free Press, 2004.

DeVoto, Bernard. *The Year of Decision, 1846.* Boston: Little, Brown, and Co., 1943.

Dictionary of American Naval Fighting Ships. http://www.history.navy.mil/danfs/s17/st_louis_i.htm/, accessed May 2, 2012

Dudley, Wade G. *Splintering the Wooden Wall: The British Blockade of the United States, 1812–1815.* Annapolis: Naval Institute Press, 2003.

Durand Florez, Luis. "La República: 1826–1899." In *Compendio Histórico del Perú, Tomo V*, edited by Carlos Milla Batres, 145–581. Lima: Editorial Milla Batres, 1993.

Dye, Ira. "Early American Merchant Seafarers." *Proceeding of the American Philosophical Society* 120:5 (October 15, 1976): 331–360.

———. *The Fatal Cruise of the* Argus: *Two Captains in the War of 1812.* Annapolis: Naval Institute Press, 1994.

———. "Physical and Social Profiles of Early American Seafarers, 1812–1815." In *Jack Tar in History: Essays in the History of Maritime Life and Labour*, edited by Colin Howell and Richard Twomey, 230–235. Fredericton: Acadiensis Press, 1991.

———. *Uriah Levy: Reformer of the Antebellum Navy.* Gainesville: University Press of Florida, 2006.

Egan, Ferol. *Frémont: Explorer for a Restless Nation.* Garden City: Doubleday, 1977.

Egerton, Douglas R. "Its Origin Is Not a Little Curious: A New Look at the American Colonization Society." *Journal of the Early Republic* 5:4 (Winter 1985): 463–480.

Eisenhower, John S. D. *So Far from God: The U.S. War with Mexico, 1846–48.* New York: Random House, 1989. Reprint, Norman: University of Oklahoma Press, 2000.

Elkins, Stanley M., and Eric McKittrick. *The Age of Federalism: The Early American Republic, 1788–1800.* New York: Oxford University Press, 1993.

Ellis, David M. *Landholders and Farmers in the Mohawk-Hudson Region, 1790–1850.* Ithaca, N.Y.: Cornell University Press, 1946. Reprint, New York: Octagon Books, 1967.

———. "Land Tenure and Tenancy in the Hudson Valley, 1790–1860." *Agricultural History* 18:2 (April 1944): 75–82.

———. "Yankee-Dutch Confrontation in the Albany Area." *New England Quarterly* 45:2 (June 1972): 262–270.

Fagal, Andrew J. B. "Terror Weapons in the Naval War of 1812." *New York History* 94:3/4 (Summer/Fall 2013): 221–240.

Fauvelet de Bourrienne, Louis Antoine. *Memoirs of Napoleon Bonaparte, Vol. IV.* Edited by R. W. Phipps. New York: Charles Scribner's Sons, 1906.

Ferguson, Eugene S. *Truxtun of the* Constellation: *The Life of Commodore Thomas Truxtun, U.S. Navy, 1755–1822.* With a new introduction by Michael J. Crawford. Baltimore: Johns Hopkins University Press, 1956, 2000.

Ferling, John. *John Adams: A Life.* Knoxville: University of Tennessee Press, 1992.

Fernández Valledor, Roberto. *El mito de Cofresí en la narrative antillana.* Mayaguez: Editorial Universitaria, Universidad de Puerto Rico, 1978.

———. *El Pirata Cofresí mitificado por la tradición puertorriequeña.* Ponce: Casa Paoli, 2006.

Fingard, Judith. "Masters and Friends, Crimps and Abstainers: Agents of Control in 19th-Century Sailortown." *Acadiensis* 8:1 (1978): 22–46.

Fogel, Robert W. *Without Consent or Contract: The Rise and Fall of American Slavery.* New York: W.W. Norton, 1989.

Foster, Charles I. "The Colonization of Free Negroes, in Liberia, 1816–1835." *Journal of Negro History* 38:1 (January 1953): 41–66.

Fowler, William M., Jr. *Jack Tars and Commodores: The American Navy, 1783–1815.* Boston: Houghton Mifflin Co., 1984.

Franklin, Wayne. *James Fenimore Cooper: The Early Years.* New Haven and London: Yale University Press, 2007.

Genovese, Eugene. *Roll, Jordan, Roll: The World the Slaves Made.* New York: Pantheon, 1974.

German, Andrew W. "Mrs. Stewart's Situation." New London County Historical Society, 2012. http://warof1812ct.org/?p=733/, accessed March 12, 2014.

Gilbert, Geoffrey. "Maritime Enterprise in the New Republic: Investment in Baltimore Shipping, 1789–1793." *Business History Review* 58:1 (Spring 1984): 114–129.

Gilje, Paul A. *Free Trade and Sailors' Rights in the War of 1812.* Cambridge: Cambridge University Press, 2013.

———. *Liberty on the Waterfront: American Maritime Culture in the Age of Revolution.* Philadelphia: University of Pennsylvania, 2004.

———. *The Road to Mobocracy: Popular Disorder in New York City, 1763–1835.* Chapel Hill: University of North Carolina Press for the Institute of Early American History and Culture, 1987.

Glenn, Myra C. "The Naval Reform Campaign against Flogging: A Case Study in Changing Attitudes toward Corporal Punishment, 1830–1850." *American Quarterly* 35:4 (Autumn 1983): 408–425.

Goetzmann, William H. *Army Exploration in the American West.* New Haven: Yale University Press, 1959.

Goldenberg, Joseph A. "Blue Lights and Infernal Machines: The British Blockade of New London." *The Mariner's Mirror* 61:4 (November 1975): 385–398.

———. "The Royal Navy's Blockade in New England Waters, 1812–1815." *The International History Review* 6:3 (August 1984): 424–439.

González, Michael J. "The Child of the Wilderness Weeps for the Father of Our Country: The Indian and the Politics of Church and State in Provincial California." In Gutiérrez and Orsi, *Contested Eden*, 147–172.

Green, Frank Bertangue. *History of Rockland County.* New York: A. S. Barnes and Co., 1886.

Groom, Winston. *Kearny's March: The Epic Creation of the American West, 1846–1847.* New York: A. A. Knopf, 2011.

Grossman, James. *James Fenimore Cooper.* New York: William Sloan Associates, 1949.

Groth, Michael. "Slaveholders and Manumission in Dutchess County, New York." *New York History* 78:1 (January 1997): 33–50.

Guernsey, Robert. *New York City and Vicinity during the War of 1812–1815.* New York: C. L. Woodward, 1889.

Guerra Martiniere, Margarita. *La República, 1827–1899: Historia General del Perú, Tomo VII.* Lima: Editorial Brasa, 1994.

Guest, Florian. "The Establishment of the Villa de Branciforte." *California Historical Quarterly* 41:1 (March 1962): 29–50.

Gutiérrez, Ramón A., and Richard J. Orsi, eds. *Contested Eden: California before the Gold Rush*. Berkeley: University of California Press, 1998. First published as *California History* 76:2/3 (Summer–Fall 1997).

Guttridge, Leonard F. *Mutiny: A History of Naval Insurrection*. Annapolis: Naval Institute Press, 1992.

———. *Our Country Right or Wrong: The Life of Stephen Decatur, the U.S. Navy's Most Illustrious Commander.* New York: Tom Doherty Associates, 2006.

Haas, Lisbeth. *Conquests and Historical Identities in California, 1769–1936*. Berkeley, Los Angeles, and London: University of California Press, 1995.

———. "War in California, 1846–1848." In Gutiérrez and Orsi, *Contested Eden*, 331–355.

Hagan, Kenneth A., ed. *In Peace and War: Interpretations of American Naval History, 1775–1984*. 2nd ed. Westport: Greenwood Press, 1984.

Handlin, Lilian. *George Bancroft: The Intellectual as Democrat*. New York: Harper and Row, 1984.

Haring, C. H. *The Spanish Empire in America*. New York: Oxford University Press, 1947.

Harlow, Neal. *California Conquered: The Annexation of a Mexican Province, 1846–1850*. Berkeley, Los Angeles, and London: University of California Press, 1982.

Hayford, Harrison, ed. *The* Somers *Mutiny Affair.* Englewood Cliffs: Prentice Hall, 1959.

Heidenreich, Linda. *"This Land Was Mexican Once": Histories of Resistance from Northern California*. Austin: University of Texas Press, 2007.

Heitzmann, W. Ray. "In-Service Naval Officer Education in the Nineteenth Century: Voluntary Commitment to Reform." *American Neptune* 39:2 (April 1979): 109–125.

Henderson, Timothy J. *A Glorious Defeat: Mexico and Its War with the United States.* New York: Hill and Wang, 2007.

Henning, G. R. "Fourpenny Dark and Sixpenny Red." *Labour History* 46 (May 1984): 52–71.

Henretta, James A. "Families and Farms: *Mentalité* in Pre-Industrial America." *William and Mary Quarterly* 3rd Ser. 35 (1978): 3–32.

Henry, Robert S. *The Story of the Mexican War.* Indianapolis: Bobbs-Merrill Co., 1950.

Hernández Ruigómez, Almudena. *Simón Bolívar.* Madrid: Ediciones Dastín Export, 2004.

Herrera Alarcón, Dante. *Rebeliones que intentaron desmembrar el sur del Perú*. Lima: Imprenta Colegio Militar Leoncio Prado, 1961.

Herring, George C. *From Colony to Superpower: U.S. Foreign Relations since 1776.* Oxford History of the United States. New York: Oxford University Press, 2008.

Hershowitz, Leo. "The Irish and the Emerging City: Settlement to 1844. In Bayor and Meagher, *The New York Irish*, 11–34.

Hickey, Donald R. *The War of 1812: A Forgotten Conflict.* Urbana and Chicago: University of Illinois Press, 1989.

High, James. "Jones at Monterey, 1842." *Journal of the West* 5:2 (April 1966): 173–186.

Hittell, Theodore Henry. *The California Academy of Sciences: A Narrative History, 1853–1906.* Revised and enlarged. Edited by Alan E. Leviton and Michele L. Aldrich. San Francisco: California Academy of Sciences, 1997.

———. *History of California, Vol. II.* San Francisco: N. J. Stone and Co., 1885.

Hobsbawm, Eric. *Bandits.* New York: Delacorte Press, 1969.

———. "Social Bandits: A Reply." *Comparative Studies in Society and History* 14:4 (September 1972): 503–505.

Hobsbawm, Eric, and Terence Ranger. *The Invention of Tradition.* Cambridge: Cambridge University Press, 1983.

Hogue, Harlan, and David J. Langum. *Thomas O. Larkin: A Life of Patriotism and Profit in Old California.* Norman and London: University of Oklahoma Press, 1990.

Hoppin, James Mason. *The Life of Andrew Hull Foote, Rear-Admiral, United States Navy.* New York: Harper Brothers, 1874.

Horsman, Reginald. *The War of 1812.* New York: A. A. Knopf, 1969.

Howe, Daniel Walker. *What Hath God Wrought: The Transformation of America, 1815–1848.* Oxford History of the United States. New York: Oxford University Press, 2007.

Hunter, Mark C. *A Society of Gentlemen: Midshipmen at the U.S. Naval Academy, 1845–1861.* Annapolis: Naval Institute Press, 2010.

Hurtado, Albert L. *John Sutter: A Life on the North American Frontier.* Norman: University of Oklahoma Press, 2006.

Huston, Reeve. *Land and Freedom: Rural Society, Popular Protest, and Party Politics in Antebellum New York.* New York: Oxford University Press, 2000.

Hutchins, John G. B. *The American Maritime Industries and Public Policy, 1789–1914.* Harvard Economic Studies, Vol. 71. Cambridge: Harvard University Press, 1941.

Jackson, Donald, and Mary Lee Spence, eds. *The Expeditions of John Charles Frémont, Vol. 2: The Bear Flag Revolt and the Court-Martial.* Urbana: University of Illinois Press, 1973.

Jackson, Kenneth T., and David S. Dunbar, "Rise to National Dominance (1782–1860)." In *Empire City: New York through the Centuries*, edited by Kenneth

T. Jackson and David S. Dunbar, 99–106. New York: Columbia University Press, 2002.

Jackson, Robert H., and Edward Castillo. *Indians, Franciscans, and Spanish Colonization: The Impact of the Mission System on California Indians.* Albuquerque: University of New Mexico Press, 1995.

Johnson, Robert Erwin. *Thence Round Cape Horn: The Story of United States Naval Forces on Pacific Station, 1818–1923.* Annapolis: Naval Institute Press, 1963.

Jordan, Douglas S. "Stephen Decatur at New London: A Study in Strategic Frustration." *United States Naval Institute Proceedings* 93:10 (October 1967): 60–65.

Kemble, John Haskell. *The Panama Route, 1848–1869.* Berkeley: University of California Press, 1943.

Kemp, Peter, ed. *The Oxford Companion to Ships and the Sea.* Oxford, New York, and Melbourne: Oxford University Press, 1976.

Kessler-Harris, Alice. "Why Biography?" *American Historical Review* 114:3 (June 2009): 625–630.

Klarén, Peter. *Peru: Society and Nationhood in the Andes.* New York: Oxford University Press, 2000.

Klement, Frank L. *Lincoln's Critics: The Copperheads of the North.* Edited by Steven K. Rogstad. Shippensburg: White Mane Books, 1999.

Langley, Harold D. "The Negro in the Navy and Merchant Service, 1798–1860." *Journal of Negro History* 52:4 (October 1967): 273–286.

———. *Social Reform in the United States Navy, 1798–1862.* Urbana, Chicago, and London: University of Illinois Press, 1967.

Langley, Lester. *Simón Bolívar: Venezuelan Rebel, American Revolutionary.* Lanham: Rowman & Littlefield, 2009.

Lavrín, Asunción, and Edith Couturier. "Dowries and Wills: A View of Women's Socioeconomic Role in Colonial Guadalajara and Puebla, 1640–1790." *Hispanic American Historical Review* 59:2 (May 1979): 280–304.

Leeman, William P. *The Long Road to Annapolis: The Founding of the Naval Academy and the Emerging American Republic.* Chapel Hill: University of North Carolina Press, 2010.

Leiner, Frederick C. Introduction and Notes to Charles Morris, *The Autobiography of Commodore Charles Morris, U.S. Navy.* Annapolis: Naval Institute Press, 2002.

Lockwood, Charles. *Manhattan Moves Uptown: An Illustrated History.* Boston: Houghton Mifflin, 1976.

Long, David F. *Gold Braid and Foreign Relations: Diplomatic Activities of U.S. Naval Officers, 1798–1883.* Annapolis: Naval Institute Press, 1988.

———. *"Mad Jack": The Biography of Captain John Percival, USN, 1779–1862.* Westport: Greenwood Press, 1993.

———. "The Navy under the Board of Navy Commissioners." In Hagan, *In Peace and War*, 63–78.

———. *Nothing Too Daring: A Biography of Commodore David Porter, 1780–1843.* Annapolis: Naval Institute Press, 1970.

———. *Sailor-Diplomat: A Biography of Commodore James Biddle, 1782–1848.* Boston: Northeastern University Press, 1983.

Lott, Arnold S. *A Long Line of Ships: Mare Island's Century of Naval Activity in California.* Annapolis: Naval Institute Press, 1954.

Loveman, Brian. *Chile: The Legacy of Hispanic Capitalism.* 3rd ed. New York: Oxford University Press, 2001.

Lubar, Steven. "'To polish and adorn the mind': The United States Naval Lyceum at the Brooklyn Navy Yard, 1833–1889." *Museum History Journal* 7:1 (January 2014): 84–102.

Lull, Edward P. *History of the United States Navy-Yard at Gosport, Virginia (Near Norfolk), for the Bureau of Yards and Docks, Navy Department.* Washington, DC: U.S. Government Printing Office, 1874.

Lynch, John. *Simón Bolívar: A Life.* New Haven: Yale University Press, 2006.

Lynd, Staughton. "Who Shall Rule at Home? Dutchess County, New York, in the American Revolution." *William and Mary Quarterly*, 3rd ser. 20:2 (July 1961): 330–359.

Maitland, Sir Frederick. *The Surrender of Napoleon.* Edinburgh and London: Blackwood and Sons, 1904.

Malcom, Corey. "Understanding the Key West Hurricane of 1846." *Florida Keys Sea Heritage Journal* 20:4 (Summer 2010): 1–16.

Mark, Irving. *Agrarian Conflicts in Colonial New York, 1711–1775.* New York: Columbia University Press, 1940. Reprint, Port Washington: Ira J. Friedman, 1965.

Marti, Werner H. *Messenger of Destiny: The California Adventures, 1846–1847, of Archibald H. Gillespie, U.S. Marine Corps.* San Francisco: John Howell Books, 1960.

Martin, Tyrone G. *A Most Fortunate Ship: A Narrative History of "Old Ironsides."* Rev. ed. Chester: Globe Pequot Press, 1982.

Marvin, Winthrop L. *The American Merchant Marine: Its History and Romance from 1620 to 1902.* New York: Charles Scribner's Sons, 1902.

Matzke, Rebecca Berens. *Deterrence through Strength: British Naval Power and Foreign Policy under* Pax Britannica. Lincoln and London: University of Nebraska Press, 2011.

May, Ernest R. *The Making of the Monroe Doctrine.* Cambridge: Belknap Press of the Harvard University Press, 1975.

McCranie, Kevin D. *Utmost Gallantry: The U.S. and Royal Navies at Sea in the War of 1812.* Annapolis: Naval Institute Press, 2011.

McCullough, David. *John Adams.* New York: Simon and Schuster, 2001.

McCusker, John J. *How Much Is That in Real Money? A Historical Commodity Price Index for Use as a Deflator of Money Values in the Economy of the United States.* 2nd ed. Worcester: American Antiquarian Society, 2001.

McEntee, M. Regina. "John McKeon: Catholic Leader and Congressman from New York, 1808–1883." Master's thesis, Catholic University, 1947.

McFarland, Philip. *Sea Dangers: The Affair of the* Somers. New York: Schocken Books, 1985.

McKee, Christopher. *A Gentlemanly and Honorable Profession: The Creation of the U.S. Naval Officer Corps, 1794–1815.* Annapolis: Naval Institute Press, 1991.

McPherson, James M. *Battle Cry of Freedom: The Civil War Era.* Oxford History of the United States. New York: Oxford University Press, 1988.

Melton, Bucker F., Jr. *Hanging Offense: The Strange Affair of the Warship* Somers. New York: Free Press, 2003.

Merrill, James. *Du Pont, the Making of an Admiral: A Biography of Samuel Francis Du Pont.* New York: Dodd, Mead, and Co., 1986.

Merry, Robert W. *A Country of Vast Design: James K. Polk, the Mexican War, and the Conquest of the American Southwest.* New York: Simon and Schuster, 2009.

Meyer, Michael C., and William H. Beezley, eds. *The Oxford History of Mexico.* New York: Oxford University Press, 2000.

Miller, Douglas T. *Jacksonian Aristocracy: Class and Democracy in New York, 1830–1860.* New York: Oxford University Press, 1967.

Miller, Robert Ryal. *Juan Alvarado: Governor of California, 1836–1842.* Norman: University of Oklahoma Press, 1998.

Milner, Clyde A., II. "National Initiatives." In *The Oxford History of the American West.* Edited by Milner, Carol A. O'Connor, and Martha A. Sandweiss, 155–194. New York and Oxford: Oxford University Press, 1994.

Monaghan, E. Jennifer. *A Common Heritage: Noah Webster's Blue-Back Speller.* Hamden: Archon Books, 1983.

Monroy, Douglas. "The Creation and Re-creation of Californio Society." In Gutiérrez and Orsi, *Contested Eden*, 173–195.

———. *Thrown Among Strangers: The Making of Mexican Culture in Frontier California.* Berkeley, Los Angeles, and Oxford: University of California Press, 1990.

Morison, Samuel Eliot. *The Maritime History of Massachusetts, 1783–1860.* Boston and New York: Houghton Mifflin, 1921.

———. *"Old Bruin": Commodore Matthew Calbraith Perry, 1794–1858.* Boston and Toronto: Little, Brown and Co., 1967.

———. *Sailor Historian: The Best of Samuel Eliot Morison.* Edited by Emily Morison Beck. Boston: Houghton Mifflin, 1977.

Moss, Richard J. *Noah Webster.* Boston: Twayne, 1984.

Mushkat, Jerome. *Fernando Wood: A Political Biography.* Kent: Kent State University Press, 1990.

———. *The Reconstruction of the New York Democracy, 1861–1874.* East Brunswick: Associated University Presses, 1981.

———. *Tammany: The Evolution of a Political Machine, 1789–1865.* Syracuse: Syracuse University Press, 1971.

Nagle, Jacob. *The Nagle Journal: A Diary of the Life of Jacob Nagle, Sailor, from the Year 1775 to 1841.* Edited by John C. Dann. New York: Weidenfeld & Nicolson, 1988.

Nasatir, Abraham P. "International Rivalry for California and the Establishment of the British Consulate." *California Historical Society Quarterly* 46:1 (March 1967): 53–70.

Neuhaus Rizo Patrón, Carlos. *Pancha Gamarra, La Mariscala.* Lima: F. Moncloa Editores, 1967.

Nevins, Allan. *Frémont, Pathmarker of the West.* New York: Frederick Ungar, 1955.

Nunis, Doyce B., Jr. "Alta California's Trojan Horse: Foreign Immigration." In Gutiérrez and Orsi, *Contested Eden*, 299–330.

Olson, Edwin. "Social Aspects of Slavery in New York." *Journal of Negro History* 26:1 (January 1941): 66–77.

Owens, Kenneth N., ed. *John Sutter and a Wider West.* Lincoln and London: University of Nebraska Press, 1994.

Painter, Nell Irvin. *Sojourner Truth: A Life, a Symbol.* New York: W. W. Norton, 1996.

Palmer, Michael A. *Stoddert's War: Naval Operations during the Quasi-War with France, 1798–1801.* Columbia: University of South Carolina Press, 1987.

Paquette, Gabriel. *Imperial Portugal in the Age of Atlantic Revolutions.* Cambridge: Cambridge University Press, 2013.

Perkins, Bradford. *Prologue to War: England and the United States, 1805–1812.* Berkeley and Los Angeles: University of California Press, 1968.

Peskin, Lawrence A. "Conspiratorial Anglophobia and the War of 1812." *Journal of American History* 98:3 (December 2011): 647–669.

Pessen, Edward. "The Egalitarian Myth and the American Social Reality: Wealth, Mobility, and Equality in the 'Era of the Common Man.'" *American Historical Review* 76:4 (October 1971): 989–1034.

———. *Jacksonian America: Society, Personality, and Politics*. Rev. ed. Homewood: Dorsey Press, 1978.

———. "Moses Beach Revisited: A Critical Examination of His *Wealthy Citizens* Pamphlets." *Journal of American History* 58:2 (September 1971): 415–426.

———. *Riches, Class, and Power before the Civil War.* Lexington: D. C. Heath, 1973.

———. "The Social Configuration of the Antebellum City: An Historical and Theoretical Inquiry." *Journal of Urban History* 2:3 (May 1976): 267–306.

———. "Social Structure and Politics in American History." *American Historical Review* 87:5 (December 1982): 1290–1325.

Phelps, Robert. "On Comic Opera Revolutions: Maneuver Theory and the Art of War in Mexican California, 1821–1845." *California History* 84:1 (Fall 2006): 44–63.

Phelps-Stokes, Isaac N. *The Iconography of Manhattan Island, Vol. 3*. New York: Robert H. Dodd, 1918.

Philbrick, Nathaniel. *Sea of Glory: America's Voyage of Discovery, the U.S. Exploring Expedition, 1838–1842*. New York: Viking Press, 2003.

Philbrick, Thomas. *James Fenimore Cooper and the Development of American Sea Fiction*. Cambridge: Harvard University Press, 1961.

Pletcher, David M. *The Diplomacy of Annexation: Texas, Oregon, and the Mexican War.* Columbia: University of Missouri Press, 1973.

Preble, George Henry. *History of the United States Navy-Yard, Portsmouth, N.H.* Washington, DC: U.S. Government Printing Office, 1892.

Prucha, Francis Paul. *The Sword of the Republic: The United States Army on the Frontier 1783–1846*. New York: Macmillan, 1969.

Pubols, Louise. "Becoming Californios: Jokes, Broadsides, and a Slap in the Face." In *Alta California: Peoples in Motion, Identities in Formation, 1769–1850*, edited by Steven W. Hackel, 131–155. Berkeley and San Marino: University of California Press for the Huntington-USC Institute on California and the West, 2010.

———. *The Father of All: The de la Guerra Family, Power, and Patriarchy in Mexican California*. Berkeley and San Marino: University of California Press for the Huntington-USC Institute on California and the West, 2009.

Randall, Peter. *Portsmouth and the Piscataqua*. Camden: Downeast Books, 1982.

Ray, Angela G. *The Lyceum and Public Culture in the Nineteenth-Century United States.* East Lansing: Michigan State University Press, 2005.

Richter, Kurt, and Nghiem Ta. "Pirates, Prizes, and Profits: Cocoa and the Early American Coastal Trade." In *Chocolate: History, Culture, and Heritage*, edited by Louis Evan Grivetti and Howard-Yana Shapiro, 211–218. Hoboken: John Wiley and Sons, 2009.

Roberts, Jerry. *The British Raid on Essex: The Forgotten Battle of the War of 1812*. Middletown: Wesleyan University Press, 2014.

Rock, David. *Argentina, 1516–1987: From Colonization to Alfonsín*. Berkeley: University of California Press, 1987.

Roland, Alexander, W. Jeffrey Bolster, and Alexander Keyssar. *The Way of the Ship: America's Maritime History Reenvisioned, 1600–2000*. Hoboken: John Wiley and Sons, 2008.

Rolle, Andrew. *John Charles Fremont: Character as Destiny*. Norman and London: University of Oklahoma Press, 1991.

Rollins, Richard M. *The Long Journey of Noah Webster*. Philadelphia: University of Pennsylvania Press, 1980.

Rosenus, Alan. *General Vallejo and the Advent of the Americans*. Berkeley: Heyday Books/Urion Press, 1998.

Rouleau, Brian. *With Sails Whitening Every Sea: Mariners and the Making of an American Maritime Empire*. Ithaca: Cornell University Press, 2014.

Royce, Josiah. *California: A Study of American Character*. Introduction by Robert A. Wells. 1886. Reprint, Santa Clara and Berkeley: Santa Clara University and Heyday Books, 2002.

Rudolph, Frederick, ed. *Essays on Education in the Early Republic*. Cambridge: Belknap Press of the Harvard University Press, 1965.

Ruttenber, E. M., and L. H. Clark, et al., comp. *History of Orange County, New York*. Philadelphia: Everts and Peck, 1881.

Rybka, Walter. "'We Have Met the Enemy and They Are Ours': The U.S. Navy brig *Niagara*." In *Coffins of the Brave: Lake Shipwrecks of the War of 1812*, edited by Kevin J. Crisman, 19–50. College Station: Texas A&M University Press, 2014.

Salomon, Carlos Manuel. *Pío Pico: The Last Governor of Mexican California*. Norman: University of Oklahoma Press, 2010.

Saltonstall, William G. *Ports of Piscataqua: Soundings in the Maritime History of the Portsmouth, N.H., Customs District from the Queen Elizabeth and the Planting of Strawberry Banke to the Times of Abraham Lincoln and the Waning of the American Clipper*. Cambridge: Harvard University Press, 1941.

Sánchez, Joseph P. *Spanish Bluecoats: The Catalonian Volunteers in Northwestern New Spain, 1767–1810*. Albuquerque: University of New Mexico Press, 1990.

Sandos, James A. "Between Crucifix and Lance: Indian-White Relations in California, 1769–1848." In Gutiérrez and Orsi, *Contested Eden*, 196–229.

Scheina, Robert L. "The Forgotten Fleet: The Mexican Navy on the Eve of War, 1845." *American Neptune* 30:1 (January 1970): 46–56.

Schlereth, Eric R. "Privileges of Locomotion: Expatriation and the Politics of Southwestern Border Crossing." *Journal of American History* 100:4 (March 2014): 995–1020.

Schroeder, John H. *Matthew Calbraith Perry: Antebellum Sailor and Diplomat.* Annapolis: Naval Institute Press, 2001.

———. *Shaping a Maritime Empire: The Commercial and Diplomatic Role of the American Navy, 1829–1861.* Westport and London: Greenwood Press, 1985.

———. "Stephen Decatur: Heroic Ideal of the Young Navy." In *Command under Sail: Makers of the American Naval Tradition*, edited by James C. Bradford, 199–219. Annapolis: Naval Institute Press, 1985.

Seal, Graham. "The Robin Hood Principle: Folklore, History, and the Social Bandit." *Journal of Folklore Research* 46:1 (January–April 2009): 67–89.

Seed, Patricia A. *To Love, Honor, and Obey in Colonial Mexico: Conflicts over Marriage Choice, 1574–1821.* Stanford: Stanford University Press, 1988.

Shaw, David W. *The Sea Shall Embrace Them: The Tragic Story of the Steamship* Arctic. New York: Free Press, 2002.

Sherman, Edwin A. *The Life of the Late Rear Admiral John Drake Sloat, of the United States Navy, Who Took Possession of California and Raised the American Flag at Monterey on July 7th, 1846.* Enlarged Monumental Edition. Oakland: Carruth & Carruth, 1905. Original edition 1902.

Sherwell, Guillermo A. *Simón Bolívar (The Liberator): Patriot, Warrior, Statesman, Father of Five Nations.* Caracas: Bolivarian Society of Venezuela, 1921. Reprint, 1951.

Shurbutt, T. Ray. "Chile, Peru, and the U.S. Pacific Squadron." In *New Aspects of Naval History: Selected Papers Presented at the Fourth Naval History Symposium, United States Naval Academy, 25–26 October 1979*, edited by Craig L. Symonds, 201–210. Annapolis: Naval Institute Press, 1981.

Silbey, Joel H. *Martin Van Buren and the Emergence of American Popular Politics.* Lanham: Rowman & Littlefield, 2002.

Skaggs, David Curtis. "Aftermath of Victory: The Perry-Elliott Controversy." *Naval History* 28:1 (February 2014): 38–45.

———. *Oliver Hazard Perry: Honor, Courage, and Patriotism in the Early U.S. Navy.* Annapolis: Naval Institute Press, 2006.

Skidmore, Thomas E. *Brazil: Five Centuries of Change.* New York: Oxford University Press, 2009.

Small, Stephen C. "The Ship That Couldn't Be Built." *Naval History* 22:5 (October 2008).

Smith, Gene A. *Thomas ap Catesby Jones: Commodore of Manifest Destiny.* Annapolis: Naval Institute Press, 2000.

———. "The War That Wasn't: Thomas ap Catesby Jones and the Seizure of Monterey." *California History* 66:2 (June 1987): 104–113, notes at 155–156.

Smith, Geoffrey S. "An Uncertain Passage: The Bureaus Run the Navy, 1842–1861." In Hagan, *In Peace and War*, 79–106.

Smith, Page. *John Adams.* 2 vols. Garden City: Doubleday, 1962.

Sobrevilla Perea, Natalia. *The Caudillo of the Andes: Andrés de Santa Cruz*. Cambridge and New York: Cambridge University Press, 2011.

Socolow, Susan M. "Marriage, Birth, and Inheritance: The Merchants of Eighteenth-Century Buenos Aires." *Hispanic American Historical Review* 60:3 (August 1980): 387–406.

Spann, Edward K. *The New Metropolis: New York City, 1840–1857*. New York: Columbia University Press, 1981.

———. "Union Green: The Irish Community and the Civil War." In Bayor and Meagher, *The New York Irish*, 192–209.

Starr, Kevin. *Americans and the California Dream, 1850–1915*. New York: Oxford University Press, 1973.

Strauss, W. Patrick. "Preparing the Wilkes Expedition: A Study in Disorganization." *Pacific Historical Review* 28:3 (August 1959): 221–232.

Stuart, Charles B. *Naval and Mail Steamers of the United States.* New York: Charles B. Norton, Irving House, 1853.

Sung Bok Kim. *Landlord and Tenant in Colonial New York: Manorial Society, 1664–1775*. Chapel Hill: University of North Carolina Press for the Institute of Early American History and Culture, 1978.

Symonds, Craig L. *Navalists and Antinavalists: The Naval Policy Debate in the United States, 1785–1827*. Newark: University of Delaware Press, 1980.

Tate, Merze. *The United States and the Hawaiian Kingdom: A Political History.* New Haven and London: Yale University Press, 1965.

Távara, Santiago. *Historia de los Partidos.* Edited by Jorge Basadre and Félix Denegri Luna. Lima: Editorial Huarascán, 1951.

Taylor, Alan. *The Civil War of 1812: American Citizens, British Subjects, Irish Rebels, and Indian Allies.* New York: A. A. Knopf, 2010.

———. *William Cooper's Town: Power and Persuasion on the Frontier of the Early American Republic.* New York: A. A. Knopf, 1996.

Thompson, E. P. *The Making of the English Working Class.* New York: Random House, 1963.

Todorich, Charles. *The Spirited Years: A History of the Antebellum Naval Academy.* Annapolis: Naval Institute Press, 1984.

Toll, Ian W. *Six Frigates: The Epic History of the Founding of the United States Navy.* New York and London: W. W. Norton, 2006.

Tucker, Spencer C. *Andrew Foote: Civil War Admiral in Western Waters.* Annapolis: Naval Institute Press, 2000.

———. *Arming the Fleet: U.S. Navy Ordnance in the Muzzle-Loading Era.* Annapolis: Naval Institute Press, 1989.

———. *Stephen Decatur: A Life Most Bold and Daring.* Annapolis: Naval Institute Press, 2005.

———. "The Stevens Ironclad Battery." *American Neptune* 41:1 (Winter 1991): 12–22.

Twinam, Ann. *Public Lives, Private Secrets: Gender, Honor, Sexuality, and Illegitimacy in Colonial Spanish America.* Stanford: Stanford University Press, 1999.

Valle, James E. "The Navy's Battle Doctrine in the War of 1812." *American Neptune* 44:3 (Summer 1984): 171–179.

———. *Rocks and Shoals: Order and Discipline in the Old Navy, 1800–1861.* Annapolis: Naval Institute Press, 1980.

Van Aken, Mark J. *King of the Night: Juan José Flores and Ecuador, 1824–1864.* Berkeley, Los Angeles, and London: University of California Press, 1989.

Van de Water, Frederic. *The Captain Called It Mutiny.* New York: Ives Washburn, 1954.

Vásquez, Josefina Zoraida. "Los primeros tropiezos." In *Historia General de México, 4ta ed.*, Vol. 2, edited by Daniel Cosío Villegas, 735–818. Mexico City: El Colegio de México, 1997.

———. "War and Peace with the United States." Translated by Michael R. Brescia. In Meyer and Beezley, *The Oxford History of Mexico*, 339–370.

Vásquez, Josefina Zoraida, and Lorenzo Meyer. *The United States and Mexico.* Chicago and London: University of Chicago Press, 1985.

Vassar, Rena L., ed. *A Social History of American Education, Vol. 1: Colonial Times to 1860.* Chicago: Rand McNally, 1965.

Wainwright, Nicholas B. "Commodore James Biddle and His Sketchbook." *Pennsylvania Magazine of History and Biography* 90:1 (January 1966): 3–92.

———. "Voyage of the Frigate *Congress*, 1823." *Pennsylvania Magazine of History and Biography* 75:2 (April 1951): 170–188.

Waldo, S. Putnam. *The Life and Character of Stephen Decatur.* Hartford: P. S. Goodsell, 1821.

Walker, Charles F. *Smoldering Ashes: Cuzco and the Creation of Republican Peru, 1780–1840.* Durham and London: Duke University Press, 1989.

Walker, Dale F. *Bear Flag Rising: The Conquest of California, 1846.* New York: Tom Doherty Associates, 1999.

Washington, Margaret. *Sojourner Truth's America.* Urbana and Chicago: University of Illinois Press, 2009.

Watson, Robert P. *America's First Crisis: The War of 1812*. Albany: State University of New York Press, 2014.

Watson, Samuel J. *Peacekeepers and Conquerors: The Army Officer Corps on the American Frontier, 1821–1846*. Lawrence: University Press of Kansas, 2013.

Weber, David J. *The Mexican Frontier, 1821–1846: The American Southwest under Mexico*. Albuquerque: University of New Mexico Press, 1982.

Weber, Jennifer L. *Copperheads: The Rise and Fall of Lincoln's Opponents in the North*. New York: Oxford University Press, 2006.

Webster, George Sidney. *The Seamen's Friend: A Sketch of the American Seamen's Friend Society*. New York: The American Seamen's Friend Society, 1932.

Wermuth, Thomas S. "The Central Hudson Valley." In *The Other New York: The American Revolution beyond New York City, 1763–1787*, edited by Joseph S. Tiedemann and Eugene R. Fingerhut, 127–154. Albany: State University of New York Press, 2005.

———. *Rip Van Winkle's Neighbors: The Transformation of Rural Society in the Hudson River Valley, 1720–1850*. Albany: State University of New York Press, 2001.

Westwood, Howard C. "Reform in the United States Navy: The 'Plucking' of Officers in the Later 1850s." *American Neptune* 50:2 (Spring 1990): 107–118.

Whitehead, Clare Beverly. *History of the Norfolk Navy Yard, Portsmouth, Virginia*. Portsmouth: Printcraft Press, 1942.

Wilentz, Sean. *Chants Democratic: New York City and the Rise of the American Working Class, 1788–1850*. New York: Oxford University Press, 1984.

———. *The Rise of American Democracy: Jefferson to Lincoln*. New York and London: W. W. Norton, 2005.

Wood, Gordon S. *Empire of Liberty: A History of the Early Republic, 1789–1815*. Oxford History of the United States. New York: Oxford University Press, 2009.

Index